Annals of the American Society for Adolescent Psychiatry

ADOLESCENT PSYCHIATRY

DEVELOPMENTAL AND CLINICAL STUDIES

VOLUME 20

Edited by
RICHARD C. MAROHN
Editor-in-Chief

SHERMAN C. FEINSTEIN
Editor Emeritus

Published by The Analytic Press, Inc.
365 Broadway, Hillsdale, NJ 07642

ISBN 0-88163-194-9
ISSN 0-226-24064-9

Printed in the United States of America
10 9 8 7 6 5 4 3 2 1

CONTENTS

PART III: GENERAL CONSIDERATIONS OF ADOLESCENCE

PART IV: SPECIFIC SYNDROMES

PART V: TREATMENT MODALITIES

EDITOR'S PREFACE

RICHARD C. MAROHN

An opportunity such as this passes to but a few and presents to one rarely in a lifetime. To become the second editor of *Adolescent Psychiatry* is an occasion to prize and cherish. It is much more than those alleged "15 minutes of fame" because its professional impact can be lasting, or so we hope. It is more because the friendships and collegial experiences it can engender linger beyond the brief or lengthy editorial encounter. It is more because the work is often protracted, the editing process sometimes extended, and the printed word relatively imperishable.

This annual has a distinguished history. It began when the American Society for Adolescent Psychiatry was but in its infancy. An organization such as ASAP would, of course, try to teach others about our exciting field, and writing about clinical work with adolescents is a necessary extension of that intent. *Adolescent Psychiatry* began in 1971, coedited by Sherman C. Feinstein, Peter L. Giovacchini, and Arthur A. Miller. Dr. Miller died that same year after completing his work on the first volume; Dr. Giovacchini continued as coeditor through Volume 7 and then as one of the senior editors for several more volumes, until Max Sugar became editor-in-chief for Volume 11 in 1983. Dr. Feinstein assumed a new role, coordinating editor, the following year, and then editor-in-chief two volumes later. The first three annuals were published by Basic Books, the next two by Jason Aronson, and the next fourteen by Chicago.

Initially, the coeditors promised

> to explore adolescence as a process . . . to enter challenging and exciting areas that may have profound effects on our basic concepts. Though our focus will be clinical and developmental, we recognize that creative ideas come from many areas and can become clinically valuable even if they do not seem to directly contribute to our needs at the moment. . . . [and they promise] a series that will provide a

forum for the expression of ideas and problems that plague and excite so many of us working in this enigmatic but fascinating field. [Feinstein, Giovacchini, and Miller, 1971, pp. xiv–xv]

The Annals had its longest convenant with the University of Chicago Press, and its distinguished reputation has cemented this publication's position in the scientific community. This volume, the 20th, stands on the solid foundation forged and built not only by these men and these publishers, but by the more than 500 authors who have presented their work in these pages; by the many editors and senior editors who have guided philosophy, creation, and development; and by the typists, copy editors, proofreaders, editors, critics, friends, and significant others who labor, live, and breathe at every step of the process. Perhaps more than anyone else, our patients have inspired, challenged, and stimulated us to write—to write so we can learn, to write so we can formulate our ideas, to write so we can teach, to write so we can think about our work, to write so we can hone our skills, to write so we can grow.

The hero of this scenario is Sherman Feinstein. In these pages, Al Schwartzberg reviews Sherman's biography, and Herman Staples counts him as one of the major figures in the history of adolescent psychiatry. I too can attest to Sherman's impact on our field—I have all the volumes there on my shelf, and I use them frequently. From the beginning, *Adolescent Psychiatry* has been a work of scholarship, a work of relevance, and a work of Sherman's judgment. He has helped novices and experienced authors alike to improve the scholarly nature of their contributions, to present material of clinical acuity, and to write well, especially to say things simply and directly. Sherman has launched many young authors; he does this with patience and kindness and an unerring eye for how to improve a submitted paper. Just as skillfully, he relies on the respect with which senior scholars in our field hold him to count on their contributions.

This volume, the 20th, illustrates that mix. It is a *Festschrift,* a celebratory collection of papers. We have tried to illustrate aspects of Sherm's impact on the previous 19 editions and to highlight his own publications, his close association with the history of adolescent psychiatry and ASAP, his interest in developmental issues, his exploration of a variety of clinical syndromes and diagnoses, and his familiarity with a spectrum of therapeutic modalities. This is a man who has done it all and helped others write about it.

As we salute our editor emeritus, Sherman Feinstein, *Adolescent Psychiatry* looks to the future. A new editor will certainly innovate and create, yet maintain a high level of respect in the professional community. A new publisher, The Analytic Press, has a solid publishing reputation in psychology, psychoanalysis, and psychiatry as the publisher of several prestigious professional journals and annals, and of many monographs in the behavioral sciences. We will continue to view *Adolescent Psychiatry* as an annual devoted to the clinical, developmental, theoretical, and philosophical interests of adolescent psychiatry.

Sherman, we hope to justify your trust!

REFERENCES

Feinstein, S., Giovacchini, P. & Miller, A. (1971), Preface. *Adolescent Psychiatry,* 1:xiii–xv. New York: Basic Books.

REFLECTIONS OF THE EDITOR EMERITUS

SHERMAN C. FEINSTEIN

In May of 1961, a group of psychiatrists mutually interested in adolescent psychiatry formed the American Society for Adolescent Psychiatry. As William A. Schonfeld (1971) wrote, it was during 1958 that a number of child and general psychiatrists met and established the Society for Adolescent Psychiatry of New York. Its aims were determined to be the provision of a forum for the exchange of psychiatric knowledge about the adolescent, to encourage development of adequate training facilities for adolescent psychiatry, to stimulate research in the psychopathology and treatment of adolescents, and to foster the development of adequate adolescent services. With the confederation of a number of local societies, the American Society for Adolescent Psychiatry was formed with its first officers: William A. Schonfeld, New York, President; Sheldon Selesnick, Los Angeles, Vice President; Sherman C. Feinstein, Chicago, Treasurer; and Herman Staples, Philadelphia, Secretary.

The Chicago Society for Adolescent Psychiatry was first organized in 1964, and an editorial committee consisting of Sherman C. Feinstein, Peter L. Giovacchini, and Arthur A. Miller was appointed to produce a *Bulletin of the Chicago Society for Adolescent Psychiatry*. This publication first appeared in April, 1967 and lasted through five volumes, edited by the editorial committee. This same committee was appointed by the American Society for Adolescent Psychiatry to explore possible publishers for a society journal.

We found several publishers that were interested, but as a result of a suggestion by Roy R. Grinker, Sr., Arthur Rosenthal, President of Basic Books, was contacted. This turned out to be a most satisfactory experience since Rosenthal was the dean of psychiatric book publishers and welcomed the idea of a series on adolescent psychiatry. What a heady experience it was for three young editors to find themselves represented by a major psychiatric publisher and featured by the prime psychiatric book club, Basic Books, a publishing phenomenon of the period.

The first volume of *Adolescent Psychiatry* was published in 1971 and consisted of 552 pages and 25 chapters. From the onset, the annual volume was a judged, peer-reviewed journal. The original editorial board consisted of a group of dedicated, hard-working psychiatrists who solicited, judged, and edited papers from established authors and meetings of the new society. The only disappointment was the sudden death of Arthur Miller on February 15, 1971, which shocked us and created a large sense of loss at the editorial level.

Miller was a gently balanced, brilliant psychoanalyst who had moved from Chicago to Ann Arbor and the University of Michigan. He contributed a basic, philosophical perspective to the definition of adolescent psychiatry and, with Giovacchini and me, wrote a statement that guided us through the developmental phases of creating a journal.

The preface of what was then being called *Annals of the American Society for Adolescent Psychiatry* contained the following proposal:

This volume, sponsored by the American Society for Adolescent Psychiatry, reflects the increasing interest in adolescence as a stage of life. This interest stems from several sources. As a clinical challenge, adolescence demands the utilization of specialized techniques. As a period of life, adolescence may be of great importance in the general understanding of development and psychopathology. Beyond the individual, adolescence is also a social phenomenon. Adolescents need to be understood for their influence on values and social institutions. . . . The purpose, therefore, of a publication such as this one is to explore adolescence as a process. We hope to enter challenging and exciting areas that may have profound effects on our basic concepts. Though our focus will be clinical and developmental, we recognize that creative ideas come from many areas and can become clinically valuable even if they do not seem to directly contribute to our needs at the moment. . . . [We hope the series] will provide a forum for the expression of ideas and problems that plague and excite [those] working in this enigmatic but fascinating field [Feinstein, Giovacchini, and Miller, 1971, pp. xiii–xv].

In reviewing Volume I of *Adolescent Psychiatry,* Daniel Offer (1971) praised the new volume in the field, which viewed youth as a unique life stage and believed that the research literature lacked an awareness of the multiplicity of routes through adolescence. He noted that little had been written on early adolescence and noncollege youth, girls rather than boys, and minority groups—particularly black teenagers. Carl Adatto (1972) wrote that the series could give professionals working with adolescents a sense of proportion regarding the magnitude of the problems of adolescence and provide connecting links between the theories and knowledge of adolescence and other stages of development.

The first volume of *Adolescent Psychiatry* was received happily by the membership of ASAP. The editorial board was selected from Society nominations and consisted of Julian Barish (New York), Peter Blos (New York), Harold Boverman (Chicago), Alfred Flarsheim (Chicago), Robert Gaukler (Philadelphia), Ghislaine Godenne (Baltimore), Robert E. Gould (New York), Eduardo Kalina (Argentina), Jerry M. Lewis (Dallas), Laurence Loeb (New York), Humberto Nagera (Ann Arbor), Leonard Neff (New York), Sol Nichtern (New York), George L. Perkins (Chicago), Daniel Offer (Chicago), Bertram Slaff (New York), Robert A. Solow (Los Angeles), Herman D. Staples (Philadelphia), Max Sugar (New Orleans), and Frank Williams (Los Angeles).

After three volumes of *Adolescent Psychiatry* were published by Basic Books, Arthur Rosenthal left Harper & Row (the owner) for the Harvard University Press. This was the second major loss we experienced in our early years that demanded decisions that were beyond our capacities. We decided to shift publishers and chose Aronson, which eventually published Volumes 4 and 5. By this time, *Adolescent Psychiatry* had achieved national recognition, and a review by E. James Anthony (1974, personal communication) discussed these developments.

Anthony called the *Annal*'s first three volumes "the most representative productions of the newest subdiscipline in psychiatry." He described the divisions of the volume into parts, each part designed to meet the interests of different readers: generalists, developmentalists, clinicians, and therapists, but "the whole organization educates us on a broader and deeper perspective." Adolescence is regarded as a singular process affecting us all directly or indirectly, perplexing us by its variability, exasperating us all by its endless provocativeness, and captivating us all in a way that no other stage in the human life cycle is able to do. He concluded that the series served as a guide to the new field of adolescent psychiatry, telling us where we have been, what is being done at present, what major developments are taking place, what we should be doing to help things move forward, and where we are going.

Volume 4 was published in 1976 and Volume 5 in 1977. An examination of the front papers and table of contents reveals authors and editors including E. James Anthony, Peter Blos, Rudolf Ekstein, M. Masud R. Kahn, Serge Lebovici, Phyllis Palgi, Chaim Potok, and Fritz Redl. In the preface to Volume 4, my coeditor, Peter Giovacchini, and I discuss the function of a society journal to be the communication of important studies of the adolescent process. We mention that editorial work is not usually associated with innovation. Such tasks involve compilation, organization, and whatever is required to achieve maximum clarity and effective communication. Each volume deals with many diverse subjects that require grouping and categorization. As editors, we have to induce order and can accomplish this by developing long-term themes and groups. The subjects of these volumes range from general cultural considerations to specific treatment issues. The former include the clash of the adolescent with his environment, and the latter may contain the biological dynamisms underlying developmental factors. The field of adolescent psychiatry, as can be seen, has many fascinating ramifications, and we strive to achieve higher states of creative imagination.

The publication of Volume 6 in 1978 by the University of Chicago Press was of particular satisfaction to me. Morris Philipson, Director of the Press, had received his tutelage under Arthur Rosenthal at Basic Books. Since Rosenthal was important to the development of *Adolescent Psychiatry,* moving to the University of Chicago Press could be seen as a homecoming. I was particularly appreciative of the efforts of Morris Philipson, John G. Ryden, T. David Brent, and Robert Sherrill in effecting the change.

The preface to Volume 6 discussed Melvin Sabshin's Schonfeld Lecture. He stressed that how a person develops has to take sociocultural variables into account. Inasmuch as the psychopathology encountered during adolescence affects the developmental process, these variables would be expected to become increasingly important for our clinical understanding. Adolescents are unique in that they can be studied from many different viewpoints, and these studies can make fundamental contributions in those areas. This also means that approaches to the study of adolescence can use methods that are appropriate to the investigating discipline. Sociology, physiology, and psychology all have their appropriate places in the investigation of the many facets that constitute the adolescent process.

Volume 6 reflects those various facets and, like previous volumes, has a general considerations section that can be considered a broad introduction to the field of adolescent psychiatry. The more specific sections focus on clinical entities and problems that are comparable to those with which clinicians, in general, are grappling. Our intentions are to use *Adolescent Psychiatry* as the frame for a textbook that uses the general discussion of field issues (i.e., eating disorders, narcissism, borderline states) as a point of reference for specific clinical and research discussions of these topics.

The United Nations General Assembly declared 1979 the International Year of the Child to focus on the concerns for children and adolescents throughout the world and to celebrate the 20th anniversary of the United Nations Declaration of the Rights of the Child. The American Society for Adolescent Psychiatry recognizes the rights and needs of young people, and, through its official publication, *Adolescent Psychiatry*, emphasizes the subtle interrelationships between current world political tides and the developmental and clinical studies with which we are occupied.

The papers in the seventh volume of *Adolescent Psychiatry* reflect the tumultuous occurrences of the recent past. It is amazing how many of these events are directly or indirectly related to adolescence. For example, we have seen the spread and felt the impact of various religious movements. The formation of such groups and the blind devotion that characterizes cults are subjects that have to be understood. Many of us suspect that the forces that are intrinsic to the adolescent process are somehow involved in the reactions of masses to charismatic and, in some instances, dangerous and destructive leaders.

Obviously, the significance of these questions transcends a particular group: we have seen how such phenomena involve nations and threaten our civilization. Alongside an interest in what have been regarded as fringe movements has been a comparable preoccupation with the impact of geographical displacement, during and following the Vietnam War, on adolescents and their families. Possibly this represents an intuitive awareness of parallel constellations intrinsic to the microcosmic cult and macrocosmic tyranny. Here is an instance in which our clinical understanding can extend to global issues.

As clinicans, we have to continue directing our attention to our patients, and the chapters dealing with diagnostic and technical problems reflect such a focus. In the clinical area, this volume represents a natural continuation of previous volumes. Quite early in the history of this publication, clinical articles tended to deal with patients suffering from structural problems. This observation undoubtedly is related to the subject itself, the adolescent patient, whose character structure is in a state of flux. Still, more is involved than the loose personality structures of adolescence in determining the types of patients that so many authors write about. Those adolescents, and adults as well, who find their way to psychiatrists' offices, increasingly reveal the manifestations of early developmental defects. We continue publishing papers concentrating on primitive fixations as seen, for example, in borderline patients in general and delinquents in particular. The emphasis is on serious psychopathology.

Perhaps we have created a full circle. The types of psychopathology we encounter may be typical of personalities that are especially susceptible to the omnipotent promises of religious and political leaders. There may be a reciprocal relationship between emotional illness and the formation of institutions that are congruent with the defensive adaptations of a large segment of the clinical population. It is unlikely that the basic structural problems of adolescence have substantially changed throughout the years. Some psychoanalysts reevaluated Freud's early cases and were able to formulate them in terms of ego defects similar to those we often discover in our adolescent patients. If anything has changed, it is the manifestations of psychopathology. This phenomenon would lead to the construction of new adaptive techniques that affect our culture, and, in turn, our culture contributes to the further elaboration of coping mechanisms. Thus, psychopathology and cataclysmic world conditions are, in some way, related. This is a subject that is much beyond the expertise of psychiatrists who treat adolescent patients. Still, our insights about the adolescent process will broaden our understanding and tolerance in many areas that are meaningful for humanistic purposes.

The beginning of a new decade (1980) with the end of a century in sight leads to appraisals of the past and perspectives for the future. The themes of appraisal and perspective are found throughout Volume 8 and are dealt with in a wide variety of approaches, always emphasizing the multidimensional manner in which adolescence may be considered by a growing number of observers.

By this time, most clinicians concerned with adolescent psychiatry are convinced that adolescence is a unique phase concerned with special developmental tasks, requiring special training and therapeutic approaches. It is a period of character consolidation that leads to the formation of the adult sense of identity. Emotional disturbances occurring during this period manifest themselves in particular forms of psychopathology, such as the identity diffusion syndrome, which is the

outcome, roughly speaking, or the breakdown, of the self-represen-
tation.

The teenage years are characterized by structural homogeneity. That is
to say, the minds of adolescents, their psychic structure, are in a
formative developmental stage. In terms of psychosexual stages, adolescents are in a postoedipal state, attempting to integrate their biologically
based sexual drives in the general ego organization. Generally, they are
acquiring adaptive techniques to cope with the external world at an adult
level. These tasks seem to be constants in the adolescent context.

At the more superficial, behavioral level, the situation admits considerable variability. There have been marked changes in the general
behavior of adolescents during the past several decades, but as far as we
can ascertain from our clinical experiences, their underlying psychic
states are more or less the same. In view of the fact that there is
practically no homogeneity to adolescent behavior, some investigators
question whether adolescence, as a phenomenon, does, in fact, exist.

A new plan adopted by the Society concerning editorial responsibiiity
resulted in the retirement of Peter L. Giovacchini as coeditor and the
appointment of John G. Looney, Allan Z. Schwartzberg, and Arthur D.
Sorosky as Senior Editors. Dr. Giovacchini was one of the founders of
Adolescent Psychiatry and was a most productive partner. He contributed in all areas of creativity and made the *Annals* a living, growing
entity. Many of his thoughts are in its words.

In a review of Volume 9, E. James Anthony (1982) commented that
Shakespeare, in middle age, was very much on the side of exasperated
parents when he wrote, "I would there were no age between sixteen and
three and twenty; or that youth would sleep out the rest; for there is
nothing in the between but getting wenches with child, wronging the
ancientry, stealing, fighting. . . ." (Shakespeare, *The Winter's Tale*).

Anthony continued:

Why I like this particular *Adolescent Psychiatry* (Volume 9) is that
the editors (Feinstein, Looney, Schwartzberg, and Sorosky), in spite
of all the psychopathology on display, have infused a sense of what
youth means or should mean to the world in general. They see not
only the destructive side of the adolescent process but also its
creativity, its adaptive attempts at mastery, its move toward independence, intimacy, and creativity, to use Erikson's phraseology,
and a period of the life cycle not only programmed for turmoil but
for high achievement in the future.

The editor's preface to that volume noted that recently published reflections of a political prisoner said that to consider suicide under stress does not necessarily mean that one attempts suicide. It may mean the introduction of thoughts on the same level as the surrounding violence. This self-imposed state functions as a compensatory mechanism and provides a potential solution, one that contains a certain amount of pride. Later, when one rejects the idea of suicide, there again comes the feeling of defeat and the threat of madness (Feinstein et al., 1981, p. ix).

With the completion of Volume 10 (1982), I had every intention of retiring as Coordinating Editor. I saw this move as an act of generativity, according to Erik Erikson an act that should encourage productivity and creativity in the younger generation. Max Sugar assumed the editorship assisted by an editorial group of the highest devotion. Unfortunately, Volume 11 (1983), with Sugar as editor-in-chief, failed to gain the approval of the ASAP Executive Committee, and I was asked to resume editorship for the next ten volumes.

Volume 12 was published in 1985 with me as Coordinating Editor, and Senior Editors Max Sugar, Aaron Esman, John G. Looney, Allan Z. Schwartzberg, and Arthur Sorosky. The United Nations had designated 1985 International Youth Year, and Beresford Hayward (France), of the Organization for Economic Cooperation and Development (OECD), spoke of the importance of adolescents in the developing nations of the world as well as in Western society. Among major social and cultural changes, unique in the extent of their generality, the emergence of adolescence was recognized as an essential stage in the life cycle. The history of the recognition of adolescence barely takes in this century, and yet the adolescent population and its social and cultural apparatus have become an international phenomenon.

Hayward (Feinstein, 1985) continued that the significance of adolescence could be obscured as being reactive or mashed, but that its real purpose is to gather together and consolidate the emotional structures and cognitive processes required to achieve individual mental maturing. Great flexibility is required for this psychic work, which can easily become brutalized and impoverished. With the establishment of the adolescent experience have come vast problems. This now-large socio-demographic group is marked by problematic and destructive trends. Adolescents have become a growth industry for commercial exploitation, leaving them notably vulnerable. Broad educational problems can be solved only by achievement of the psychic aim of adolescence—emergence of the individual into adult mental maturity—still an enigma for science and society. If the general progress of modern society and culture is to be equated with higher levels of achievement, the enormous importance of adolescence becomes apparent.

The year 1985 also marked the establishment of the International Society for Adolescent Psychiatry, a confederation of societies from Europe, North and South America, and Asia. In 1987, an annual journal, the *International Annals of Adolescent Psychiatry,* was begun with Aaron H. Esman, editor-in-chief, and Sherman Feinstein and Serge Lebovici, senior editors. A second volume was published in 1992 with Allan Z. Schwartzberg, editor-in-chief and Aaron Esman, Sherman Feinstein, and Serge Lebovici, senior editors.

The 13th volume of the *Annals* was described as celebrating a *rite de passage,* the psychological entry into adolescence of this series of clinical and developmental studies. This dynamic approach was taken by Daniel Offer, past president of ASAP, who had the foresight to have a sociologist, Paul Dommermuth, study the organizational efforts of a group of young psychiatrists with a growing interest in adolescence. Dommermuth (Feinstein, 1986) observed that segmenting and branching in a valid profession is continuous and involves redefining the divisions of labor and developing new missions. This volume of *Adolescent Psychiatry* also reflected the fulfillment of the prediction that new subgroups or segments within the Society would emerge, emphasizing a wider range of clinical and research explorations. It was described as representing a panoramic display of the vicissitudes of adolescent development: normative and pathological; family reactions and supports; cultural aspects; creativity; regression; contributions and hindrances to diagnosis; and treatment, both inpatient and outpatient.

Volume 14 (1987) was dedicated to the memory of two friends of ASAP and *Adolescent Psychiatry,* Margaret S. Mahler and Dana L. Farnsworth. Two new senior editors, George H. Orvin and John L. Schimel, were appointed, joining Aaron H. Esman, John G. Looney, Allan Z. Schwartzberg, Anthony D. Sorosky, and Max Sugar. The preface pointed out that the 1980s reflected growing concerns in the financial aspects of psychiatry. I saw the problem as a growing shortage of adequately trained child and adolescent psychiatrists. The gap between child and adolescent patients and the availability of trained psychiatrists to treat them will continue to expand. We are concerned that the shortage will lead to expansion of nonmedical, behavioral approaches, with inadequate medical supervision as a byproduct of governmental health care reform.

Another aspect of these concerns is the preventive aspects of psychiatry, the examination of the demographics and epidemiology of emotional disorder in children and adolescents. Previous volumes of *Adolescent Psychiatry* have illustrated the enormous vulnerability for mental illness in adolescents, but there is widespread concern that many accepted interventions are not effective and are prematurely accepted without scientific scrutiny. Volume 15 (1988) examined female psychosexual development in chapters by Susan M. Fisher and Roberta J. Apfel with a discussion by the late Norman R. Bernstein. The success of special sections in earlier volumes flowered in a conference on creativity and adolescence and is presented in depth with Harvey A. Horowitz as special editor.

Volume 16 (1989) featured two exciting chapters that reflected the growing sophistication of our production. Senior Editor Peter Blos presented a reworking of his ideas about sexual development in his paper "Masculinity: Developmental Aspects of Adolescence," and Lois T. Flaherty outlined "A Model Curriculum for Teaching Adolescent Psychiatry," thoughts about a training and certification program in adolescent psychiatry.

With the publication of Volume 19 in 1993, the last volume of *Adolescent Psychiatry* under my editorship was produced. This same year marks the death of Roy R. Grinker, Sr. at age 92, to whom Volume 19 was dedicated. He, along with the University of Chicago Press, was greatly responsible for the support and encouragement I needed to produce the *Annals* of the Society.

My deepest appreciation is extended to my senior editors Aaron Esman, Harvey A. Horowitz, John G. Looney, George A. Orvin, Allan Z. Schwartzberg, Arthur Sorosky, and Max Sugar. Over the years they made major contributions to *Adolescent Psychiatry*. The editorial board shouldered the burden of the peer-review process and unfailingly produced reviews, evaluations, and a sparkling series of special projects. The group that produced these efforts over the years included Irving A. Berkovitz, Adrian Copeland, Dave Davis, Leah J. Dickstein, Carl Feinstein, Lois T. Flaherty, Peter T. Knoepfler, Saul Levine, John E. Meeks, Lillian H. Robinson, Richard Rosner, Moisy Shopper, and Myron Weiner. Last, but not least, is the group of consulting editors and authors who unstintingly invested their energies in making *Adolescent Psychiatry* the vital, living entity it became. I particularly want to mention E. James Anthony, Peter Blos, Rudolf Ekstein, Eduardo Kalina, Moses Laufer, Serge Lebovici, James F. Masterson, Daniel Offer, Bertram Slaff, and the late Herman D. Staples.

REFERENCES

Adatto, C. (1972), Review of *Adolescent Psychiatry. Psychoanal. Quart.,* 41:455–456.

Anthony, E. J. (1982), *Behavioral Science Book Service Review,* as quoted on book jacket of *Adolescent Psychiatry,* volume 9, 1981.

Feinstein, S. C. (1985), Preface, *Adolescent Psychiatry,* 12:ix–x. Chicago: University of Chicago Press.

_____ (1986), Preface, *Adolescent Psychiatry,* 13:xi–xii. Chicago: University of Chicago Press.

_____ Giovacchini, P. L. & Miller, A. A. (1971), Preface, *Adolescent Psychiatry,* 1:xiii–xv. New York: Basic Books.

_____ Looney, J. G., Schwartzberg, A. Z. & Sorosky, A. D. (1981), Preface, *Adolescent Psychiatry,* 9:ix–x. Chicago: University of Chicago Press.

Offer, D. (1971), *Adolescent Psychiatry: The Myth That Has Become a Reality. Psychotherapy and Social Science Review,* as quoted on book jacket, *Adolescent Psychiatry,* volume II, 1973.

Schonfeld, W. A. (1971), Foreword, *Adolescent Psychiatry,* 1:vii–viii. New York: Basic Books.

PART I

ADOLESCENCE: GENERAL CONSIDERATIONS

Appropriately, Allan Schwartzberg, Editor of the *International Journal of Adolescent Psychiatry* and a member of the Editorial Board of *Adolescent Psychiatry* since Volume 7, introduces us to the life and work of Sherman Feinstein, including his roles in helping to found the American Society for Adolescent Psychiatry and the International Society for Adolescent Psychiatry. Then we have the chance to see Sherman the author at work, presenting two papers about adolescent affective disorders, an important area in which Sherman has made significant contributions as a clinician, teacher, and writer.

1   SHERMAN C. FEINSTEIN, M.D.: EDITOR, *ADOLESCENT PSYCHIATRY,* 1973 TO 1994

ALLAN Z. SCHWARTZBERG

Volume 20, a Festschrift, honors Sherman C. Feinstein, Editor-in-Chief of *Adolescent Psychiatry*. This volume is a rich harvest of his own contributions, as well as papers reflecting special interests such as affective disorders, eating disorders, and bipolar illness. Sherman, an editor since 1970, became editor-in-chief in 1987.

During the past several decades, the Annals have developed and maintained a consistent standard of excellence highly regarded by all professionals in the field of adolescent psychiatry, both nationally and internationally. They have come to rely on the Annals as a unique authoritative storehouse of knowledge in our specialty with special emphasis on developmental issues, psychopathology, and treatment of the various emotional disorders of adolescents. The development of special sections has allowed readers the opportunity to pursue topics with unusual breadth and depth.

The development of the Annals has been uniquely intertwined with the growth and development of the American Society of Adolescent Psychiatry (ASAP). Sherm, as he is affectionately called by many friends and colleagues, was well positioned to serve not only as an original editor but also as an organizer and leader in the development of the society during its early stages, serving as the second president of the ASAP. With the advent of the Vietnam War, the rising tide of opposition and the growth of the drug and counter culture, the need for an organization devoted to the interests of psychiatrists who had special interest and expertise in working with adolescents became apparent.

In 1967 a loose confederation of societies from Chicago, New York, Philadelphia, and Los Angeles coalesced to form ASAP. Sherm was in the forefront of these organizing efforts, wearing many hats as leader, organizer, educator, researcher, and clinician. These same talents and his natural ability to network with colleagues and friends was most helpful in the development of the International Society of Adolescent Psychiatry. In 1973, while serving a World Health Organization Fellowship in Paris, he became acquainted with Serge Lebovici, a renowned French psychoanalyst. Together they dreamed of an international organization dedicated to the diagnosis and treatment of the special mental health needs of adolescents worldwide. With careful nurturing of the seeds germinated through meetings in Paris and Dublin in 1973, the efforts of the next 12 years reached fruition in the founding of the International Society of Adolescent Psychiatry in Paris in 1985. Sherman Feinstein played a key role in the development of this Society when serving as the second president.

Sherm's early interest in a writing career began in early adolescence with a fascination with printing. This interest subsequently led to the expression of a talent for writing, when he served as editor of his award-winning junior high school newspaper. He continued to write in high school and college. The early fascination of printing persisted, leading eventually to the development of a small printing business, which he shared with his sons. Old printing presses abound in the Feinstein basement as a testimony to this venture.

Sherm was born and raised in New Haven, Connecticut, with three brothers and one sister. Early in his career he moved to Chicago, graduating from the Chicago Medical School in 1948. During that year he married his loving wife, Sara, in Minneapolis, her home town. Following army service, where he was head of psychiatry in a maximum security multimilitary-force prison while Sara did parole work, he served an adult residency at the University of Michigan followed by a return to Chicago and child psychiatric training at the Institute for Juvenile Research.

In the mid-50s, child and adolescent psychiatry was a relatively new discipline, without formal recognition as a specialty. Sherm was invited by Roy Grinker, M.D., director of the Psychosomatic and Psychiatric Institute at the Michael Reese Hospital, to develop an adolescent psychiatric program. Thus began a 40-year relationship with Michael Reese Hospital, continuing to the present. Sherm pioneered the development of an adolescent psychiatric treatment program in a general hospital, one of the first programs of its type in the nation. In addition to serving as director of Child and Adolescent Psychiatric Training, he has served as director of Child Psychiatric Research for the past 35 years. During these three decades he has continued in the forefront as a key figure in the development of adolescent psychiatry as a subspecialty, both nationally and internationally.

Much of the foregoing provides information about Sherm that might be found in a standard curriculum vitae. A more complete portrait would describe him not only as a scholar and humanist but also as a personal friend and colleague. Indeed, this brief biography would not be complete without mention of Sherman's strong network of family, friends, and colleagues. Sherm and Sara have been blessed with two sons and nine grandchildren. Their older son, Joel, currently in private pediatric practice, also specializes in child abuse research and is medical director of a child sexual abuse program at Christ Hospital in Oak Lawn, Illinois. Joel and his wife, Joan, have eight children. Paul, their younger son, is a domestic law attorney in Chicago. He and his wife, Andrea, have a 3-year-old son.

Despite the time spent on all his professional accomplishments, Sherm has managed to share with his sons an early interest in scouting, as well as scuba diving, chess playing, tennis, and attending many sports events.

Editing, adolescent psychiatry, and ASAP have been important parts of Sherm and Sara's lives. They have traveled to virtually every meeting of ASAP and ISAP during the past 20 years. Sherm has worked tirelessly for the society, not only through his meeting and organizational efforts but often beginning to edit during the very early morning hours, a time he finds most productive. Through their involvement in *Adolescent Psychiatry* they have made close, lifelong friends throughout the United States and the world. His involvement with the field has been informed by a true sense of mission, passion, and caring.

Despite all the demands on his time, he has maintained a remarkable humility, high energy level, warmth and good humor, often acting as mediator and conciliator at difficult times, helping to mediate strongly conflicting views. His willingness to make himself available to past ASAP presidents, colleagues, residents, medical students, patients, and families, is legendary. Throughout he has shown qualities of dedication, trustworthiness, curiosity, calmness, and dependability. He has been a mentor to countless colleagues and friends.

I have been fortunate to have had the opportunity to work with Sherm during the past 18 years as colleague and friend. As we mark the occasion of his retirement as editor-in-chief, the society is fortunate that his energy, dedication, intellect, commitment, leadership, and editorial skills will continue to be available for many years to come.

SHERMAN C. FEINSTEIN

Affective disorders are described as disturbances of mood, prolonged emotions that "color the whole psychic life" and generally involve either extreme depression or elation (American Psychiatric Association, 1980). Major affective disorder, in which there is a full affective syndrome, includes bipolar disorder and major depression (no history of manic disorder). Less pervasive affective disorders include cyclothymic (manic and depressive symptoms), hypomanic, and dysthymic (depressive) states.

Although age-specific associated features of affective disorder may color the general disorder, essential features can be recognized in infants, children, and adolescents, making the diagnosis of masked disorder no longer necessary (Carlson and Cantwell, 1980; Cytryn, McKnew, and Bunney, 1980).

Manic episodes feature an elevated, expansive, or irritable mood. Associated symptoms may include increased activity, pressure of speech, flight of ideas, inflated self-esteem, decreased need for sleep, distractibility, and excessive involvement in activities that have a high potential for painful consequences. The intrusive and demanding nature of these interactions is usually not recognized by the individual. Lability of mood may be present with shifts to anger or depression. Suicidal ideation may be present, and suicidal actions can occur during these periods. Alterations of consciousness with thought disorder can manifest delusions or hallucinations along with other psychotic impairment of reality testing and bizarre behavior.

Depressive disorder may erupt in children and adolescents as separation anxiety, reluctance to attend school, or fear of the death of parents. Negativistic or antisocial behavior may appear at times with severe acting out. Identity disorder with retreat from family involvement, interference with time sense, school or work difficulties, deterioration of personal appearance, substance abuse, and development of a negative identity can serve as associated features of a major depressive episode.

Eventually, dysphoric mood or loss of interest or pleasure manifests itself as sadness, irritability, vegetative changes, decreased energy, worthlessness, concentration difficulties, and suicidal thoughts or attempts. In children, dysphoric mood may be characterized by sadness, particularly about friends, and episodes of being scapegoated may surface. Appetite can decrease or increase; sleep patterns may manifest initial, middle, or terminal insomnia or hypersomnia. Hyperactivity or hypoactivity may be seen. Thoughts of death or suicide are common and may be communicated through friends, diaries, or subtle acting out. Malmquist (1971) includes unhappy appearance, withdrawal and inhibition, somatizing, a quality of discontent, a feeling of rejection, negative self-concept, low frustration tolerance, clowning, denial of feelings, provocativeness, and acting out among the symptoms of childhood depression.

Adolescent Bipolar Affective Disorder

In adults the essential feature of bipolar affective disorder is a disturbance of mood that may assume full or partial manic or depressive symptoms. In adolescents, bipolar affective disorder, manifesting a manic-depression pattern, may show specific equivalent behaviors that are the precursors of the cyclothymic personality and manic-depression disorders of adulthood. Recent findings (Youngerman and Canino, 1978; Feinstein, 1980; Kestenbaum, 1980) suggest that the affective system of patients with manic-depressive disorder may have a basic vulnerability which, when overstimulated, begins a discharge pattern that does not respond easily to autonomous emotional control. Some biological variation (probably genetically based) leaves the affective system with specific vulnerability to affective stress. The typical bipolar cyclic states of adulthood, therefore, may be considered illness patterns rather than minimal criteria for diagnosis (Feinstein, 1973; Feinstein and Wolpert, 1983; Feinstein, 1980).

CLINICAL FEATURES

Manic-depressive disorder during puberty and adolescence may manifest some of the following behavior patterns:

1. Severe adolescent rebellion manifested by negativism, overconfidence, and an insistence on a feeling of well-being.
2. Exaggerated self-esteem with grandiose conceptions of physical, mental, and moral powers and overcommitment to adolescent tasks.
3. Heightened motor activity manifested by restlessness, hyperactivity, and compulsive overactivity. Several patients with anorexia nervosa were later discovered to have manic-depressive disorder.
4. Exaggeration of libidinal impulses may surface as a sudden change from an inhibited child to an aggressive, sexually acting-out adolescent. Puberty, particularly in girls, may be seen as a great threat to the body image. In one case a period of amenorrhea after menarche resulted in a manic-depressive episode with delusions of being pregnant.
5. Gradual emergence of a cyclic, bipolar pattern of affect disorder but often manifesting itself as marked instability with short periods of depression and mania rather than the longer periods typical of adult manic-depression. Suicidal ideation is frequently noted.

DIAGNOSTIC ASPECTS OF MANIC-DEPRESSIVE DISORDER

The identification of manic-depressive disorder in childhood has been a matter of some controversy, subject to changes in diagnostic fashion (Anthony and Scott, 1960). This ambiguity stems from a multiplicity of sources, both theoretical and practical. Traditional analytic thinkers have been particularly reluctant to acknowledge the existence of childhood affective disorders because, by psychoanalytic definition, clinical depression presupposes the development of superego structures. Psychodynamic theorists, such as Klein (1934), meanwhile, have postulated mania as an inherent infantile coping mechanism — not necessarily an aberrant state.

Resolution of this conflict has not been forthcoming, in part because of inconsistent diagnostic criteria for assessing affective illness and a concomitant lack of observational agreement. Failure to identify depressive equivalents in the behavior-disordered child is one such limitation. Flight of ideas and pressured speech, commonly associated with manic-depression, have been considered by others to be pathognomonic of schizophrenia (Carlson, 1979). Similarly, such behavioral characteristics as distractibility, lability of affect, and irritability — which would seem to be definitional of manic-depressive disorder — are often interpreted as hyperactivity, clearly not a psychotic state.

The criteria usually employed for the diagnosis of manic-depressive illness reflect Kraepelin's (1921) early descriptive studies. By utilizing end states as criteria, such as a full-blown manic episode, this system overlooks important developmental changes in affect and thus would seem to preclude the diagnosis of manic-depressive illness in children. The diagnostic requirement that there should be both a distinct and marked phasic disturbance of affects and evidence of a state approximating the classical description (Anthony and Scott, 1960) frequently delays the diagnosis for many years.

Klein (1934) contended that the child during early development passes through a transient manic state that she considered a defense against early infantile depression. The basis for this inference was her observation of the infant's feeling of omnipotence and control over objects. In normal children, however, this natural overreaction typically disappears by the age of 2 as they develop a sense of separateness from mother and a self-concept. The persistence of mood extremes, coupled with a family history of affective disorder, could be considered consistent with early indications of affective illness.

Davis (1979) described what he calls a specific manic-depressive variant syndrome of childhood that requires the presence of affective storms; a family history of affective disorder; mental, physical, or verbal overactivity; troubled interpersonal relationships; and no formal thought disorder, in children who respond to lithium carbonate.

The frequency of breakdown in manic-depressive illness increases with the development of puberty and the onset of adolescence. Again, the affective reactions are age appropriate and emphasize those defenses that are critical at a particular stage of life.

The question of the timing of the breakdown is of great interest. Both the loss of a loved object and the transition from childhood to adolescence are considered major demands on the gradually emerging adolescent ego. Mourning and progression through transitional developmental states require the capacity to utilize ego defenses in the mastery of the loss. A fundamental defect in the affect system, probably genetically determined, overwhelms the ego defenses, and the resultant affective reactions may be characterized as manic-depressive, essentially indicating exaggerated or blocked capacities to deal with the normal affective response to the perception of a loss. If the intensity of the stimulation is too great, or the environmental supports are sadomasochistic rather than accepting and supportive, an alteration of consciousness may result, manifested by psychotic thinking or behavior.

Schizophrenia in adolescents is frequently a difficult diagnosis to make, and as Masterson (1967) points out, only in 25% of seriously disturbed adolescents can the diagnosis be made at the onset; the long-term picture of the disease process emerges slowly during the diagnostic and therapeutic process. Stone (1971) discusses the dilemmas of making a definite diagnosis of manic-depressive illness and the present tendency to call a patient "schizophrenic till proven otherwise." The diagnosis of manic-depressive illness in adolescents is made by keeping in mind adolescent behavioral equivalents of the classical results of a bipolar affective disorder.

Anthony and Scott (1960) believe that a genetic clock is operative in an individual who is genetically predisposed or environmentally handicapped. Gershon et al. (1976) reviewed genetic markers used in studies of psychiatric illness and studied red-green color blindness, Xg blood group antigen, and histocompatibility lymphocyte antigen (HLA). The evidence has been against close linkage for each of these markers. The most promising prediction of vulnerability in adult life is the presence of subclinical affective disturbance in childhood (McKnew et al., 1979).

TREATMENT OF ADOLESCENT MANIC-DEPRESSIVE ILLNESS

A major advance in the treatment of manic-depressive disorder is the present extensive use of lithium carbonate. Lithium carbonate is considered a safe drug and functions without blunting of perception or intellect (Kline, 1969). The common toxic symptoms of the fine hand tremor, anorexia, nausea, and diarrhea rapidly disappear if the dosage is reduced (Wolpert and Mueller, 1969).

The use of lithium carbonate has been reported in young children and adolescents, with promising results (Feinstein and Wolpert, 1973; Youngerman and Canino, 1978; Carlson, 1979). Careful medical cooperation is necessary, and the dosage and lithium blood level studies must be carefully monitored. Even though the use of lithium in cases of affective illness frequently leads to a rapid resolution of the manic attack, the importance of concomitant psychotherapy should not be overlooked.

CLINICAL MANAGEMENT

A thorough medical survey should be conducted with careful attention to cardiac, renal, liver, and thyroid function. An electroencephalogram should be secured if there is any history of convulsive disorder, because lithium may lower the convulsive threshold. Continuous monitoring of thyroid function is necessary because of the thyroid-suppressing effects of lithium. None of our patients have been affected, but several adults being observed have developed hypothyroidism.

The average daily dosage of lithium ranges from 750 to 1800 mg (or higher), depending on the blood level. The general therapeutic range is 0.8 to 1.4 mEq/L, with the most comfortable range between 1.0 to 1.2 mEq/L. Patients in a manic phase usually require a higher dosage to maintain therapeutic levels, which can be reduced with symptom remissions (Carlson, 1979).

Lithium carbonate is now available as tablets, capsules, and in the liquid as lithium citrate. The drug is well absorbed by the gastrointestinal tract: the blood level peaks in 1 hour after ingestion, and half-life in adolescents is 18 to 24 hours. Many complain of gastric irritation, and it is recommended that lithium be taken with food. Small, more frequent doses may also minimize the distress. Blood samples should be obtained weekly to check lithium concentration for the first month or until a stable therapeutic dose is achieved, then monthly or bimonthly.

Side effects are minor (nausea, fine tremor, polyuria, polydipsia, weight gain, and toxicity) and are usually controlled by slight dosage reduction (Carlson, 1979). Uncontrolled symptoms of affective disorder or psychotic reaction may require additional use of tranquilizers and antidepressants with appropriate attention to the toxic effects of these drugs, especially haloperidol.

PSYCHOTHERAPY

Our long-term experience with a group of adolescent manic-depressives had led us to recommend ongoing supportive psychotherapy to help them accept the disorder as well as more intensive psychoanalytic psychotherapy in the presence of developmental defect. The affective lability of childhood may be considered a traumatic factor in early development and often causes developmental interferences resulting in borderline personality organization. Many of our study group demon-

SHERMAN C. FEINSTEIN

strated personality organization, as described by Kernberg (1978), Masterson (1978), and Schwartzberg (1978), manifesting broad interference with self-development and distortions in object relationships.

Adolescent Depression

Depression remains one of the most common, but still not clearly defined, emotional reactions in childhood and adolescence. Depressive reactions are manifestations of conflicts in object relationships and, when they occur during adolescence, are indicative of and contribute to difficulties in psychic development. Object loss is particularly traumatic to the adolescent and makes a deep impact on the still developing psychic structure.

TYPES OF ADOLESCENT DEPRESSION

"NORMAL" ADOLESCENT DEPRESSIVE MOOD

The adolescent with multiple developmental tasks is subjected to a wide range of experiences, both intrapsychic and interpersonal. Partial regressions in the service of mastering ego stresses related to the necessary loosening of ego structures subject the adolescent to frequent loss experiences. Because adolescence contains a renegotiation of both the original separation-individuation efforts and previous oedipal resolutions, the capacity to mourn is considered to be in a state of relative incompleteness.

It is because of this state of affairs that Anna Freud (1958) believed all adolescents could be thought of as being in a state of mourning and, in fact, longing for the periods of childhood when solutions were relatively simple. Denial, depression, separation anxiety, and rage at the lost object may be mobilized when the teenager perceives an object loss. However, the final stage of reconstitution can be only partially resolved, leaving the adolescent confused, ambivalent, and at times fearful of diffusion of the ego. It is during these states that the adolescent frequently reaches out for help. Unfortunately, at times the plea is not a direct attempt to secure counsel but may be expressed in aggression, suicidal gestures, wandering, and various action fads or religious explorations.

Charles, a self-referred teenager, complained of fatigue, inability to concentrate, loss of appetite, and severe anxiety. He was worried about ruining his excellent high school record. Following an episode of

13

infectious mononucleosis, he was unable to function and became depressed. He had felt positive about himself until the present episode and believed he had been able, at age 10, to handle his parents' divorce. In three sessions of psychotherapy, he was able to trace his current depression to regression to earlier periods of helplessness and particularly to feelings of loss of his father at the time of the divorce. He was able to deal with his rage over the loss of his intact family and the anxiety of completing high school and leaving for college. He called to cancel his next session because he now had a job, had made up his course work, and was feeling much better.

The adolescent is capable of resolving a normal depressive reaction by self-therapy, by support received from peers or meaningful adults, and particularly by intelligent counseling. The realization that the feelings of the depressive reaction are normal responses to a loss or the fear of a loss is reassuring and can provide the support needed for ego mastery.

ADOLESCENT DEPRESSION WITH OEDIPAL AND LATENCY FIXATIONS

Depressive reactions in adolescents are frequently characterized by a notable absence of phase-appropriate behavior, and a remarkable immaturity of the mourning capacity. Anthony (1970) has described a type of adolescent depression that has marked oedipal characteristics and manifests significant guilt and moral masochism derived from a punitive superego. Anger, reserved for the parents, is turned back on the self, and the self-destructive trends are ultimately related to the wish to destroy the parents by whom the child feels betrayed. During the mourning process, this hostility, which normally is directed toward the lost object, may be misdirected because of the guilt involved in unacceptable direction of the rage. The hostility may then be directed toward a surviving parent or the self, resulting in provocative, argumentative behavior, or masochistic or suicidal attempts at handling depressive affects.

The difficulties involved in the treatment of these depressions are many. The adolescent is already struggling with oedipal fixations that he is using to defend himself against the fear of loss of controls inherent in the preadolescent and adolescent process. At the same time, however, the adolescent is developmentally able to move out of the depressive phase of mourning into the phase of separation-individuation. This allows him to make a powerful treatment alliance and to attempt to deal with depressive elements with some confidence in his own survival capacities. The difficulties involved relate to the narcissistic defenses the adolescent is forced to use, which include omnipotence in evaluating his own efforts and a shattered idealism in the adults with whom he is involved. An early interpretation of the normal aspects of rage toward the lost object can be most helpful in providing a structure for the adolescent struggling with still unresolved oedipal-latency development.

Ralph entered treatment after making a serious suicidal attempt. He had been selected for a special tutorial program, had become guilty about whether he deserved the honor, and after struggling with course choices and a growing feeling of isolation had tried to hang himself. Adolescence was an uncomfortable period as he struggled with feelings of inadequacy. He felt he had "peaked" at age 10 when he was considered a genius, but his father had suffered financial reverses and Ralph withdrew during junior high school with deep feelings of humiliation. Therapy was frequently intellectualized as Ralph would gleefully point out an error his therapist had made in some fact. At times he had a sneering, hostile attitude but denied any feelings of anger or disappointment. Gradually, he began to deal with his deep feelings of emptiness and fears of masculine inadequacy. He realized he was hoping to receive something from his therapist that would allow him to cope with his separation anxieties—then he became aware of his childhood, his competitive struggles with his father, and undertook the task of developing a more autonomous sense of self.

ADOLESCENT DEPRESSION WITH DEFECTIVE SEPARATION-INDIVIDUATION RESOLUTION

From a clinical point of view, adolescent depression in which preoedipal features predominate manifests itself in highly volatile fluctuations of mood and dependency. Early interferences with separation-individuation are characterized in adolescence as immaturity, lack of consistency, and a shallowness of character structure. Such adolescents show a remarkable degree of unresolved dependency that places the demand for dealing realistically with loss phenomena on their parents and surrogates. The lack of firm, constant introjects prevents them from completing that stage of mourning that reaffirms their own intactness. Frequently, an intense dyadic relationship exists with the mother, resulting in a dependent, symbiotic-type bond manifested by clinging, or sometimes in a sadomasochistic relationship replete with hostile attacks on the family and external authorities. Malmquist (1971) describes these children as being aware of their needs to become emancipated as they struggle with despair over their incapability. They are frequently

15

hypochondriacal or manifest psychosomatic disorders. Acting-out behavior, with verbal as well as physical violence, is seen; it has a symbiotic quality and alternates with clinging demands for reassurance and protection.

Fluctuations of mood, which are mentioned by Malmquist (1971) and Anthony (1970) as important in adolescent depression, are a frequent component of depressions with early developmental fixations. Phenomena of mood are critical during early child development. Until age three, most children demonstrate major periods of exhilaration or relative elation. This mood alternates with low-key periods when they become aware that mother is absent from the room (Mahler, 1972). Fixations during this period of mood-control development leave the adolescent with defective controls that reappear during adolescent depressions as marked rapid fluctuations of mood between despair and elation. Characterologically these adolescents are considered to manifest borderline personality organization (Kernberg, 1978; Masterson, 1967).

Jill, age 18, attended a small college near her home because of an inability to separate. She had few defenses to deal with her depression, was anxious continuously about being away, and struggled with suicidal thoughts. The oldest of two, she was obsessively concerned with her relationship with her mother. She demanded evidence that her therapist cared for her by asking for additional appointments frequently. Jill had a difficult early life because of multiple infections and a severe depression mother experienced after the family moved when Jill was age 1. When she was age 2 her mother had surgery and several deaths occurred in the family. Jill became serious and was usually unhappy and easily frustrated. Psychotherapy was a continuous battle, with the patient railing over every absence or interruption. There was a continuous gloom as she whined and complained over every aspect of her miserable existence. Her life was dominated by obsessive and compulsive rituals that were attempts to handle her severe anxiety. The use of imipramine finally helped regulate her functions and she was able to make a positive commitment to treatment. She became more able to concentrate and began to show strength through tolerating increased separation and individuation experiences.

TREATMENT OF ADOLESCENT DEPRESSION

The treatment of depression during adolescence can be very effective, since the adolescent patient is continuously struggling with regressive phenomena, and depressive reactions are only an exaggeration of the normally dealt-with vicissitudes. In those cases where there is early ego damage, however, serious clinical depressive reactions can be very difficult, and the danger of suicide is always a critical issue.

Phase-appropriate depressive reactions are dealt with by a variety of therapeutic techniques; they usually respond well to reassurance or short-term psychotherapy. The depth of mourning varies with the stimuli. Parent loss through death or divorce calls forth deep mourning, which may result in temporary incapacitation. Adolescents, however, can be helped to resolve the mourning by making them aware of the stages of the process and reassuring them of the normality of their reactions. Of particular importance are comments about the stage of rage toward the lost object. Since this stage depends on the resolution of the oedipal complex and the superego negotiations of latency, adolescents may still be actively struggling with these issues. Helping them to deal with the rage directly and to discourage the frequent use of projection or displacement will help in the eventual resolution.

Self-therapy is described by Anthony (1974) as a common phenomenon during adolescence. He concludes that it can be included among the classic therapeutic processes and that it may result in desirable expansion of the ego and a moderation of the superego. The dangers, however, may be great because of possible incompleteness of resolution. Josselyn (1978) believes that the relatively normal adolescent who is able to verbalize his turmoil is a legitimate treatment prospect because of the advantages to the adolescent in minimizing the energy investment in resolving developmental conflicts.

The treatment of adolescent depressions with fixations at oedipal and preoedipal stages of development calls for intervention and requires a total approach to the individual, including the family or milieu that is interacting with the adolescent. There are essentially two phases to the treatment. First, the depression must be relieved so that the ego defenses can become operative. Antidepressant medication may be of great help. Second, an effort must be made to locate the early fixations and conflicts and to attempt the resolution and working through of these developmental defects.

The establishment of a therapeutic alliance and overcoming of normal resistances is at times very difficult with the adolescent. It has been found helpful, however, to approach the adolescent as though one were responding to a plea for help. Aggressive and sadomasochistic defenses are used for mastery and become overwhelming. Accepting the manifest behavior as an attempt at adaptation and proceeding directly to the depressive core with an interpretation of the depression frequently will relieve the despair and communicate to the adolescent that you have received his message.

With the child struggling with an anaclitic depression, the role of the therapist is to serve as a facilitator of the mourning reaction. The therapist's support and analysis of the interfering conflict will help the patient to proceed with the mourning process and, in those patients in whom early defects are present, will serve as a surrogate ego. Because the complete range of mourning defenses is not available until adulthood, the therapist working with an adolescent must always be prepared to use supportive treatment parameters along with the gradual development of insight gained through analysis. This careful balance of support and insight therapy is one of the most crucial characteristics of therapy with adolescents and demands flexibility and resourcefulness on the part of the therapist.

The relief of acute depression is only the first step in dealing with the depressive character structure. This is a dangerous stage in the therapy insofar as the removal of the surface conflict leaves the still-undeveloped underlying structures vulnerable to further loss reactions, and the patient has little to support him except the newly established therapeutic relationship. It is at these times that a suicidal gesture, acting out, or impulsive termination of treatment is likely to occur. Active intervention — such as mobilizing the family into a therapeutic team, or hospitalization, which serves as an artificial stimulus barrier until the character defenses can deal with sensitive conflict issues — may be required.

Once it is demonstrated that he in fact has the capacity to deal with loss, the adolescent's capacities to neutralize affects and utilize ego observation grow. The question of whether loss has actually occurred becomes a crucial issue. The possibility of a cognitive affective distortion has to be considered, particularly during adolescence, when unfulfilled wishes frequently are interpreted as losses, with the precipitation of subsequent depression.

The working through and modification of depression proneness and depressive character structures is a difficult procedure and requires insight techniques. The recapitulation of earlier relationships in the transference and the careful analysis of the preoedipal and oedipal elements slowly relieves the use of depressive defenses. The patient begins to become aware of the deep infiltrations made into his character defenses by the depressive process. He sees how the fear of loss colors his everyday dealings.

Treatment of the adolescent requires modification of the techniques used in child and adult therapy. Gitelson (1948) observed that while the role of the therapist with the child or the adult is clearly defined as the adult helper or parent, the adolescent allows no such definition. He reacts frequently to the current situation (vis-à-vis the therapist) and experiences much anxiety. The emotional attitudes of the patient are not merely a repetition of the past, they also deal with the here-and-now. The therapeutic role with adolescents requires dependability, controls through the intelligent use of authority, and the providing of an ego-ideal. Gitelson (1948) saw the goal of therapy with adolescents as facilitating a character synthesis rather than an analysis, and the special therapeutic skills required were the ability to tolerate mistrust, the capacity to develop empathy, and the making of narcissistic contact, especially in crisis situations. The adolescent's establishment of identification and reformation of the ego-ideal leading to final consolidation of the superego is crucial and allows the adolescent to begin to interact with his peer group. This therapeutic process must be carried out at an optimum ego distance, which allows the therapist to support and encourage the patient during his explorations.

The use of antidepressive medication can be of major assistance in the treatment of adolescent depressive disorders. The reactive depressions usually do not require medication but may respond to psychotherapeutic efforts. However, a reactive depression may trigger a deeper, endogenous state that can only be recognized after a period of therapy with no improvement. Depressive disorders with earlier fixation points, a history of recurrent episodes, or a clear family history of affective disorder should be considered definite indications for the use of antidepressive medications.

REFERENCES

American Psychiatric Association (1980), *Diagnostic and Statistical Manual of Mental Disorders, 3rd ed. (DSM-III)*. Washington, DC: American Psychiatric Association.

Anthony, E. J. (1970), Two contrasting types of adolescent depression and their treatment. *J. Amer. Psychoanal. Assn.*, 18:841–859.

———— (1974), Self-therapy in adolescence. *Adolescent Psychiatry*, 3:6–24. New York: Basic Books.

19

_____ & Scott, P. (1960), Manic-depressive psychosis in childhood. *J. Child Psychol. Psychiat.*, 1:53–72.

Carlson, G. A. (1979), Lithium use in adolescents: Clinical indications and management. *Adolescent Psychiatry*, 7:410–418. Chicago: University of Chicago Press.

_____ & Cantwell, D. A. (1980), Unmasking masked depression. *Amer. J. Psychiat.*, 137:445–449.

Cytryn, L., McKnew, D. H., & Bunney, W. E., Jr. (1980), Diagnosis of childhood depression: A reassessment. *Amer. J. Psychiat.*, 137:22–25.

Davis, R. E. (1979), Manic-depressive variant syndrome of childhood. *Amer. J. Psychiat.*, 136:702–702.

Feinstein, S. C. (1973), Diagnostic and therapeutic aspects of manic-depressive illness in early childhood. *Early Child Devel. Care*, 3:1–12.

_____ (1980), Why they were afraid of Virginia Woolf: Perspectives on juvenile manic-depressive illness. *Adolescent Psychiatry*, 8:332–343. Chicago: University of Chicago Press.

_____ & Wolpert, E. (1973), Juvenile manic-depressive illness: Clinical and therapeutic considerations. *J. Amer. Acad. Child Psychiat.*, 12:123–132.

Freud, A. (1958), Adolescence. *The Psychoanalytic Study of the Child*, 13:255–278. New York: International University Press.

Gershon, E. S., Bunney, W. E., Leckmen, J. F., Van Eerdewegh, M. & Debauche, B. A. (1976), The inheritance of affective disorders: A review of data and hypothesis. *Behavior Genetics*, 6:227–261.

Gitelson, M. (1948), Character synthesis: Psychotherapeutic problems of adolescence. *J. Amer. Orthopsychiat. Assn.*, 14:422–431.

Josselyn, I. M. (1978), Etiology of three current adolescent syndromes: An hypothesis. *Adolescent Psychiatry*, 6:298–319. Chicago: University of Chicago Press.

Kernberg, O. (1978), The diagnosis of borderline conditions in adolescence. *Adolescent Psychiatry*, 6:298–319. Chicago: University of Chicago Press.

Kestenbaum, C. J. (1980), Adolescents at risk for manic-depressive illness. *Adolescent Psychiatry*, 8:344–366. Chicago: University of Chicago Press.

Klein, M. (1934), The psychogenesis of manic-depressive states. In: *Contributions to Psycho-Analysis*. London: Hogarth Press.

Kline, N. S. (1969), *Modern Problems in Pharmacology*. White Plains, NY: Phiebig.

Kraepelin, E. (1921), *Manic-Depressive Insanity and Paranoia*. London: Livingstone.

Mahler, M. (1972), On the first three subphases of the separation-individuation process. *Internat. J. Psycho-Anal.*, 53:333–338.

Malmquist, C. P. (1971), Depressions in childhood and adolescence. *New England J. Med.*, 284:887–893; 955–961.

_____ (1977), Childhood depression: A clinical and behavioral perspective. In: *Depression in Childhood*, ed. J. G. Schulterbrandt & A. Raskin. New York: Raven.

Masterson, J. F. (1967), *The Psychiatric Dilemma of Adolescence*. Boston: Little, Brown.

_____ (1978), The borderline adolescent: An object relations view. *Adolescent Psychiatry*, 6:344–359. Chicago: University of Chicago Press.

McKnew, D. H., Cytryn, L., Efron, A. M., Gershon, E. S. & Bunney, W. E., Jr. (1979), Offspring of patients with affective disorders. *Brit. J. Psychiat.*, 134:148–152.

Schwartzberg, A. Z. (1978), Overview of the borderline syndrome of adolescence. *Adolescent Psychiatry*, 6:286–297. Chicago: University of Chicago Press.

Stone, M. A. (1971), Mania: A guide for the perplexed. *Psychother. Soc. Sc. Rev.*, 5(10):14–18.

Wolpert, E. A. & Mueller, P. (1969), Lithium carbonate in the treatment of manic-depressive disorders. *Arch. Gen. Psychiat.*, 21:155–159.

Youngerman, J. & Canino, I. (1978), Lithium carbonate use in children and adolescents: A survey of the literature. *Arch. Gen. Psychiat.*, 35:216–224.

3 ASSIMILATING PIAGET: COGNITIVE STRUCTURES AND DEPRESSIVE REACTION TO LOSS

SHERMAN C. FEINSTEIN AND DAVID J. BERNDT

Jean Piaget has had an enormous impact on child psychiatry and occupies a crucial position in the systematic probing of the mind of the child and elucidating intellectual development. He combined his knowledge of biology, logic, and psychology with detailed observations and penetrating insights to provide us with a rich lode of theory and data about intellectual development. But his curiosity cont nued unabated, and he always continued to be interested in the more primitive mechanisms illustrated by infantile perceptions.

Although Piaget was relatively uninterested in pathological behavior per se, one can gain from his theories a better understanding of psychopathology since he provides valuable guidelines for how children may interpret or conceptualize events by understanding the intellectual options available (Harter, 1968). For example, the depressive reaction illustrates Piaget's observations of the egocentrism displayed during the sensorimotor period, an egocentrism that is characterized by a lack of differentiation between self and world, namely, the "absence of both self-expression and objectivity" (Piaget, 1954). Depression remains one of the most common but still not clearly defined emotional reactions in childhood and adolescence. Depressive reactions (an affect integral to psychic life) are manifestations of tensions in self and object relationships (particularly object loss) and contribute to difficulties in psychic development. From these reactions various depressive manifestations emerge that tend to make the true diagnosis of childhood depression difficult because of the ubiquitousness of its expressions (Feinstein, 1975).

This paper focuses on developmental, cognitive, and affective issues of depression and how Piaget's (1963) theories help in the understanding of the process. Depressive reaction is viewed as the usual method for integrating the cognitive and affective recognition of loss. The ego's perception of loss demands an immediate reintegration of ego structures, since the affective elements that accompany the recognition of an object or self loss render the ego helplessly vulnerable to feelings of abandonment and fears of annihilation. This reintegration, the product of successful growth and development, is the process of mourning.

Beck (1971), in describing a cognition-affect chain, states that there is an intimate connection between cognition and affect. A particular cognitive content produces affects that are congruent with it. Therefore, ideation arising from a fantasied or symbolic loss produces the same affect as an actual loss. The converse is also true—affects can act as stimuli in the same fashion as an external stimulus. Affects can be subjected to the cognitive processes of monitoring, labeling, and interpretation with the result that, to a patient, dysphoric affects can suggest a loss or produce the fear that a loss may occur.

The impact of these cognitive perceptions (either primitively realistic or in error) is to bring about partial regression to the stage of growth that exists at the symbiotic level of interpersonal development (Geleerd, 1961; Mahler, 1972). The developmental achievements of the ego determine whether the resolution of the depressive reaction is immediate, delayed, or results in a clinical depressive disorder.

Piaget's concern with the basic epistemological question of how one acquires knowledge about the world is of significance in understanding the cognitive and affective aspects of childhood depression. His theory of intellectual, or cognitive, development begins with the central postulate that motor activity is the primary source from which thoughts (mental operations) eventually emerge. Developmentally, cognitive activity more and more replaces motor activity. During the sensorimotor stage (birth to two years), the infant moves from being a primarily reflexive organism responding in an undifferentiated way to his environment to being a relatively coherent organization of sensorimotor actions (Flavell, 1963). This leads to the stage of preoperational thought (two to seven years) during which the child makes an attempt to master the world of symbols and representational thought. His conceptual framework, however, is grounded in the reality of his own subjective and egocentric perceptions, and his judgments are neither reflective nor logical. We shall illustrate briefly two areas of interest to Piaget and investigators of the phenomenon of depression for the purpose of opening up a discussion that may contribute some ideas about central depressive ideation as a complication of bonding as well as the role of affects in the development of psychic structure.

Depressive Ideation

Among the earliest of the developmental achievements necessary to reaching propositional or formal operations is separation-individuation and attainment of object constancy. For Klein (1948), a normal developmental stage that manifests central anxiety is the "depressive position," a period during which the infant experiences "sorrow and desolation over the loss of good objects." The infant interprets every absence as a loss until "his good objects are secured within himself" and he develops "feelings of trust and belief in his objects and his own capacity to love." Failing to do so, the child is "particularly liable to depressive episodes," to "feelings of loss and sorrow and guilt and lack of self-esteem."

Piaget (1963) traces the earliest intelligence forms to similar issues:

> The earliest forms of intelligence already aim at the construction of certain invariants . . . [but] of the invariants which arise at the sensorimotor stage perhaps the most important one is the all schema of the permanent (constant) object . . . that object which continues to exist outside of the perceptual field.

He differentiated the permanent object from a "perceived object," in the sense that there would be no "schema of a permanent object" if the child no longer reacted once the object had disappeared from the perceptual field (was not visible, could no longer be touched, or is no longer heard). There is already an invariant, or schema, of the permanent object if the child begins to search for the vanished object. This does not occur by four and one-half months, as Klein (1948) would have it, but by nine to ten months (Piaget, 1963). At first there is a period when the "object is not yet a mobile thing, capable of movements and correlated displacements in an autonomous system in space. Rather the object is still an extension of the action itself. . . ." Finally, toward the end of the first year, the object comes to have a degree of independent existence.

For Piaget, a cognitive schema and an affective schema may be analogous but are not identical. Intellectual representation finds its counterpart in affective acknowledgement. Piaget (1953–1954) prefers to discuss affective and cognitive elaborations of the object that involve

25

cognitive decentration of external space, affective decentration of external space, and affective decentration of interests in sources of gratification distinct from one's own actions.

Object permanence is accomplished through five transformations. The first is the construction of the object, in which the object becomes a permanent element that is independent of its perceptual discovery. A second transformation Piaget identified as the objectification and spatialization of causality. This allows the infant to recognize that an object, independent of the infant, can affect another object. Third, people acquire the same properties as objects, rather than transitory, unvocalized, perceptual entities. A fourth transformation involves imitation of others, one consequence of which is that the infant becomes more familiar with its own body. in the fifth transformation, one becomes consciousness of oneself.

For Piaget (1954) consciousness of the self, of others, and of analogies between the self and others appear simultaneously. Furthermore, affective and cognitive constructions occur simultaneously, and consequently all objects exist both cognitively and affectively. Feelings, however, are not conserved without the aid of intellect, but are reconstructed: "Feeling . . . appears, disappears, and oscillates in intensity not because it sinks into or emerges from the unconscious but because it is created, then dissipates, then is recreated."

A depressive reaction may reflect, in part, a state of disequilibrium due to unsuccessful adaptation to loss. During mourning, loss must be assimilated or accommodation of structure is necessary. What, however, is lost? The question is dependent in part on level of development.

Will and Mourning

Mourning can be defined as the psychological process that is instantaneously set in motion to deal with the affective response to the perception of loss. This process may be considered the recipient of the ego defenses developed by successful resolution of psychosocial and intrapsychic development during childhood and adolescence.

Piaget (1962) approaches the affects by considering will as an affective operation that bears on the conservation and coordination of values and on reversibility in the domain of values. Intellectual operations, in contrast, bear on the coordination and conservation of verifications or of relations. An act of will reverses tendency (impulse): it reinforces the weak and thwarts the strong, actually inferior, impulse (helplessness, vulnerability, and fear of annihilation).

Piaget shows how, by the act of decentration, one can deal with a strong but inferior tendency—by calling upon the conservation of values one can free oneself by a double act of reversibility: recalling the past or anticipating the future. From the moment one includes the actual tendency in the permanent scale of values, the conflict is resolved and the initially strong impulse becomes the weaker one.

Affects, then, are feelings that are not conserved but are transformed and submitted to indefinite fluctuations. Affects, however, according to Piaget, can be conserved by the imposition of moral feelings. He implies that by using a synthesis of the superego (or morality as a whole) it becomes an apparatus of conservation of affect and allows resolution of primitive tendencies. In an advanced state this becomes the process of mourning—the reconstitutive reactions by the ego mechanisms available to resolve the depressive reaction as part of the total process of reaction and reconstitution.

Conclusions

Piaget's concern with the basic epistemological question of how one acquires knowledge about the world is of significance in understanding the cognitive as well as the affective aspects of childhood depression. Depressive reactions reflect tensions in object and self-relations stimulated, particularly, by the perception of object loss. The affective elements that accompany the recognition of an object or self loss render the ego helplessly vulnerable to feelings of abandonment and fears of annihilation.

Piaget outlines how cognitive structures are maintained through the construction of certain invariants, especially the schema of the permanent object. The affective components, feelings that are not conserved and result in depressive dysphoria, can be conserved by the imposition of moral feelings mediated by the superego. This matrix, and the permanent schema eventually become elements of the mourning process.

REFERENCES

Beck, A. T. (1971), Cognition, affect, and psychopathology. *Arch. Gen. Psychiat.*, 24:495–500.

Feinstein, S. C. (1975), Adolescent depression. In: *Depression and*

Human Existence, ed. E. J. Anthony & T. Benedek. Boston: Little, Brown.

Flavell, J. H. (1963), *The Developmental Psychology of Jean Piaget.* Princeton, NJ: Van Nostrand.

Geleerd, E. (1961), Some aspects of ego vicissitudes in adolescence. *J. Amer. Psychoanal. Assn.,* 9:394–405.

Harter, S. (1968), Piaget's theory of intellectual development: The changing world of the child. *Conn. Med.,* 444–456.

Klein, M. (1948), *Contributions to Psycho-Analysis, 1921–1945.* London: Hogarth Press.

Mahler, M. S. (1972), On the first three subphases of the separation-individuation process. *Internat. J. Psycho-Anal.,* 53.

Piaget. J. (1953–1954), *Intelligence and Affectivity.* Palo Alto, CA: Annual Reviews, 1981.

_____ (1954), *The Construction of Reality in the Child.* New York: Basic Books.

_____ (1962), Will and action. *Bull. Menninger Clin.,* 26:138–145.

_____ (1963), The attainment of invariants and reversible operations in the development of thinking. In: *Piaget Sampler,* ed. S. F. Campbell. New York: Wiley, 1976.

PART II

HISTORY

The history of adolescent psychiatry in the United States is incomplete without mention of William Schonfeld, a friend and colleague of Sherman Feinstein. Dr. Schonfeld, as a leader of the New York Society for Adolescent Psychiatry, collaborated with Sherman and others in establishing the American Society for Adolescent Psychiatry. Here we present an unpublished paper of Dr. Schonfeld's delivered during a series of meetings with South American adolescent psychiatrists in 1968. The late Herman Staples's survey of American adolescent psychiatry includes the contributions of both Dr. Schonfeld and Dr. Feinstein; of course, Dr. Staples is also part of that history.

Siegfried Bernfeld is a towering figure in the history of psychoanalysis and of the study of adolescence; his concept of "prolonged adolescence" is pivotal in our history even though his ideas about the topic have never been presented until this publication. Presented here for the first time is Bernfeld's "Prolonged Adolescence." After having reflected on our illustrious past, it is only fitting that we reassess our current state and look to the future; Adrian Copeland facilitates this in his chapter.

4   DEPRESSION IN ADOLESCENTS

WILLIAM A. SCHONFELD

Depression in adults is a well-known psychiatric condition, usually with rather well-defined, recognizable symptoms. In adolescents, however, depression is often masked by symptoms not readily identified with this state. Thus, until recently, we did not recognize depression as a clinical entity in adolescents.

To illustrate the adolescent's reaction against depression, four cases are presented here. In general, adolescents have great difficulty in experiencing and controlling the affects of depression. They try to protect themselves against it by acting out—a denial by action. The depressive feelings may be shown in any number of ways: temper tantrums, disobedience, truancy, failing school and dropping out, stealing, running away from home, accidents, promiscuous sexual involvement, use of drugs, and a wide range of other delinquent behavior. Some show their depression by eating disturbances, particularly anorexia, but at times by overeating and general hypomotility.

Of course, acting out as a symptom complex is not specific to depression. It is evident in a variety of other psychiatric disorders and as an expression of conflict. Severe disturbances of behavior in adolescents, however, are frequently due to depression, and a youth will leave clues that will enable you to develop the diagnosis and treat him definitively. Of 121 adjudicated delinquents studied by Chwast (1967), 10% showed no depression, but 80% were depressed, half of them severely.

Most adolescents, as previously noted, are unable to contain their depressive feelings. To them, anything is better than being depressed. An adolescent will not tell you that he is depressed and, if confronted, will deny it. Thus in each case, we have to look for signposts that will enable us to make some shrewd guesses as to what is going on under the surface. At times, the depression will be revealed only after the behavior has been controlled through psychotherapy or institutionalization. I have often

31

found acting-out behavior to be a youth's call for clinical help to relieve his underlying depression.

The depressive elements usually evidenced in the psychopathology are unwarranted feelings of inadequacy, worthlessness, helplessness, hopelessness, rejection by others, and loneliness. According to Sugar (1968), the dynamics of depression and the maladaptive defense in adolescents seem to be best explained by Bowlby's theory of the process of mourning, namely, separation and protest, disorganization, and reorganization.

The hostility felt toward the depriving parent, who is also a loved object, makes the adolescent feel terrible and increases his depression and guilt. Why one adolescent can contain his depression through acting-out behavior while another needs to atone for and expiate his sins and turn his aggression upon himself, we do not know. The youth, however, who has a great need to preserve the image of a kind, loving parent will often protect that parent and turn his rage away from the parent to himself.

Now, what are the clues to look for in the clinical situation? There are four main categories: (1) type of psychopathology; (2) a "loss" as a precipitating factor; (3) past history; and (4) parental relationship. We search for the events that may have triggered the depression and the secondary acting out. It may be an obvious loss, like a parent's death, divorce, or remarriage. But at times it may be the parents who have become otherwise preoccupied, so that the adolescent has lost their attention, or a sibling who has gone off to college or gotten married.

Sometimes it is the loss of a maid or governess on whom the youngster depended. Often it is the loss of a love object. Separation from any person who plays an important part in his life may be the trigger. At times it may be the loss of status, physical prowess, or self-esteem.

The adolescent may be quite unaware of the connection between his psychopathology and the precipitating factor and a great deal of probing may be required to bring him to this insight. On the point of past history, invariably, in the cases I have treated, I have found different degrees of emotional deprivation. As a result, the adolescent goes through childhood without achieving the necessary emotional development and is unable to cope with frustration or control his impulses.

As for parental relationship, most of the parents of the depressed adolescents I studied were rejecting. Unconsciously, they tried to find outlets for their own neurotic and antisocial needs, attempted to work out their own neurotic conflicts through their children, and were unable to perceive and respond to their children's needs. The adolescent usually felt that his parents did not care for him and had abandoned him.

To recapitulate, with a background of emotional deprivation, the adolescent patient experiences a loss of a person who has been one of the few pillars of support to his immature personality. He then becomes depressed and starts to act out to protect himself from this feeling. By the time he is referred, he may have embarked on his acting-out behavior.

Clinical Examples

EXAMPLE 1

The first case in point is John, age 16. His father received a phone call from his ex-wife, from whom he had been divorced for the last four years. He was dismayed and shocked to learn that his son, who was then a student at prep school, had been arrested for breaking into houses and stealing.

About three months earlier, John returned from a Christmas holiday, bored, withdrawn, and uninterested in his work, although in the past he had been a good student and quite friendly. Each night, when the others in the dormitory were asleep, he would sneak out, enter a different building, and steal several small objects. Then one night he walked right past a policeman while carrying a large painting under his arm. Of course, he was apprehended. He then freely admitted his guilt and took the policeman back to his dormitory, where he had carefully wrapped and stored all the other articles he had stolen.

What were the precipitating events here? John's mother and father were divorced when he was 12. He spent most vacations with his mother, but when he came home for Christmas this year, he got into a fight with his mother. She threw him out and told him to go to his father. The father, living with a mistress, had no room for John, and so he put him up at a hotel for the duration of the holiday. John spent his two weeks sitting in this hotel room reading and watching television.

As to past history and parental relationships, John's father was a cold, withdrawn man, who was rarely at home; and his mother was an unstable, nagging, and controlling woman. John was always used as the scapegoat by both parents. When they were divorced, he was sent on to prep school where he made a good adjustment. When his mother threw him out of the house and his father also rejected him, however, he was catapulted into a depression from which he found release in acts of thievery. At the same time, it served as an act of retaliation, as well as a plea for help.

EXAMPLE 2

The second case is Fred, age 17. His father, in contrast to John's, was not surprised to receive a call from the police to the effect that his son had been arrested for possessing narcotics. The father had been having trouble with Fred for at least four years; Fred had been involved in many episodes of stealing, truancy, and using marijuana.

Fred had always been a discipline problem, both at home and at school. His real difficulties, though, began when he was around 12 years of age and was apprehended for vandalism. He was taken to a psychiatrist for a few sessions, but the summer vacation intervened. As is typical of many cases, the patient behaved a little better during the summer, so his parents failed to follow through with treatment.

The next year his school grades began to fall, and he went on senseless stealing sprees. As he grew older, his behavior got worse. He was sloppy and undisciplined at home, truanted, took up with some hippies, and turned to marijuana, LSD, and methedrine. He often left marijuana and pills around the house, but the family ignored them.

What were the precipitating events, past history, and parental relationships here? Fred's mother was a very aggressive, domineering, anxious woman who controlled both her husband and the rest of the family. During therapy, she revealed that she had once stolen as a child and had been embarrassed when her mother made her return the article. She was determined not to subject her son to the same humiliation. Unconsciously, she may have encouraged her son to act out her own repressed impulses to steal.

Fred realized that his father was extremely passive and willingly allowed his wife to dominate him. When the patient was 12, his mother became involved in an affair and had little time for her family. Here again, we find a background of emotional deprivation and an immature personality. The patient experienced his mother's withdrawal as abandonment and went into a depression, with which he attempted to cope by antisocial behavior and drug abuse.

EXAMPLE 3

The third case is Betty, age 15, who was hospitalized for an appendectomy. The day before she was due to be discharged from the hospital, she attempted suicide by swallowing a liquid detergent from the cart holding the maid's cleaning materials.

Betty's father was a cold, withdrawn fellow who had been disappointed in life and could never accept Betty as he had been forced into marriage as a result of the unwanted pregnancy. Her mother, for her part, pampered the patient. Betty had a disturbance of self-concept and marked feelings of inadequacy brought on by the rejection by her father.

When Betty was hospitalized, the resident surgeon devoted a great deal of attention to her. He was the first male ever to show any concern for her. She responded by getting a crush on him and fantasied staying in the hospital, becoming a nurse, marrying the doctor, and never having to go home again. When the surgeon discharged her, she once again felt rejection, and a depression set in. She reacted with a feeble attempt at suicide, not really wishing to die, but only to stay a while longer in the hospital.

On her discharge, I saw her in psychotherapy, and she made an effective transference. She responded well and developed an insight into her father's attitudes as being a symptom of his own sickness, rather than a rejection of her. She became more outgoing and receptive to attention from boys her own age, graduated from high school, and is now employed as a secretary and doing well.

EXAMPLE 4

The fourth case is Mary, age 19, who phoned her family from college to announce that she was dropping out of school because she was pregnant. She had had a disturbed home life as a child, and her mother had died when she was 12. Several years later, her father remarried. Her sense of being deserted by both father and mother threw her into a state of utter loneliness and depression to which she reacted by acting out through sexual promiscuity, her quest for love and acceptance. Her pregnancy was premeditated and planned as an act of desperation to shock her father into acknowledging her existence.

Thus we see that depression is a frequent syndrome in adolescents, seen not directly but rather through defenses against it in the form of acting-out behavior. There are several clues to look for in making the diagnosis: (1) the type of behavior; (2) the precipitating event of loss; (3) the background of emotional deprivation; and (4) difficult relationships with parents.

Usually, the syndrome responds well to psychotherapy. The first step in treatment is to try to get the adolescent to control his behavior by establishing a relationship and developing an insight about the self-destructive nature of his actions. Each time he controls a bit of behavior, he becomes more depressed. This he is unable to tolerate. So it is at this point that you have to give him insight into his state of depression, but not before. If you attempt too soon to explain to an adolescent that he is acting out because he is depressed, he will deny it and never come back.

When the adolescent is going through his depression, the therapist must become much more supportive and point out all his secondary levels of defenses against depression. The aim of psychotherapy is to replace the feeling of hopelessness with a sense of hope. Always bear in mind that before the adolescent will respond to treatment, he has to be convinced that you understand him, that you accept him, and that you know what you are doing. When the behavior is controlled, the depression comes to the fore. When the depression is worked through in psychotherapy, there is no longer a need to act out, and the patient is able to function effectively.

I should like to emphasize that I feel that electroconvulsive therapy (ECT) and MAO Inhibitors are contraindicated in adolescents. Neither do I recommend the routine use of other antidepressants since they may remove the incentive to change and create symptomatic improvement that will later deteriorate if the basic problems have not been worked through.

Although not all suicides are a result of depression, suicidal attempts frequently indicate a serious degree of depression. Motives for suicide and ways of attempting it are varied, and there are no set rules for preventing it. One thing is certain, however: any adolescent who talks about committing suicide has to be taken seriously. This does not mean he must always be institutionalized, at one extreme, or indulged, at the other. Each youth who talks about suicide or attempts it must be evaluated individually as to whether he is in need of outpatient care or requires protective confinement.

When I see such a youngster in therapy, I usually keep the parents alerted, ask them to dispose of guns and all poison that may be in the home, and direct them to keep syrup of ipecac in the house, because of the possibility of a suicidal attempt by ingestion of drugs. I also urge the patient to call me any time of the day or night if he feels upset.

The number of persons who toy with the idea of committing suicide is many times greater than the number that actually attempt it; the number that attempt it is several times larger than the number that succeed. For obvious reasons, the exact figures are unknown, but estimates in the literature range from 6 to 50 attempts for every completed suicide. The suicide rate in the United States for adolescents is about 5 to 20 per 100,000, depending on the statistics one uses in the 15 to 24 age group and is exceeded only by accidents and homicides as a cause of death among nonmilitary youth.

Two studies of suicidal adolescents (Gould, 1965; Teicher and Jacobs, 1966) found that suicide is seldom spontaneous and impulsive. Two-thirds of the adolescents had made previous attempts, and all had seriously considered suicide for a long time as a solution to their troubles. These adolescents had a history of problems accentuated during the previous five years. Many of them found they had cut themselves off from parents, friends, teachers, and had no one to talk to. Suicide is often precipitated by a chain reaction cutting of ties with the adolescent's few remaining associates. Many had a romantic attachment that ended in disappointment or pregnancy. Others lost an older sibling or a close friend.

Suicide attempts do not necessarily indicate the existence of a psychosis, although schizophrenia should be considered in the differential diagnosis. Not all suicides are the outcome of depression, but it is not possible to predict which adolescent depression may escalate to a degree where the youngster will attempt a solution through suicide. When the adolescent finds that the acting out has not controlled his depression, he may find his discomfort so intolerable that he will attempt suicide, either to call attention to his plight or actually to put himself out of his misery.

In the suicidal act, the unconscious hatred of his frustrating, depriving parent also gives rise to the need to punish the depriver by making him feel sorry, guilty, and responsible for the youngster's death. There is also a desire to make the parent change his ways of relating to the child and prove his love.

Social and cultural factors are important in determining whether a youth will attempt to solve his problems through suicide. Teicher and Jacobs's (1966) study shows that a high percentage of youths who attempt suicide have had a friend or parent who attempted suicide before. Certain cultural groups tend to have higher rates of suicide than others. Farnsworth (Braceland and Farnsworth, 1969) has commented on the "contagion" of suicide. If one suicide occurs on a college campus, or the news media report a suicide, invariably several others follow in its wake.

Conclusions

Depression is a syndrome frequently manifested in adolescents through acting-out behavior, often delinquent in character. Clues to look for are: (1) the type of behavior; (2) the loss of someone close, resulting in feelings of abandonment, inadequacy, and aloneness; (3) a background of emotional deprivation; and (4) a difficult relationship with parents.

Depression is almost always a part of the underlying psychodynamics of suicide in adolescents. It is not, however, possible to predict which adolescent will find that acting out does not serve to contain his depression and whose discomfort is so intolerable that he will attempt suicide to call attention to his plight or sink into oblivion. Factors that contribute to such a decision include a build-up of disappointments, a dissolution of significant relationships, the loss of a love object due to the breaking up of a romance or a pregnancy, and being part of a sociocultural climate that condones suicide.

Psychotherapy is effective when directed first toward containing the acting-out symptoms and then toward working out the depression. Anxiety-relieving and antidepressant drugs are often helpful and should be integrated with psychotherapy.

REFERENCES[1]

Braceland, F. J. & Farnsworth, D. L. (1969), Depression in adolescents and college students. *MD State Med. J.*, 18:67–73.

Chwast, J. (1967), Depressive reactions as manifested among adolescent delinquents. *Amer. J. Psychother.*, 21:575–584.

Gould, R. E. (1965), Suicide problems in children and adolescents. *Amer. J. Psychother.*, 19:228–246.

Sugar, M. (1968), Normal adolescent mourning. *Amer. J. Psychother.*, 22:258–269.

Teicher, J. D. & Jacobs, J. (1966), Adolescents who attempt suicide: Preliminary findings. *Amer. J. Psychiat.*, 122:1248–1257.

[1]Because Dr. Schonfeld did not complete his work on this paper, the references cited in the manuscript are incomplete and have been reconstructed by the Editor (RCM).

5 REFLECTIONS ON THE HISTORY OF ADOLESCENT PSYCHIATRY

HERMAN D. STAPLES

The entire history of adolescent psychiatry lies in this century, with most of it concentrated in the years since World War II. It is sobering to think that I was an eyewitness to a good deal of it. My remarks, therefore, will be my personal reflections rather than a scholarly treatise.

Necessarily, the history of adolescent psychiatry must emerge from our understanding of childhood and adolescence from the physiological, psychological, and sociocultural perspectives. Physiologically, growth processes in the first two decades of life have remained relatively the same throughout the ages, with the possible exception of the decreasing age of menarche and, less well-documented, spermarche. Socioculturally, the changes have been enormous, influenced so much by the doubling, and perhaps tripling, of the average expectable life span; by the revolutionary changes in labor practices; by economic, legal, and educational factors; by changes in customs and attitudes toward the young. It wasn't too long ago that a 13-year-old bar mitzvah boy could declare with a straight face, "Today I am a man." Indeed, the very concept of adolescence seems to be a modern invention when one considers that, until recently, a human being was regarded as either a child or an adult, with a changeover at somewhere between 7 to 14 years of age. At the turn of this century, one could say that public education was still a new concept, that age 16 was a top age for most youngsters to leave school, and only a few going on to college. Child labor laws were beginning to appear, postponing the time of entry into the labor market, and conditions ripened for the advent of an adolescent period of time to be carved out between carefree childhood and responsible adulthood. In the medical world, in the latter part of the 19th century, pediatrics was split off from what is now internal medicine. The subspecialty of adolescent medicine is much newer and is contemporaneous with adolescent psychiatry.

In the field of psychiatry in the first decades of the 1900s, the title "alienist" was giving way to the designation of "psychiatrist," although much of practice still dealt with psychotic patients. Many psychiatrists were really "neuropsychiatrists," which indicated the dual origin of the specialty. Freud was a good example of someone who began in neurology and then broke away into psychiatry, where he created such a vast enlargement of our understanding of psychoneuroses and character disorders. It is interesting that Dora (Freud, 1905), the first in a series of case studies of patients generally considered to be adults, was 18 years old when her three-month treatment took place in 1899. By our standards, she would be designated an adolescent, but in 1905, when the case was published, she may well have been considered an adult. Given our penchant for finding firsts, Dora could lay claim to being the subject of the first adolescent case history.

Another first would have to be the two-volume classic on adolescent psychiatry written in 1904 by G. Stanley Hall, who is generally regarded as the father of adolescent psychiatry. This text emphasizes the *Sturm und Drang* of adolescence. Freud (1909) is also famous for writing the first psychoanalytic child case, that of Little Hans. Of course, Freud worked entirely with the physician/father and saw Little Hans only once and briefly in the waiting room. Child psychiatry, as we understand it, simply did not exist in the early 1900s.

Most of the attention that was focused on young people in those years had to do with juvenile delinquency. William Healy, a general psychiatrist, founded the Chicago Institute for Juvenile Research in 1909, largely to try to meet the challenge of delinquency in youngsters. It is to his credit that he recognized the need to broaden the aim when he established the Judge Baker Clinic in Boston in 1917.

Another area of concern and some progress was the field of mental retardation or mental deficiency. In 1905 Binet and Simon developed the first standardized test of IQ. In the 1910s the development of psychoanalysis and work with delinquency continued and expanded. August Aichhorn of Vienna seemed to be able to bridge both streams; he was an analyst with a special gift for working with juvenile delinquents by applying analytic principles. His book, *Wayward Youth* (Aichhorn, 1936), is still worth reading.

In psychiatric circles less affected by psychoanalysis, those psychiatrists working with emotionally disturbed children saw that they would need to alter the child–parent relationship and to deal with other aspects of the child's social and educational environment. The extent of this undertaking favored the involvement of psychologists and social workers to share the work load. This could best be done in a clinic with a team approach to working with children and parents. The 1920s saw a proliferation of child guidance clinics with the financial stimulation of the Commonwealth Fund; governmental funds for mental health were virtually unheard of in those days. The influx of social workers, psychologists, and, to a lesser extent, nurses and teachers, all as members of a team, usually under the leadership of a psychiatrist, led to the formation of the American Orthopsychiatric Association in 1926 with William Healy as the first president.

Jean Piaget, of Geneva, began his groundbreaking studies in the 1920s on the development of cognition and judgment in children and adolescents. In Vienna, Anna Freud began to adapt psychoanalytic principles to children and to develop the field of child analysis based on direct work with children.

Standard-setting and certification of competency in various specialties began in the 1930s. The American Board of Psychiatry and Neurology was established in 1934, granting certification in the one type of psychiatry that existed officially, that of general psychiatry. The first children's psychiatric ward was set up at Bellevue Hospital in New York in 1923, and the first adolescent psychiatric clinic was established, also in New York, 14 years later in 1937. In general, the 1930s were years of consolidation and slow growth with few new gains. With the rapid escalation of demand brought on by World War II, however, the 1940s touched off far-reaching changes and explosive growth. The American Psychiatric Association appointed its first Committee on Child Psychiatry in 1949. The National Institute for Mental Health was formed that same year with Robert Felix as its first Director. The need to have an organization to speak for children's clinics resulted in the formation of the American Association of Psychiatric Clinics for Children in 1948 with Fred Allen as its first president. The A.A.P.C.C. began the process of setting standards for each discipline in child guidance clinics; this function was later taken over for child psychiatry by the American Board. The 1940s also saw the introduction by Leo Kanner of a new and puzzling diagnostic category of childhood autism. Erik Erikson was formulating his ideas on the psychosocial stages throughout the life cycle, ideas on Identity, and psychohistory.

The 1950s marked the dawn of a new age of psychopharmacology with the introduction of chlorpromazine in 1953. It was a decade, too, when family therapy came into its own. And after several decades of increase in the number of psychiatrists working predominantly with children and accumulating more and more knowledge of the basic core of such work, the American Academy of Child Psychiatry was formed in 1953, with George Gardner as its first president. It is noteworthy that a Child Psychiatry Board was first recommended but officially rejected in the 1940s. By 1957, however, the APA Council allowed it, and the first board exams were given in 1959. The first local Society for Adolescent Psychiatry was formed in New York in 1958 with James Masterson as first president. This is part of a story within-a-story that I will go into later, but for now I want to complete the decade-to-decade survey.

The 1960s were turbulent but creative years. The Association for Child Psychoanalysis was formed by Anna Freud, Marianne Kris, and others in 1965. The American Society for Adolescent Psychiatry was formed in 1967 with William Schonfeld as the founding president. The American Academy of Child Psychiatry liberalized its membership in 1969. The field of group therapy made important strides. Peter Blos published his monumental, definitive text, *On Adolescence,* in 1962. Margaret Mahler began to publish her seminal research findings on separation/individuation theory.

The 1970s was another era of consolidation and steady growth. Interest increased in adolescent psychiatry and in geriatric psychiatry. The first volume of the *Annals of Adolescent Psychiatry* appeared in 1971 as an annual publication of the American Society for Adolescent Psychiatry, guided until this volume by Sherman Feinstein as the editor-in-chief.

I would single out two important developments in the 1980s: one is salutary; the other, much less so. The first is the increasing interest in infant psychiatry; the second is the rise of managed care with its far-reaching effects on adolescent psychiatry practice. Organizationally, the World Association for Infant Psychiatry was formed in Portugal in 1980 with Eleanor Galenson and Justin Call as the first copresidents. The International Society for Adolescent Psychiatry was organized in Paris in 1985 with Serge Lebovici as honorary president and Sherman Feinstein as First President. In 1987, the American Academy of Child Psychiatry changed its name to the American Academy of Child and Adolescent Psychiatry.

In 1992, the first examinations were given by the new Board of Adolescent Psychiatry. Beginning in the mid-1980s, there was a growing trend to downplay the predominant role of infant psychiatrists and psychoanalysts in the field of infant psychiatry and to upgrade the role of the "developmentalists," culminating in an organizational name change to the World Association for Infant Mental Health. In the meantime, the effects of managed care have been intensifying with, at best, mixed results.

So far, I have outlined mostly social and organizational events. Now to elaborate on some points of tension that have surfaced during our history. To do this, I will play the role of a commentator writing with personal views and biases, rather than a completely objective historian. As I thought about the last 50 years in our field, certain aphorisms kept coming to mind, such as ying/yang or the back-and-forth swing of the pendulum; the truism that every one is a lumper or splitter; the cynical saying that "what goes around, comes around"; the view that if you live long enough, you see that everything repeats itself. I was impressed when I contemplated that the only evolutionary change in the territoriality of our field that had occurred painlessly was the progression from neuropsychiatry into a separate neurology and psychiatry. I attribute this division to the growth of knowledge in each specialty to the point that a split became inevitable. With the recent work in neurobiology, however, we may, if we live long enough, see a resynthesis—the old lumpers-and-splitters doctrine at work.

When progress in the art of working with children suggested it was time for a split and a breaking away, we found that general psychiatry fiercely resisted and delayed this process. When the inevitable split did occur, those who had broken away into child psychiatry were perhaps overzealous in guarding their guild identity. We saw that the American Academy of Child Psychiatry became an elitist organization with very strict entrance requirements to keep the membership "pure." After 16 years of mounting pressure and the threat of the formation of a new, broader-based child psychiatric organization, the Academy reformed itself in 1969 to liberalized membership criteria. Its health flourished and its size grew to where it is now comparable to the size the American Psychiatric Association was in the not-too-distant past. Sidney Berman, an Academy president and a prime mover in the changeover, described the events in the January/February 1993 issue of the Academy's *Newsletter*.

While the liberalization of membership requirements did bring in those with special training in child psychiatry, it did nothing for psychiatrists without formal child training who felt comfortable working with adolescents. During the years when the Academy was so exclusive, there arose another response to the problem. As we have seen, the concept of adolescence was a long time being established. Without a biological marker for the end of adolescence, at midcentury child psychiatry included all the years up to 18, with the years from about 16 to about 22 in a kind of no man's land. Child psychiatrists were usually involved more with prelatency and latency children and with young adolescents, while some general or adult psychiatrists liked working with older adolescents and young adults, roughly the latter years of high school and the college years. Accordingly, it was only natural for a movement to start to organize a group to speak for, and deal with, older adolescents. William Schonfeld, a former pediatrician with a special interest in adolescents, and several other New Yorkers, James Masterson and Bert Slaff, organized the New York Society for Adolescent Psychiatry in 1958. Similar groups soon formed in Philadelphia, Chicago, and Southern California. Joining these four basic groups the American Society for Adolescent Psychiatry was founded, in 1967, as a confederation of local societies. The large increase in the numbers of adolescents in the population and the striking ways in which they called attention to themselves in the 1960s may have touched off concern on the part of some child psychiatrists that their field might be splitting, with the creation of a public image that their role would be limited to children under the age of puberty.

I do not mean to ignore the theoretical basis for claiming that a thorough knowledge of childhood is highly desirable for working with adolescents. Indeed, we all know that knowledge about childhood and adolescence is critical for working with adults. Historically, the concept of child psychiatry has always included adolescence, and I know of no attempt to change that. However, there began a series of name changes in the 1970s and 1980s to add the words "and Adolescent" to the title of child psychiatric organizations, beginning with the International Association of Child and Adolescent Psychiatry and Allied Professions (IA-CAPAP), the American Academy of Child and Adolescent Psychiatry, the American Board of Child and Adolescent Psychiatry, the various publications, — all to make sure that everyone knew that adolescence was included with childhood. It is interesting to me that only the analysts have so far resisted this movement — the Association for Child Psychoanalysis has not changed its title even though it often devotes meetings to adolescence.

I mentioned, "what goes around, comes around." I cannot help but see a repetition of history when I think of the resistance of general psychiatry to the birth of child psychiatry, followed by the opposition of child psychiatry to the birth of adolescent psychiatry. Another historical saying is that the past is prologue to the future. It is ironic that a similar conflict may yet develop on the lower end of childhood with the emergence of the subspecialty of infant psychiatry, which first formed its own organization in 1980—the splitting process all over again.

The tensions in our field that have been described are largely interorganizational. There is another type of tension that should be noted, the sometimes subtle and sometimes acute tension between disciplines involved in mental health. While the relationship of the two national organizations dealing with children and adolescents and with adolescents exclusively has occasionally been a bit strained, they have in common restricting full membership to psychiatrists. This restriction seems to be less rigid in Europe and in international organizations, for example, IACAPAP and ISAP, the International Society for Adolescent Psychiatry. It is well known that Freud welcomed nonmedical colleagues into the field of psychoanalysis, but the American Psychoanalytic Association had many restrictions until a few years ago, when a long and costly law suit filed by the American Psychological Association changed all that. Again, the Association for Child Psychoanalysis, probably owing to the influence of Anna Freud, always accepted nonmedical child analysts as full members.

As we head toward the next century and are on the threshold of sweeping changes in mental health practice, it remains to be seen whether the fundamental changes forced on all of us will push the pendulum toward the splitters or the lumpers. Will we be shoved in the direction of interdisciplinary strife as we compete for a share of the health dollar? Or will we gravitate toward unity in the face of a common enemy—the politicians, bureaucrats, insurance companies, and the ilk who have carved out a large place for themselves in what used to be our field of mental health?

One last cliché—time will tell.

REFERENCES

Aichhorn, A. (1936), *Wayward Youth.* New York: Putnam's Sons.
Freud, S. (1905), Fragment of an Analysis of a Case of Hysteria. *Standard Edition,* 7:7–122. London: Hogarth Press, 1953.
_____ (1909), Analysis of a phobia in a five-year-old boy. *Standard Edition,* 109:5–149. London: Hogarth Press, 1955.
Grun, B. (1975), *The Timetables of History.* New York: Simon & Schuster.

APPENDIX I: PIONEERS AND IMPORTANT FIGURES IN ADOLESCENT PSYCHIATRY

G. STANLEY HALL - Credited with being the Father of Adolescent Psychiatry. 1904 - Published first textbook on Adolescent Psychiatry; mentioned the *Sturm und Drang* of Adolescence.

SIGMUND FREUD - 1905 - Published first Adolescent Case Study, "Fragment of an Analysis of a Case of Hysteria" (Dora, 18 years old). 1909 - "Analysis of a Phobia in a Five-Year-Old Boy" (Little Hans)

ANNA FREUD - Wrote "Introduction to the Technique of Child Analysis," "Ego and the Mechanisms of Defense," many others, including several on Adolescence.

AUGUST AICHHORN - Vienna - Psychoanalytically oriented treatment of delinquents. *Wayward Youth.*

WILLIAM HEALY - 1909 - Founded the Institute for Juvenile Research in Chicago for the treatment of juvenile delinquents. First President of the American Orthopsychiatric Association.

JOHN BOWLBY - England - Wrote about maternal care, attachment, separation, etc.

JEAN PIAGET - Swiss - Illuminated many aspects of the cognitive and moral development of children and adolescents.

ERIK ERIKSON - Introduced the concept of identity formation, psychosexual stages throughout the life cycle, etc.

PETER BLOS - Pioneer developer of the psychoanalytic understanding of adolescence and the treatment of adolescents. Wrote the landmark text, *On Adolescence.*

MARGARET MAHLER - Introduced the concept of separation-individuation as a stage in ego development with reverberations throughout childhood, adolescence, and adulthood.

LEO KANNER - Introduced the condition of infantile and childhood autism.

FRITZ REDL - Original work in the group approach with delinquent youth and research-oriented residential treatment.

WILLIAM SCHONFELD - Founder and first president of the American Society for Adolescent Psychiatry.

JAMES MASTERSON - First president of the New York Society for Adolescent Psychiatry.

DANIEL OFFER - Important research on normal adolescents.

SERGE LEBOVICI - Paris - Founder and honorary president of the International Society for Adolescent Psychiatry.

SHERMAN FEINSTEIN - Cofounder and first president of the International Society for Adolescent Psychiatry, long-time editor of *Annals of Adolescent Psychiatry*.

AARON ESMAN - Editor of the first *Annals of International Adolescent Psychiatry* and other important books on adolescent psychiatry.

APPENDIX II: TIMETABLES OF ADOLESCENT PSYCHIATRY HISTORY[1]

YEARS	EVENTS	ISSUES	ORGANIZATIONS	TEXTBOOKS/PAPERS
1900s	Wm. Healy founded the Institute for Juvenile Research, Chicago, 1909	Early emphasis on juvenile delinquency; early psychoanalytic case studies; Binet & Simon developed 1st IQ test, 1905	First textbook of adolescent psychiatry by G. Stanley Hall; first adolescent case study (Dora, 18 years old) by Sigmund Freud, 1905	
1910s	Wm. Healy established the Judge Baker Child Guidance Clinic, Boston, 1917	August Aichhorn worked with delinquents in Vienna *The Individual Delinquent* by Wm. Healy, 1915		
1920s	Eight child guidance clinics established with aid of the Commonwealth Fund; first children's psychiatric ward at Bellevue Hospital, New York City, 1923	Work with adolescents went beyond delinquency to treat all types of emotional and behavioral conditions; Jean Piaget began studies of early child development	American Orthopsychiatric Association founded, first president, Wm. Healy, 1926	*Wayward Youth* by August Aichhorn, 1925; *Introduction to the Technique of Child Analysis* by Anna Freud, 1928
1930s	American Board of Psychiatry and Neurology established, 1934; first adolescent psychiatry clinic, New York City, 1937			
1940s	First American Psychiatric Association Committee on Child Psychiatry appointed, 1949; National Institute for Mental Health established, first Director, Robert Felix, 1949	Emphasis on Group Work with delinquents; Child Psychiatry Boards recommended but not approved	American Association of Psychiatric Clinics for Children founded, first President Fred Allen, 1948	*Childhood Autism* by Leo Kanner, 1944
1950s	Chlorpromazine begins to revolutionize psychopharmacology, 1953; APA Council allows Child Psychiatry Boards, 1957; first Child Psychiatry Boards given in 1959	Family Therapy comes into its own	American Academy of Child Psychiatry founded, first President George Gardner, 1953; New York Society for Adolescent Psychiatry formed, first President James Masterson, 1958	

	Events	Issues	Organizations	Textbooks
1960s	American Academy of Child Psychiatry liberalized its membership requirements, 1969	Group Therapy comes into its own	Association for Child Psychoanalysis founded by Anna Freud & Marianne Kris, 1965; American Society for Adolescent Psychiatry formed, first President William Schonfeld, 1967	*On Human Symbiosis and the Vicissitudes of Individuation* by Margaret Mahler, 1968; *On Adolescence* by Peter Blos, 1962
1970s		Decade of increased interest in adolescent psychiatry and in geropsychiatry	AAPCC changes its name to American Association for Psychiatric Services for Children and gives up standard setting	First volume of *Adolescent Psychiatry*, 1971 (ASAP annual publication)
1980s	Founding Congress of the International Society for Adolescent Psychiatry, Paris, 1985	Decade of increased interest in infancy; managed care begins to affect adolescent psychiatric practice	World Association for Infant Psychiatry & Allied Disciplines formed, first Copresidents, Eleanor Galenson & Justin Call, 1980; International Society for Adolescent Psychiatry formed, Honorary President Serge Lebovici & President Sherman Feinstein, 1985; AACP changed name to . . . Child *and Adolescent* Psychiatry, 1987	
1990s to date	Third ISAP Congress, 1992, Chicago; first examinations given by the new American Board of Adolescent Psychiatry, 1992	Continuation and intensification of impact of managed care on adolescent psychiatry	World Association for Infant Psychiatry changes its name to World Association for Infant Mental Health	

[1] In trying to outline the history of Adolescent Psychiatry, I adapted the format used by Bernard Grun (1975) in *The Timetables of History*. You will find in the appendix a chart showing decade by decade what occurred under Events, Issues, Organizations, and Textbooks. In addition, I listed some of the most outstanding pioneers and leaders in the development of our field.

VIENNA PSYCHOANALYTIC SOCIETY

MINUTES— FEBRUARY 15, 1922

(TRANS. JULIE WINTER AND RICHARD C. MAROHN)

CONCERNING A TYPICAL FORM OF

MALE PUBERTY

DR. SIEGFRIED BERNFELD

(TRANS. JULIE WINTER AND RICHARD C. MAROHN)

COMMENTS ON DR. SIEGFRIED BERNFELD'S

PAPER, "CONCERNING A TYPICAL FORM OF

MALE PUBERTY"

RICHARD C. MAROHN

Vienna Psychoanalytic Society Minutes— February 15, 1922*

11TH MEETING, FEBRUARY 15, 1922

Present: Prof. Freud, Aichhorn, Storfer, Nunberg, Deutsch, Schmiedeberg, Dr. Steinberg, Hoffman, Dr. Folschauer, Dr. Fennichel, Dr. Bychowski, Assistant Prof. Schilder, Dr. Gohl, Dr. Kaplan, Dr. Bernfeld, Dr. Klug, Dr. Mitschermann, Ruth, Rauh, Dr. Bold, Dr. Bibering, Miss Adrian, Dr. Keitzt, Assistant Prof. Pappenheim, Dr. Winterstein, Dr. Federn, Dr. Sadiger, Dr. Sperber, Dr. Reuch, Fennichel, Assistant Prof. Friedjung.

*From the Siegfried Bernfeld Papers, Container #8, Manuscript Division, Library of Congress. Translated by Julie Winter and Richard C. Marohn.

NEXT MEETING ON MARCH 1, 1922

Asst. Prof. Schilder and Dr. Federn on Schilder's *Wesen der Hypnose* [The Essence of Hypnotism]
Dr. Bernfeld: concerning a typical form of male puberty.
Physiological and psychological puberty. Extended puberty as a social phenomenon. Idealistic interests and a productive interest in the goal, great deal of self- consciousness and symptoms of the onset of repression, tendencies to depreciate others with the exception of the friend, since personal love of the friend is said to be developed. The self is extraordinarily cathected at the expense of object choice. Conflict between the ideal self and the real self typical of puberty.
Dr. Oberholzer: Concerning a case of inferiority in neurosis.
Clinical _____ concerning a case of an oversized penis.
Dr. Mitschermann: An oversized organ unsuitable for use is not necessarily experienced as overvalued.

Concerning a Typical Form of Male Puberty*

SIEGFRIED BERNFELD

Studying the literature on sexual behavior and psychology readily demonstrates that the investigations and conclusions of these sciences do not apply equally to all stages of the nonadult. In particular, adolescence has until now received little consideration and is less well described and still less understood than the earlier periods of psychic and sexual development. This fact can arouse all the more astonishment and can stimulate one to further scientific work because a specifically human phenomenon presents itself in adolescence. The development of animal sexuality and psychology knows no such stage with similar qualities inserted between childhood and adulthood.[1] The few investigations of primitive peoples[2] seem to show that adolescence may not be a psychological characteristic of human development, but the result of "cultural" or "social" factors.

One reason for this astonishing absence in the scientific literature must

*Presented at the Vienna Psychoanalytic Society, February 15, 1922. Translated by Julie Winter and Richard C. Marohn.

Translation notes: *puberty* has been replaced by *adolescence, extended* has been replaced by *prolonged, ego* has been replacec by *self*, usually, *ideal ego* has been translated *ego ideal*.

emanate from the subject itself. Puberty is associated with extraordinarily complex phenomena, expressed in the most diverse realms: physiological, psychological, and, not the least, sociological. The psychological and psychophysical phenomena alone encompass a [host of areas.] The subject matter, however, is not the only complexity; the structure of adolescent phenomena is also complex. Because of the many individual, social, cultural, historical, and physical differences these phenomena exhibit, the scientist is not inclined to group them under a single term. Yet it seems justified to speak of *adolescence*, its determinants, and its function. Researchers also share this naive idea of the subject, and *adolescence* is used colloquially in common speech.

Psychoanalysis provides another decisive scientific reason for conceptualizing the manifestations of adolescence as a unitary process. Libido theory maintains that all simultaneous [psychosomatic or psychosexual processes] are mutually interdependent and are the result of the preceding stages. At the same time, psychoanalysis describes precisely the essentials of a given stage of development and distinguishes among the various parts, because object libido and self libido remain central and motivating, even when one is exploring very remote psychical and physical regions. Certainly, psychoanalysis has not tried to show that all the phenomena of adolescence can be seen as a coherent unity, and perhaps cannot do so; however, psychoanalysis does enable us to achieve coherence for the libidinal processes of adolescence. Freud[3] formulated the characteristics of adolescence, its phenomena as well as its psychosexual functions: in adolescence, infantile sexual life undergoes two important changes, which transform it into its more definite adult form. First of all, "the subordination of all other sources of sexual excitement under the primacy of the genital zones" takes place. This change "is realized by means of the mechanism of exploitation of forepleasure (*"Vorlust"*), whereby the otherwise independent sexual acts, which are tied together with pleasure and excitement, become preparatory acts for the new sexual goal, the expulsion of the sexual products." Second, the "process of object finding" is completed in adolescence. And, to be sure, this final, second object choice occurs, "led by means of the infantile manifestations of the child's sexual inclinations toward his parents and those who take care of him which are reawakened in adolescence, and by means of the prohibitions on incest which have in the meantime been erected and redirected from these people onto other similar ones."

Our way of considering the problem, as demonstrated by these formulations, has several important advantages over the usual ways proposed by many authors. Our viewpoint sees adolescence as a functional process whose beginning and end points are given and whose duration and form are essentially determined by these two factors. Furthermore, our perspective embraces the problem psychologically and thus eliminates the difficulties that are introduced by the physiological concept "puberty." Finally, the concept of "normal adulthood" qualifies for scientific usage, precise and value free, by emphasizing a characteristic and normal attribute. However, as also noted by Freud, this perspective provides neither a description nor a clarification, nor even a criticism of the phenomenon, but leads only to a new project.

Above all, however, one important fact is clear, even though no one has drawn any definite conclusions from it: the duration of adolescence is subject to extraordinary variation. It is not merely a matter of definition or lack of it when authors differ in estimating adolescence to last from two or three to seven or eight years. Certain definitions, such as the physiological or the sociological-historical, make it possible to specify a more precise duration. The other psychic developmental stages exhibit variations in length, but they are relatively narrowly defined. According to the Freudian formulation, which we endorse, duration is not a significant characteristic of adolescence, but rather a principle for classifying the various forms and types of adolescence.

Accordingly, the possible duration of adolescence is theoretically unlimited. Some people never reach the end stage of the object-finding period of their lives. Convention, or nonscientific usage, dictates whom we will call "neurotic" and whether we say that the "normal" person of this group experiences "permanent adolescence" or whether we can use a completely different term. The difficulty is derived, in any case, from a fixation of the libido that could no longer be undone.

The beginning of adolescence is more sharply drawn, because the sexual goal, for which the task of adolescence is to lay the foundation and to reach, is tied to physical conditions whose maturation takes a certain number of years. Therefore, we will accept two years as an average estimate given by these authors. From this point onward, one moves toward the end point of adolescence. Not reaching the end point must be the result of a fixation of the libido or to some turn of fate that for a period of time has a similar result.

We can, then, distinguish two different developmental processes: (1) ϕ [sexual capacity], sexual capability, the result of a physiological process and Φ [genital maturation], the ability to have an erection, to ejaculate, and to experience appropriate stimuli as sexual excitement in the genital apparatus; (2) ψ [libidinal sexual needs], the sexual needs that correspond to Φ [genital maturation], the result of a definite libido development, and Ψ [appropriate sexual gratification], whereby appropriate stimuli for sexual excitement is habitually employed and the resulting tension seeks to find resolution through an object.* Thus, adolescence can be conceptualized in two phases: the beginning, occurring when prior development divides into a ϕ [sexual capacity] and a ψ [libidinal sexual needs] line; the pivotal point occurs when ϕ [sexual capacity] becomes Φ [genital maturation], the end point when ψ [libidinal sexual needs] becomes Ψ [appropriate sexual gratification].

The duration of the first part (Φ [genital maturation]) is relatively constant. Fluctuations can certainly not be ruled out, but the amount of variation is normally quite small. The development of sexual capability is bound to physiological processes, whose conditions are more or less the same in all normal individuals. The second part of adolescence is the adaptation of the sexual need to the new situation, the part of adolescence that actually varies, and the degree of variation is large, larger than in other developmental processes that run a regular course. This is the psychical portion of adolescence. According to this formulation, the duration of adolescence is psychically determined.

Theoretically, the shortest adolescence would be Ψ [appropriate sexual gratification], the necessary, physically determined adolescence, and, accordingly, ψ [libidinal sexual needs] adolescence of any duration would be designated as *prolonged adolescence*, a psychical phenomenon. According to our current state of empirical knowledge, this would seem to be beyond dispute. The attentive student of adolescence, however, notices that this frequent complication is a generally valid process, namely, that ψ [libidinal sexual needs] is always somewhat longer than Φ [genital maturation], and that the adaptation of the psychical to the physical, which is expressed through this difference ($\psi - \Phi$ [libidinal sexual needs] – [genital maturation]), always takes a certain amount of time, even if small.

In the balance of this paper, we will be concerned only with that form of adolescence which we designate as *prolonged adolescence*, whose end lies in the normal range but only after the conclusion of the development

*The authors have devised and inserted key words in brackets [. . . .] after Bernfeld's Greek symbols, in the hope of simplifying understanding of the text. Thus, Φ = genital maturation and ϕ = sexual capacity, the two physiological parameters; Ψ = appropriate sexual gratification and ψ = libidinal sexual needs, the two psychological parameters; and ψPb = prolonged adolescence.

of the sexual capability (Φ [genital maturation]), along with the shortest adaptation of the sexual need to the developed sexual capability, which can be empirically ascertained. We will symbolize *prolonged adolescence* as ψPb [prolonged adolescence]. Prolonged adolescence is a form of adolescence that certainly appears often enough to designate it as typical. Of course, it would be preferable to speak of the range of kinds of prolonged adolescence, because the course of ψPb [prolonged adolescence] is never the same in all cases, but, rather, there are also many varieties that can be delineated and described.

We will now try to delineate one type of ψPb [prolonged adolescence] and characterize its noticeable features, but not without difficulty, because there are no carefully selected, well-studied individual cases to undertake such a demarcation and description. The literature offers no suitable material for this, and the detailed representation of even one well-developed case of ψPb [prolonged adolescence] would require a publication of great size. Sooner or later such case reports will be necessary.[4] In anticipation, it makes sense to describe clinical vignettes based on impressions and observations of many youths, from personal knowledge or from literature.

The most noticeable and clamorous form of adolescence is an example of ψPb [prolonged adolescence], evident in a visible and striking way in today's "Youth Movement" ("*Jugendbewegung*") of Germany and Austria. In other countries, this form of adolescence has shown itself in similar, but less well-known and less famous, movements and, as a student organization, has attracted a certain degree of recognition and respect for centuries. Of course, all these social movements are as little psychically identical as the youths who are active within them. To make distinctions within ψPb [prolonged adolescence], however, it is necessary to grasp it as a whole in all of its appearances. Therefore, we mean ψPb [prolonged adolescence] whenever we speak of "youth" in a cultural sense, the youth of a political party, the youth of an artistic movement, youth in a revolution, and so on. We do not use the word youth in a metaphorical sense but, rather, mean a particular phase of life, one that is similar to the adult phase, but, in other respects, nonadult.

Youth has a direct, active, cultural meaning, whether one considers it progressive or harmful, because it participates in the substance of culture and in its transformations. The cultural realms of youth participation have not always been the same; religion, politics, art, science, "social life," sports, and so forth, may be alternately or at the same time affected. ψPb [prolonged adolescence] does not always appear in cultural life strongly and clearly; there have been eras when it was not at all evident (where ψPb [prolonged adolescence] had not yet developed or had not appeared in enough people to come under sociological purview). Usually, the cultural manifestations of ψPb [prolonged adolescence] are the same, a revolutionary effect, raising challenges and promoting causes, points of view, and ways of doing things that contradict those of the adults of the time and are therefore relatively new. This is not necessarily the case, however, for each ψPb [prolonged adolescence] generation or for all of them. In another sense, the cultural function is quite general (although certainly each ψPb [prolonged adolescence] individual is not necessarily involved in it). When ψPb [prolonged adolescence] occurs is the time when certain aspects and forms of cultural life are "propagated." It is during ψPb [prolonged adolescence] that a person first, and in an enduring way, develops an interest in certain aspects of culture and allows them to have a considerable role in his psychical make-up. Never before and rarely afterwards does this happen and then only under particular and not entirely normal conditions. Individuals who do not develop a ψPb [prolonged adolescence] are deprived of these experiences and their psychical and spiritual consequences and the important role they play. Pedagogy and the cultural politics ("*Kulturpolitik*") for that reason have always given ψPb [prolonged adolescence] special attention—naturally without getting into scientific methods of examination. We hope to have shown at the end of this investigation that the introduction of a scientific perspective demonstrates the problem to appear much more complex, and the pedagogical conclusions much more reckless, than was suspected before.

While ψPb [prolonged adolescence] is characterized as a social phenomenon, it is not so easily characterized from an individual psychological perspective. Of course, very heterogeneous individual types can appear as a relatively unified group. All individuals who generate the social phenomenon ψPb [prolonged adolescence] do not necessarily also participate in the psychical phenomenon ψPb [prolonged adolescence]. From our psychoanalytic perspective, the social sense serves to define sharply the psychological type, and it is this type which we will encounter among the dominant persons of the ψPb [prolonged adolescence] generation. Among the young leaders of the current ψPb [prolonged adolescence] generation, we can easily designate a group that shares a number of characteristics.

First, this type is striking because of his many interests in things or behaviors that do not ordinarily receive such attention. As diverse as these interests may be, they tend to be idealistic in nature. They serve neither a sublimated libido nor the satisfaction of the ego (self-preservative) instincts directly. Frequently, the objects of these interests are the foregoing "spiritual values"—art, politics, humanity, and such— but also more individually colored, eccentric, or specialized values. In any event, these interests are different from the customary objects of the two basic drives: property and woman; often, they develop in such a way that they have little or nothing to do with these drives. In extreme, but not at all uncommon, cases, the whole strength of the libido and ego instincts is directed toward those "spiritual" goals; usually, however, only a variable, though large, amount is so allocated. Other interests and goals are concealed, kept secret, distorted, or indirectly pursued, and they never appear as components of the ego ideal of youth.

Second, the person's relationship to his goals is characteristically productive, but it is difficult to describe the appearances of this relationship. The ψPb [prolonged adolescence] youth who is interested in art is not satisfied with enjoying the art of others or with believing in the higher meaning of art, but he tries to create such works himself, to realize the higher meaning of art through his own activity. This tendency does not necessarily produce actual works of art (to say nothing of whether they have any artistic worth, for this is outside the realm of psychology), because there are many factors and situations that can hinder artistry; however, ψPb [prolonged adolescence] youth never lack this tendency toward productivity. The concept of productivity is complex, especially when art, philosophy, or science is not the central interest and when this interest does not know or give rise to concrete "works." {But here also we see a tendency that would be analogous to that of "Works - Production - Willing."} This is what happens when two 17-year-olds, devoted to the "idea of humanity," found a "Free Society of Those Becoming"[5] than has and can have no real function and can be understood only in terms of the longing of these two youths to achieve something, anything at all, for their idea, even if it is the partial, illusory[6] realization of a fantasy game. In a general sense, ψPb [prolonged adolescence] productivity is significant in two ways: to show one's idealism to the outside world and to effect it in a personal, spontaneous, and original manner.

This superficial characterization might depict underlying motives but does not do this for every instance, and does not even intend to do this.

Third, the youth is usually profoundly self-conscious of these two characteristics, or else they evade repression. The person himself and his works are highly esteemed and taken seriously, overesteemed according to everybody except for his closest friends. Usually, this esteem refers only to single physical or character traits, only to certain works or some of their qualities. Sometimes, self-esteem appears to be missing, since many expressions of the "sense of inferiority" and of self-hate are apparent. Psychoanalysis is not necessary to recognize the ambivalent nature of this behavior or its genesis from repressions, indeed from very superficial repressions. In addition, these youths demonstrate an exaggerated self-esteem, by slighting either the older generation or their peers, at least the majority of them. We usually find both to the same degree.

To this triad we add other characteristics, atypically and incompletely expressed, but frequently part of the manifest form of ψPb [prolonged adolescence]. Two are especially worth mentioning because of their theoretical value, and we will discuss them later.

Fourth, while the need to depreciate others is sometimes intense and can be directed against all personal acquaintances, against "man" in general, or especially against one's own generation and against the authorities, one or a few of one's contemporaries and of the older generation are excluded, such as a friend or teacher, not necessarily still living. Love and respect are given only to these two, or to a very few.

Fifth, the creation of a loving friendship {ideologically} and to expand it to a whole circle of friends of similar orientation, same status, equal worth, and comparable sensitivity occurs frequently in the ψPb [prolonged adolescence] in question.[7] How this tendency manifests itself and whether it occurs at all depends on currently unknown psychical and social conditions. While this tendency is frequently seen, it is even more typically wished for. In addition, we should include not only those instances of true companionship or of the wish for it, but also the many situations in which there is not a physical coming together: For example the contributors to a student newspaper form no group with one another, perhaps do not even know one another, but still feel themselves bound together by a certain something that they all share, something like: "We have the duty, since the inquiry into the soul . . . could not be purely accomplished, to try to do this by other means. . . ."[8] or "We merely want to have peace and time . . . to be able to come to terms with ourselves."[9]

In describing this form of ψPb [prolonged adolescence], we intentionally avoided more precise terms. We cannot assume that our readers have a broad understanding of adolescence. To substitute debates about correct theory for relative degrees of ignorance was not possible for various reasons, and so we tried to tie together memories and experiences with a symbol (ψPb [prolonged adolescence]), which does not generate abstract and definite formulations. This method does not facilitate further study. Understanding is achieved only by a precise psychoanalytic classification. Our first attempt at "translation" already demonstrates this because a number of the aforementioned characteristics have a common root, "narcissism."

This ego experiences an exceptionally strengthened libidinal obsession in comparison to the latency period and the other forms of adolescence, and, to be sure, this occurs at the cost of the object. As a result, phenomena appear that are similar to those of the psychoses, but the difference is clear enough: the objects do not become completely empty of libido, for even true love is not uncommon in the ψPb [prolonged adolescence] way of thinking and certainly cannot be excluded. In this context, frequent, but not essential, phenomena of this form of adolescence become understandable, like the frequent, if transitory, narcissistic homosexual fixation.

Theoretically, this attachment is quite important and, as far as we can tell, insufficiently appreciated. The recognized task in Freud's formulation quoted at the beginning runs into trouble; instead of the sexual drives attaching to an object, a considerable portion is transformed into narcissism and thus produces a secondary—if you will, also a tertiary— narcissistic situation, alongside the remaining object libidinal attachment, which probably does not always stay in a constant relationship to it.

This pubertal narcissism is distinguished very sharply from the infantile by means of an economic moment. It is not pleasurable, or is pleasurable only to a small degree, and is very reminiscent of melancholic conditions; in any case, it is accompanied by many deep depressions. The reason for this is that an ego ideal is formed, one which binds a great deal of libido to itself; and the stronger this tie becomes, the more the ego ideal becomes distanced from the real self and, as is absolutely characteristic of ψPb [prolonged adolescence], stands in opposition to it. The conflict, which in ψPb [prolonged adolescence] always emerges between real self and the ego ideal and sometimes takes on considerable strength, allows for different outcomes, which until now have been little studied. For that reason, we can hardly accomplish more than to see whether a typical resolution of the conflict corresponds to the typical form of ψPb [prolonged adolescence] under consideration.

One can describe the conflict approximately in this way: the libidinal strivings, which reinvest the self or develop within it, are prevented by the ego ideal from binding themselves to the self; they are diverted from their goal and seek possibilities for satisfaction which the ego ideal can allow. Endopsychic forms offer themselves as such possibilities: fantasies, judgments, ideas, which through the narcissistic satisfaction they offer become a kind of object. Of course, they become objects that differentiate themselves from those occupied with object libido in a way that is not easy to formulate. One calls such "also objects" ideal ones. The undisturbed satisfaction is tied together with pleasure; the sexual activity — also the diverted type — that is possible toward them is, however, different from that of the object libido toward its object. We can get a sense of this contradiction by means of the following adage: "The stars, one does not desire them, one is happy about their brilliance, and one looks with pleasure into each clear night." From a somewhat different perspective, this contradiction can be formulated in a way similar to Freud's when he described the difference between identification and object choice using the example of the identification with the father: "In the first case, the father is that which one would like to be, in the second, that which one would like to have."[10]

To excuse the lack of precision in this explanation, consider that we are moving to new, as yet unresearched, ground and attempting to initiate those investigations that Freud postulates when he says: "Let us think about the fact that the self steps now into the relationship of an object to the ego ideal that developed from it, and that possibly all mutual effects, which we have come to know between the outer object and the total self in the study of the neuroses, come to be repeated on this new stage within the ego.[11] In addition, one must also consider that a precise discrimination between the narcissistic and object libidinal strivings is very difficult, because we have to deal with subtle differentiations, which must seem contrived to the reader, since we cannot present the material out of which the differentiations clearly, although not effortlessly, arise. The formation of the ideal, as far as it occurs by means of diversion of the goal of narcissistic strivings under the pressure of failure of the ego ideal, is the fate of narcissism (a process analogous to sublimation, if one, as I have suggested,[12] uses the word sublimation in a narrow sense, as the fate of the object libido). That with formation of the ideal sublimation also plays a part, or in considerable measure could play a part, hardly needs mentioning. This conflict and its described outcome is accordingly for our form of ψPb [prolonged adolescence] characteristic and essentially encompasses its appearances causally and in a unitary way. Other conflicts, above all between ego (ego ideal) and sexuality, naturally play a part as well. Especially the Oedipus and the castration complexes, in a certain mutual relationship, are among the necessary factors in its representation.

These relationships, some of which are well known, some very complex, will be saved for another context. Here I will comment only about a remarkable and essential characteristic of our ψPb [prolonged adolescence]. We spoke earlier about the tendency toward productivity that is not always typical of the ψPb [prolonged adolescence]-form in question, although it always accompanies this (ψPb [prolonged adolescence]) to a certain degree. And, indeed, in a distinctive way: production, the creation of products—the attempt to do this, the wish to do it—is at the pleasure of the ego ideal. Production is a means to become or appear true to the ideal. The product itself as a true-to-the-ideal endopsychic object binds narcissism (and often ego-drive constituents as well). Production itself or the completed product—sometimes both—often belong, to a not inconsiderable degree, to the real world; production is a true object and therefore makes sublimations possible. At the same time, however, the work has possibilities—at least fantasized ones—to bind libido of unknown persons; with that it becomes the middle member between the self, which finds itself in introversion, and the potential sexual objects in the real world. Accordingly, the product regularly plays a large and typical role at the conclusion of ψPb [prolonged adolescence], about which we will later have something to say.

Now that we have come to know something about the economics and dynamics of ψPb [prolonged adolescence]-form, we may inquire about the conditions under which adolescence takes such a course. Apparently, a failure at the beginning or during the course of adolescence forces the object libidinal strivings to turn themselves back into the self. We know from Freud[13] which factors regularly bring about such a failure. The libido, reawakened in adolescence, must revive the infantile incestuous strivings, and the incest prohibition, which has been constructed in the intervening years, opposes the renewed wishes of the libido. Only one other condition is needed to clarify the fact of ψPb [prolonged adolescence] in general: the incest wish and incest prohibition must possess a strength that goes beyond the ordinary.

The foregoing is not sufficient for an understanding of the described form of ψPb [prolonged adolescence]. Clearly, particular moments determine its specific course. First of all, we notice something that might be responsible in a general way for prolonging adolescence. The discrepant relationship between ψ [libidinal sexual needs] and Φ [genital maturation], which is usually characteristic of adolescence, is in fact merely a reversed repetition of a condition that had an important consequence at an earlier period of life. Early infantile sexual activity ends owing to the fact that at that time the development along the ψ-line was way ahead of the slow (self-) development along the Φ-line.

It would be astonishing if the outcome of the infantile conflict did not have an impact on the course of the essentially identical conflict in adolescence. For that reason, we are even more inclined to attribute to it a role in the causation of ψPb [prolonged adolescence], as indeed this is a narcissistic phenomenon and that trauma at the beginning of the latency period was a narcissistic injury. Perhaps we find that the condemnation of the self by means of the ego ideal is based on the experiences and narcissistic limitations that the individual had to undergo through the early infantile ψ-Φ discrepancy. Had that discrepancy become a powerful shock to narcissism, a disposition might have developed to create an ego ideal that is sharply distanced from the self, one that severely criticizes and judges it. In addition, the trauma when the discrepancy is revived contributes in a general way to the failure of the final ψ development, especially because that narcissistic injury stands in intimate relation to the Oedipus complex.

In a strictly demanding and judging ego ideal lies one of the conditions of adequate ideal formation. Because this is so significant for our ψPb [prolonged adolescence], we need to determine the strength of its ego ideal. Related to this, one easily observes that the attack by the ego ideal is, above all, directed against specific qualities—real or imagined—for which there are real models or precursors in formerly loved persons. So one person fights against the father, the other against the brother or teacher in himself. In early infantile love, as well as in the oedipal situation, identification is a very important mechanism. If this identification in the unconscious lasted longer that usual—and that could well be with a strong incestuous fixation, which is indeed a cause of ψPb [prolonged adolescence]—then the pubertal Oedipus finds father, who has been consciously rejected actually to be nearer and more within himself than had been suspected; and the ego ideal, which is differentiated from the father (for example), has every cause for a relentless fight.

Without presenting explicit material, I cannot go into a typical case. We should simply point out several reasons for the vigorous differentiation of the ego ideal. One situation is, however, so frequent and includes such complex conditions for the rich development of our typical form of ψPb [prolonged adolescence] that I will describe it. Well known

63

is the identification of the boy with his mother, as well as the feminine tendency in the character and life of numerous men that is tied to this identification (as everyone knows not to confuse with homosexuality). Indeed, this "feminine" tendency is very characteristic for the ψPb [prolonged adolescence] in question; and closer analysis of youths who represent our ψPb [prolonged adolescence] form shows clearly in many ways a well-formed identification with the mother. What may now seem very contrived in a theoretical formulation presents as a strong inference in a clinical study. If the object libido turns to such a mother-identifying ego, then incest threatens a bit within one's own self, which danger can call forth a strong defensive response by the ego ideal and determine its clear formation and its strict discipline. This outcome involves so many complications that it is easy to see how it might take several years to achieve equilibrium, and the longest ψPb [prolonged adolescence] cases are often included in this grouping.

You will have noticed that this phenomenon, ψPb [prolonged adolescence], remains constant in its essential characteristics particularly among creative people, especially poets. Frequently, these people demonstrate the fight with mother-identification and its interpretation by the ego ideal as incestuous. In fact, I believe that much of what I have said here is also a contribution to the psychology of the artist or of the creative person in general. To some extent, one can fruitfully state that the creative person does not complete adolescence during his whole life. Certainly the youth of all artists belongs to the ψPb [prolonged adolescence] type, and often to the one described here; and the youth who fits this description always appears (and not only to his relatives – or perhaps least of all to them) to promise a great future. A promise that of course few keep, for ψPb [prolonged adolescence] is not genius, as much as it may be similar to it in many respects. From these facts, we could call the ψPb [prolonged adolescence] form we are dealing with here the "genius form." If one wants to compare adolescence and pathology, one could also call the genius ψPb [prolonged adolescence] the "paraphrenic."

This digression into the psychology of the artist draws our attention to an aspect of the process of "ideal formation" to be considered further. The early maturation of the artistic youth is often mentioned. We are not surprised to find that the "genius ψPb [prolonged adolescence]" generally, although not invariably, matures early; that is, the latency period has already proceeded a little differently than schematically established, when a ψPb [prolonged adolescence], at least a genius ψPb [prolonged adolescence], emerges. There are two kinds of differences: 1) sexual activity during latency in this case tends to be greater than usual because the presumed narcissistic injury did not lead to complete paralysis of the sexual interest and sexual activity, but rather to the persistence of both; however, 2) already in the latency period and in preadolescence, an increase of narcissism and an intensification in its activity can be noticed, as well as the development of the ego ideal as a consequence of the experienced restriction of narcissism. Thus the youth entering adolescence already has a formed ego ideal to deal with, which opposes the adaptation of the ψ development to the beginning changes of the Φ-line.

Let us briefly summarize this presentation, which is sometimes unclear. Among the complex features of male adolescence, a realm of phenomena can be distinguished that share this characteristic: the psychical phenomena of adolescence last longer than the period of physiological adolescence. We designate this *prolonged adolescence* (ψPb). We called one of the many forms of ψPb [prolonged adolescence] the "genius adolescence," which we found characterized by a number of constant or very frequently coincident features, such as ideals, productivity, self-esteem, veneration of a friend or leader, and group formation.

We believe we have found the common basis of these features in the transformation of certain significant quanta of object libido back into narcissism; in the presence of a well-formed ego ideal, sharply differentiated from the real self and strongly and strictly condemning it; and in the compulsion coming from the ego ideal to form ideals, to which the introverted libido yields to a great extent.

As conditions for this form of progression we noted: 1) the disruption of early infantile sexuality, which leaves behind it a considerable and lasting narcissistic wound; 2) a strong and persistent incestual fixation during the latency period; and 3) beginning ego ideal-formation in the latency and pre-pubertal periods.

NOTES

1. Cf. Mitchell, Die Kindheit der Tiere. (*The Childhood of Animals*)

2. Cf. Erich Franke, "Die Entwicklung der zeichnerischen Begabung bei Negerkindern." (*The Development of Drawing Talen in Negro Children*)

3. *Drei Abhandlungen zur Sexualtheorie. (Three Essays on a Theory of Sexuality)*

4. Partial attempts in this direction are made in my "Beitraege zur Jugendforschung" (*Contributions to Adolescent Research*), the first vol.

of which appeared under the title "Vom Gemeinschaftsleben der Jugend" ("The Social Life of Youth") in the Psychoanalytical Press, 1922, and the second with the title "Vom dichterischen Schaffen der Jugend" ("The Literary Creativity of Youth") is in preparation.

5. See my essay "Über Schülervereine" ("Concerning Student Associations"). *Zeitschrift für angewandte Psychologie,* SVI. Also Gerhard Fuchs: *Ein Schülerverein, Beiträge zur Jugendforschung (A Student Association, Contributions to Adolescent Research).*

6. For understanding such behavior see preliminary remarks of W. Hoffer, "Kinderspiel" ("Child Play"), Ph.D. diss., University of Vienna, 1922.

7. A selection of examples for the motives and forms of this tendency is found in the quoted *Beiträgen zur Jugendforschung (Contributions to Adolescent Research).*

8. *Der Anfang; Zeitschrift der Jugend (The Beginning: A Journal About Adolescence),* edited by Georges Barbizon and Siegfried Bernfeld. Verlag die Aktion, Berlin, 1913/14, p. 45.

9. *Der Neue Anfang (The New Beginning)*; edited by Hermann Schlicht. Munich. 1919, p. 1090.

10. Freud, *Massenpsychologie und Ichanalyse,* p. 68 ("Group Psychology and the Analysis of the Ego").

11. Freud, *Massenpsychologie,* pp. 114–115 ("Group Psychology . . .").

12. Bernfeld, "Bemerkungen über Sublimierung" ("Remarks Concerning Sublimation"), *Imago,* 1922.

13. Freud, *Drei Abhandlungen zur Sexualtheorie* ("Three Essays on the Theory of Sexuality").

Comments about Dr. Siegfried Bernfeld's Paper

RICHARD C. MAROHN

Siegfried Bernfeld[1] was born in 1892 in the Ukraine and was raised in Vienna, the first-born of a Hungarian Jewish clothing merchant and his younger wife. He had a younger brother and sister. In the gymnasium in 1907, he first read Freud's *Interpretation of Dreams* because of his interest in psychology; in 1910, he entered the University of Vienna, studying plant physiology and psychology. He was active in the Zionist and the socialist youth movements and for a while was Martin Buber's

---

[1]This summary of Siegfried Bernfeld's life and career is taken from Benveniste (1920).

secretary. He was a productive writer and at age 21 had his first article published in the *International Journal of Psycho-Analysis*. He married in 1914 and had two daughters. In 1915, he received his Ph.D. in pedagogy and psychology and became a guest of the Vienna Psychoanalytic Society in May, becoming a full member in 1919. He had studied under Freud and was analyzed by Hanns Sachs.

During the period 1919–1922, he also founded a residential school for Jewish war orphans, based on psychoanalytic and progressive education principles. In 1922, he began analytic practice and started teaching at the psychoanalytic institute in association with Herman Nunberg, Theodor Reik, Eduard Hitschmann, and others. He was also publishing articles and books about childhood, adolescence, and alternative education. In 1926, he and his wife separated, and he moved to Berlin, where he married an actress and began analytic practice and institute teaching there. In 1931, Freud wrote of him:

He is an outstanding expert of psychoanalysis. I consider him perhaps the strongest head among my students and followers. In addition he is of superior knowledge, an overwhelming speaker and an extremely powerful teacher. Thus I can say all in all only the very best about him and we deeply regretted it when he left for Berlin [quoted in Benveniste, 1992].

Because of his natural science background, he was interested in measuring libido (thus the Greek symbols in our paper!) and in 1930 published *Energie und Trieb* (Energy and Drive), a part of which appeared in 1931 in the *International Journal of Psycho-Analysis* as "The Principle of Entropy and the Death Instinct." In 1932, he left his second wife and returned to Vienna, where he associated with Anna Freud, August Aichhorn, and Willi Hoffer, who met in a weekly study group focused on psychoanalytic pedagogy and helped found a journal, which reappeared after World War II as *The Psychoanalytic Study of the Child*.

In 1934, Bernfeld moved to France with his new wife, the daughter of a Berlin art dealer, his two daughters, and her two children from a previous marriage. His wife was a practicing psychoanalyst, Suzanne Cassirer Paret, analyzed by both Sachs and Freud. As the political situation worsened, he and his family first went to England, then to New York, where he was encouraged to go to San Francisco. They arrived there in August 1937 and found one American-trained psychoanalyst, one Berlin-trained analyst, and two lay students. They all participated in seminars under the auspices of the Chicago Institute, and in 1942 the San Francisco Psychoanalytic Society was formed under the umbrella of the Topeka Society. Bernfeld was always considered an inspiring teacher and lecturer — in Vienna, Berlin, and San Francisco. He was irritated with the M.D. requirements of the American Psychoanalytic Association, which meant that he could be only an Honorary Member, and he eventually split off from the APA. For a while he conducted study groups in his home. He continued to write on the field of child and adolescent studies and about Freud's work and life and assisted Ernest Jones in preparing his biography of Freud. Bernfeld died in 1953, his wife in 1962.

While working on some presentations, as yet unpublished (Marohn, 1987a, b), and rethinking the paradigm of adolescence as a second separation–individuation phase (Blos, 1967), I also reconsidered the concept of "prolonged adolescence," attributed to Bernfeld (Blos, 1954), but could find no English translation of Bernfeld's (1923) source paper, "Concerning a Typical Form of Male Puberty." There is a review of the *Imago* article in the 1925 *International Journal of Psycho-Analysis,* where the reviewer, Katherine Jones (1925), noted that Bernfeld was suggesting an alternative view of adolescent development, different from Freud's displacement-of-libido model and focused on transformations of narcissism as important adolescent transformations, extending well into the third decade of life.

Bernfeld's paper was presented to and discussed at the February 15, 1922 meeting of the Vienna Psychoanalytic Society. The minutes of 1922 have not been published, but unpublished minutes for 1923–1924 have been translated (Lobner and Rose, 1978; Rose, 1988). Ernst Federn (personal communication, 1989) directed me to the Siegfried Bernfeld Archives at the Library of Congress, which contacted the "donor" for access permission. Permission was granted, and a photocopy of the minutes of the February 15, 1922 meeting, handwritten by Theodore Reik (1922), was sent.

Freud was at the meeting, as were about 30 others, and Bernfeld presented his paper, but the notes are scant. The conflict between narcissism and object choice is recounted, and mention is made of the "conflict between the ideal self and the real self" being "typical" for adolescence.

Bernfeld wrote a paper that purported to be scientific, with its dissection of puberty and adolescence into aspects and parameters depicted by Greek symbols: *PHI,* Φ = genital maturation and *phi,* ϕ = sexual capacity, the two physiological parameters; *PSI,* Ψ = appropriate sexual gratification and *psi,* ψ = libidinal sexual needs, the two psychological parameters; and psiPb, ψPb = prolonged adolescence. Briefly, he reiterates that the psychological and psychophysical aspects of adolescence are complex and to understand adolescence requires a complex approach; hence the symbols. He also reiterates Freud's contributions that adolescence involves the achievement of genital primacy and of nonincestuous object choice. The duration of adolescence is variable, from two to eight years. Adolescence cannot be defined by its duration, but it can be described thereby. When libidinal needs persist, and the duration is highly variable, we speak of *prolonged adolescence,* as seen in the youth movement of the time.

Then Bernfeld describes at length transformations of narcissism as seen in adolescence and young adulthood, in self-expression, the realization of ambition, and self-esteem regulation; in the achievement of values and goals and in relationships to idealizable others; and in the various twinship experiences of youth who are pursuing careers. Reik's (1922) notes certainly focus on these narcissistic struggles:

Idealistic interests and a productive interest in the goal, great deal of self-consciousness and symptoms of the onset of repression, tendencies to depreciate others with the exception of the friend, since personal love of the friend is said to be developed. The self is extraordinarily cathected at the expense of object choice. Conflict between the ideal self and the real self typical for puberty.

Jones (1925) notes that the essence of prolonged adolescence is that the psychological transformations last longer than the physiological, which Bernfeld seems to find "typical." She too recounts various narcissistic aspects of these youth:

1. The interests of this type are turned towards "ideal" objects like art, politics, humanity, etc. 2. The relation to these objects is productive. The youths try to produce a work of art, a new form of politics, etc. 3. There is always present a good deal of self-confidence or many symptoms of a repression that has failed. This is expressed in different ways; with the high opinion of oneself goes a low opinion of one's companions. 4. One outstanding individual—the friend or master—is loved and revered. 5. Often this love for the friend is extended on to a whole group.

Jones notes that this description of puberty is different from Freud's because libido is not used to find an object but shifted into the ego ideal and a secondary narcissism.

69

Bernfeld does not see puberty as devoid of object relating and views it as secondary or tertiary narcissism. Yet, it is not simply a repetition of infantile narcissism because it is painful, especially because it involves the discrepancies between the ego ideal and the real self. A new object relationship is established, between the self and the ego ideal. Bernfeld (1923) notes that

a precise discrimination between the narcissistic and object libidinal strivings is very difficult, because we have to deal with subtle differentiations, which must seem contrived to the reader, since we cannot present the material out of which the differentiations clearly, although not effortlessly, arise. . . . The formation of the ideal, as far as it occurs by means of diversion of the goal of narcissistic strivings under the pressure of failure of the ego ideal, is the fate of narcissism. . . . Other conflicts, above all between ego (ego ideal) and sexuality, naturally play a part as well. Especially the Oedipus and castration complex . . . [pp. 15–16].

At first, it seems that Bernfeld is proposing that, in order to understand the complexity of adolescence, one must embrace both libidinal (object libido) and narcissistic (ego libido) aspects, not a revision of Freud's ideas, simply an emendation. When Bernfeld speaks of the etiology of prolonged adolescence, however, he speaks of what "forces the object libidinal strivings to turn themselves back into the self" (p. 17). It is indeed a narcissistic injury early in life, only partly related to the oedipal period, that leads to the formation of the ego ideal and the subsequent sense of failure and conflict.

Bernfeld's summarizing statements are illuminating:

Among the complex features of male adolescence a realm of phenomena can be distinguished which share this characteristic: the psychical phenomena of adolescence last longer than the period of physiological adolescence. We designate this *prolonged adolescence* (ψPb). One of the many forms of ψPb [prolonged adolescence] we called the "genius adolescence," and we found it characterized by a number of constant or very frequently coincident features, such as ideals, productivity, self-esteem, veneration of a friend or leader, and group formation.

We believe we have found the common basis of these features in the transformation of certain significant quanta of object libido back into narcissism; in the presence of a well-formed ego ideal, sharply differentiated from the real self and strongly and strictly condemning it; and in the compulsion coming from the ego ideal to form ideals, to which the introverted libido yields to a great extent.

As conditions for this form of progression we noted: 1) the disruption of early infantile sexuality, which leaves behind it a considerable and lasting narcissistic wound; 2) a strong and persistent incestual fixation during the latency period; and 3) beginning Ego Ideal-formation in the latency and pre-pubertal periods [pp. 21–22].

COMMENTARY

Although Bernfeld felt impelled to maintain Freud's dichotomy between ego libido and object libido, he did not necessarily subscribe to the dichotomy between narcissism and object relating. Instead he suggested that a number of adolescent and young adult relationships are characterized by transformations of narcissistic bonding, as with a friend or master. What is most important is that Bernfeld did not characterize prolonged adolescence as a pathological outcome but as a fairly typical variant.

This is "most important" because when Blos (1954) wrote about "Prolonged Male Adolescence" he noted that Bernfeld had investigated a "social phenomenon observed in European youth movements after the First World War" whose members "presented a strong predilection for intellectualization and sexual repression, thus delaying the resolution of the adolescent conflict and, in consequence, the personality consolidation of late adolescence" (p. 38). Blos described his own example of prolonged adolescence: "the American middle-class young man, roughly between eighteen and twenty-two, who usually attends college or has, at any rate, some professional aspirations; this fact, more often than not, makes him financially dependent on his family during the years of early adulthood" (p. 38). In a 1979 footnote, Blos said that, although the phenomenology had changed radically, for example, the "drop-out" and the "alternative life style," and despite the general acceptance of Erikson's concept of "psychosocial moratorium," the dynamics he had described earlier remained valid.

Prolonged adolescence is

> a static perseveration in the adolescent position which under normal circumstances is of a time-limited and transitory nature. A developmental phase which is intended to be left behind after it has accomplished its task has become a way of life. Instead of the progressive push, which normally carries the adolescent into adulthood, prolonged adolescence arrests this forward motion with the result that the adolescent process is not abandoned but kept open-ended. In fact, the adolescent crisis is adhered to with persistence, desperation, and anxiousness. . . . The fervent clinging to the unsettledness of all of life's issues renders any progression to adulthood an achievement which is hardly worth the price. This dilemma leads to the contrivance of ingenious ways to combine childhood gratifications with adult prerogatives. The adolescent strives to bypass the finality of choices and options exacted at the close of adolescence [p. 39].

Because these young men do not conform to Blos's ideas of genitality and autonomy but continue to work on narcissistic transformations utilizing parental and new selfobjects, he labels this process as a pathological variant. Blos's view of adolescence relies heavily on the separation–individuation model and on the apparent antithesis between narcissism and object relations. He does not accept the coexistence of libidinal and narcissistic attachments, with each playing a vital role in adolescent and young adult development. He views Freud's concept of adolescent displacement of libido from incestuous to nonincestuous objects as detachment and the achievement of psychological structures and an illusory autonomy, rather than focusing on transformations in one's attachments to the parental selfobjects.

Blos's "prolonged adolescence" is not a psychopathological state, but the result of limited theories applied to reliable data, the separation–individuation paradigm, and the libido–narcissism dichotomy. The reliable data show that, well into the third decade of life, people continue to work on the so-called adolescent transformations of their narcissistic structures and their selfobject ties. What is "prolonged" is that these transformations continue beyond the close of the physiological changes of puberty/adolescence. Because any relationship with a libidinal (sexual) object involves narcissistic ties to the lover as selfobject, how ψ (libidinal sexual needs) are fulfilled involves slowly evolving modifications of one's narcissistic structures and use of selfobjects.

Blos's (personal communication, 1987) comments are informative:

My "Prolonged Adolescence" concept of 1954 was based on the avoidance of oedipal conflict resolution by the perseveration on adolescent phase and postponement of advance to adulthood. In my 1962 book there are echoes of all this, but soon I abandoned "Prolonged Adol." as a useful concept (theoretical and technical) and soon never mentioned it again. That makes it difficult to discuss it again. I turned to the investigation of the adolescent process as a phase-appropriate psychic restructuring in order to terminate the pre-adult cycle of life. In fact, if the restructuring process is delayed, impeded or diverted beyond a certain time limit, a psychopathological condition sets in, manifested in a characterological condition or in the consolidation of a neurosis. I then speak of an aborted adolescence. I have studied these developmental events as the constituents of the adol. process. . . . I attributed (as a factor primum inter pares) the failure in adol. psychic restructuring to the incapacity to surrender infantile object — and self-idealization. Without this shift in internal reorganization the progression to maturity and to adult object relation is seriously impeded. This statement is so grossly open-ended that it provokes more "discussion points."

Blos is no longer concerned with the avoidance of heterosexual object choice but with delays in restructuring that should be completed with the close of adolescence. Yet others would contend that these transformations continue well into young adulthood and, in greater or lesser degree, thoughout adult life.

In a later paper, Bernfeld (1935) renames "prolonged" adolescence as "neurotic" adolescence where

the transition to adult thinking, feeling and acting is delayed far beyond physiological sexual maturation. . . . with noticeably strong inclinations towards activities in art, literature, and philosophy, frequently linked with a specific feeling of self-esteem, as well as with an urge toward "youthful communal life" . . . [p. 114].

While Bernfeld adheres to the displacement paradigm, he notes the importance of adolescent transformations of narcissism both in the self-esteem and twinship needs of the "neurotic" (formerly "prolonged") adolescent who suffers from "inner anxiety" and in the "simple" adolescent for whom "the central affect to be mastered and avoided is narcissistic injury" (p. 116).

SUMMARY

In his paper "Concerning a Typical Form of Male Puberty," Bernfeld implies that adolescence does not necessarily and exclusively involve at its core libidinal changes and heterosexual object choice. Bernfeld maintains some dichotomy between narcissism and libidinal relating but speaks clearly of narcissistic object choice in idealization as well as ego ideal formation. Bernfeld gives greater importance to narcissism and narcissistic transformations in understanding adolescent development than previously described and delineates "prolonged adolescence" not as a pathological outcome, but as a variation of adolescent development.

REFERENCES

Benveniste, D. (1992), Siegfried Bernfeld in San Francisco, *Amer. Psychoanalyst,* 26:12–13.
Bernfeld, S. (1923), Über Eine Typische Form der Männlichen Pubertät, *Imago,* 9:169–188.
Bernfeld, S. (1935), On simple male adolescence (trans. R. Ekstein), *Seminars Psychiat.,* 1:113–126, February, 1969.
Blos, P. (1954), Prolonged male adolescence. In: *The Adolescent Passage.* New York: International Universities Press, 1979, pp. 37–53.
_____ (1967), The second individuation process of adolescence, *The Psychoanalytic Study of the Child,* 22:162–286. New York: International Universities Press.
Jones, K. (1925), Abstracts/Sexuality, *Inter. J. Psycho-Anal.,* 6:477–478.
Lobner, H. & Rose, L., trans. (1978), Discussions on therapeutic technique in the Vienna Psycho-Analytic Society (1923–1924), *Sigmund Freud House Bull.,* 2:15–33.
Marohn, R. C. (1987a), A re-examination of Peter Blos's concept of prolonged adolescence. Presented to annual meeting of American Society for Adolescent Psychiatry, Chicago, May 9.
_____ (1987b), The renaissance of adolescence: A reassessment of separation–individuation theory. Presented to Dept. of Psychiatry Grand

Rounds, University of New Mexico School of Medicine, Albuquerque, November 13; and as Joel Handler Memorial Lecture, Chicago Society for Adolescent Psychiatry, November 18.

Reik, T. (1922), Minutes of the Vienna Psychoanalytic Society, February 15, 1922, from the Siegfried Bernfeld Papers, Container #8, Manuscript Division, Library of Congress, Washington, DC.

Rose, L. (1988), Freud and fetishism: Previously unpublished minutes of the Vienna Psychoanalytic Society, *Psychoanal. Quart.,* 57:147–166.

7   ADOLESCENT PSYCHIATRY:
PRESENT STATUS AND FUTURE TRENDS

ADRIAN D. COPELAND

Youth constitutes a large and important segment of the general population. There is considerable evidence that it is a group currently under a great deal of stress with the problems of drug abuse, emotional breakdown, gang violence, educational default, and dropping out. They have been profoundly influenced by parlor devices and television that have beamed continuous messages of violence and destruction for as long as this generation can remember. Contemporary life stresses have been considerable, with many adolescents disassociating themselves from the everyday problems of survival and adaptation, thus reducing their overall stress in an increasingly demanding, oriented society that provides technologically an inadequate place for them in the labor force. Dissolution of the traditional supports of family and institutions have placed additional burdens on the adolescent. We are the clinicians that must respond to their needs [Copeland, 1974].

Although the figures vary, Jensen (1993) indicates that the prevalence of serious mental disorder for this group averages about 12%, with some estimates both in the United States and abroad being as high as 37%. Epidemiological studies (Rosario, Kapur, and Kaliaperumal, 1990; Anseri, 1987) also show that psychopathology is greater in adolescence than in latency, lending credence, if not to "Sturm und Drang," at least to notions of chaos and confusion.

Current Status of Adolescent Psychiatry

Psychiatry in general and adolescent psychiatry in particular have developed greatly since World War II. A comparison of the original

Diagnostic and Statistical Manual of Mental Disorders with *DSM-IV* (American Psychiatric Association, 1994) gives moot testimony to this advancement. However, despite these gains, the field has not yet achieved scientific parity with the rest of medicine.

The Medical Model

Use of the medical model for disease provides a convenient frame of reference with which to measure the progress of the subspecialty of adolescent psychiatry. Medical disease description is usually divided into 1) chief complaints; 2) the physical examination and laboratory findings; 3) a differential diagnosis followed by a diagnosis; 4) epidemiology and prevalence of the diagnosed disease; 5) etiology; 6) treatment; 7) course of illness; and 8) prognosis. In some disorders, information about prevention is included. Although important differences exist between physical medicine and psychiatry, this model can nonetheless be helpful in measuring progress.

1) CHIEF COMPLAINTS

Presenting chief complaints about children and adolescents are usually derived from multiple sources that do not always concur (Bird, Gould, and Staghezza, 1992; Sanford et al., 1992). For instance, parents may complain of the child's oppositionalism; the teacher may report attention deficit; the psychological exam may indicate depression; and the adolescent may complain only of parental intrusiveness. This disparity often presents problems of diagnosis and management that are significant and, at times, difficult to reconcile.

2) THE PHYSICAL EXAMINATION AND LABORATORY FINDINGS

The results of the physical examination and various studies provide the foundation on which medical diagnosis is made. Most psychiatrists, however, eschew physically examining their patients, and in the vast majority of mental disorders, physical signs and positive laboratory findings are absent. Child abuse, however, is one glaring exception in which the physical examination is essential (Dejong, 1985). While current research is making exciting new anatomic and genetic discoveries associated with mental illness in Alzheimer's disease, schizophrenia, and other disorders, pathognomonic biological markers are, however, not yet available. Although psychological examinations are helpful, reports are often equivocal, and few if any psychodiagnostic tools exist that can provide the kind of precise information that is typical of an electrocardiogram or magnetic resonance imaging.

3) DIAGNOSIS AND DIFFERENTIAL DIAGNOSIS

The introduction of *DSM-IV* (American Psychiatric Association, 1994) has advanced psychiatric nosology in a number of ways: it more closely reconciles the American *Diagnostic and Statistical Manual* with the *International Classification of Diseases 10* by adding such syndromes as childhood disintegrative disorder and Rett's disorder. It will further validate some diagnoses via field trials, as with autism, and for simplification certain categories will be dropped or consolidated; for instance, overanxious disorder of adolescence will be eliminated and subsumed under the adult, generalized anxiety disorder.

But if gains have been made, major nosological problems still exist. The *DSM*s are based on diagnostic categories derived from cumulative clinical experience and current consensus. These categories are not usually empirically derived, scientifically validated, nosological entities. Some work toward validation has been done, however, as with hypochondriasis (Noyes et al., 1993). Thus, frequent revisions in the *DSM*s are necessary as new data are obtained and invalidated concepts are revised. In addition to invalidity, other categorical problems are noted and include imprecise definitions leading to misdiagnosis, as in the case of bipolar disorder. Comorbidity of diagnoses instead of mutual exclusivity is another problem, causing blurring of boundaries and problems of differentiation (Anderson et al., 1987), as in the cases of schizophrenia and major affective disorder (schizoaffective disorder), and attention-deficit disorder and hyperactivity disorder (ADHD). Also certain categories may have been inappropriately eliminated, as in the case of identity disorder. This is elaborated in Case Example 2.

In contradistinction to the categorical approach of *DSM*s the dimensional approach of Achenbach et al. (1989) and others uses empirically based behavioral scales to develop valid and mutually exclusive categories or typologies. This approach, however, does not take into account the rich, cumulative experience of traditional psychiatry, and the categories derived are often devoid of relevance to current diagnostic entities.

Obviously both the dimensional and categorical approaches have merit, and both need to be reconciled in order for adolescent psychiatry to mature and diagnostic categories to be less ephemeral. Development of biological markers would also constitute a major nosological advance.

4) EPIDEMIOLOGY

The epidemiologic database for child and adolescent psychiatry is poor for a number of reasons, with estimates of psychopathology varying greatly. A major deterrent to obtaining accurate prevalence information is underreportage because of social stigma: people are reluctant to recognize mental illness in their children and to seek help; moreover, adolescents themselves do not readily request therapy; and consequently only those with glaring pathologic behaviors are identified. It is estimated that as many as one-third of all seriously disturbed youth are undetected and go without needed care. Another important epidemiologic problem is that of methodology. Many studies focused on clinical populations exclusively, with insufficient focus on the community, thus providing skewed data (Jensen, 1993). Lastly, insufficient attention has been paid to subcultural variables in our pluralistic society, creating problems in differentiating between true psychopathology and sociopathy. Patterns of sexual behavior, violence, and drug use are illustrative of this gray area. Thus, epidemiologic data about the prevalence of adolescent psychopathology is soft and research methodology needs to be improved.

With these caveats having been stated, the following generalizations may be made about adolescent epidemiology: psychopathology is more prevalent in adolescence than in latency, reaffirming Hall's (1904) observation that this adolescent phase of development is a turbulent one; gender differences exist, with a higher prevalence of acting-out behaviors in boys, such as conduct disorders and substance abuse disorders, and a higher prevalence of "acting in" disorders in girls, such as depression and anxiety (Florenzano, 1991; Kessler et al., 1994). As already noted, prevalence rates vary widely. A very conservative estimate, however, is that at least 1 in 10 adolescents suffers from a serious mental illness, not only in the United States but internationally as well.

OTHER SIGNIFICANT FINDINGS

In a community study of blue-collar adolescents, prevalences of mental disorders were alcohol abuse 32%, phobias 28%, drug abuse 9%, major depression 9%, posttraumatic stress disorder 6%, and obsessive compulsive disorder 2%. In another community study, 7% of the adolescent population had attempted suicide. Key risk factors were a) being fatherless and b) having a concurrent mental disorder (Andrews and Lewisohn, 1992). In a national survey, severity of mental illness was associated with comorbidity (Kessler et al., 1994). With regard to chronic mental illness in older adolescents, hospital admissions for schizophrenia ranged from four to nine per 100,000.

Child sexual abuse was seen to be etiologic in 3.9% of all adult psychopathology (Scott, 1992).

In two studies, adolescent psychopathology was found to be widespread, with much comorbidity and impairment; only a minority of adolescents were in treatment (Grant, Offord, and Blum, 1989; Sutton, 1991).

An Australian study found that mental illness was positively correlated with poverty in a population of school children (Sawyer et al., 1990).

5) ETIOLOGY

The etiology of adolescent mental disorders is not always clear and does not follow the traditional model of medicine in which one cause creates one disease. Rather, two concepts seem appropriate to explain adolescent psychopathology: nonspecific psychopathogenicity, in which one stressor or etiologic factor can produce various kinds of mental disorders, and multicausality, the biopsychosocial model, in which one mental disorder can be caused by varied and different psychopathogens.

With regard to nonspecific psychopathogenicity, incest has been associated causally with anxiety disorders, substance abuse, and depression (Pribor and Dinwiddie, 1992). Psychic trauma is described as etiologic for posttraumatic stress disorder, which manifests a wide variety of symptoms, including anxiety, depression, cognitive dysfunction, and return of repressed memories. Parental loss has been associated with depression, panic anxiety, and phobia in women (Kandler et al., 1992); and children subject to family relocations showed significant behavioral and learning disorders (Wood et al., 1993). Thus, a specific stressor is associated with not one but a number of different mental disorders.

As to multicausality and the biopsychosocial model, an Israeli study of adolescent suicide cited narcissism, reactive depression and schizoid personality disorders as etiologic (Apter et al., 1993). In schizophrenia, heredity (Parnas et al., 1993) and temporal lobe abnormality (Johnstone et al., 1989) have been implicated, as well as abnormal family rearing (Lidz and Fleck, 1965). Depression is reported to be caused by genetic dysfunctions, pathology of the basal ganglia (Hussain, McDonald, and Doraisavany, 1991), and by sexual abuse (Livingston, 1987).

Thus, in this case, a mental disorder is seen to be attributable not to one factor but to different ones, perhaps working confluently and in three different spheres: hence, multicausality and the biopsychosocial model. These concepts are still loosely formulated, and much needs to be discovered before theories about the causes of adolescent psychopathology can be validated.

PROGNOSIS

The clinical course and prognosis of many adolescent mental disorders are difficult to predict. Phasic stress reactions and deep-seated psychopathology often present similarly and are difficult to differentiate. In some cases, however, certain early symptoms and syndromes have been linked with later psychopathology and may be of prognostic significance. For instance, *pavor nocturnus* has been associated with later affective disorders: child sexual assaultiveness, firesetting, and ADHD were linked with adult antisocial personality disorder. Copeland (1993) found that clusters of certain specific symptoms of childhood maladjustment such as firesetting, enuresis, nail biting, and animal cruelty were associated with major psychopathology of adolescence, to a statistically significant degree, but differentiation between phasic stress reactions and deep-seated psychopathology is complex and very difficult, posing a diagnostic and prognostic challenge and requiring longitudinal studies for resolution (Myers, Burket, and Otto, 1993).

The following case vignettes illustrate some of the structural problems of adolescent psychiatry:

Case Examples

1 MADELINE

Madeline is a 14-year-old white female who was seen in an outpatient clinic postdischarge from an inpatient unit with the diagnosis of atypical psychosis. She had been prescribed haloperidol, two milligrams twice daily. Initially, she presented with depression, flat affect, anxiety, and the chief complaint, "I'm getting pains: I'm starting to become a woman." Symptoms of childhood maladjustment included nail biting, prolonged enuresis, nightmares that caused awakening, and extreme weight variations. Symptoms lessened greatly and haloperidol was eventually replaced with buspirone. Madeline soon returned to school. Her affect remained flat, and she appeared somewhat anxious and depressed but showed no further signs of psychosis. What initially presented as a major affective disorder with psychotic features became a case of mild mixed anxiety and depression. How she will fare 5 years hence is anybody's guess. Differential diagnosis is lengthy, and includes atypical psychosis, major affective disorder, early-onset schizophrenia, or some form of adjustment disorder. The case of Madeline illustrates problems of diagnosis and prognosis in adolescent disorder.

2 BRUCE

Bruce is a 13-year-old black male who came into treatment after he induced a 5-year-old boy to perform fellatio on him. He showed markedly effeminate traits and immediately became the masochistic scapegoat of his peers at the group home. It was later revealed that he was a victim himself of sexual abuse at age 7, by a teenage male cousin. Projective testing confirmed traits of feminine identification and conflict about his own masculinity. Intense prolonged individual, group, and milieu therapy produced gradual changes. His behavior with peers changed first, from that of a masochistic victim to that of a hyperaggressive bully. This was then followed by more normative, age-appropriate behavior, which included participation in organized sports, dating, and peer acceptance. From a diagnostic standpoint, he would fit into the category of gender identity disorder of adolescence, but this category has been dropped from *DSM-IV*. While he would also fit the criteria for a pedophile diagnosis, there is no diagnosis reflecting his own sexual victimization and its relationship to having been an abuser. More research needs to be done etiologically: nosology needs further refinement.

3 IRENE

Irene, a 15-year-old female, was first seen in the outpatient clinic with her mother, whose major complaint was of Irene's obsessiveness, compulsivity, panic, and phobia. She indicated that Irene could not remain in a room with the door closed, because she panicked. Mother spoke volubly not only of Irene's mental problems but also of her own back difficulties. She took much medication herself and would not allow treatment for Irene that did not include medication. Given the mother's intransigence, small doses of hydroxyzine were prescribed, producing a dramatic, immediate reduction of all of Irene's symptoms; only mild anxiety and some obsessive compulsive traits remained. When mother was absent, Irene never had trouble sitting with me in a room with a closed door.

Diagnosis posed a problem in terms of the lability and authenticity of Irene's symptoms. Some form of compliant folie à deux or malingering also needs to be considered. The comorbidity of obsessive compulsive, phobic, and panic symptoms, though all subsumed under panic disorders, pose questions about the interchangeability and coexistence of symptoms in adolescence. Finally, the apparent dramatic remission of symptoms after medication was prescribed further obscures diagnosis and prognosis.

Conclusions

The use of the medical model for classifying and describing mental disorders of adolescence provides a convenient frame of reference and perhaps a difficult standard with which to measure progress in adolescent psychiatry.

Indeed, many advances have been made since World War II. Nosology has become much more sophisticated both quantitatively and qualitatively, with greater appreciation of biopsychosocial factors as etiologic. Increasing use of field trials has improved the validity of many categories, and longitudinal studies are just beginning to emerge that will clarify the vicissitude of mental disorders occurring in childhood and adolescence. Much remains to be accomplished, however, in making diagnosis, etiology, epidemiology, treatment, and the prognoses of adolescent psychiatry more scientific.

REFERENCES

American Psychiatric Association (1994), *Diagnostic and Statistical Manual of Mental Disorders, 4th ed.* (DSM-IV). Washington, DC: American Psychiatric Association.

Achenbach, T., Connors, C., Quay, J. & Howell, C. (1989), Replication of empirically derived syndromes as a basis for taxonomy of child/adolescent psychopathology. *J. Abn. Child Psych.*, 17:299–323.

Anderson, J., Williams, S., McGee, R. & Silva, P. (1987), DSM-III disorders in preadolescent children: Prevalence in a large sample from the general population. *Arch. Gen. Psychiat.*, 44:69–76.

Andrews, J. & Lewisohn, P. (1992), Suicidal attempts among older adolescents: Prevalence and cooccurrence with psychiatric disorders. *J. Amer. Acad. Child Adoles. Psychiat.*, 31:655–662.

Anseri, A. (1987), Trends of psychiatric disorders among children and adolescents in Bahrain. *Internat. J. Social Psychiat.*, 33:46–49.

Apter, A., Bleich, A., King, R., Krou, S., Flluch, A., Kutler, M. & Cohen, D. (1993), Death without warning. *Arch. Gen. Psychiat.*, 50:138–152.

Bird, H., Gould, M. & Staghezza, B. (1992), Aggregating data from multiple informants in child psychiatry epidemiological research. *J. Amer. Acad. Child Adoles. Psychiat.*, 31:78–85.

Copeland, A. (1974), *Textbook of Adolescent Psychopathology and Treatment.* Springfield, IL: Charles C Thomas.

—— (1993), Childhood symptoms of maladjustment. *Adolescent Psychiatry*, 19:394–400. Chicago: University of Chicago Press.

Dejong, A. (1985), The medical evaluation of sexual abuse in children. *Hosp. Comm. Psychiat.*, 36:509–512.

Florenzano, R. (1991), Chronic mental illness in adolescence: A global overview. *Pediatrician*, 18:142–149.

Grant, N., Offord, D. & Blum, J. (1989), Implications for clinical services, research and training. *Canadian J. Psychiat.*, 34:492–499.

Hall, G. S. (1904), *Adolescence*, 2 vols. New York: Appletree.

Hussain, M., McDonald, W. & Doraisavany, P. (1991), A magnetic resonance imaging study of putamen nuclei in major depression. *Psychiat. Res.*, 40:95–99.

International Classification of Diseases, 10 (1993), *International Classification of Mental and Behavioral Disorders: Diagnostic Criteria for Research.* Geneva: World Health Organization.

Jensen, P. (1993), Epidemiology of childhood disorders. Presented at annual meeting of the American Society of Adolescent Psychiatry, San Diego.

Johnstone, E., Owens, D., Crow, T. et al. (1989), Temporal lobe structure as determined by nuclear magnetic resonance in schizophrenia and bipolar affective disorder. *Neurol. Neurosurg. Psychiat.*, 52:736–741.

Kandler, K., Neala, M., Kessler, R., Heath, A. et al. (1992), Childhood *parental loss and adult psychopathology in women. Arch. Gen. Psychiat.*, 49:109–116.

Kessler, R., McGonagle, K., Zliao, S., Nelson, C. et al. (1994), Lifetime and 12-month prevalences of DSM-III-R psychiatric disorders in the United States. *Arch. Gen. Psychiat.*, 51:819.

Lidz, T. & Fleck, S. (1965), *Schizophrenia and the Family*. New York: International Universities Press.

Livingston, R. (1987), Sexually and physically abused children. *J. Amer. Acad. Child Adoles. Psychiat.*, 3:413–415.

Myers, W., Burket, R. & Otto, T. (1993), Conduct disorders and personality disorders in hospitalized adolescents. *J. Clin. Psychiat.*, 54(1):21–26.

Noyes, R., Kathol, R., Risher, M., Phillips, B. et al. (1993), The validity of DSM-III-R hypochondriasis. *Arch. Gen. Psychiat.*, 50:961–970.

Parnas, J., Cannon, T., Jacobson, B., Schulsinger, H. et al. (1993), Lifetime DSM-III-R diagnosis outcomes in the offspring of schizophrenic mothers. *Arch. Gen. Psychiat.*, 50:707–714.

Pribor, E. & Dinwiddie, S. (1992), Psychiatric correlates of incest in childhood. *Amer. J. Psychiat.*, 149:52–56.

Rosario, J., Kapur, M. & Kaliaperumal, D. (1990), An epidemiological survey of prevalence and pattern of psychological disturbance of schoolgoing early adolescents. *J. Personality Clin. Stud.*, 6:165–169.

Sanford, M., Offord, D., Boyle, M. & Peace, A. (1992), Ontario Child Health Study: Social and school impairments in children aged 6 to 16 years. *J. Amer. Acad. Child Adoles. Psychiat.*, 31:60–67.

Sawyer, M., Sarris, A., Baghurst, P., Cornish, C. & Kalucy, R. (1990), The prevalence of emotional and behavior disorders and patterns of service utilizations in children and adolescents. *Austral. New Zealand J. Psychiat.*, 24:323–336.

Scott, K. (1992), Childhood sexual abuse: impact on a community's mental health status. *Child Abuse Neglect*, 16:285–295.

Sutton, B. (1991), Psychiatric hospitalization of children and adolescents. *Tex. Med.*, 87(8):83–86.

Wood, D., Halfon, N., Scarlata, D., Newacheck, P., et al. (1993), Impact of family relocations on children's growth, development, school function and behavior. *J. Amer. Med. Assn.*, 270:1334–1338.

PART III

GENERAL
CONSIDERATIONS
OF ADOLESCENCE

This section contains papers by some of the pivotal figures in adolescent psychiatry. Once again, Aaron Esman displays the wise perspective on adolescents and adolescence that has made him a respected teacher, writer, and clinician. Vivian Rakoff's erudition is legendary, the stuff that audiences are made of, and he again fulfills our expectations in his consideration of the role of trauma in the transition to adulthood.

Clarice Kestenbaum discusses types of psychic trauma and how they might occur in adolescents, while Max Sugar considers the equally important contributions of sexuality to that process. Daniel Offer and his colleagues, Kimberly Schonert-Reichl and Kenneth Howard, continue the study of adolescent help-seeking behavior in an important contribution by Dr. Schonert-Reichl.

AARON H. ESMAN

Probably the outstanding fact about contemporary adolescents is their visibility. Never before in history have young people, at least in the industrialized world, been so blatantly present in their modes of dress, their hairstyles, their musical tastes. As communication becomes faster, transportation easier and cheaper, and the spread of new ideas and new fashions from one center to another ever more rapid, it becomes more and more difficult for the observer to distinguish indigenous national trends. How are we to understand this apparent evolution of a global adolescent culture? Does it reflect universal biopsychological needs? Is it the consequence of media influences? To what degree are socioeconomic forces at play here, in contrast to intrinsic developmental pressures?

Classical psychoanalytic theory has emphasized the central role of biological factors in the adolescent process; puberty—the maturation of the sexual apparatus and its consequent impact on drive/fantasy formation—has been viewed as the critical determinant of changing patterns of object relations and behavioral trends (Freud, 1905; A. Freud, 1958; Blos, 1962). Adolescence has been described as the adaptation to puberty. Social science, however, has emphasized the determining influence of changing social role expectations in the transition from child to adult status in society. Erikson (1950) sought to integrate these perspectives, creating a psychosocial model that emphasizes the consolidation of a sense of "identity" as the nuclear developmental issue of adolescence in any cultural setting.

All of these viewpoints—psychoanalytic, social science, psychosocial—take as their starting point the notion that adolescence is, in fact, a defined and definable phase of human development. It is useful, however, to review this assumption in a historical perspective. Has adolescence always and everywhere been so recognized? When did our present conception of adolescence emerge? The French cultural historian

*This chapter is abstracted from the author's book, *Adolescence and Culture* (1990).

Philippe Ariès (1962) maintained that, at least in Western Europe, until the eighteenth century, adolescence was confused with childhood. Ariès pointed out that the schools, until the seventeenth century, did not distinguish between the child and the adult.

In the sixteenth and seventeenth centuries, Ariès said, children from ages 10 to 13 sat in the same classes with adolescents aged 15 to 20. "People went to school when they could, early or late." This situation is reminiscent of the rural American one-room schoolhouse, in which age levels were merged and which children attended when and as their duties on the farm permitted. It was only in the eighteenth century, Ariès stated, that a "new sensibility" emerged, marked by the appearance of two cultural prototypes, the "Cherubin" and the "conscript" — the former, as delineated by Beaumarchais and immortalized by Mozart, a love-struck, dandyish, pre-Romantic courtier; the latter, the young soldier, more virile, emphasizing hardiness and bravery.

Questions do arise, however. For instance, Shakespeare deals with adolescents in varied ways; most familiar, perhaps, is the oft-quoted passage from *The Winter's Tale*: "I would there were no age between ten and three-and-twenty, or that youth would sleep out the rest, for there is nothing in the between but getting wenches with child, wronging the ancientry, stealing, fighting." Even more telling, perhaps, is *Romeo and Juliet*, not merely a tale of star-crossed lovers, but one of street fighting between what we would now call adolescent gangs warring over turf and reacting with fatal violence to slights and challenges to their virility. Even in *Hamlet*, the University of Wittenberg seems to have been a setting in which Rosencrantz and Guildenstern, along with the ambiguously aged protagonist, enjoyed some period of a "psychosocial moratorium" before the bloody events at Elsinore led the prince to his fatal "identity crisis."

Kris (1948) and others have pointed out that Shakespeare's account, in *Henry IV*, of the adventures of Prince Hal is a classic depiction of mid-to-late adolescent development in an Eriksonian framework. At first, in his youthful carousings with Falstaff and his gang of thieves and highwaymen, Hal is experimenting with what Erikson called "negative identity" fragments through trial identifications with antisocial figures who, at least in the case of Falstaff himself, served as father surrogates as well. Hal even plays with an overt oedipal triumph with distinct patricidal overtones when he prematurely tries on his dying father's crown. But when Henry IV dies, Hal immediately takes on his destined adult identity as king; he dramatically, even cruelly, rejects Falstaff and, in doing so, casts off the negative identifications with which, in his irresponsible adolescent years, he could afford to toy. In short, he becomes Henry V. Thus, at least according to Shakespeare, in the circle of the royal court it was possible even in late-medieval England for something resembling a modern adolescence to be lived out—or at least imaginatively reconstructed. Time and the wealth with which to purchase it were the necessary conditions—then as now.

Ariès's picture of the emerging conception of adolescence in Europe is complemented by Kett's (1977) comprehensive and scholarly review of the history of adolescence in the United States. Like Ariès, Kett concludes that adolescence arrived late in American consciousness and that the adolescent as a personality type appeared on the scene even later. In the largely rural America of the seventeenth and eighteenth centuries one was a "child," a "youth," or "young person," perhaps, but at least after the age of 7 or 8 one mixed with adults in many settings, attended school at unfixed times with school fellows of varied ages, and often left home early to find work or enter apprenticeship. The 14- to 16-year-old was an economic asset, even an economic necessity, in the large families of the time and, except for a small elite group, did not enjoy the luxury of a "psychosocial moratorium."

It was, Kett pointed out, only in the nineteenth century, with increasing urbanization and industrialization, that regular school attendance became the rule up to age 14 and that specific institutions for youth, like the high school, the YMCA, and church youth groups, became established. It was with the codification of age grading in the schools and the spread of the high school as a setting for the education and retention of older teenagers that the term "adolescence" came into general currency in the mid-nineteenth century, a time when, as Kett notes, moralists were becoming concerned about the frailty of youth in the face of the "temptations" of urban life.

Meanwhile, significant changes were occurring in the structure of the family. Greater longevity, along with fewer children more closely spaced, led to the proliferation of families in which both parents lived to see their children pass, often simultaneously, through the teen years and to lavish parental concern upon them. At the same time, technological change was drying up vocational opportunities for those in the 12- to 14-year age group, with the consequence that the age of home leaving advanced progressively. "Today," says Kett (1977) "parents look at middle age as a time when their teenage children will place an extraordinary drain on family resources. In nineteenth-century families the opposite was true: teenage children were economic assets and were expected to compensate by their earnings for the fact that they had been economic liabilities when young" (p. 169).

In most cultures, adolescence is associated with a major change in social status, and it is this social adolescence that is marked by a wide variety of rites of passage that serve to institutionalize the transition from child to adult role and its specific meaning in each society. To deviate from or to rebel against such rites is unknown and unthinkable in preliterate cultures; to do so would be to divorce oneself totally from the society.

The process of transition from child to adult status in such societies is generally brief. For the most part children learn their occupational and social roles during later childhood (what Freud called the latency period), and the limited technology of the culture is transmitted either by parents or by designated surrogates. The rites of passage may last from hours to days, less often weeks, rarely longer—certainly not the years that are required in our culture.

Rites of passage do, as a culture changes in response to new conditions, take on new meanings as they lose their original significance. A case in point is the Jewish rite of bar mitzvah, which in its historically obscure origin marked the pubertal transition of the boy from child to adult status in the Jewish community, including the assumption of familial and economic as well as religious responsibilities.

The gain for the boy was substantial—the right to participate, along with adult men, in learned discussions of the Law and its interpretation: to play a part, that is, in the central concern of Jewish cultural life. The bar mitzvah persists in our time as a formalized rite of passage (Arlow, 1951), but except in the most orthodox subcultures its meaning has become not only attenuated but transformed. The passage at age 13 into "adult" status in nonorthodox or secularized middle-class Jewish society is essentially meaningless, since neither psychosexually nor economically is the boy prepared to participate in adult life. And in most cases his bar mitzvah represents the end, rather than the beginning, of his involvement in the religious community. The bar mitzvah thus has become largely an occasion for social display and conspicuous consumption—a kind of middle-class potlatch. Lavish gift giving maintains in vestigial form some of the original symbolism.

What, then, are we to conclude about adolescence as a developmental phase? The bulk of evidence supports the view that adolescence, as we know it, is a cultural invention (Stone and Church, 1957)—a product of industrialization, of the need to extend the period of education and training for adult roles in the face of expanding technology, and of the need to keep young people out of the labor force in order to assure job opportunities for adults in times of scarcity. The "moratorium of choice" of which Erikson speaks is conceivable only in a culture in which choices are available; for the child in a preliterate or traditional culture the choice is to follow one's predestined way or to leave the society altogether.

Now to focus on secular western culture: In 1904 G. Stanley Hall, professor of psychology at Clark University, where 5 years later Freud was to make his momentous debut on American soil, published a two-volume tome under the imposing title of *Adolescence: Its Psychology and Its Relation to Anthropology, Sociology, Sex, Crime, Religion, and Education.* Hall's encyclopedic study became the established source for conceptualization and description of adolescent behavior for generations to come. In particular, Hall's model of adolescent "Sturm und Drang" became the prototype for later psychiatric and psychoanalytic representations of the normal adolescent as tempest-tossed, torn by unmanageable passions, impulsive, rebellious, and given to florid swings of mood. His relations with parents and the adult world in general were seen as antagonistic and conflict-ridden.

This picture of "normal adolescent turmoil" was epitomized, a half century later, by Anna Freud, who in a series of papers (1958, 1969) spoke of adolescence as a "developmental disturbance" and declared that it was frequently impossible to distinguish aspects of normal adolescent behavior from severe psychopathology of the neurotic, borderline, or even psychotic type. The force of Hall's and Miss Freud's authority and the predominance of clinical experience as the source of data for the psychoanalyst established the hegemony of this viewpoint for several decades. It was not until the 1960s that reports began to emerge of systematic studies of normative populations of adolescents. Studies such as those of Douvan and Adelson (1966), Symonds and Jensen (1961), Offer (1969), and Offer and Offer (1975) cast new light on the process of normal adolescent development. The thrust of most, if not all, of these normative population studies has been that, as Oldham (1978) put it, normal adolescent turmoil is a "myth" (p. 267). The researches of Offer and his associates, based on the work of more than two decades, are probably the most extensive and certainly the most psychoanalytically informed of these investigations. Overall, at least two-thirds of their total group developed in a manner inconsistent with the classical picture of "adolescent turmoil."

Another staple of the popular literature on adolescence and youth, particularly in the 1960s and 1970s, was the concept of the "generation gap"—an ostensibly unbridgeable chasm between the values, attitudes, tastes, interests, styles, and behavior of young persons and those of their parents, between the rising generation and those already in authority or decline. The weight of evidence, too extensive to cite here, seems to argue against the existence of a true generation gap. In fact, most adolescents in most cultures conform rather quietly to the expectations of their elders. From the normal population studies one gains a picture of general compliance and identification with adult standards, with, perhaps, brief and sporadic flurries of rebelliousness around nonessential issues. Indeed, the logic of cultural continuity demands that this be so; were each generation truly to reject or rebel against the values and ideologies of its parents, only chaos could result. From the body of the data derived from the study of normal adolescents in the range of industrialized societies it appears, again, that the classical picture of "Sturm und Drang" is an inaccurate one—or, at least, that it describes only a minor, rather than the major, segment of the adolescent population. This is not intended to minimize the stressful character of adolescence in developed and developing societies. The young person traversing this phase is confronted by a number of crucial developmental "tasks". He must experience and adapt to the biological changes of puberty, with its attendant impact on the body and drive organization. He must learn to deal with new patterns of social relationships, tinged as they are increasingly with sexual feelings and fantasies and the definition of sexual role patterns. The adolescent must also undergo significant changes in his relations with parents and other family members, as he tests out his capacity for autonomous living while learning to come to terms with residual dependent wishes and feelings of attachment to parents who are no longer seen as omnipotent, idealized figures (Esman, 1982). Decisions must be made about future life plans, particularly in areas of education and vocation, involving identification with actual or fantasized models.

Most adolescents, even in our society, seem to have developed during their latency years coping capacities (or "ego resources") that permit them to undergo a rather quiet transition from childhood to adulthood, marked by mild rebelliousness regarding some outward trappings of independence in early adolescence, and with transitory moodiness with depressive undertones as they live through the transposition of their principal attachments from parents to age-mates. The presence of two supportive parents who are themselves able to adapt progressively to their adolescent's growth seems clearly to facilitate such an equable transition. The flamboyant behaviors of the minority, whether rebellious, delinquent, hypersexual, or merely noisy, provide for adult minds an ideal focus for the projection of their own imperfectly repressed or renounced impulses; it is then the "younger generation" that becomes the repository for these "bad" parts of the self (Anthony, 1969).

Culture and Adolescent Behaviors

The influence of culture on adolescent thought and behavior can be conceptualized in two ways: 1) cross-cultural variations; 2) changes within a society as cultural changes occur. In a sense these perspectives fall within the purview of, respectively, ethnology and sociology. Above all, works of imaginative literature in the form of the Bildungsroman or barely fictionalized reminiscences (typical of the "first novel") provide further perspectives.

Of these, perhaps the greatest, certainly the most evocative of time, place, and culture, is Joyce's *A Portrait of the Artist as a Young Man*. Joyce (1916) brilliantly and touchingly portrays the torments of a boy tortured by his guilt-laden sexual longings in a priest-ridden Catholic society. Stephen Dedalus's terrors about the hellfire that awaited him after masturbation, and his mingled triumph and shame after his first encounter with a prostitute, were surely typical for adolescent boys in turn-of-the-century Dublin — all the more so at a time when the popular and "scientific" literature were everywhere virtually unanimous in their insistence on the moral evils and medical risks associated with masturbation.

There is virtually universal agreement among social scientists that the phenomenology of adolescence — its duration, its behavioral characteristics, its place in family and social organization — is in large measure culturally determined.

Adolescence as we know it in modern societies is a creature of the industrial revolution and it continues to be shaped by the forces which defined that revolution: industrialization, specialization, urbanization, rationalization and bureaucratization of human organizations and institutions, and continuing technological development [Hill and Mönks, 1977, pp. 14–15].

The image of the adolescent that emerges from the psychoanalytic and related literature — the experimentalist struggling toward the achievement

95

of a sense of personal autonomy and individuation and a sexual relationship based on romantic love—is bound to that culture. As Baumrind (1975) says, "personal autonomy and individuation are not universally accepted defining characteristics of the mature person, a fact that American behavioral scientists are prone to overlook" (p. 118).

In fact, the definition of a "mature person" is itself widely variable. As Sebald (1984) points out, in rural Ireland a male is not considered an adult until his father dies; this cultural pattern is sharply dramatized in Synge's *The Playboy of the Western World*, in which the protagonist, by falsely claiming that he has killed his father, achieves the admiration of the crowd and the love of a beautiful woman—until his lie is discovered.

Even the forms of sexual adolescence are cast in the mold of culture. The more or less exclusive heterosexuality that is normative and idealized in Western societies, particularly those dominated by Christian morality, stands in sharp contrast to the institutionalized homoeroticism of young males in classical Athenian culture. More striking, however, is the pattern described by Stoller and Herdt (1982) among the Sambia of New Guinea. In this culture boys remain with their mothers well into middle childhood; fathers are distant, engaging in hunting, warriorhood, and ritual. At the first initiation, which occurs between ages 7 and 10, the boys are abruptly separated from their mothers and begin their indoctrination into the world of men, actively—and at times brutally—encouraged to identify with their fathers' male roles. At this time the young boy begins to suck older boys' penises, in order to accumulate the semen that, the Sambia believe, will make him a man. At puberty he changes roles and becomes the one whose penis is sucked by younger boys. Finally in his late teens he marries and becomes actively, aggressively, and exclusively heterosexual. This homoerotic behavior of late childhood and adolescence is culturally normative and is experienced as an aspect of acquiring masculine identity, of becoming like the father and assuming his social and sexual role. Remarkably, a mode of mutual male sexual gratification that is anathematized in Western societies is here raised to the level of a cultural imperative, buttressed by a belief system that, however bizarre to the Western scientific mind, achieves for those who hold it sufficient internal coherence and plausibility to provide a rationale for this unique approach to the process of becoming a man.

Becoming a woman is, of course, also a process shaped by cultural rituals and mores. Muensterberger (1961) cites the instance of the Nandi in Central Africa who, at least in earlier times, imposed on pubertal girls a system of elaborate rites that culminated in the excision of the clitoris by cauterization with a red-hot coal. This operation, conducted by a woman initiator and accepted without complaint, was followed by a period of isolation and enforced inactivity "in order to [make the girl] round and voluptuous and more desirable when she is married" (p. 362). (Note here the variation from current Western criteria for female "desirability".) In other cultures (notably feudal Europe) the girl's entrance into sexual adolescence was effected by the *droit de seigneur* or *jus primae noctis*, in which the lord — or more often an older male relative — maintained and exercised the prerogative of "initiating" all new nubile females.

The Question of "Youth Culture"

Along with the concept of the generation gap there arose, in the middle years of this century, the notion of a special "youth culture," standing in opposition to and definable from the prevailing and dominant adult culture throughout the Western industrialized world. There is much controversy about the actuality of such youth cultures, but whether a matter of adult perception or of "objective" reality, certain adolescent and youthful behaviors are so flamboyant and so widely diffused as to suggest the existence of definable subcultures. A brief weekend visit to London's Trafalgar Square, for instance, would yield an intense impression of black-clad youth of both sexes parading varicolored coiffures, elaborately sculpted in the manner of "primitive" tribes. European journalists proclaim the advent on the continent of the Skinheads — violent adolescents and "youths" of the kind that in England descend violently on soccer matches and in Germany commit outrages of racism and anti-Semitism. Los Angeles has for years been plagued by large violent gangs of black and Hispanic adolescents who have at times engaged in random shooting sprees.

It is tempting to perceive these phenomena as diversified manifestations of a particular malaise of our time. Sebald (1984) reminds us, however, that in 1857 the state militia was called out to quell the violence of adolescent gangs on the streets of New York City and that, according to Macaulay, youthful gang behavior was rife in seventeenth-century London; indeed, one of the more violent gangs of the period was known as the Mohawks. And as noted earlier, Shakespeare depicts in *Romeo and Juliet* the "turf" wars of Veronese adolescents in the late Middle Ages. Even before the Industrial Revolution, it would appear that urbanization and its attendant evils — poverty and family disorganization among them—generated some of the features of adolescent subcultures with which we have become familiar.

But there is general agreement among social scientists that as a fixed star on the social horizon, "youth societies" are a product of industrialization. Indeed, the very concept of "youth" can be seen as a metaphor for social change. This can be seen most sharply in the developing nations of the so-called third world, in which rapid (if chaotic) industrialization is coupled with a large population of late adolescents with rising expectations but only modest prospects for fulfillment. The political ferment of these youth groups—generally identified as "students"—has led to major revolutionary change in many such societies and threatens (or promises) to do so in others.

For adolescents growing up in the dominant middle-class culture of the West, the situation is somewhat more subtle and complex. The life of the middle-class adolescent in Western society is shaped by, and serves to reflect, deep-seated trends in the economic and moral crises of contemporary capitalism—trends that are spreading even into the "socialist" world as it seeks to improve the lot of its citizens by adopting "capitalist" principles. And in the culture of late capitalism, the primary role of the adult citizen is that of consumer, and adolescence has become, more and more, a training for the assumption of that role. Traditional nineteenth-century values have informed and continue to inform psychoanalysis and its view of the healthy personality. They are enshrined in Erikson's epigenetic sequence of developmental achievements, which include such "virtues" as autonomy, industry, generativity, and wisdom. These "virtues" seem, however, less and less relevant in a culture that prizes above all self-gratification and in which, Bell (1978) says, "more and more individuals want to be identified not by their occupational base but by their cultural tastes and life-styles" (p. 38). "Shop till you drop" is the slogan. In a culture dominated by a "fun" morality, the old values do not hold; psychoanalysis is increasingly seen as irrelevant.

Training for consumerism begins, of course, well before adolescence. At the very least it begins with the child's exposure to television and the relentless barrage of commercial messages it purveys. In the past 40 years television has become the primary educative and socializing instrument of the culture. The average child in the United States and Britain devotes as much time to watching TV as to school attendance—indeed more, since on weekends and holidays he or she may devote the entire waking day to it—and if the medium has one message, that message is "consume."

By the time they become adolescents, these children not only have begun their own careers as consumers but also have acquired a significant influence on the consumption patterns and preferences of their parents. If they are girls they have become the targets of a vast literature of style and fashion journals, fan magazines, and "life-style" periodicals, all geared toward the promotion and shaping of their consuming habits. The popular music business depends for its very life on the consuming habits of adolescents. The industry has therefore developed highly sophisticated marketing strategies that astutely capitalize on well-recognized aspects of adolescent development. The prototypical popular music performer, particularly in the rock genre, is a late adolescent or postadolescent male who adopts the stance of a rebel against conventional adult mores (long hair, bizarre and/or "macho" dress, the use of street language, ostentatious use of drugs) designed to appeal to and vicariously gratify the phallic narcissism of young adolescent males. "The trick," says the English social critic George Melly (1970), "is to shift the emphasis so that the pop idol, originally representing a masculine rebel, is transformed into a masturbation-fantasy object for adolescent girls" (p. 40). In short, Melly concludes, "what starts as revolt finishes as style."

The impact on adolescence of culture and cultural change is nowhere more dramatically demonstrated than in the case of anorexia nervosa. For generations after its first description by Gull (1874) it remained a relatively rare disorder, affecting white middle-class adolescent girls and young women. Today the picture is very different. Anorexia nervosa, along with its companion disorder, bulimia, has become a plague of the young generation of women of a wide range of social and class backgrounds. Thus, from a rather obscure illness known primarily to physicians, anorexia nervosa has become a staple of popular journalistic interest, with frequent newspaper and television coverage.

One is pressed to search for explanations of this fact in the sociocultural sphere, and one finds little difficulty in doing so. Young women in our society—and this appears to be a universal feature of industrialized nations—are exposed to no message more clearly and unremittingly repeated than that of the urgent necessity for social and sexual success of being thin. Both among peers and at home the girl who fails to conform to this distorted ideal is likely to be teased and criticized—made, as a patient remembers having being made, to feel that she could not possibly be loved by her weight-conscious parents or accepted by her peers if she were "fat."

Still another example of the acute susceptibility of adolescents to cultural—that is, economic—pressures is the pattern of tobacco use. As is well known, smoking was primarily a masculine habit early in this century; in the wake of the feminist movement of the past 30 years and in the face of growing male concern about the link between lung cancer and smoking, the tobacco industry has aggressively directed its message toward adolescent girls and young women with such slogans as "You've come a long way, baby" and with the production of "slim" and "light" cigarettes. The results are demonstrated in recent studies that show that both in the United States (Pirie, Murray, and Luepker, 1988) and Italy (Monarca et al., 1978) the incidence of smoking among high school girls is significantly higher than in boys. A substantial change in cultural attitudes and in adolescent behavior is apparent.

These illustrations of commercial manipulations should not be taken to suggest that all aspects of adolescent behavior or the patterns of youthful subcultures should be ascribed to marketing pressures. It is in the interaction of normal developmental forces, broad scale socioeconomic tendencies, and specific cultural influences that patterns of adolescent behavior and youth subcultures are forged. In particular, the characteristic modes of adolescent behavior in industrialized societies are a function of the tension between youthful aspiration and social possibility, between young people's desire for adult status and the marginality that their society imposes on them.

The values of the dominant adult culture impose themselves on adolescents in other situations that to the superficial observer appear to represent typical adolescent issues and (mis)behaviors. A recent case in point is that of five middle-class adolescent boys who were accused of sexually abusing a 17-year-old mentally retarded girl while eight male peers stood by and cheered them on. Several of these boys were star athletes—captains of the football and baseball teams at their local high school. Remarkably, expressions of outrage by students and adults in the community were as often directed at the girl and her defenders as against the boys who allegedly perpetrated the offense. One student reported receiving death threats from the "friends" of the accused boys; many adults expressed concern primarily that publicity about the case would reflect badly on the community. What appeared to some to be an adolescent sexual prank, a piece of adolescent "acting out," exposed a system of community values that distinctly favored sexually aggressive male athletes over handicapped females and, characteristically, tended to place blame on the victim. The boys' high status as "jocks" thus tended to make them immune to criticism in the eyes not only of their adolescent classmates but also in those of many adults in a community steeped in the American idealization of the athlete.

Adolescents as Instruments of Change

Today's adolescents are, as noted, on the front lines of cultural change. In that position they are not only vulnerable to the impact of socioeconomic and cultural perturbations; they also serve as messengers to those behind the lines who more or less eagerly await the latest dispatches from the front.

The impact of adolescents on the larger culture is not so easy to delineate. Particularly is this true because the very definition of adolescents as a group with possible agency is, in historical perspective, quite recent; further, in much of the world the pace of cultural change has, at least until the post-World War II era, been slow indeed. Thus adolescents have emerged as instruments of cultural change largely in the past four decades in developed and developing societies whose histories are still being written.

None have been more aware of the potentiality of youth as agents of cultural transformation than the leaders of the totalitarian regimes of the twentieth century. Nazi Germany's Hitler Youth, the Soviet Komsomol, and Mao Zedong's Red Guard all represent efforts — generally successful ones — to harness the energy, activism, and ideological fervor of adolescents to the cause of revolutionary social change.

Erikson has, in a series of studies (1964, 1968), detailed the appeal of ideology for adolescents. He refers to the "totalistic" quality of their thinking, the narcissistic satisfaction derived from the sense of knowing the "truth," the restitutive value, at a time of developmental flux and of revision of attitudes toward relations with the adult world, of a firm and categorical system of beliefs. "Where historical and technological development . . . severely encroach upon deeply rooted or strongly emerging identities . . . on a large scale, youth feels endangered, individually and collectively, whereupon it becomes ready to support doctrines offering a total immersion in a synthetic identity" (1968, p. 89).

It was in just such a historical context, Erikson (1968) points out, that Hitler "established an organization, a training, and a motto, 'Youth shapes its own destiny' " (p. 309). It was in a similar context that Mao Zedong enlisted Chinese adolescents in the service of his Cultural Revolution, creating the Red Guard, which served as the primary enforcers of doctrinal purity and "proletarian consciousness." Thus, during the ascendancy of their adult mentors, these young people exerted a powerful influence on the culture in which they lived. By projecting their own fantasies of infantile omnipotence onto their charismatic leaders, the youthful totalitarians could recapture, by means of identification, a sense of unlimited power and unchallengeable authority.

Meanwhile, during the 1960s and early 1970s, in the United States, in France, in Germany, in Japan, and elsewhere, groups of students and in some cases pseudostudents rose against both the educational and political institutions, demanding "reforms" and a greater voice in the formation and execution of official policies. To many of the participants, and to some of the bemused adults that observed them, this revolt contained the seeds of a true revolution.

Now, over two decades later, it is clear that no revolution occurred, nor did the basic structure of the society or its institutions undergo much in the way of fundamental change. And yet important consequences did emerge from the youth-powered upheavals of the 60s and 70s. The civil rights of minority groups in the United States were measurably strengthened and legislatively reinforced; the Vietnam War was brought to its inglorious close. In both cases the political leadership of the movements was, as would be expected, in the hands of adults, but the labor power, the fervor, the relentless pressure of ardent numbers, and the dedicated commitment to the ultimate goal came from the ranks of adolescents and that even newer social grouping, "youth" (Keniston, 1971).

In the aftermath of those passionate years, the culture is vastly different from what it had been before the 1960s. New styles, new folkways introduced by the young have come to pervade the society and have spread downward to the children and upward toward the adult world. Indeed, many of the new mores introduced by the young and the rebellious have been co-opted by the most conservative elements in the culture; the blue denim and long hair that emerged on the college campuses of the 60s have become the uniform not only of the construction workers and teamsters but of residents of Park Avenue as well.

Many commentators have deplored the current American fashion for violent, obscene, and abusive language, displayed both in films and television and in general social discourse. Blame for this turn has been laid by some at the feet of Freud, to whose discovery of the role of repression in the generation of neurosis is ascribed the popular misconception that the uninhibited expression of "feelings" is healthful. Although it is true that "traditional" (i.e., Victorian) standards of propriety began to crumble during the "jazz age" of the 1920s, it was most particularly during the 1960s, in the context of the social turbulence accompanying the civil rights movement and the anti–Vietnam War demonstrations, that the barriers that maintain civility and social discourse truly crumbled away. Student protesters chanting "Off the pigs" set the tone for the increasing acceptance of expressions of naked violence in public utterance; at the same time overt sexual appeal (as opposed to innuendo) began to appear in music and lyrics addressed by youthful performers to younger audiences.

The loosening of standards of civility pervades the culture, of course, and cannot be ascribed entirely to the influence of adolescents and youth. They are as much the patient as the agent of the social changes that have induced this process. Among these the simultaneous emergence of the women's liberation movement, spearheaded by young women of college and graduate school age under the tutelage of their older "sisters," has intensified the pervasive spread of uninhibited speech, giving women the "right" to use freely words and phraseology formerly reserved, at least in public, to men. Thus a recent 18-year-old college freshman (freshwoman?) patient of impeccable upper middle-class background habitually expressed herself quite matter-of-factly, unselfconsciously, and with no sense of either exhibitionism or shame in language that would, a generation ago, have made a stevedore blush.

It may be fruitless to pursue the question of priority in this matter; whether, for instance, the pervasiveness of scatological and copulatory idiom in adult-made films is a stimulus and a model for the language patterns of their largely adolescent audiences, or whether the filmmakers are simply responding to preexisting changes in the standards of verbal usage among the members of their intended market. In all likelihood it is a spiraling process of mutual influence that continues to propel movie dialogue to greater heights of vulgarity or, if one will, openness. Similar questions may arise regarding popular music performances, where the harmlessly screaming teenage girls of the 30s and 40s contrast sharply with the violent, at times murderous, throngs of male and female adolescents at the rock concerts of more recent decades. To what degree, that is, this difference is the result of the manipulative tactics of adult promoters, publicists, and drug peddlers and to what extent it represents an autonomous change in adolescent behavior patterns is beyond determination.

Conclusions

These reflections, I believe, support the thesis that adolescence is a — perhaps the—barometer of culture. Its very transitional status illuminates the particular characteristics of the stages that precede and follow it — childhood and adulthood — and the process and meaning of passage from one to the other.

Every culture evolves a system of child-rearing practices designed, consciously or unconsciously, to produce the kind of adults that it needs and values. Certain basic biologically determined aspects of human nature are, in Melford Spiro's (1987) expression, "pan-human"; it is in the interplay between these human universals and the particularities of familial and cultural variability that personalities are formed, traditions are transmitted, and, where desired, innovations are introduced. Much of this process goes on, of course, in early childhood; indeed, by the time the child reaches puberty he or she has already been indoctrinated with major elements of cultural lore. This is, after all, what education, formal or informal, is all about.

Still it is adolescence — or its analogues — that, as Erikson showed, puts the definitive cultural stamp on the evolving character and that serves as the weathervane to the observer of the cultural climate. The Nandi girl's silent, stoic submission to the excision of her clitoris epitomizes the role she as a woman will play in a highly patriarchal culture; in contrast, the American Jewish girl's celebration of the bat mitzvah ceremony (a recent noncanonical innovation) betokens the increasing equalization of gender roles in middle-class Western societies.

As large-scale mechanized commercial agriculture replaces the family farm all over the industrialized world, more and more once rural families, including their adolescent children, are being swept into the expanding urban culture, with all its benefits and disadvantages. For, as we have seen earlier, it is urbanization above all that creates the conditions that define adolescence as we know it, that demarcates industrial and postindustrial societies from the traditional ones. It is precisely the character of adolescent life, the definition of an institutionalized adolescent stage, that most sharply distinguishes these cultural forms.

In *The Satanic Verses*, Rushdie (1988) depicts with hallucinatory clarity and mordant wit the adaptation of an immigrant Bangladeshi family — and, in particular, of their adolescent daughters — to the alien mores and institutions of present-day London. Unlike the compliant, unaggressive, traditional adolescent described by Sinha (1965), these girls are swept up in the freewheeling, verbally explicit, rebellious, and sexually uninhibited behaviors that have characterized Western urban working and lower middle-class youth in the latter half of the twentieth century. "Bangladesh," says one, "ain't nothing to me. Just some place Dad and Mum keep banging on about" (Rushdie, 1988, p. 259), while their mother complains, "It seems everything I used to know is a lie, such as the idea that young girls should help their mothers, think of marriage, attend to studies" (p. 276).

Coincidentally, in a BBC television talk show at about the time of the novel's publication nature imitated art: an immigrant Indian mother bemoaned the impact of London life on her adolescent daughters—in particular, on their relations with boys—and, to the dismay of her more acculturated husband, announced her firm intention to take them back to their native soil so that they could grow up as proper Indian girls should. This implied not only submission to traditional conventions but specifically their acceptance of arranged marriages. The clash of cultures thus finds its most intense and strident expression in the conflict around the behavior of adolescents. It is in such situations that the concept of the "generation gap" takes on genuine meaning. Rushdie's adolescents, with their bare midriffs, their disdain for formal learning, their spiked and multicolored hairdos, and their blatant sexuality, throw into sharp relief the values of the mass culture into which they are assimilating and into which, willy-nilly, their parents are being reluctantly drawn.

We began this survey with a casual impression of homogeneity. We end it with a sense of diversity, a diversity based on differences in social class, cultural tradition, and socioeconomic development. It is clear that any formulation of the psychology of "normal" adolescence that suggests pan-human uniformity or biologically based universality is open to serious doubt. Puberty is, of course, a human universal. But adolescence—becoming adult—is more than the adaptation to puberty. It is molded by the very nature of adulthood as that varies from culture to culture, by the ecological and economic realities that characterize each society, and by the sanctions and prohibitions that each society imposes on drive expression and the possibilities for self-realization. The transition from the status of child to that of adult may be brief or protracted; it may be marked by defined rituals or by indefinite and conflicting social markers; it may require unquestioning adherence to traditional role behaviors or encourage open, exploratory pursuit of goals self-chosen through complex processes of "identity formation."

It would be foolish to define Western adolescence in terms of the fads and fashions that come and go from year to year, from place to place. "Rebelliousness," "conformity," long hair, short hair, political commitment, political apathy—these shift and fluctuate like skirt lengths, according to the state of the economy and the vagaries of intercurrent events. What demarcates adolescence in industrialized societies is precisely this lack of definition, this openness to change, this susceptibility to the influence of political and technological developments. It is just this openness that is the despair of the elders, who wish to see their children's adolescence as an enactment of the retrospectively distorted memory of their own and who are eternally discomfited by the cultural changes of which their adolescent offspring are the barometers. But such intergenerational continuity can occur only in the rapidly disappearing isolation of the desert or the rain forest. As even the gerontocracy of the People's Republic of China is coming to see, one cannot have the benefits of industrialization and international communication without the price of cultural transformation, and it is the students—the adolescents and "youth"—who carry the banners that mark such inexorable change.

REFERENCES

Anthony, E. J. (1969), The reactions of adults to adolescents and their behavior. In: *The Psychology of Adolescence*, ed. A. Esman. New York: International Universities Press, pp. 467–494.

Ariès, P. (1962), *Centuries of Childhood*. New York: Knopf.

Arlow, J. (1951), A psychoanalytic study of a religious initiation rite: Bar Mitzvah. *The Psychoanalytic Study of the Child*, 6:353–374. New York: International Universities Press.

Baumrind, D. (1975), Early socialization and adolescent competence. In: *Adolescence and the Life Cycle,* ed. S. Dragstedt & I. G. Elders. New York: Wiley, pp. 117–143.

Bell, D. (1978), *The Cultural Contradictions of Capitalism*, 2d ed. London: Heinemann.

Blos, P. (1962), *On Adolescence—A Psychoanalytic Interpretation*. New York: Free Press of Glencoe.

Douvan, E. & Adelson, J. (1966), *The Adolescent Experience*. New York: Wiley.

Erikson, E. (1950), *Childhood and Society*. New York: Norton.

_____ (1964), *Insight and Responsibility*. New York: Norton.

_____ (1968), *Identity, Youth, and Crisis*. New York: Norton.

Esman, A. (1982), Fathers and adolescent sons. In: *Father and Child,* ed. S. Cath, A. Gurwitt & J. Ross. Boston: Little, Brown, pp. 265–274.

Freud, A. (1958), Adolescence. *The Psychoanalytic Study of the Child*, 13:255–278. New York: International Universities Press.

_____ (1969), Adolescence as a developmental disturbance. In: *The Writings of Anna Freud*, 7:39–47. New York: International Universities Press, 1971.

Freud, S. (1905), The transformations of puberty. (Three essays on the theory of sexuality.) *Standard Edition*, 7:207–243. London: Hogarth Press, 1953.

Gull, W. (1874), Anorexia nervosa (apepsia hysterica, anorexia hysterica). *Trans. of the Clinical Society* (London), 7:22–28.

Hall, G. S. (1904), *Adolescence*. New York: Norton.

Hill, J. & Mönks, F. (1977), *Adolescence and Youth in Prospect*. Guildford, UK: IPC Science & Technology Press.

Joyce, J. (1916), *A Portrait of the Artist as a Young Man*. New York: Viking.

Keniston, K. (1971), Youth as a stage of life. *Adolescent Psychiatry*, 1:161–175. Chicago: University of Chicago Press.

Kett, J. (1977), *Rites of Passage*. New York: Basic Books.

Kris, E. (1948), Prince Hal's conflict. *Psychoanal. Quart.*, 7:487–506.

Melly, G. (1970), *Revolt into Style*. London: Penguin.

Monarca, S., Modolo, M., Sopponi, V., Catanelli, M., Romizi, R. & Santi, L. (1978), Alcohol, tobacco and psychoactive medicine consumption among high school students of 10 Italian towns. *Internat. J. Addictions*, 22:1243–1254.

Muensterberger, W. (1961), The adolescent in society. In: *The Psychology of Adolescence*, ed. A. Esman. New York: International Universities Press, 1975, pp. 12–44.

Offer, D. (1969), *The Psychological World of the Teenager*. New York: Basic Books.

_____ & Offer, J. (1975), *From Teenager to Young Manhood*. New York: Basic Books.

Oldham, D. (1978), Adolescent turmoil: A myth revisited. *Adolescent Psychiatry*, 6:267–282. Chicago: University of Chicago Press.

Pirie, P., Murray, D. & Luepker, R. (1988), Smoking preference in a cohort of adolescents, including absentees, dropouts, and transfers. *Amer. J. Pub. Health*, 78:176–178.

Rushdie, S. (1988), *The Satanic Verses*. New York: Viking Press.

Sebald, H. (1984), *Adolescence: A Social Psychological Analysis*. Englewood Cliffs, NJ: Prentice-Hall.

Sinha, T. (1965), Psychoanalysis and the family in India. *Bull. Phila. Assn. Psychoanal.*, 15:114–116.

Spiro, M. (1987), *Culture and Human Nature: Theoretical Papers*, ed.

B. Kilborne and L. Langness. Chicago: University of Chicago Press.

Stoller, R. & Herdt, G. (1982), The development of masculinity: A cross-cultural contribution. *J. Amer. Psychoanal. Assn.*, 30:29–59.

Stone, L. & Church, J. (1957), Adolescence as a cultural invention. In: *The Psychology of Adolescence*, ed. A. Esman. New York: International Universities Press, 1975, pp. 7–11.

Symonds, P. & Jensen, A. (1961), *From Adolescent to Adult*. New York: Columbia University Press.

9   TRAUMA AND ADOLESCENT RITES
OF INITIATION

VIVIAN M. RAKOFF

In this paper I try to address a widespread and essentially mysterious form of trauma primarily associated with what van Gennep (1960) labeled the *"rites de passage"* of adolescence—the willfully imposed, and usually voluntarily accepted, cruelties of initiation rites, which, far from destroying the social fabric, appear to sustain society. As Frazer (1922) observed, the essence of the rite of initiation is trauma—"the essence of these initiatory rites, so far as they consist in a simulation of death and resurrection" (p. 802).

The mystery? Why is the adolescent, prepubertal, pubertal, and postpubertal person not simply welcomed to full membership in a society with welcoming feasts and songs, without the necessity of mutilation, trial, difficult tasks, or public displays of mastery? Why must adolescents be starved, isolated, humiliated, or mistreated before they are accepted as adults? And—to shift the question— how do these adolescent trials appear in our society, apart from the obvious, to be benign and attenuated displays of mastery in, say, the bar mitzvah or the driver's license test? What, if any, are the contemporary manifestations of the cruel, dangerous, trauma-inducing, and highly symbolic initiation rites of simpler exotic societies? What may be the relevance of such "primitive" rituals to the complex process of acculturation in our pluralist communities?

Symbols are often not clear in their reference; the original source of the symbol may be lost in time. The Union Jack may stir British hearts, but not every Englishman so stirred knows that the design derives from a layering of the crosses of St. Andrew, St. George, and St. Patrick; nor does every U.S. citizen who responds to the almost sacred image of the Stars and Stripes know its exact relationship to the original colonies and the accumulation of states. And in long-continued, symbol-laden social

109

ritual, the original source of that ritual may also become obscure—so obscure that the origins of the customs are then liable to endless speculative interpretation of the kind so vividly illustrated in Freud's (1913) *Totem and Taboo* or the anthropological essays of Theodore Reik (1964). Thus, frequently we can only guess at the unconscious or preconscious meaning of the rituals constituting a particular rite de passage.

There are, however, some positivist phenomenological data that will serve to anchor speculation and remove the topic from fanciful, unsupported theorizing: some form of adolescent entry ritual appears to be socially universal (as far as one can make any statement of social universality, since there is sure to be some remote island where it apparently doesn't happen—the anthropologists' "but not in Samoa") and across cultures the form, if not the specific content, of these rituals is similar.

It may be useful to remind ourselves what these are like and to note that these ceremonies are (were?) found in very different societies, on different continents. The Wongi or Wongikon of New South Wales knock out a tooth and are given a new name. Thuremlin the God supposedly takes the youth to a distant place, kills him, cuts him up, and restores him to life—away from the women. Other Australian Aboriginal rites involve circumcision and subincision (Frazer, 1922). Similarly, in New Guinea many tribes require circumcision as the rite that confers full manhood, accompanied by a rite of being swallowed and disgorged by a mythical monster. "Sometimes," Frazer laconically observes, "they die" (p. 802). They are covered in a crust of white chalk, in a manner reminiscent of the white-clay body painting characteristic of the Abekweta ceremonies among the Southern Bantu. Among the people who live on the largest Fijian island of Viti Levu (Frazer, 1922) the drama of death and resurrection takes the form of terrorizing the initiates rather than wounding them: they are brought before a row of apparent corpses who seem to have been brutally murdered and left covered in blood with their entrails exposed. The "corpses" then arise, as if from the dead. The blood and guts, being those of pigs, are washed away. The "corpses" then return to welcome the youths to manhood.

Rites of particular violence were practiced by the Kakian association in West Ceram. The boys were kept in a dark hut, where they are supposed to have been swallowed by the devil. They were painted yellow and tattooed. When they were not sleeping they had to crouch without moving a muscle. The women of the community mourned them as though they had died. The boys, having become men, were then brought back into the community. They had "died" and been "resurrected." The youths feigned confusion (or indeed after their confinement they may have been confused) and had to be taught ordinary behavior. After a period of 20 to 30 days, they were permitted to wash, a lock of hair was cut off, and they were allowed to marry (Frazer, 1922).

The themes are repeated, far away from the islands of the Pacific and Australia. In Africa the secret society "Ndembu" plays out a death and resurrection ritual with adolescent males and females, at the end of which they are "brought back to life" and given new names (Frazer, 1922, p. 809). And in North America the Dakotas, Sioux, and Ojibway practiced parallel rituals of death and resurrection.

This has been a relatively quick world tour of simple societies, and it will, I hope, underline the near universality of the practices, which court or simulate death and resurrection. Practices that are nearly universal and are found in very different societies, in very different circumstances, are likely to serve fundamental social/psychological functions. And, to anticipate myself, their absence may produce a variety of personal and public forms of dysfunctional behavior. They will almost certainly be "overdetermined" or "polysemous," and therefore no single simple explanation will fully address the full range of needs and reasons that generate these practices.

As one might expect, the explanations of both origin and function of these rituals that have been advanced range from the simpleminded (but not necessarily invalid for being so) to the mystical (also not necessarily invalid).

The most immediately apparent reason for the rites seems to be Darwinian: a winnowing out of the weak and the identification of the most powerful and talented warriors, protectors, heroes; an acid test of survival capacity. In that sense, the adolescent rituals of endurance are an elaboration of the custom of exposure so that the group will be protected by the strongest and not have to carry the liability of the fragile. Death and torture in this explanation are not metaphors or symbols, but a trial with immediate physical consequence. While rituals in some societies do encompass actual mutilation and trial, however, many other groups enact more abstract or more symbolic challenges in which the ancient physical challenge has been abstracted. The latter become a test of worthiness of an intellectual, social, or moral kind, rather than brute physical survival. Thus customs range from close-to-danger to the merely trying; from hunting, starvation, and exposure to

111

the bar mitzvah and the driver's license. Darwinian survival is not a sufficient explanation for these attenuated versions of induction ceremonies. Indeed, it does not encompass the full nature of the ceremonies as they proceed beyond trials to a more complex social purpose.

Understanding the rites as a simple physical weeding out misses the component of resurrection, which in most rituals moves beyond the celebration of survival to something closer to the sacred. In Weber's (1963) formulation, the survivor of the charismatic education does not simply gain acceptance. The initiate is admitted not only to membership but also to knowledge of the sacred rituals of the community. Weber proposed a model that embraced both the physical trial and the transmission of sacred lore:

> At the root of the oldest and most universally diffused magical system of education is the animistic assumption that just as the magician himself requires rebirth and the possession of a new soul for his art, so heroism rests on a charisma which must be aroused, tested and controlled in the hero by magical manipulations. In this way therefore the warrior is reborn into heroism. Charismatic education in this sense, with its novitiates, trials of strength, tortures, gradations of holiness and honor, initiation of youths, and preparation for battle is an almost universal institution of all societies which have experienced warfare [pp. 67–68].

And which society has not at one time or another experienced warfare? Furthermore the "war" may become more and more symbolic, the trial increasingly abstract. The warrior may be transformed into a pilgrim in pursuit of sacred goals—Christian in the *Pilgrim's Progress* or the journey through stages of magic ritual as in *The Magic Flute*, which is based on the ceremonies of progress in Free Masonry.

In addition to securing the maturation of the novitiate, the rites are mechanisms for bringing the individual into the continuity of the group. The scarifications and wounding—among the most common is circumcision—may be seen as ways of writing on the body of the individual, a metaphorical text of the fundamental beliefs of the society. For example, in an examination of patterns of tattoos, Claude Lévi-Strauss (1963) makes explicit the sacred messages contained in ritual body adornments:

> Among the Maori and the natives of the Paraguayan border facial and corporal decoration is executed in a semi-religious atmosphere.

Tattooings are not only ornaments . . . they are not only emblems of nobility and symbols of rank in the social hierarchy; they are also messages fraught with spiritual and social significance. The purpose of Maori tattooings is not only to imprint a drawing on to the flesh but also the stamp on to the mind all the traditions and philosophy of the group [p. 257].

He cites as an example the conventions of representation which involve the symmetrical splitting of animals as motifs. "Split representation can be explained as a function of a sociological theory of the splitting of the personality" (p. 259).[1]

The huge constructs of death and resurrection may seem too much for the ceremonies during which youths are transformed into adults. But would one think that all this is fanciful, that there are words and customs that link the "theatrical" miming of death and resurrection to explicit formulations, as Victor Turner (1991) clearly describes in his account of symbols in Ndembu Rituals. He refers to a milk tree that has white sap and a tree with red sap that grow on the site of the initiation ceremonies. The milk tree "stands for" breast milk. That is clear and understandable, as is the convention that the red sap is a symbol for blood. But more than that, he writes, "At its highest level of abstraction . . . the milk tree stands for the unity and continuity of Ndembu society" (p. 21). Through the symbolic milk and blood of the trees, both men and women are signified as components of that spatiotemporal continuum. And, to nudge it closer to our time and culture, Turner quotes an "educated Ndembu," who explained that the milk tree was like the British flag above the colonial administrative headquarters: "Mudyi (the milk tree) is our flag." The formulation resonates with and establishes a kinship between the cloth, dye, and imagery of the flag and the customs of near-death, real trauma, and metaphorical resurrection and social continuity of what we like to call primitive rites. It illuminates the nonpositivist and, sometimes, sadly nonsensical excitement surrounding "the

---

[1]I am reminded of the executing machine in Kafka's "In the Penal Colony," in which the written record of crime and sentence of the victim is tattooed on his body by an ingenious machine. The text is elaborated into ornament so complex that the words are difficult to decipher. Kafka's example is remarkably apposite because the original text and meaning of the social and sacred customs is often lost and is an example of how the patterns and rituals become an end in themselves — mechanisms of social bonding and history validated by constant repetition without the freight of explicit meaning that may have originally informed the practice.

flag," "the chalice," "our language," and "our bones." The members of a society are in this sense not only bonded by symbols, but in part *consist* of their symbols, which are *like* blood or limbs or flesh, not an "add-on" to be shed at will, but part of a continuum of psyche and soma—a single entity—not to be lightly dismembered.

Characteristically, such symbols begin with the simplest things, such as blood and food, and they cluster around inescapable biological events that must happen with or without ritual. We *must* eat, we *do* bleed, we *must* die, we *will* pass from childhood through puberty to adolescents without *rites de passage*. The symbolic transformation of these inescapable things and events makes them efficient platforms for a sense of significance and social bonding. Food in particular is a force field akin to gravity in its power to attract symbolic transformation. The Catholic Mass transforms the biological necessity of eating into a ritual symbolizing the sacred redemption of humankind; the bread becomes the flesh of the Redeemer and the wine his blood. Kashruth in the Jewish tradition makes every mouthful eaten an homage to God's immanence. Every meal is in this way a constant reminder of the moral existence, and the believer is saved from a depleting sense of the frivolity and meaninglessness of existence. Beyond these clear examples drawn from our society, there are countless instances of food as intensely connected with taboos and the sacred.

The question concerning the characteristic actual and symbolic violence of rituals and trials persists even more powerfully after these things are taken into account. A tree may be sacred, bread may be sacred; but in addition to these benign transformations of the quotidian into the hieratic, there remains real violence, real blood. It will in the ritual take on expanded meaning, but the pain, the wounding are real and threatening. Turner (1991), in his elaborate exegesis of Ndembu pubertal-adolescent rites, picks up the theme. Circumcision is perceived not only by the imaginative as a small death: the place of circumcision and, indeed, the place of trial for females where they must lie immobily is referred to as "the killing ground." Somewhere in the past was there a real killing ground from which the child/children to be killed were sometimes snatched and then rescued? Is a real, terrifying custom the source of the mitigating myths of Isaac redeemed from sacrifice, or Joseph pulled from the well, or Moses saved from the water, or the Children of Israel saved by blood on their doorposts, or Christ not really dead but risen to eternal life? Everywhere the drops of blood: the ram caught in the thicket, Joseph's blood-stained robe, the blood on the doorposts; "saved by the blood of the lamb"—Christ. In all these examples, the blood signals not only death and wounding, but also life and resurrection. The wound is both sacrificial and redemptive, and in the religious traditions the savagery of the act is denied and turned into its opposite.

Yet other subcomponents of meaning have been suggested as factors in the polysemous braid of adolescent *rites de passage*: an essential feature is the separation of the "youth" or "maiden" from a particular family of origin to group membership, a new extended family defined both by the historic lineage of the group/tribe and the present members of the community. Freud (1910) points to the mechanism.

> The protection against neurotic illness which religion vouchsafes to those who believe in it, is easily explained: It removes their parental complex, on which the sense of guilt in individuals as well as in the whole human race depends, and disposes of it, while the unbeliever has to grapple with the problem on his own [p. 123].

"On his own" is the telling phrase for our purposes. During the initiation rite young men who have been hurt and wounded by their fathers and cut off from their protection, while ostensibly being permitted to join them, will never be "on their own." They are bonded not only to one another in a boot-camp experience but are defined as separate from the elders and indeed from those who will follow them. Not bonded in rebelliousness — they *are* welcomed into the society at the termination of the rites — but by a protective shared survival of threat and trial. At the end, the group is a new "us" within a society that is both "us" and "them."

This process may also be perceived as a playing out of the putative oedipal drama for males. The jealous fathers wound their potential rivals and welcome them afterwards not only as group members, but as wounded men, who may now be weaker and less threatening. Consider that in hunter/gatherer groups, some of the fathers are likely to be in their 20s, men who would be very jealous of robust teenagers, sexual and social competitors. It isn't hard to imagine that ancient rituals of child sacrifice, rationalized as offerings to the gods, may have been a socially valid way of reducing the competition. This notion, too, however, has been elevated and imagined into metaphor-breeding ritual: the place where all the ladders start, "the rag and bone shop of the heart" (Yeats, 1979, p. 375).

While the rituals are apparently gender specific, connected as they usually are with menarche and puberty, and while the trials frequently involve genital mutilation, there is enough evidence to support a significant modification of the notion that the end of the rites produces an adult man or an adult woman somehow alienated and separated from the opposite sex. For example, during the circumcision rites of the Ndembu, the instructor in circumcision techniques is referred to as "the mother of circumcision medicine" (Turner, 1991, p. 22). Similarly, Turner reports that significant male figures, when they function as major social figures, become androgynous. "A chief is often referred to as 'the mother of his people' while the hunter doctor who initiates a novice into a hunting cult is called 'the mother of huntsmanship'" (p. 22). The receiving group of membership may therefore be seen as consisting of all individuals in the community, male and female.

Perhaps this explains the profound paradox in the recognition of sexual maturation that is an integral part of many initiation rites. The men and the women may literally be genitally wounded to become "less man" and "less woman"; the ritual creates a smaller penis through loss of the prepuce, or a wounded vulva and therefore a lesser organ of procreation. Furthermore, in the symbolic rebirth of many pubertal rites, the physical pain of the males mimics the pains of labor: the males become female in the process of giving birth to themselves, a point also made by Comoroff (1985); the females cited by Turner (1991) must be stoical and immobile for hours on end—they must behave in stereotypically male fashion. There is a blurring of sexual particularity at the same time as adult sexual identity is ritually affirmed. This too is a mechanism for assuring a bond to the entire community: past, present, old and young, male and female. The danger of a single-sex bond is thus reduced; and the society as a whole is perceived as kin, and the initiate is not only a member of a particular cohort.

The uninitiated, by contrast, are marginal and are never fully adult in the society; they remain "boys" and "girls." Jean La Fontaine (1977) takes this point further and, commenting on a study of Gisu, adds that "the uninitiated males may also be said to be women, that is like women they lack the power to command" (p. 423). Among the Gisu, the authority-conferring mechanism of "*ritual*" circumcision is a "validation of male authority." A youth circumcized in hospital is not thereby made a man, for he has not withstood the ordeal. The circumcision in the hospital is simply an operation, not a component of a significant ceremony.

Until now I have concentrated on the role of pain, trial, and mutilation, but the passing on of "secret knowledge" is also a common component of the ritual. Characteristically, people are forbidden to come near to the site of the initiation ceremonies; fearful consequences are threatened if the secrets are communicated to the uninitiated, and so on. Yet objective evidence suggests that the "secrets" are seldom astounding. It is as though secrecy and trial were inversely proportional to the content of the revealed truth, as La Fontaine (1977) notes (again citing studies of Gisu), the endurance with unexpected stoicism of unanticipated pain may, in fact, be the knowledge that cannot be communicated — *the remarks of the newly-initiated make clear that the secret is the experience itself"* (p. 424, italics added). And as Richards (1956) pointed out for the Bemba, the initiates may learn little or nothing from the ritual. In spite of this, the Bemba say that in the *Chisungu* (the initiation rite), "We teach and teach and teach the girl" (p. 424). La Fontaine (1977) identifies the nature and significance of the communication of secret knowledge: "What is significant is not *what* is secret but that there *are* secrets, the possession of which separates the initiates from others. The knowledge transmitted is in effect that outsiders do not know the truth." (A contemporary example among black youth — the T-shirt that reads, "You wouldn't understand — it's a black thing" — echoes the idea of secret knowledge gained through initiation.) La Fontaine cites Barth regarding systems of secret knowledge: "Such systems establish bonds between persons on the basis of their common knowledge and in the process of the rituals a socially important lesson is imparted 'knowledge is greater than force; authority is greater than power'" (p. 425).

Whereas ritual focuses on the trial of the initiate, the elders who conduct the ceremonies and the society that will welcome the candidates at the conclusion of the process constitute an integral part of the complex event (La Fontaine, 1977). "In Gisu initiation rituals, two elements are said by Gisu to be effective: the First, teachers and elders, who direct the second; the powers inherent in the dancing of the ignorant" (p. 430), that is, the uninitiated. La Fontaine's emphasis on the power bequeathed by knowledge is persuasive although it apparently neglects the important role of "the knowledge" in anomie reduction and the social membership component of initiation rituals.

First I argued that initiation rituals are concerned with the transfer and vindication of traditional knowledge and not primarily with the change of status of the individuals who pass through the rituals. Ordeals and oaths can be seen as the proof that the knowledge

117

condensed in ritual has indeed effected a change. The ritual is self-validating but in a way that demolishes any distinction we might wish to make for societies other than our own between religious and secular thought. The proof rests on a double acceptance of traditional wisdom and the authority of the wise. This is the second strand: that since the elders claim to authority is legitimized by their greater knowledge the validation of that knowledge also supports their position. This form of political legitimacy distinguished in the ritual from the power to coerce or inherent force, is entirely consistent with a mode of explanation by antecedents and epistemology which guarantees truth by specifying its origins. Initiation rituals create occasions in which the traditional wisdom is communicated, tested and vindicated as the source of the power of rights [p. 430].

Or as Comoroff (1985) writes, "Ritual was the mode of practice most forceful in its transformative capacity, especially when performed on behalf of the community as a whole, by those who were its living embodiments" (p. 80).

While one may be skeptical about the significance of a tree in a village as an umbrella for ceremonies of transformation, it may strain an urban westerner a little less to remember the intense attachment we show to cathedrals, temples, cemeteries, and the like. Having agreed that this phenomenon exists in sophisticated, technologically advanced societies, we may more easily empathize with people who feel affronted when an ancient burial site is bulldozed to make way for a shopping center. When quotidian sites are invested with the power to transform simple actions into metaphor, they become "laboratories" that are invested, through the peculiar magic of the sacral, into great engines that can move personal lives, public lives, whole societies, indeed, all of humankind, into different — and characteristically more significant — modes of existence. As I have noted, the Christian Mass is a ritual during which incantation of texts, usually ornamented and dramatized by solemn music, accompanies the eating of a holy biscuit and the drinking of holy wine, which either represent (in reformed ritual) or actually become (in orthodox Catholic ritual) the body and blood of Christ. In this blood-drinking and cannibalistic ritual the redemption of the human race is signaled and mimetically performed. And, most significantly for purposes of this discussion, participation in these rituals establishes "communion," membership, with large, historically continuous, and meaning-giving tradition. The life of the individual is saved from frivolity and meaning-lessness by this association.

To summarize: most, perhaps all, societies perform *rites de passage* accompanying adolescence. Many of these rituals include ceremonies that in ordinary life would be considered traumatic and abusive. But through the transforming function of the ceremonies, the trials and suffering become the channel for full membership in the contextual society. Indeed, being welcomed into the community at the end of the traumatic component of the ritual is an integral part of the rite; the pain is followed by a celebratory recognition of a change in status. Membership then is achieved both into the contemporary context of the peer group and the whole contemporary community and also into the continuing historical identity of that community. The secret knowledge that is supposed to have been imparted during the rituals is ultimately only the knowledge of belonging, truly belonging. The individual's life has been given meaning, continuity, and pattern.

Since these ceremonies are almost universal, I will make the leap (a leap only in the formal sense—less of a leap when one considers ordinary social existence) and suggest that they probably derive from a universal human need: the need of the individual for a social context that defines and shelters private existence.

The relevance of these ceremonies to contemporary technological "Western" societies is not always immediately obvious. Fragmentary benign and diluted customs do come to mind; the bar mitzvah, the sweet sixteen party, the driver's license, the high school prom, the first cigarette. Apart from the bar mitzvah, which in spite of its religious setting has become highly secularized, none of these carries the explicit mythical and historical components of the ceremonies I have described. They are metaphorically thin and do not express membership achieved within a powerful and continuing tradition.

Paradoxically, the sense of shared danger, the serious hurt, and the bonding through costume and language are more apparent among socially marginal youth. The emotional weight of membership in a cohort of initiates is more evident in the behavior of these marginal youth than in those who clearly "belong" in the majority society. Gang membership may be seen as similar to membership in the suffering cohort of initiates in which trauma and trial are frequently the passport to acceptance. The violent punitive group activity confirms a sense of belonging.

A question forms itself out of a horrified and bewildered contemplation of self-inflicted trauma among 15- to 25-year-old youths in the developed world. Coming to mind immediately are the suicide rate in this group, which has become increasingly prone to suicide since World War II (Klerman, 1988), and the increased incidence of anorexia nervosa (Garner and Garfinkel, 1978). Is there in the adolescent period a need for some form of physical challenge for suffering, for danger—as a component of the entry into biological adulthood? One recoils from such an idea. After all, most people in the vulnerable decade make their way to functional adulthood without mutilating themselves through starvation, tattooing, or, at its most extreme, suicide. But the mystery remains in the case of the large numbers of those who do these terrible things to themselves.

Expanding the question makes one ask, "How does a universal need for belonging become associated with pain?" After all, the human organism is essentially programmed to avoid pain. Durkheim's classic formulation associating suicide with anomie may make the increased rate of suicide among alienated youth understandable. If one's life has no meaning or context, the effort to remain alive may be perceived as pointless (Marks, 1974). The suffering of the anorectic, however, like the voluntary acceptance of deprivation and submission to irrational authority of the cult member, makes little positivist sense. One must invoke the black box of the unconscious, or the even more capacious black box of psychobiological hard wiring, to make sense, even hypothetical sense, of these pathological attempts to cope with the tasks of the middle- to late-adolescent phase.

But the many examples of rites previously referred to may provide a normative key to at least some of the mystery. In particular—as one recalls—circumcision is sometimes referred to as "killing" and the place of circumcision is "the killing place." Real death hovers close to the metaphorical death of many mutilating customs, and this frequent association suggests an unconscious or preconscious tropism to a real death. Tiano (1992) has written about the rebirth of a new self during adolescence in the same vein as Rakoff (1967) wrote. Adolescence may be viewed as a process of the birth of an adult self from the childhood self. Does rebirth imply a death of the previous self—the death of the child self, a need to moult a previous physical self. Does the metaphor need to be enacted?

While the small ceremonies and the dangerous customs of gang membership, impregnating a young woman, tattooing, cult membership, anorexia nervosa, motorcycle roving, fraternity hazing, even drunken partying and horrifying suicide all share some components of socially validated *rites de passage*, these bits and pieces of peer-group customs are fragmentary, *formes frustes* of fully realized customs. The inescapable imperative toward peer-group bonding and trial is unformed and decontextualized, a kind of postmodern deconstruction of ancient need. Most significantly, although they may express an explicit or implicit yearning for belonging, because these ceremonies are not integrally associated with social acceptance and the establishment of meaningful social communion, they leave the individual without a realized membership in a supporting society. They are the resorts of the vulnerable, who indulge in a form of behavioral pica; and when the age-limited period of trial and, with luck, survival is passed, there is no social mechanism for acceptance into productive adulthood on "the other side."

Of what use is this formulation to the clinician who must deal with the needs of anomic youth in a pluralist, nontraditional society, a society that does not pay much explicit respect to a shared history; or to youths such as Native Canadian aboriginals, whose suicide rates are the highest in Canada, youths who are doubly anomic. Their own society's history and customs are recently lost, and they have no place in the mainstream society, which is dangerously centrifugal even for those who claim apparent membership (Eastwood, unpublished).

If only proper rituals of meaningful affiliation could be created at will, some of the problems might perhaps be dealt with. But the essence of ritual is repetition, and not merely repetition, but repetition hallowed by long history and meaningful association. One cannot by an act of will create ceremonies leading to group affiliation. If, however, one accepts the Durkheimian formulation that lack of significant identity with one's society leads to anomie, then some modest beginnings may be proposed. Such proposals cannot undertake to restore a past history or to reinstate customs that have lost vitality and validity, and they will only too easily be dismissed as "willed," lacking in spontaneity, failing to address such other problems as poverty, racism, and so on. Indeed, some of these criticisms may be true, but the need is tremendous, and something should be proposed, and some social engineering should be devised that will build on the mix of affiliative need and the courting of "trials."

The range of remedial proposals will cover small-group activity and larger national schemes, for example, among isolated native youths, specific programs to teach the youths their history and folkways, accompanied by skills training that will have relevance to the dominant society's economy and technology.

But for native youth in particular the study of history and folkways without a sense of relevance to the world seen on television will probably lead to a sense of artificiality and irrelevance. Participation in customs that have lost their validity may also produce a subtle falsification of that history, tainting it with romanticism and a reactionary nostalgia. Furthermore, it may consign native peoples to a stifling tie to a particular physical circumstance without portability, flexibility, or the ability to share in the historical movements of increasingly pluralist societies. Education in the lore of a past without sharing in a present-day secular reality may consign people to the status of inhabitants of an ethnographic zoo.

The experience in Israel, which has had to assimilate immigrants from many backgrounds, may provide a model for a wider scheme. The army in Israel, in addition to being a conventional military machine, is also an instrument of social integration. By the sharing of the experience of a boot camp, the privation, and ceremonies of army induction, a bond is created among recruits. Amos Elon (1990) cites Avishai Margalit: "Army service here is often like a primitive tribal initiation rite. It is a main socializing experience" (p. 99). Can this model be transferred to our societies? Would a nonmilitary national service, applicable to all youths without discrimination, serve? It would provide the opportunities for difficult shared experience; it would allow an appreciation of national ideals; it could be used to educate the participants in the cultures of other group members; it could be used for the performance of socially useful work; above all, it would give to an entire generation the matrix for a shared identity; and it would identify specific educational needs. At the end, through ceremony and recognition, the society would welcome the young people into full membership.

This is not to suggest that everything is solved by shared experience. Poverty remains a terrible problem and is the background for much destructive adolescent behavior. But poverty alone is not "sufficient cause." Cairo has millions of poor people, but the urban crime rate is among the world's lowest. It can be argued that Egyptians still feel a profound sense of unity with their society, to which they are bonded by shared customs, religion, and language. On the other side of the scale, the alienating effects of a modern technological society are also not "sufficient cause." Tokyo, which is as high-tech as any city on earth, also has a low urban crime rate. The society is as unitary and bonded as Cairo's.

Can we recreate the *rites de passage* for vulnerable youths and restore the painful trials to their status of instruments of growth and adult identity rather than mere accompaniments to destructiveness and identity diffusion?

REFERENCES

Comoroff, J. (1985), *Body of Power, Spirit of Resistance*. Chicago: University of Chicago Press.

Eastwood, R. (1967), Epidemiology of suicide. Unpublished report.

Elon, A. (1990), Letter from Jerusalem, *New Yorker*, April 23, p. 99.

Frazer, J. G. (1922), *The Golden Bough*. New York: Macmillan. (1913), *Totem and Taboo*. *Standard Edition*, 13:1–161. London: Hogarth Press, 1953.

Freud, S. (1910), *Leonardo da Vinci and a Memory of his Childhood*. *Standard Edition*, 11:3–137. London: Hogarth Press, 1957.

Garner, D. M. & Garfinkel, P. E. (1978), Sociocultural factors in anorexia nervosa. *Lancet*, 2:674.

Klerman, G. (1988), Youthful melancholia. *Brit. J. Psychiat.*, 152:4–14.

La Fontaine, J. (1977), The Henry Myers Lecture. *Man*, 12:423–425, 429.

Lévi-Strauss, C. (1963), *Structural Anthropology*, trans. C. Jacobson & B. Grundfest Schoepf. New York: Basic Books.

Marks, S. R. (1974), Durkheim's theory of anomie. *Amer. J. Sociol.*, 80:329–363.

Rakoff, V. M. (1967), Adolescence as rebirth. In: *Adolescent Psychiatry*, ed. J. Shamsie. Montreal: Schering, pp. 60–67.

Reik, T. (1964), *Pagan Rites in Judaism*. New York: Farrar Straus.

Richards, A. I. (1956), *The Chisungu*. London: Faber & Faber.

Tiano, S. (1992), The adolescent and death: The fourth organizer of adolescence. Unpublished manuscript.

Turner, V. (1991), *The Forest of Symbols*. Ithaca, NY: Cornell University Press.

van Gennep, A. (1960), *The Rites of Passage*, trans. M. B. Vizedom & G. L. Caffee. Chicago: University of Chicago Press.

Weber, M. (1963), *Sociology of Religion*, trans. E. Fischoff. Boston: Beacon Press.

Yeats, W. B. (1979), The circus animals' desertion. In: *Collected Poems*. New York: Oxford University Press.

10　CHILDHOOD TRAUMA REVISITED: INTERRUPTION OF DEVELOPMENT

CLARICE J. KESTENBAUM

The belief that childhood experience determines adult behavior is so widespread that it has become an integral part of every major developmental paradigm. Theoretical considerations about particular childhood experience and subsequent sequelae, however, have greatly changed during the past decades. Researchers in the 60s challenged the prevailing view that a single event—such as primal scene observation or punitive toilet training—could have an unvarying effect on behavior; rather, overall parental style was considered more significant than the occurrence of a specific event unless the event was perceived as traumatic enough to derail the child from the path of normal development.

The concept of trauma concerns the impact of overwhelming life stressors and their effects on physical and psychological functioning. But how much stress is necessary to produce a trauma in any given individual? Obviously, an individual's coping mechanisms and resilience and the presence or absence of support systems determine the outcome. Determinants of psychopathology in childhood include multiple risks factors: environmental, including parental psychopathology, alcoholism, family disorder, family size and socioeconomic status; and individual characteristics, such as genetic predisposition, temperamental traits, and physical illness, to name but a few. Certain children have experienced such severe stress as air raids or earthquakes with equanimity because of the perception that their caretakers remained calm in the face of disaster; others, on the other hand, have, under far less stressful circumstances, exhibited manifestations of posttraumatic stress disorder.

In attempting to clarify the concepts of risk, vulnerability and resilience, E. James Anthony (1974) used the analogy of three dolls made of glass, plastic, and steel. When exposed to the blow of a hammer the glass doll shatters; the plastic doll is bent out of shape; the third doll "gives off a fine metallic sound." The last doll, for constitutional reasons (a steel ego) is like the child who responds to stress by maintaining mastery over his environment and developing the ability to cope; that doll demonstrates "relative invulnerability" to the vicissitudes of life.

Kiser et al. (1991) have studied the reactions of children and adolescents to physical and sexual abuse. Over half their sample developed symptoms of posttraumatic stress disorder: they exhibited heightened anxiety, hypervigilance, and impaired impulse control. Those children and adolescents who did not develop the characteristic symptoms exhibited more depression, delinquency, and aggression. Many developed personality disorders — schizotypal, paranoid, and especially borderline personality disorder, a finding corroborated by Ogata et al. (1990), Nigg et al. (1991), and Stone (1981, 1987).

Van der Kolk, Perry, and Herman (1991) concluded from their studies that childhood trauma and physical and sexual abuse contributed to the initiation of self-destructive behavior, particularly in a nonnurturing environment. Incest has been implicated, particularly by Green (1984), as leading to borderline personality disorder and multiple personality (1984). We all recall the case of "Nicole," Dick Diver's hapless patient in Fitzgerald's *Tender Is the Night:* paternal sexual abuse resulted in psychosis and institutionalization. Again, we are led to believe that a single traumatic event resulted in severe mental illness in a seriously vulnerable young woman.

Lenore Terr (1991) has been studying the effects of trauma on the developing child. She wrote:

> If one looks only at the clinical manifestations of traumas in a given day in the life of the traumatized child, one could diagnose conduct disorder, borderline personality disorder, major affective disorder, attention deficit-hyperactivity disorder, phobic disorder, dissociative disorder, obsessive-compulsive disorder, panic disorder, adjustment disorder . . . and precursors of multiple or acute dissociative disorder, and not be wrong [p. 11].

In attempting to sort out multiple sequelae of specific types of traumatic events, Terr postulated two types of trauma: Type I, resulting from a single overwhelming event that originates from an external source and renders the child temporarily helpless and unable to cope; and Type II stemming from long-standing, repeated ordeals similar to Kahn's (1963) concept of cumulative trauma, as in cases of physical and sexual child abuse. Terr found several characteristics common to most cases: "thought suppression, sleep problems, exaggerated startle responses, developmental regressions, fears of the mundane, deliberate avoidances, panic, irritability and hypervigilance" (p. 12).

Four characteristics were particularly significant in Type I cases: (1) strongly visualized memories; (2) repetitive behaviors, (repetition compulsion); (3) trauma-specific fears; and (4) hopelessness about the future. A failure of repression was evident in most cases. Terr did not find either traumatic dreams or amnesia for the event to be a hallmark of traumatized young children, as is usually reported in cases of adult PTSD.

The Type II traumas were those which resulted in maladaptive character formation. Defense mechanisms of denial and repression, identification with the aggressor, and turning against the self are paramount. Terr describes an unremitting sadness alternating with outbursts of rage; and a seeming absence of feeling suggestive of a psychic numbing; and repeated experiencing of depersonalization (removing oneself from the scene) in these children.

Reports of amnesia following a single traumatic event in childhood are rare, notwithstanding the movie *Spellbound,* in which total amnesia persisted until a second traumatic event reevoked the locked secrets in adult life. Who can forget Gregory Peck's struggle to recover his memory with the help of psychiatrist Ingrid Bergman, who observed that her patient became anxious when around certain linear patterns of black and white? (Recall that the character felt that he had actually caused the death of his younger brother, who was impaled on a spike fence when his sled ran amok.) Such repression, Terr found, does not usually occur in Type I trauma.

Case Examples

MARIA

My first experience with a conversion reaction occurred when I was a first-year child psychiatry fellow on the pediatric consultation liaison service. I had been asked to consult on an eight-year-old girl referred by the ophthalmology inpatient unit for hysterical blindness. No medical reason could be found for the sudden seeming loss of vision in both eyes three days prior to my consultation. The notes said that she displayed typical tubular vision on examination. I found Maria sitting in bed "watching" an animated television program. I introduced myself and told her that I had been asked to consult on her case. She exhibited the classical *belle indifference* found in adult patients I had seen in the emergency room (more prevalent then than now). She smiled politely in my direction and pointed to an empty chair. She didn't seem distressed in any way.

"Can you tell me what happened three days ago, Maria?"

"I don't know. I just couldn't see any more."

"What were you doing just before you stopped seeing?"

"Nothing special. I was sitting on the stairs next to my apartment playing with my girlfriend, the way we always do after school."

"And then what?"

"I don't know. Nothing special."

I questioned her about home, school, friends. She lived with both parents and a younger sister in a four-room apartment not far from the hospital. She was in the third grade in a parochial school, was doing well, and had many friends. I continued to inquire about other aspects of her life. She spoke of her Italian-born grandparents and extended family—many cousins and aunts—with warm feelings. Nothing seemed amiss. In desperation, I asked if she ever remembered any dreams.

"I remember the one I had last night." she said. "I was running over a bridge. A man was chasing me with a knife. Then I woke up."

I asked her if she could draw a picture of the dream. Despite her "blindness," she took my pencil and sketched the scene. A stick-figure man was chasing a girl over a bridge. He had dropped a knife into the water below. She could recall no more details except that the dream was scary and woke her up.

I told her I would come back the following day and suggested that little by little she would begin to see things more clearly. I was puzzled. I could detect no overt psychopathology in the child to account for the hysterical symptom. My next move was to contact Maria's mother.

Mrs. T was a middle-aged Italian-American woman, very upset about her daughter's condition.

"Can you think of anything that might have brought this on?" Nothing came to mind.

"Did the neighbors see anything unusual?" Not that she knew.

That evening, however, Mrs. T called me at the hospital and asked to meet with me as soon as possible. The next morning she reported that the neighbor's child with whom Maria had been playing had told her mother that the building superintendent's 18-year-old son had exposed himself on the stairwell. Why had the neighbor's child run home to tell her mother while Maria had said nothing to anyone, had become amnesiac, and in fact gone blind?

I continued my investigation.

"Mrs. T, did anything ever happen to Maria when she was younger? Did she see something sexual that might have frightened her?"

Mrs. T crossed herself. She was certain that Maria had never seen her husband and herself making love. She had never discussed sexual matters with her because she was too young.

I was sure the man with the knife in Maria's dream was a memory of an actual event, one of which Mrs. T may not have been aware.

"Are you sure nothing ever happened to her?" I asked.

At this point Mrs. T broke down in tears. She looked terrified.

"Something did happen — when Maria was two and a half. But she was too young to remember. I was at church one Sunday. My husband was away, and I left her at home with my brother, who is slightly retarded. When I came home, I saw that he had tried to have sex with Maria because her diaper was soiled with semen. I took her to the doctor, but she hadn't been hurt. I never told anyone except the priest. We sent my brother to live with some cousins in the country. I never told my husband. I was sure Maria remembered nothing about it."

I explained to Mrs. T what I thought had happened. In language she could understand, I told her that Maria had pushed out of her conscious memory the incident until the forbidden memory suddenly returned when she saw the young man's exposed penis (screen memory). In a religious household, where even discussion about sex was considered "bad," Maria "shut off" her perception and memory by the sudden "forgetting," and hysterical blindness followed.

I went back to see Maria and told her gently that her friend had explained that a man was on the stairwell with them that day. She didn't remember anything at all. I told her that he was a sick man who scared little girls but that the police were taking him away to help him with his problem. Each day Maria's vision became sharper. By the end of the week, Maria could distinguish my features from across the ward.

I made arrangements for outpatient follow-up visits, but the family never kept the appointments. In fact, I learned shortly afterward that the family had moved away and were lost to follow-up.

CAROL

Carol was completing her sophomore year in an Ivy League college. She was a brilliant student and had an active social life, but only with girls. She was extremely pretty, but her weight problem interfered with her relationships with boys. She had never had a date. She sought therapy at the urging of her parents, who were certain that Carol would never find a husband.

I found Carol to be engaging and bright in every area of discourse *except* the subject of dating. She seemed unconcerned that no one had ever invited her out. She preferred to spend time with family members and girlfriends. I wondered if she could be homosexual, but she denied having any sexual fantasies or dreams and stated that never in her life had she masturbated.

Carol was the youngest child of American-born Jewish parents. The father was a successful businessman, the mother a high school teacher. She had a married sister, aged 31, and two older brothers, aged 30 and 27 years. All three were partners in the family business. Despite Carol's academic success (she was a prelaw student), she was surprisingly "boring" in sessions; she seldom reported dreams and had few associations when she did. Despite seemingly serious efforts to diet, she was 60 pounds overweight in her physician's judgment; he insisted that she join Weight Watchers to bring down her borderline high blood pressure.

Therapy proceeded for several months without change. Carol had lost 10 pounds and was slowly attempting to lose more when an event occurred that changed the course of therapy. Her parents had presented her with a ticket for a Greek-island cruise as a reward for high academic achievement. (They undoubtedly hoped she would meet someone special.) Carol actually did meet someone, a Greek waiter on shipboard who didn't mind her avoirdupois at all. In fact, he seemed absolutely smitten. Carol was flattered but remained somewhat aloof and unapproachable. One night she had too much to drink and allowed him to fondle her. Suddenly she experienced a panic of overwhelming proportions. (She was almost unable to describe the scene.) A vivid memory flooded her consciousness. She was six, and her 13-year-old brother with whom she was playfully wrestling was suddenly lying on top of her holding her down. He was forcing his penis between her thighs and laughing while he held her mouth shut. After he ejaculated he warned her never to tell anyone or he would "get her" when she was asleep. Carol believes the rape only occurred once. "I guess I blotted it all out — I've never spoken of it again."

During the subsequent session Carol described how she had wanted to become fat. She didn't understand the reason why her overweight had never troubled her: that the fatter she was, the safer she felt.

Several months after the return of the repressed memory, Carol confronted her brother. He broke down and wept. He admitted that he had felt guilty for the 12 years since he had abused her and worried that he had ruined her life forever.

Carol did lose the weight; she began dating, slowly, and by the end of the treatment, which concluded with college graduation, she had a steady boyfriend and was sexually fulfilled. She was actually able to reestablish a warm and loving relationship with her brother, whom she had avoided since she was six years old.

PATRICK

Patrick was a 16-year-old boy referred for evaluation by his parochial school teacher because of deteriorating academic performance. Although I usually see a patient and his family before obtaining psychological tests, in this instance the tests had been ordered and sent to me in advance. I could see at a glance that Patrick was a very bright boy—his verbal IQ was 130, indicating that he was in the superior range of intelligence. His performance IQ, however, was 83—a very large gap in someone for whom organic pathology has been ruled out. The psychologist was perplexed. She wrote, "Patrick was impersonal and distant. When questioned at the end of testing he denied all conflicts and problems." She felt he needed to control motor impulses at the expense of his intellectual functions.

The psychologist's impression was that Patrick's severe overcontrol was due to enormous rage. "Anger is something that he thinks about, but it is unlikely that he allows himself to feel it." She also noted that he had difficulty responding to the Rorschach card that is most frequently related to the mother. She wrote, "After considerable blocking and an inability to respond, Patrick replied that it looked like two four- or five-year-old angry girls' faces. His view of women is a severely distorted one; women provoke in him a considerable amount of anxiety."

Armed with the psychologist's impression, I made an appointment to see Patrick alone in order to establish rapport and trust.

I found Patrick to be a tall, handsome teenager who looked somewhat younger than 16. He did not object to the consultation but said he didn't think it could help much. "I just can't study! I get bored pretty fast, and my mind just wanders in class or when I'm doing homework," he said.

He was failing all but two of his subjects, math and English, both of which he barely passed.

"What would you rather be doing?" I asked.

"Just hanging out. Watching T.V."

He was not really involved in after-school sports, other kids, or any absorbing interests or hobbies; he had no real friends. I questioned him further about his life story. He told me his mother died when he was seven, but he didn't remember much about it. He thought she had a heart attack and fell from a window to her death. I was surprised, but he didn't elaborate. He and his sister had been sent to a Catholic boarding school until the father remarried when Patrick was 11. His recollections of those years were filled with stories of severe punishment by teachers, "getting hit on the head when you talked out of turn or being humiliated if you wet your bed." (Apparently this was a frequent occurrence at age eight.)

Patrick's father, Mr. W, was a 47-year-old businessman whose first wife had died nine years earlier. He had been remarried five years prior to the consultation to a woman 15 years younger than himself. There was one sibling, a 12-year-old girl who was functioning well. Mrs. W was quite beautiful but seemed depressed and withdrawn. They corroborated Patrick's story that life in the boarding school had been difficult for Patrick, who was mischievous and disrespectful of authority.

"Even now I can never get him to take out the garbage or clean up his room," Mrs. W complained. "Lately, he seems to have undergone a personality change — so listless, not interested in anything, always in his room," she added.

I realized Patrick was depressed and explained that I wanted to see him twice a week before deciding what further steps to take. Patrick did not balk at coming to his sessions; but he lacked spontaneity, answering my questions but not contributing more information. He talked about current problems with mean teachers and recalled events in his past, but he seemed to have little memory about his life prior to boarding school. I asked about his mother. He had a picture of her "in a drawer somewhere," but he rarely thought about her. He felt ashamed, somehow, that she was dead. He told people that Mrs. W was his real mother although his friends joked that she looked more like a sister than a mother.

During the first weeks of treatment, I had the feeling that Patrick, so self-contained, was doing his best to keep at a safe distance, that opening the smallest crack in the seemingly inpenetrable facade could let loose a torrent of emotions. I inquired about his early memories.

"I don't remember much. I think I was king of the wild, playing tricks, always getting into trouble. I think I used to be happy," he added wistfully.

"What about now?"

"Well, I hate my school. The nuns are really jerks. I hate religion too. My parents don't understand. I'd rather go to a regular school."

"If you could change anything about yourself or your life what would it be?" I asked several weeks later.

"I guess I'd change my face. I look in the mirror and I don't like my face. I hate my glasses. I feel alone—not like other boys. I wish I could get good grades. I can't seem to concentrate. Sometimes I wonder if life has a purpose—about why we're here, not that I would ever kill myself or anything," he added quickly.

"But you do think about death sometimes?"

"Yeah, kind of wondering about what it must be like to just disappear."

I ascertained that Patrick had never seriously considered suicide but that he did think about death, especially his own, a great deal. He never discussed these thoughts with anyone.

"My stepmother is too giddy and childish; she just laughs, and my father would probably only nod and pick up the newspaper. That's what he usually does when a serious conversation comes up."

I realized that Patrick was lowering his guard. He began asking me about other patients he'd seen in the waiting room.

"What do they talk about? Do you ever hypnotize them?"

"Why do you ask about hypnosis?" I asked.

"Maybe you could find out what makes them tick."

"Often people tell me their dreams," I responded. "Then we can figure out what's bothering them without needing to hypnotize them"

"I heard people can't be hypnotized against their will," he said.

"That's true. I've only done it when someone needed to find out some answers really fast and wanted to be hypnotized, but usually we can work out problems without hypnosis."

"I had a dream last week," Patrick volunteered.

"I'd really like to hear it," I said. "You know, dreams are a key to unlocking a door where many secrets are hidden. If you remember it and want to share it with me, it may mean that you might be ready to find some answers to your problems in school or why you feel so down most of the time."

"Well," he began, "there were a lot of people milling about; some men wearing black. My mother—my real mother—was sitting at her night table fixing her hair. She was sad and said she had to go to Paradise. I was sad too. I said, 'Why do you want to leave me Mother?'"

I was surprised by the emotion I felt as Patrick related the dream. It seemed more like a memory that had not faded with time.

"What does the dream remind you of?"

"Well, I do think about her lately. I was even wondering why she had to die."

Suddenly Patrick seemed to become frozen in his chair—his face contorted—and fell to the floor.

I was shocked. Patrick lay on the floor, sobbing uncontrollably. I knelt down beside him.

"Tell me everything you remember," I suggested gently.

His words came tumbling forth.

"She didn't fall. I saw her go to the window and jump out. It was my fault because I got a D on my report card, and she was upset."

He rocked back and forth. "Everybody said I was wrong, but I saw her. I remember it now."

"And you didn't remember until now that she jumped to her death?"

"Yes. My father came running in. He looked down below—police were there and an ambulance. He said she had a heart attack and fell. I tried to tell him what I saw, but he yelled, 'No, it didn't happen that way Patrick.'"

I helped Patrick back into the chair and brought him a drink of water.

"And all those years you had to keep that secret hidden. No wonder you were confused and unhappy believing that a bad mark on a seven-year-old's report card could cause your mother to kill herself. Obviously she was ill."

Patrick was still crying quietly now. Memories came pouring forth. It was as if a veil had been lifted. I reached for the telephone and called Patrick's father at work. I asked him to come in alone the next day to discuss the events surrounding his first wife's death. I explained to Patrick that I need to discuss the true facts with his father alone but that we would have a family session as soon as I myself knew the truth about his mother's suicide.

Mr. W was visibly shaken. "We could never have buried her in consecrated ground if it had been known she committed suicide," he admitted.

It seems that Patrick's mother had a psychotic depression when Patrick was born and again when he was six. She had been consulting a psychiatrist and was taking medication, but both she and the family refused hospitalization.

I told Mr. W that he could not go on denying the true events, that Patrick had to be told that she jumped out of the window because she was sick (not that she had had a heart attack) and that it was not his fault. He asked me to discuss the case with the family priest, which, of course, I did with alacrity.

The next week Patrick began sessions with a new approach—he needed to be told the truth he had always known and deal with his loss by mourning his mother. He remained in therapy for two years with a successful outcome. His grades were markedly improved; he developed friendships and entered the world of adolescence. On graduation from high school he left home for an excellent university and was graduated with honors.

Discussion

Each of the three vignettes describes a single traumatic event in childhood (Type I) that resulted in disorientation with amnesia and subsequent symptomatology: hysterical blindness, obesity, and depression with academic inhibition. These symptoms, according to Terr (1991), are usually observed when Type II trauma, or cumulative trauma, has occurred, followed by dissociative states, numbing, withdrawal and characteristic personality disorders, particularly borderline psychopathology. Terr's interest in childhood trauma stemmed from her study of the Chochilla kidnapping of 20 pre-schoolers who exhibited a wide range of posttraumatic behaviors and from her study of several hundred children evaluated for a variety of traumatic experiences who suffered from posttraumatic stress disorder.

How does one explain the difference in symptom choice? Anthony (1974) has observed that a strong support system may protect against later events. In Terr's cases, the children shared a common experience. They could talk about it together and had a strong supportive intervention network. In my three cases, and most cases of sexual abuse, the events are secrets not shared with others and felt to be shameful.

In reexamining the psychoanalytic concept of trauma, Dorpat (1985) observes that the basic function of the mental apparatus is reestablishment of stability following an external disturbance. The ego avoids trauma by anticipating the noxious event in mastery play and fantasy. In most cases, traumatized children with PTSD repeat the stressful event in an effort to master it. But what brings about the sudden amnesia I described earlier? Dissociation involving denial—the most primitive, the earliest of the mental mechanisms of defense.

Dorpat describes denial as a "fuzzy, complex concept"—an unconscious defense mechanism against unpleasurable ideas, affects, and

135

perceptions, an unconscious repudiation of some or all of the meaning of an event to allay anxiety or other unpleasurable affects—or, as Brenner (1981) noted by way of Freud, "an unconscious protective response to psychic pain—a reaction to anxiety, guilt, sorrow or *trauma*" (p. 561).

"Denial, together with the disorganizing emotional turmoil at the time of trauma, prevents individuals from forming accurate representational memories and reality-syntonic meanings regarding the traumatic experience" (Dorpat, 1985, p. 25). The cognitive psychologists have described a similar mechanism as the arrest of cognition of something threatening and the shifting of attention to something less threatening.

Research in perception and focal attention has described hypnotic states in which a person perceives and at the same time does *not* perceive. For example, hypnotized subjects who were told that they would not see a particular chair when they were awakened from their trance all avoided the chair as they walked through the empty room. In other words they "registered" its presence and had a visual awareness of the object while denying its existence. Certain stimulus inputs reach *unconscious* levels of registration but are blocked from *conscious* perception (Neisser, 1967).

Dorpat (1985) contends that denial prevents the formation of representational memories and arrests the normal process of thinking and percept formation and brings about *pathological* memory activity. When the traumatic memory actually breaks through years after the event, the past experience is vividly recalled "as if it occurred yesterday." There is not the normal wearing-away process by which recollections of things past are assimilated and fade away. (Patrick's aberration occurred in exactly this way.)

When an event as traumatic as the death of a parent by suicide occurs, irrational guilt, rage, and helplessness are often defended against by denial. Complete dissociation with amnesia, however, is not the usual consequence of childhood trauma, as I noted earlier. The death of a parent can bring about partial dissociation with memory distortion, depersonalization, and affective blunting.

A 40-year-old female patient once described the reaction of her six-year-old daughter's classmate who had just learned that her terminally ill mother was dying. Her father had come to school to take her to the hospital; her friends and teachers were standing around her crying. "I saw her face suddenly change. The wall went up, shutting her away from the others. She had learned in one moment how to wear the mask before the world, covering over the pain and hurt. I went over to her and told her that I too had lost my mother when I was her age and that I understood." My patient then recalled how she herself had pushed out of consciousness feelings that did not emerge until she left home for college, when waves of grief over her mother's death overwhelmed her.

The therapeutic process requires working through emotional responses to the trauma hitherto blocked out in the relationship with the analyst. Reconstruction of the event is of primary importance in arriving at reconceptualization of past experiences. Trauma in childhood that results in complete or partial dissociation represents a serious interruption of development and needs to be dealt with through psychoanalytic psychotherapy, in my opinion, so that the child or adolescent can rid himself of the noxious memory (at best unconscious) and return to the path of optimal development.

REFERENCES

Anthony, E. J. (1974), A risk-vulnerability intervention model. In: *The Child in His Family,* ed. E. J. Anthony & O. Kapernick. New York: Wiley, pp. 529–545.

Brenner, C. (1981), Defense and defense mechanisms: *Psychoanal. Quart.*, 50:557–569.

Dorpat, T. L. (1985), *Denial and Defense in the Therapeutic Situation.* New York: Aronson.

Green, A. H. (1984), Child abuse by siblings. *Child Abuse Neglect,* 8:311–317.

Khan, M. M. (1963), The concept of cumulative trauma. *The Psychoanalytic Study of the Child,* 18:286–306. New York: International Universities Press.

Kiser, L. J., Heston, J., Millsap, P. A. & Pruitt, D. B. (1991), Physical and sexual abuse in childhood: Relationship with post-traumatic stress disorder. *J. Amer. Acad. Child Adoles. Psychiatry,* 30:776–783.

Neisser, U. (1967), *Cognitive Psychology,* New York: Appleton Century-Crofts.

Nigg, J. T., Silk, K. K., Westen, D., Lohn, R. E., Gold, L. J., Goodrich, S. & Ogata, S. (1991), Object representations in the early memories of sexually abused borderline patients. *Amer. J. Psychiat.,* 148:864–869.

Ogata, S. N., Silk, K. K., Goodrich, S., Lohn, N. E., Weston, D. & Hill, E. M. (1990), Childhood sexual abuse and physical abuse in adult patients with borderline personality disorder. *Amer. J. Psychiat.,* 147:1008–1013.

Stone, M. H. (1981), Borderline syndromes: A consideration of subtypes and an interview: directions for research. *Psych. Clin. N. Amer.* 4:3–23.

_____ (1987), A psychodynamic approach: Some thoughts on the dynamics and therapy of self-mutilating borderline patients. *J. Personal. Dis* 1:347–349.

Terr, L. C. (1991), Childhood trauma: An outline and overview. *Amer. J. Psychiat.* 148:10–20.

Van der Kolk, B. A., Perry, C. & Herman, J. L. (1991), Childhood origins of self-destructive behavior. *Amer. J. Psychiat.* 148:1665–1671.

MAX SUGAR

Although there is an abundant literature on adolescent sexuality and behavior, there are some factors that have not been accorded their appropriate significance. In order to clarify further sexual behavior among different groups of typical adolescents in the United States, this paper attempts to present a wider view of many facets that appear to have a bearing on female and male biological and emotional development.

Sexual Development

IN FEMALES

The sporadic self-stimulation that begins in females at about nine to eleven months may increase until the middle of the second year or may be absent. Between 16 and 19 months, during the early genital phase (Roiphe, 1968), girls manifest increased genital sensitivity with repetitive direct (manual) or indirect (rocking, thigh pressure) masturbation, with erotic arousal and accompanying pleasurable facial expressions (Galenson, 1979; Roiphe, 1979). Then there is curiosity, with visual and tactile exploration of their own and peers' genitals, followed by a distinct, mild preoedipal castration reaction. Girls turn from mother to father and manifest coyness and increased erotization to him. With the awareness of the sex differences, there is a decrease in direct, but an increase in indirect, masturbation, along with a greater attachment to dolls and doll play.

From my observations of girls at this age, a girl at this time may show an innate supine passive-receptive posture, a broad smile, and even leg raising on seeing father or a father substitute to whom she feels very close.

139

A girl's discovery of her anatomical differences from the boy is not necessarily experienced as a narcissistic injury, but a girl who does have such a reaction has a prephallic disturbance in object relations (Galenson and Roiphe, 1976).

Girls first become interested in babies around 12 months, and dolls begin to represent babies primitively. Around the beginning of the third year, girls show a marked excitement and interest in babies and wish to have one; they are already "dominated by a heterosexual drive pressure" (Parens, 1990, p. 757).

In the phallic-oedipal phase, girls have an increase in masturbation, exhibitionism, and a preoccupation with their own and others' genitals. This preoccupation may lead to mutual exploration with the same- and opposite-sex peers in the sexual play of this period. With the oedipal phase, girls have a heightened interest in father as their love object. This phase gives way to the castration complex, in which they give up father and return to mother.

Latency girls are "often a caricature of femininity; yet a variety of preoedipal conflicts, unresolved penis envy and phallic exhibitionism is also frequently apparent" (Tyson, 1982, p. 80). For females in early latency, sleepovers and "secret" talks about the origin of babies are based on bisexual conflict and are a defense against oedipal issues.

With increasing hormone levels come heightened bodily sensations and sexual excitations as females' bodies begin to change in late latency. These girls also have many sexual thoughts and feelings, engage in masturbatory activities, and have thoughts about having babies; and they have some bisexual conflict (Harley, 1971; Tyson, 1982; Almond, 1990). The pubertal female's sexual feelings and masturbatory fantasies are very arousing and cause some conflict for her, although usually not at clinical levels. The expressions of phallic strivings are often and regularly direct, more than they usually are before or after this period, when they are disguised (Harley, 1971).

Harley observed that girls at this time talk of dirty secrets, have mutual urination and defecation, and "scorn boys for their more open filthiness and thus aim to establish their own superiority over the male sex" (p. 387). She also suggests that girls' castration complex accounts for their ruthlessness and cruelty in their interpersonal relations, not seen in boys. These phallic strivings appear to be the basis for girls' assertiveness at 11 in contrast to later behavior (Gilligan, 1982). The resurgence of the oedipal conflict is evident again in puberty and early adolescence with figure comparisons, slumber parties, sex secrets, and "dirty talk."

140

Zilbach (1993) posits a female line of development, with specific emphasis on breast development and menarche, and their particular meanings for the girl. Menarche is an important marker of issues between mother and daughter, separation-individuation, and preoedipal conflicts (Whisnant, Brett, and Zegans, 1979). Tampon use involves a readiness or a growth toward fostering autonomy and individuation and learning to touch and explore one's external genitalia (Shopper, 1979).

Adolescent girls' masturbation is also related to exploration and autonomy. At age 15, about 33% of girls masturbate, and at age 20 this number increases to about 60% (Chilman, 1983). In 1986 (Masters, Johnson, and Kolodny, 1986) the percentage was over 75%. Masturbation promotes females' sexual responsiveness, orgasmic capability (Kinsey et al., 1953; Masters and Johnson, 1966), and activity (Chilman, 1983). Adolescent females visually undress males and have many erotic thoughts and fantasies about them, just as males do females (Sugar, 1990), and they are sexually active (Hass, 1979; Zelnik and Kantner, 1980; Coles and Stokes, 1985; Wyatt, 1990). The unconscious wish for a baby needs emphasis as a determinant in the girl's affiliative and sexual endeavors with males beginning in early adolescence.

IN MALES

Males have sporadic sexual self-stimulation beginning between seven and ten months until the middle of the second year. Between 16 and 19 months, boys show direct repetitive manual or indirect self-stimulation with erotic arousal with or without erections. This behavior is followed by visual and tactile curiosity and exploration of their own and peers' sex differences. Then a mild preoedipal castration reaction occurs, and boys show denial of anatomical differences and avoid female genitals. They now become very interested in transportation toys and are increasingly active (Roiphe, 1979).

Masturbation, exhibitionism, and curiosity about genitals increase with the phallic-oedipal phase. Exploration of same- and opposite-sex differences is very much involved in play. With the oedipal phase, the intensely increased interest in mother is followed by castration anxiety, and the boys leave mother and turn to father. When early latency boys play "church on fire" or compete about length of urinary stream, they are expressing thinly disguised bisexual conflict and identification with males. With increasing testosterone levels in late latency, boys have erections and masturbate, although they do not ejaculate.

141

At puberty and early adolescence, castration anxiety, bisexual conflicts, and oedipal issues are prominent. Reflections of these issues are seen in boys' increased involvement with same-sex peers (comparing penis size, mutual masturbation, and homosexual experimentation), avoidance of females, and identification with males.

Masturbation in adolescence is phase specific (Blos, 1962) and the major sexual outlet, along with sexual fantasies, for males. The bisexual conflicts are commonly managed and resolved through a revision of the infantile ego ideal and emulation of new heroes. With ejaculation, there is a need to manage impulses and deal with sexual fantasies, thoughts, and functions. Then there is a surging of testosterone-driven sexual activity accompanied by a great need to demonstrate heterosexual performance ability to themselves and others.

For males there is thus a continuous line of sexual activity, curiosity, exploration, denial, and avoidance in an almost wavelike form, from no interest or activity to a surge, followed by a period of denial and avoidance of mother and genitals, and then a relatively quiescent period with avoidance of females. Following hormonal level increases and the resurgence of the oedipal issues in early adolescence, defenses and activity to defend against them are evident. Then there is another, higher amplitude wave with a surging of testosterone-driven sexual activity accompanied by a great need to demonstrate heterosexual performance ability to themselves and others.

Generative Aspects

Adrenarche, which occurs at age six to eight years in both sexes and reaches its peak in late adolescence, refers to the maturation of adrenal androgen secretion and involves the hypothalamic-pituitary-adrenal axis and normal pubertal development.

Gonadarche, which refers to activation of the hypothalamic-pituitary-gonadal axis and maturation of gonadal sex steroid secretion, occurs at ages nine to thirteen. These steroids are responsible for the development of secondary sex characteristics (with testosterone and dihydrotestosterone masculinizing boys and estradiol feminizing girls) and reach asymptote in midadolescence (Nottelman et al., 1990). Males' testosterone level is eight times more than females', and males have five times as much testosterone as weak adrenal androgens. Females have five to ten times more of the weak adrenal androgens than testosterone (Udry, Talbert, and Morris, 1986).

Although menarche and ejaculation are very significant as physical events and as major intrapsychic organizers, they do not herald puberty. Puberty begins with genital enlargement. This period varies greatly, and there are marked individual and gender differences.

In 1950, menarche in the United States was at 13.6 years for whites and 13.1 for blacks; and the age at first marriage was 21.4 years for whites and 21.9 years for blacks (Hofferth, 1990). The current average ages of menarche (12.7), ejaculation (13.9), and marriage (26.3 for men and 24.1 for women) (Mesce, 1992) immediately point to one of the problems facing adolescents today in contrast to 140 years ago—the time span between the onset of reproductive ability and the age of marriage. This span was about two years in 1850, when the average onset age of puberty was 16 or 17 and the average age of marriage was 18 or 19 (Money and Tucker, 1975). In 1950, this span was 7.8 years for white females and 8.8 years for black females. Currently the span is about 11 years for white and 14 years for black females (Hofferth, 1990).

FEMALE PUBERTAL CHANGES

For females, puberty begins with breast bud development, which occurs anywhere from age eight to thirteen. Then there is rounding of the hips and development of pubic hair, along with beginning of the growth spurt at about 9.5 years of age. Female pubertal events have about an eight-year range (Tanner, 1978). Menarche is a relatively late marker, with an age range of 10.5 to 15.5 and a current mean age of 12.8 years for white females and 12.5 years for black females (Dubas and Petersen, 1993). There is a period of anovulatory menses for perhaps a year or more, but this is not reliably evident or present in all. Females attain sexual maturity at age 13 to 18 years (Tanner, 1978).

MALE PUBERTAL CHANGES

Males may have a four-year span for pubertal changes, with an onset as early as age 9.5 years (range 9.5 to 13.5) with the beginning enlargement of the testes. The mean age for this enlargement is a bone age of 12 years (Kelch, Grumbach, and Kaplan, 1972). The more overt changes may begin as early as 10.5 years with a height spurt. Pubic hair may occur at about the same time, whereas axillary hair and deepening of the voice are relatively late developments (Tanner, 1978). The onset of ejaculation is at 13.9 years (mean) with a range of 11 to 15 years. The

143

first nocturnal emission occurs about one year after the first ejaculation (Kinsey et al., 1948). There are fewer total and viable sperm in early adolescence than in early adulthood, and consequently there may be a relatively sterile period for males. Sexual maturity for males is achieved at age 13.5 to 17 years (Tanner, 1978).

Cultural Aspects

There is a multiplicity of factors that enhance or delay the initiation of sexual relationships in adolescence among which a precondition is the youngster's cultural background. Hotvedt (1990) points out that "the emergence and expression of sexual behavior in each culture are shaped by that culture to multiple purposes" (p. 157). Premarital sex is expected and approved among adolescent females in 21% of the worldwide cultures she studied. In 75% of the cultures, it is not a serious matter for girls to engage in sexual activity, whereas 25% strongly disapprove. Female premarital sex was common in 49% of the cultures, but in 20% it occurred seldom or never.

Premarital sex for males was universal in 60% of the cultures, and in 12% it was considered uncommon or rare. In 35% of the cultures, premarital sex was male initiated, and in 18% it was female-initiated (Hotvedt, 1990). Trost (1990) points out that the cumulative teenage abortion and birth rates in the United States indicate that 17% of youngsters have had an abortion or a child before the age of 18 and that possibly, when a pregnancy is the result of intercourse to keep a boy friend, it is not specifically due to unprotected intercourse but to "existing received social norms within the social group of the adolescent" (p. 175). That contraceptive use depends on group norms holds true even in countries where contraceptives are easily available and free, such as the Netherlands or France, and unlike the United States.

The United States does not have one cultural ethos but a diversity, since there are many groups with varying cultural issues related to adolescent sexual functioning. These differences show up when Hispanic-Americans are compared with Anglo-Saxon Americans, African-Americans, or other adolescents. Scott et al. (1988) feel that there are marked cultural differences between African-Americans and Hispanic-Americans, and they describe concepts that are very important among Latin-American women. Among these are *marianismo*, which involves submission and chastity, and its opposite, *verguenza*, which refers to shame and the fact that good girls should not know about sexuality. In

144

their study, female Hispanic-American adolescents had the lowest scores of knowledge about body parts, their functions, and contraceptive methods.

Adolescents' behavior and sexuality are not isolated from the society in which the youngsters live but, as a part of its woof and warp, reflect that society. Consider that in the past three decades adults in this country have experienced a higher divorce rate, increased sexual permissiveness, later marriages, lower fecundity, and open cohabitation of unmarried adults. We can readily see that adolescents have simply followed suit and imitated their elders with earlier sexual activity, postponement of marriage, cohabitation for short periods, or serial monogamy, if they are not openly having many relationships.

This is similar to the sexually permissive climate of the "Roaring 20s" before the crash of 1929 and great depression of the 30s. Perhaps there is a jubilee cycle in which economics affects a culture and sexual license every 50 years.

Family Aspects

Furstenberg, Brooks-Gunn, and Morgan (1987), Inazu and Fox (1980), and Thornton and Camburn (1987) noted that where communication about sex increases between youth and parents, sexual activity decreases. Thornton and Camburn (1987) indicate that there is a positive correlation between the sexual behavior of mothers during their adolescent years and that of their daughters, which conclusion reinforces similar findings by Newcomer and Udry (1984) and O'Connell and Rogers (1984).

Children in stable families have lower levels of premarital sexual intercourse and an older age at first intercourse (Zelnik, Kantner, and Ford, 1981; Hogan and Kitagawa, 1985; Mott, cited in Thornton and Camburn, 1987). Moore, Peterson, and Furstenberg (cited in Thornton and Camburn, 1987) suggested that frequency of dating by a single mother is related to the sexual experience of her children and that teenage girls whose mothers cohabited without marriage are more likely to have early sexual intercourse.

The simultaneous increased premarital sexuality, divorce, and remarriage of the 60s and 70s may not have been independent of each other. More divorce and remarriage may be partly responsible for some of the increased premarital sexuality during the period. From their study of whites born in 1961 and interviewed at age 19 in 1980, Thornton and

Camburn (1987) concluded that parental and family attitudes influenced adolescents' attitudes more than they influenced adolescent behaviors, and that the age of the mother was positively and significantly related to the children's sexual attitudes and behavior, but not to the attitude of the mother. The percentage of adolescents who experienced coitarche was 60% (64% for males and 54% for females), which is similar to the figures of Zelnik and Kantner (1980).

Horowitz et al. (1991) found that among a group of black females who were followed from the late 60s as young mothers, the majority of the offspring had not become parents by age 19. The majority of those who became parents had mothers with lifetime depression and had moved out of their mother's home within 26 months of the child's birth. The authors felt that emotional deprivation at an early age predisposed these adolescents to seek emotional closeness through sexual activity and parenthood.

By contrast, Fingerman (1989) considered that sexually active adolescents seem to come from families with liberal sexual ideals and that the mother's profession influenced the sexual behavior and sex role attitudes of both sons and daughters. In Fingerman's study, the daughters of working mothers thought of the ideal woman in our present society as having potency, activity, and independence. Those girls whose mothers were in nontraditional professions were less traditionally sex typed. Fingerman felt that the mother's profession, not the mother's presence in the home, influenced the child's perception of women in society.

Yarber and Greer (1986) suggested that mothers with the most positive attitudes toward a sexual self had daughters who were "the most responsive relative to personal sexual expression, that is, greater frequency of masturbation and orgasmic experiences, but who were not any more involved heterosexually" (p. 71) in terms of the frequency of partners or of coitus. In contrast, fathers' sexual attitudes have little relationship to the sexual attitudes and behavior of the offspring. In addition, none of the male student sexual behaviors were related strongly to parents' sexual attitudes.

Banks and Wilson (1989) found that the extended family among blacks is viable as a family structure and that there are healthy family nurturing units made up of extended, instead of nuclear, family units in which single people are maintained. Twenty-six percent of the boys and 15% of the girls in their study were living with grandparents and other relatives before age 12, but after that age almost 20% of the boys and 11% of the girls resided with relatives other than their biological parents. In a nuclear family with two parents, or with one biological parent and a stepparent, there is probably more consistency and stability, compared with an extended family, with its multiple changes and substitute parents.

The education and socioeconomic status (SES) of families were associated with the age of first sexual experience for black and white females in Wyatt's (1990) cohorts. Daughters of professionals or semi-professional families had a later onset age of first sexual relationship, with a range of 18.3 to 18.8 years, while the daughters of the skilled or semiskilled had coitarche at 16.4 to 17.3 years of age. The number of parenting figures in the home before age 12 had no relation to coitarche.

The number of parenting figures after age 12 was significant for the onset of sexual activity. For females with biological or stepparents at age 13 to 17, sexual relations began at 17.2 years; for those with single or multiple parents, consisting of one biological and one other parenting figure present from age 13 to 17, coitarche was at age 16 (Wyatt, 1990).

Consistency in parenting prior to age 17, regardless of the number of parents, delayed first intercourse for black and white females. An inconsistency in parenting before age 16 had the opposite effect (Wyatt, 1990). This finding supports Banks and Wilson's (1989) data indicating that delay in coitarche depends in part on residence with parents until age 16. Minority-group members, however, attain less education than whites and have higher unemployment rates. It is well known that birth rates go up with unemployment (Sugar, 1991).

Sexual Desire

FEMALES

Smith, Udry, and Morris (1985) noted that the motivation for adolescent girls age 12 to 15 to initiate sex was primarily related to their friends' sexual behavior and social processes, although estrogen effects (i.e., hip and breast development) and androgen effects (i.e., pubic hair development) were also contributors to sexual motivation.

Udry (1990) found that there were many sources of social influence on white girls' initiation of coitus but none for black girls. DuRant and Jay (1989), however, found that the black girls' sexual behavior was influenced by their female friends just as it was with white girls.

According to Rosenblum (1990), the best indicator of sexual involvement for females was type of friends; there was some association between androgen levels and sexual interest; and social learning had an increasing influence on sexual development of females.

Harvey's (1987) investigation of women age 18 to 34 found that women experienced increased sexual arousal and sexual pleasure as they progressed from the menses to the premenstrum. The author concluded that human female sexual behavior may be influenced by hormonal fluctuations and cognitive factors accompanying the menstrual cycle. This study, however, relied on basal temperature and reports from the subjects without hormonal level assays.

MALES

Udry (1990; Udry, Talbert, and Morris, 1986) observed that sexual motivation and behavior (intercourse) are related to testosterone levels in male adolescents but that the influence of social processes for white boys was minimal. Their data for black boys were inadequate since most of the boys were sexually experienced at the time of the first interview between age 11 and 15. Udry (1990) felt that androgens were necessary for normal sexual desire in males. Rosenblum (1990) considered that the best predictor of sexuality in early adolescence for the male was the level of free circulating testosterone.

Early and midadolescents have many questions and concerns about many subjects—especially sex. In a survey over a number of years, 59% of early adolescents had questions about sexual matters (with a large focus on anatomy and physiology); 55% of midadolescents' questions were about sex (mostly about contraception, pregnancy, sexually transmitted disease [STD] and abortion [Sugar, 1990]). Fears of fusion with the same-sex parent and of closeness with the opposite-sex parent lead the early adolescent to increased closeness with same-sex peers as an anxiety-reducing device.

The anthropological literature suggests that only rarely do parents provide sex education. Hotvedt (1990) writes: "It is as if a taboo exists against parental involvement, and other members of society are considered as more appropriate providers of post-pubescent training" (p. 168). She points to the frequent initiation of younger adolescents into sexuality by older peers, who set the rules and pace of sexual initiation. The literature repeatedly cites peers as the prime source for teenagers' knowledge about sexuality, more so than parents, siblings, or sex-education classes.

Precoital Behavior

Smith and Udry (1985) noted that whites are more likely than blacks to engage in a series of noncoital, predictable behaviors that continue for a period of time before first intercourse. In contrast, the precoital experiences of black teens were less predictable and often involved only necking.

Among white adolescents, intercourse was the least frequent sexual behavior of males and females, while necking was the most frequent, followed by feeling breasts clothed, then feeling breasts directly, and so on. Smith and Udry felt that the sequence of noncoital behavior by whites extended over a period of time and may serve as an adjustment period for the girl and boy to come to recognize the increased likelihood of intercourse.

The order of behaviors for the black females was the same as that for black males. The highest to lowest percentages of most frequent sexual behavior were as follows: necking for both males and females; then feeling breasts clothed; and then intercourse. This pattern applied to 75% of the males and 40% of the females. These figures constitute almost more than twice the rate for white males and four times the rate for white females (Smith and Udry, 1985).

In Wyatt's (1990) research, there was no difference between blacks and whites in the sequence of noncoital sexual behaviors and the onset of sexual intercourse. Where there was necking before or at age 13, coitarche was at 16.5 years (mean); but if it was at 14 or 15, intercourse was delayed until 16.7 years. If necking did not begin until age 16, coitus did not begin until age 18.2 years. If petting onset was at or before age 15, coitus occurred at 16.4 years; while, if petting onset was at 16 or later, coitus began at 17.8 years. Thus, again, SES enters into the sexual behavior pattern.

Coitarche and Ethnicity

Kinsey et al. (1953) noted that 50% of white middle-class females had intercourse before age 20. Gebhard et al. (1958) found that black females initiated intercourse before white females did, and 82% of black females were sexually experienced at or before age 20. Here also SES was a contributing factor.

From the data of Wyatt (1990) and Zelnik and Shah (1983), 50% of females and 70% of males, age 15 to 19 and 17 to 21, respectively, had

had sexual intercourse if they were living in a metropolitan area. The average age at their first sexual experience was 16.2 for the young women and 15.7 for the young men. Blacks generally had coitarche at a younger age than whites did, and twice as many black males and females had intercourse before age 15 compared with whites.

Over half the young females said that they were going steady with their partners at the time, while a quarter said they were dating. The remainder claimed engagement, or being with friends, or only recently having met the person. Black females were more likely than whites to say they were dating. Among the males there were less frequent statements about being engaged or going steady and more that they were just friends, thus supporting to some extent the inference of Whatley et al. (1989) that adolescent males regard their sexual partners as mostly casual. The older the female at the time of first intercourse, the more likely she was to be engaged; whereas the younger she was, the more likely it was that her partner was someone she had just met. This finding applied to both blacks and whites (Wyatt, 1990).

Zabin et al. (1986) indicate that among inner city black teens, 61% of males claimed that intercourse preceded their first wet dream; the authors concluded that 41% of the young men had their first hetero-sexual relation in prepuberty. The mean age of first intercourse for males was 12.0. First ejaculation and coitarche were at the same time (mean, 13.5 years). In their female cohort, 13% had had coitarche preceding menarche. Over 75% of the females had initiated intercourse at 14.4 years, approximately two years after their menarche. Finkel and Finkel (1983) observed that coitarche had occurred at age 11.6, 13.0, and 14.5 among black, Hispanic, and white adolescents, respectively.

Rickert et al. (1989) observed that in their survey of females age 14 to 16 (of whom 50% were white and 50% were black; 84% in school), the median onset age for sexual intercourse was 13, and 85% of respondents reported sexual activity.

Getts (1988) recorded that dating among military dependents began for 50% of males and 40% of females at 13 to 14; 90% and 80%, respectively, at ages 15 and 16; and 95% and 96%, respectively, at 17 and 18. Fifty percent of females and males were sexually active at age 16 to 17. By age 19 to 20, 91% of the females and 71% of the males were sexually active.

Among students age 14 through 19, in three different high schools in a rural area, 40% were virgins. The others had intercourse sporadically with an average of twice a month. Very religious students were not any more likely to abstain from sexual intercourse than were the less religious students (McCormick, Izzo, and Folcik, 1985), which is counter to the findings by DeLamater and MacCorquodale (1979).

From a number of sources (Forrest and Singh, 1990; Sonnenstein, Pleck, and Kuo, 1991), it appears that females age 15 to 19 have had increasing rates of coitarche (from 47% in 1982 to 53% in 1988), as have males age 17 to 19, for whom the percentage increased from 66% in 1979 to 76% in 1988.

In self-reported data of 1990 among high school students across the country in grades nine to twelve, 54% reported sexual experience and 40% reported sexual intercourse in the three months before the survey. More males had sexual experience than did females (61% to 48%), and black students were more likely than whites or Hispanics to be sexually experienced, with percentages of 72, 52, and 53, respectively. The percentages of youth having coitarche increased by grade from ninth to twelfth (Center for Disease Control, 1992).

Among college women (79% white and 21% black, mean age 21.4 years), of whom 80% were undergraduates, 87% were sexually experienced and 81% had had one or two sexual partners in the previous year (DeBuono et al., 1990).

In her retrospective study of 18- to 26-year-old females, Wyatt (1990) found that coitarche was at 16.7 among black females and 17.2 years among whites; the overall mean was 16.9, but there was no significant ethnic difference. The range for coitarche was age 10 to 27, with 13% reporting it as at or before age 14. Black females who were initiated at or before age 15 constituted 31%, compared with 23% among whites. At age 16, 48% of black females had been initiated, compared with 39% of whites. By age 17, 67% of black females were sexually experienced, compared with 52% of whites; at age 18, 80% of both groups were initiated; by age 19, the numbers were the same for both groups (91%). The data from Zelnik and Kantner (1980) that the recent increase in premarital adolescent coitarche is derived from the activities of white youths is supported by Wyatt's (1990) statement that ethnic differences are disappearing and the earlier onset of sexual intercourse continues among black and white females.

Socioeconomic Status and Onset of Sexual Intercourse

It has long been observed that lower SES youth are out of school and have had coitarche much earlier than the higher SES youth, especially if the latter go on to college.

Orr et al. (1989) observed that in a blue-collar junior high school population, virginal males were in the minority by age 13, and sexually inexperienced females were in a minority by age 15. The school population consisted of 77% whites and 19% blacks with a mean age of 13.6, among whom 70% of males and 41% of the females were sexually experienced. The figures for the sexually experienced increased from age 12 in a cohort of 37% of nonvirginal males and 24% of nonvirginal females to age 16, when 70% of the males and 41% of the females were sexually experienced. Of the black males, 80% were sexually experienced, compared with 63% of the white males. In a higher socioeconomic group of college youth, Darling, Davidson, and Passarello (1992) found that the mean age of first intercourse was 17.7 for females (60%) and 17.8 years for males (84%).

Most studies are of low SES groups but the contributions of SES, race, and ethnicity need clarification and separation. Wyatt's (1990) findings show a difference for different SES groups for coitarche. The findings by Zelnik and Kantner (1980) were for a low SES group, as were those by Zabin et al. (1986).

Without specifying SES it is inaccurate to say that blacks have earlier coitarche than whites do. Similarly, to say that among blacks there is generally less concern about adolescent pregnancy does not coincide with clinical experience. Black and white parents are equally disappointed when a single daughter is pregnant. The family has various options available then, depending on religious beliefs, SES, values, and the like. Regardless of SES, white families have one more option than black ones do: if a white girl chooses to deliver and give up the child for adoption, there is an eager reception awaiting the white child. This is not necessarily the case for a black child. Therefore, it seems to me that in the United States, in the face of the realities, low SES black families are resigned and disappointed.

Adolescent Coital Frequency

FEMALES

Hofferth (1990) observed that among all teenage females age 15 to 19 in metropolitan areas the percentage of sexually experienced changed from 27.6 in 1971 to 39.2 in 1976, to 46 in 1979, and to 42.2 in 1982. Her most recent figures showed a percentage change among experienced whites from 42.3 in 1979 to 40.3 in 1982, and an even larger shift among blacks from 64.8% in 1979 to 52.9% in 1982. In 1982, 18% of the youngsters had had no sex in the past three months, 16% had it once a month, 25% had it three times a month, 21% experienced it weekly, 16% more than twice a week, and 3% had sex daily.

In the cohort studied by Rickert et al. (1989), 62% of equal numbers of white and black females age 14 to 16 had relations two to three times per month.

MALES

Sonnenstein et al. (1991) found that, on average, the sexually experienced youth had spent six of the past twelve months without a sexual partner and that only 21% of sexually active males had had more than one partner in any one month of the preceding year. Although proportionately more adolescents were now sexually experienced compared with 1979, fewer white males had had coitarche before their 15th birthday. The number of partners since first intercourse and in the past four weeks appears to have decreased, as had the frequency of intercourse in the last four weeks. From their data, Sonnenstein et al. concluded that "young men have surprisingly conservative sexual behaviors and have relatively few periods of multiple partners" (p. 166).

Strunin (1991) reported that adolescent blacks have less intercourse per month than whites and less in the previous month than whites; blacks have intercourse six times less per month than whites; and blacks have fewer sexual partners than whites. These data support the findings by Zelnik and Kantner (1980) that the overwhelming number of teenagers are not promiscuous.

Risk-Taking Behavior

Risk-taking behavior is part and parcel of adolescence, and sexuality is just one of the areas in which risk taking may occur. Part of the risk taking is based on ignorance, denial, grandiosity, and a lack of information (Sugar, 1991). Sarrel and Sarrel (1990) and Valois and Waring (1990) found that college youngsters have much uncertainty, ignorance, and anxiety about sexual functioning. These factors lead to sexual difficulties with partners or unintended pregnancy as a result of denial or omnipotence.

Females still do not attend to the risk of STD including AIDS, even after exposure to HIV infection (Grace, Emans, and Woods, 1989). For youngsters with STDs there is increased risk to their fertility as well as increased morbidity. There is also a higher risk of somatic illness and for suicide attempts by youngsters who are unintentionally pregnant. Adolescents usually avoid health professionals and do not depend much on them for information about sexuality or about ordinary care for their bodies. Part of this aversion may be due to their avoidance of authorities as representative of parents, their concerns involving oedipal issues, and their need to distance themselves from their infantile objects (Sugar, 1990). Many college students have little sexual knowledge and do not appreciate it for a change in behavior (Roberts, 1992). College athletes appear to be at high risk for some maladaptive lifestyle behaviors such as having sex with many more sexual partners, STDs, and riding with an intoxicated driver (Nattiv and Puffer, 1991).

Sexuality and Social Values

In a blue-collar sample, there was no difference in self-esteem among virginal and nonvirginal adolescent males. Males had more self-esteem in general than females did. The nonvirginal female in the same cohort had less self-esteem than did the virginal females in a statistically significant number. Virginal males equaled virginal females in self-esteem (Orr et al., 1989).

College females experienced feelings of guilt more often than males did, but for females there was less guilt surrounding continuing or current intercourse (Darling et al., 1992). Juhasz and Sonnenshein-Schneider (1987) found significant gender differences in decision making reflected in the male–female double standard in sexual behavior. Males were high on self-enhancement through sexual intercourse and hence were more oriented toward sexual-impulse gratification. For females, intimacy considerations regarding sexual intercourse were more important, with emphasis on the relationship aspect of sexual behavior.

Spanish-speaking adolescents were mostly influenced by others—parents, peers, and religious authorities; blacks were the least influenced by others. Spanish-speaking males and black females tended to show most concern over pregnancy. The Spanish-speaking adolescents, especially the males, displayed a need for intimacy as a precursor to sexual intercourse. They also showed the least sexual liberality and autonomy, whereas black adolescents displayed the most. The authors comment: "Traditionally, for the female, being a good girl sexually has had high value, which may account for the gender variation" (Juhasz and Sonnenshein-Schneider, 1987, p. 385).

Robinson, Ziss, and Ganza (1991) observed that over the past 25 years there has been an increase in the number of young men and women who feel that premarital sex is immoral. In 1985, 17% of women and 16% of men agreed that premarital sex is immoral. Those confirming that a promiscuous man is immoral decreased from 57% in 1965 to 30% in 1975, but rose to 52% in 1985. The percentage in accord with this about women fell from 91% in 1965 to 41% in 1975, but increased to 64% in 1985. For male respondents, a promiscuous man was thought to be immoral by 35% in 1965, 19% in 1975, but 32% in 1985. The percentage who felt a promiscuous woman is immoral fell from 42% in 1965 to 29% in 1975, but went up to 51% in 1985. These findings seem to indicate that there was higher disapproval of promiscuity in the 1980s than in the 1960s and the 1970s (Robinson et al., 1991). These changes seem to parallel the findings by Hofferth (1990), Strunin (1991), and Sonnenstein et al. (1991) about the recent decrease in sexual initiation and activity.

Inasmuch as these changes preceded the AIDS epidemic and awareness, the stimulus for them needs to be sought elsewhere. Perhaps this is part of the jubilee cycle similar to the conservative social-sexual attitudes of the 30s and 40s after the very permissive "Roaring 20s."

Conclusions

Sexuality in adolescence is built on the preceding phases and follows a rather regular development with increases in hormones, body changes, and attendant anxieties. Input from society and effects of psychosocial development allow or inhibit the expression of sexuality in an appropriate fashion. Society reaps the kind of adolescents that it sows. Although adolescents are not promiscuous, even in the current atmosphere of sexual permissiveness, society has viewed them as such, although adults have been licentious in the last several decades.

The family has a strong effect on postponing or advancing coitarche. Social values about sexual activity are a product of the culture and family, which also undergo change in different eras. Without specifying SES, it is inaccurate to compare the sexual activity of different groups.

Some suggestions are offered to distinguish female from male sexuality on a biological and emotional developmental line. The catalyst for, and basis of, adolescent male heterosexual behavior is the level of testosterone; the relationship aspect is the source of females' motivation for sexual behavior. Although the onset age of sexual relations is earlier now for males and females, and a larger number are sexually experienced compared with several decades ago, females and even adolescent males are largely conservative sexually. Sexual initiation and activity are dependent on such factors as culture, family, education, socioeconomic status, and ethnicity, as well as psychosexual development.

REFERENCES

Almond, B. (1990), The secret garden. *The Psychoanalytic Study of the Child*, 45:477–494. New Haven, CT: Yale University Press.

Banks, I. W. & Wilson, P. I. (1989), Appropriate sex education for black teens. *Adoles.*, 24:233–246.

Blos, P. (1962), *On Adolescence*. Glencoe, IL: Free Press.

Center for Disease Control (1992), *Morbidity and Mortality Weekly Report*, 40:885–888. Atlanta, GA.

Chilman, C. S. (1983), *Adolescent Sexuality in a Changing American Society*. New York: Wiley.

Coles, R. & Stokes, G. (1985), *Sex and the American Teenager*. New York: Harper & Row.

Darling, C. A., Davidson, J. K. & Passarello, L. C. (1992), Mystique of first intercourse among college youth: The role of partners, contraceptive practices, and psychological reactions. *J. Youth Adoles.*, 21:97–117.

DeBuono, B. A., Zinner, S. H., Daamen, M. & McCormack, W. H. (1990), Sexual behavior of college women in 1975, 1988, and 1989. *New Eng. J. Med..*, 322:821–825.

DeLamater, J. & MacCorquodale, P. (1979), *Premarital Sexuality*. Madison: University of Wisconsin Press.

Dubas, J. S. & Petersen, A. C. (1993), Female pubertal development. In: *Female Adolescent Development* (2nd ed.), ed. M. Sugar. New York: Brunner/Mazel, pp. 27–42.

DuRant, R. H. & Jay, S. (1989), The adolescent heterosexual relationship and its association with the sexual and contraceptive behavior of black females. *Amer. J. Dis. Child*, 143:1467–1472.

Fingerman, K. L. (1989), Sex and the working mother: Adolescent sexuality, sex role typing and family background. *Adoles.*, 93:1–18.

Finkel, M. L. & Finkel, E. J. (1983), Male adolescent sexual behavior, the forgotten partner: A review. *J. School Health*, 53:544–547.

Forrest, J. & Singh, S. (1990), The sexual reproductive behavior of the American woman, 1982–1988. *Family Planning Perspect.*, 22:206–214.

Furstenberg, F. F., Brooks-Gunn, J. & Morgan, S. P. (1987), *Adolescent Mothers in Later Life*. New York: Cambridge.

Galenson, E. (1979), Development from one to two years: Object relations and psychosexual development. In: *Basic Handbook of Child Psychiatry*, Vol. I, ed. J. D. Noshspitz. New York: Basic Books, pp. 144–156.

_____ & Roiphe, H. (1976), Some suggested revisions concerning early female development. *J. Amer. Psychoanal. Assn.*, 24(5):29–57.

Gebhard, P., Pomeroy, W., Martin, C. & Christensen, C. (1958), *Pregnancy, Birth and Abortion*. New York: Harper.

Getts, A. G. (1988), Dating and sexual behaviors in military dependent adolescents. *Military Med.*, 153:614–617.

Gilligan, C. (1982), *In a Different Voice*. New York: Harper & Row.

Grace, E., Emans, S. J. & Woods, E. R. (1989), The impact of AIDS awareness on the adolescent female. *Adoles. Pediat. Gynecol.*, 2:40–42.

Harley, M. (1971), Some reflections on identity problems in prepuberty. In: *Separation-Individuation*, ed. J. B. McDevitt & C. Settlage. New York: International Universities Press, pp. 385–403.

Harvey, S. M. (1987), Female sexual behavior: Fluctuations during the menstrual cycle. *J. Psychosom. Res.*, 31:101–110.

Hass, A. (1979), *Teenage Sexuality*. New York: Macmillan.

Hofferth, S. L. (1990), Trends in adolescent sexual activity, contraception, and pregnancy in the United States. In: *Adolescence and Puberty*, ed. J. Bancroft & J. M. Reinisch. New York: Oxford University Press, pp. 217–253.

Hogan, D. P. & Kitagawa, E. M. (1985), The impact of social status, family structure, and neighborhood on the fertility of black adolescents. *Amer. J. Soc.*, 90:825–855.

Horowitz, S. M., Klerman, L. V., Kuo, H. S. & Jekel, J. F. (1991), Intergenerational transmission of school-age parenthood. *Fam. Plan. Perspect.*, 23:168–172.

Hotvedt, M. E. (1990), Emerging and submerging adolescent sexuality: Culture and sexual orientation. In: *Adolescence and Puberty,* ed. J. Bancroft & J. M. Reinisch. New York: Oxford University Press, pp. 157–172.

Inazu, J. K. & Fox, G. L. (1980), Maternal influences on the sexual behavior of teenage daughters. *J. Fam. Issues*, 1:81–102.

Juhasz, A. M. & Sonnenshein-Schneider, M. (1987), Adolescent sexuality, values, morality, and decision-making. *Adoles.*, 22:579–590.

Kelch, R. P., Grumbach, M. M. & Kaplan, S. L. (1972), Studies on the mechanism of puberty in man. In: *Gonadotropins,* ed. B. B. Saxena, C. G. Belling, & H. M. Gandy. New York: Wiley, pp. 524–534.

Kinsey, A., Pomeroy, W. & Martin, C. (1948), *Sexual Behavior of the Human Male*. Philadelphia: Saunders.

_____ _____ _____ & Gebhard, P. H. (1953), *Sexual Behavior in the Human Female*. Philadelphia: Saunders.

Masters, W. & Johnson, V. (1966), *Human Sexual Response*. Boston: Little, Brown.

_____ _____ & Kolodny, R.C. (1986), *Masters and Johnson on Sex and Human Loving*. Boston: Little, Brown.

Mesce, D. (1992), 90s families to be stable but different. *New Orleans [LA] Times-Picayune*, p. A-3.

McCormick, D. O., Izzo, A. & Folcik, J. (1985), Adolescents' values, sexuality, and contraception in a rural New York county. *Adoles.*, 20:385–395.

Money, J. & Tucker, P. (1975), *Sexual Signatures: On Being a Man or Woman*. Boston: Little, Brown.

Nattiv, A. & Puffer, J. C. (1991), Lifestyles and health risks of collegiate athletes. *J. Fam. Pract.*, 33:585–590.

Newcomer, S. F. & Udry, J. R. (1984), Mothers' influence on the sexual behavior of their teenage children. *J. Marriage Fam.*, 46:477–485.

Nottelman, E. D., Inoff-Germain, G., Sussman, E. J., & Chrousos, G. P. (1990), Hormones and behavior at puberty. In: *Adolescence and Puberty,* ed. J. Bancroft & J. M. Reinisch. New York: Oxford University Press, pp. 188–123.

O'Connell, M. O. & Rogers, C. C. (1984), Out-of-wedlock births, premarital pregnancies and their effect on family formation and dissolution. *Fam. Plan. Perspect.*, 16:157–162.

Orr, D. P., Willowbrandt, M. L., Brack, C. J., Rauch, S. P. & Ingersoll, G. M. (1989), Reported sexual behaviors and self-esteem among young adolescents. *Amer. J. Dis. Child.*, 143:86–90.

Parens, H. (1990), On the girl's psychosexual development: Reconsideration suggested from direct observations. *J. Amer. Psychoanal. Assn.*, 38:743–773.

Rickert, V. I., Jay, M. S., Gottlieb, A. & Bridges, C. (1989), Adolescents and AIDS: Females' attitudes and behaviors toward condom purchase and use. *J. Adoles. Health Care*, 10:313–316.

Roberts, L. W. (1992), America responds to AIDS: But did college students? *AIDS Educ. Preven.*, 1:18–28.

Robinson, I., Ziss, K. & Ganza, B. (1991), Twenty years of the sexual revolution, 1965–1985: An update. *J. Marriage Fam.*, 53:216–220.

Roiphe, H. (1968), On an early genital phase: with an addendum on genesis. *The Psychoanalytic Study of the Child*, 23:348–365. New Haven, CT: Yale University Press.

_____ (1979), A theoretical overview of preoedipal development in the first four years of life. In: *Basic Handbook of Child Psychiatry*, Vol. I., ed. J. D. Noshspitz. New York: Basic Books, pp. 118–127.

Rosenblum, L. A. (1990), A comparative primate perspective on Adoles.. In: *Adolescence and Puberty,* ed. J. B. Bancroft & J. M. Reinisch. New York: Oxford University Press, pp. 63–69.

Sarrel, L. J. & Sarrel, P. M. (1990), Sexual unfolding in adolescents. In: *Atypical Adolescence and Sexuality*, ed. M. Sugar. New York: Norton, pp. 18–43.

Scott, C. S., Shifman, L., Orr, L., Owen, R. G. & Fawcett, N. (1988), Hispanic and black American adolescents' beliefs relating to sexuality and contraception. *Adoles.*, 91:677–688.

Shopper, M. (1979), The rediscovery of the vagina and the importance of the menstrual tampon. In: *Female Adolescent Development*, ed. M. Sugar. New York: Brunner/Mazel, pp. 214–233.

Smith, E. A. & Udry, J. R. (1985), Coital and noncoital sexual behaviors of white and black adolescents. *Amer. J. Public Health*, 75:1200–1203.

_____ _____ & Morris, N. M. (1985), Pubertal development and friends: A biosocial explanation of adolescent sexual behavior. *J. Health Soc. Behav.*, 26:183–192.

Sonnenstein, F. L., Pleck, J. H., & Kuo, L. C. (1991), Levels of sexual activity among adolescent males in the United States. *Fam. Plan. Perspect.*, 23:162–167.

Strunin, L. (1991), Adolescents' perception for risk for HIV infection: Implications for future research. *Soc. Sc. Med.*, 32:221–228.

Sugar, M. (1990), Developmental anxieties in adolescence. *Adolescent Psychiatry*, 17:385–403. Chicago: University of Chicago Press.

_____ (1991), Adolescent pregnancy in the U.S.A.: Problems and prospects. *Adoles. Pediat. Gynecol.*, 4:171–185.

_____ (1992), Late adolescent development and treatment. *Adolescent Psychiatry*, 18:131–155. Chicago: University of Chicago Press.

Tanner, J. M. (1978), *Foetus into Man*. Cambridge, MA: Harvard University Press.

Thornton, A. & Camburn, D. (1987), The significance of the family on premarital sexual attitudes and behavior. *Demog.*, 24:323–340.

Trost, J. E. (1990), Social support and pressure and their impact on adolescent sexual behavior. In: *Adolescence and Puberty*, ed. J. Bancroft & J. M. Reinisch. New York: Oxford University Press, pp. 173–181.

Tyson, P. (1982), A developmental line of gender identity, gender role and choice of love object. *J. Amer. Psychoanal. Assn.*, 30:61–86.

Udry, J. R. (1990), Hormonal and social determinants of adolescent sexual behavior. In: *Adolescence and Puberty*, ed. J. B. Bancroft & J. M. Reinisch. New York: Oxford University Press, pp. 70–87.

_____ Talbert, L. M. & Morris, N. M. (1986), Biosocial foundations for adolescent female sexuality. *Demog.*, 23:217–230.

Valois, R. F. & Waring, K. A. (1990), An analysis of college students' anonymous questions about human sexuality. *J. Amer. College Health*, 39:263–268.

Whatley, J., Thin, N., Reynolds, B. & Blackwell, A. (1989), Problems of adolescents' sexuality. *J. Royal Soc. Med.*, 82:732–734.

Whisnant, L., Brett, E. & Zegans, L. (1979), Adolescent girls and menstruation. *Adolescent Psychiatry*, 7:157–171. Chicago: University of Chicago Press.

Wyatt, G. E. (1990), Changing influences on adolescent sexuality over the past forty years. In: *Adolescence and Puberty,* ed. J. B. Bancroft & J. M. Reinisch. New York: Oxford University Press, pp. 182–206.

Yarber, W. L. & Greer, J. M. (1986), The relationship between the sexual attitudes of parents and their college daughters' or sons' sexual attitudes and sexual behavior. *J. School Health*, 56:68–72.

Zabin, L. S., Smith, E. A., Hirsch, N. B. & Hardy, J. B. (1986), Ages of physical maturation and first intercourse in black teenage males and females. *Demogr.*, 23:595–605.

Zelnik, M. & Kantner, J. F. (1980), Sexual activity, contraceptive use and pregnancy among metropolitan area teenagers 1971–1979. *Fam. Plan. Perspect.*, 12:230–237.

_____ _____ & Ford, K. (1981), *Sex and Pregnancy in Adolescence*. Beverly Hills, CA: Sage.

_____ & Shah, F. K. (1983), First intercourse among young Americans. *Fam. Plan. Perspect.*, 15:64–70.

Zilbach, J. J. (1993), Female adolescence: toward a separate line of female development. In: *Female Adolescent Development* (2nd ed.), ed. M. Sugar. New York: Brunner/Mazel, pp. 45–61.

PART IV

SPECIFIC
SYNDROMES

This section considers a variety of pathological conditions adolescent psychiatrists encounter. The late Paul Trad's paper on the vicissitudes of adolescent motherhood presents a significant way of reconceptualizing the treatment process. Only recently, the incidence of dissociative disorders in the adolescent population has begun to be recognized; William Fleisher and Geri Anderson discuss the prevalence and implications of this disorder for practitioners.

Benjamin Garber has long worked with casualties of parent loss and takes an informative look at the literature written for children and adolescents to deal with the death of a parent. Derek Miller reconsiders the nature of the borderline syndrome and its relevance to the adolescent period. There follows a paper by a definer of the borderline syndrome in adolescence, James Masterson, who considers not only the bulimia syndrome but also illusory narcissistic psychopathology; while the problem of eating disorders in adolescents is considered in considerable scope by Lynn Ponton.

12 SEEKING HELP FROM INFORMAL AND FORMAL RESOURCES DURING ADOLESCENCE: SOCIODEMOGRAPHIC AND PSYCHOLOGICAL CORRELATES

KIMBERLY A. SCHONERT-REICHL, DANIEL OFFER,
AND KENNETH I. HOWARD

Research on the emotional problems of adolescents is emerging as a compelling area of investigation. It is only recently, however, that researchers have begun to examine the coping behaviors that adolescents employ in dealing with these emotional problems as well as the individual variation that exists with regard to their specific coping behaviors (e.g., Compas, 1987; Compas and Phares, 1991; Frydenberg and Lewis, 1993; Ebata and Moos, 1994). Clearly, at some point in time, all adolescents are confronted with situations and problems that cause them to experience emotional pain. While some adolescents may prefer to try to handle these problems by themselves, others may attempt to alleviate their distress by approaching some type of helping agent, informal (family, friends) or formal (school counselors, mental health professionals). These attempts to cope with emotional problems by approaching a helping resource are labeled as "help-seeking."

In recent years, a growing body of empirical literature on help-seeking has addressed the question of how people utilize different service agencies and social support in their efforts to cope with emotional problems (DePaulo, Nadler, and Fisher, 1983). Although this research has yielded some important insights with regard to help-seeking behaviors, little of this work has examined the help-seeking behaviors of adolescents and instead has focused on those of adults (see Brown, 1978). Moreover, researchers interested in examining the help-seeking behaviors of adolescents have conducted needs assessment surveys in order to uncover the health and illness concerns of adolescents and have not

165

examined the association between help-seeking and important individual and personal characteristics, such as race, gender, and self-image, as well as indices of unhealthy functioning, such as symptomatology, and delinquency (e.g., Sternlieb and Munan, 1972; Radius et al., 1980; Riggs and Cheng, 1988). In addition, the majority of researchers examining adolescent help-seeking have investigated adolescents' *perceptions* of the helping agents that they would use if they were experiencing problems rather than adolescents' *actual* help-seeking behaviors (Marks et al., 1983; Feldman et al., 1986; Riggs and Cheng, 1988; Seiffge-Krenke, 1989; Dubow, Lovko, and Kausch, 1990; Whitaker et al., 1990; Windle et al., 1991). Finally, few attempts have been made to differentiate those adolescents who seek help from informal helping sources from those who seek help from *both* informal and formal helping sources.

Adolescence appears to be a crucial time for mental health intervention because of the several behavioral and emotional difficulties that increase from childhood to adolescence (e.g., suicide, delinquency, drug and alcohol abuse) and because some adult disturbances, such as schizophrenia, are first seen during adolescence (Seiffge-Krenke, 1989). Further understanding of the help-seeking behaviors of adolescents may greatly enhance our ability to reach adolescents in order to intervene and prevent problems that would lead to poor adult adjustment (Kohlberg, Ricks, and Snarey, 1984; Offer and Spiro, 1987).

The focus of the present investigation, therefore, was to identify those variables that are associated with adolescents' seeking help from formal and informal helping agents so as to provide much needed information to those concerned with helping adolescents cope adequately.

Specifically, the questions this research addressed are:

1. At what rates do adolescents seek help from each type of helping resource (i.e., friends, family, mental health professionals, school counselors)?

2. What are the relationships between sociodemographic characteristics, self-image, symptomatology, and delinquency and help-seeking from formal and informal helping agents?

3. What are the differences in demographic and background characteristics between those adolescents who seek help from only informal sources and those who seek help from *both* informal and formal sources?

4. What are the differences between those adolescents who seek help from only informal sources and those who seek help from *both* informal

and formal sources with regard to self-image, symptomatology, and delinquency?

Method

SAMPLE

Three high schools in a large metropolitan area in the Midwest were identified. The high schools were chosen to reflect contrasting demographic statuses; two were located in the suburbs and one within the city. The students from one suburban school were predominantly white and from upper middle-class homes, and the students from the other suburban school were also mostly white and were from middle-class homes. The students from the urban school were mostly black and from lower- and working-class homes. From each school a complete list of juniors and seniors was obtained, and random samples were drawn.

Altogether 497 adolescents participated in the present investigation. The students tested represented 83% of the students initially contacted for the study. The sample obtained included 249 males and 248 females. There were 261 whites, 213 black and 23 adolescents from other racial backgrounds (i.e., Asian, Hispanic). Fifty-nine percent of the adolescents were from intact (i.e., both biological parents) families, and the remainder were living in either reconstituted (i.e., one biological parent and one stepparent) or single-parent families. Approximately 7% of the fathers had not graduated from high school; 17% of the fathers had a high school education only; and 76% of the fathers had some college. The mean age of the sample was 17.40 years (SD = .59), with a range of 15.70 to 19.75 years.

MEASURES

Demographic Variables. The demographic questionnaire consisted of 39 items designed to elicit information regarding the adolescent's sex, age, racial background, academic achievement, family structure (i.e., intact versus reconstituted or single-parent), and parental educational level. Father's educational level was used as an index of socioeconomic status rather than reported familial income because other researchers have found that students are most knowledgeable about their father's education (Dubow et al., 1990). We grouped father's educational level into three categories as follows: (1) less than high school graduate, (2) high school only, and (3) some college. Reported high school grades served as an index of academic achievement, ranging from mostly A's (10) to mostly D's (1). Race was grouped into two categories: (1) whites, and (2) blacks, Asians, and Hispanics. Finally, the adolescents provided information on their current family structure, which was then used to group them into two categories: intact (living with both biological parents) and reconstituted or single-parent families.

Utilization of Formal and Informal Helping Agents. A modified version of the Mental Health Utilization Questionnaire (MHUQ; Veroff, Douvan, and Kulka, 1981) was employed to assess adolescents' utilization of formal and informal helping-agents. The MHUQ is based on a survey developed by the Institute for Social Research. This questionnaire comprises 53 items exploring the extent to which the adolescent has felt the need to use various kinds of treatment programs. Specifically, adolescents were asked questions regarding their use of formal (i.e., alcohol/drug abuse centers, teenage drop-in centers, mental health professionals, school counselors, clergy, crisis hotlines) and informal (i.e., teachers, coaches, parents, friends, siblings) helping agents. For the purposes of the present study, only mental health professionals (i.e., psychiatrist, psychologist, social worker), school counselors, parents, and friends are discussed because these groups had sufficient numbers for statistical analyses. Determination of help-seeking from mental health professionals and school counselors was elicited by the following probe: "Have you used _____ for help with an emotional problem during the last year?" Response options included the following: (a) no, (b) yes, one time, (c) yes, two times, (d) yes, three times, (e) yes, more than 3 times. These response options were then dichotomized to reflect two contrasting groupings, with no as one category and all of the yes responses as another. With regard to seeking help from parents and friends, subjects were asked, "Do you discuss emotional problems with your parents?" and "Do you discuss emotional problems with your friends?" Response options for both of the parents and friends helping categories were (a) no, (b) yes, a little of the time, (c) yes, some of the time, (d) yes, a lot of the time, and (e) yes, most of the time. As with the formal helping agent categories, these response options were also dichotomized to reflect two contrasting groupings: those who had not sought help from friends and parents and those who had sought help from friends and parents.

Self-Image. The Offer Self-Image Questionnaire (OSIQ; Offer, Ostrov, and Howard, 1981) is a self-report questionnaire that measures adjustment in areas relevant to an adolescent's life. It inquires about such areas of functioning as relationships with parents, the adolescent's body, and how he or she copes with the internal and external world. The OSIQ's reliability and validity has been repeatedly demonstrated. For the purposes of the present study, all scale scores were added together to yield a total score with a higher score representing healthier functioning.

Symptomatology. The Symptom Checklist (SCL) used here is a modified version of the SCL-90 (Derogaitis, 1977). This SCL version consists of 46 items presented with response alternatives ranging from 1 = "not at all" to 3 = "a lot" and covers a wide range of symptomatology and psychopathology (e.g., somatization, depression, anxiety) that the respondent has experienced during the last year. A higher score on this scale represents more symptomatology. In a factor analysis based on the data collected, three factors for boys (i.e., low energy, depression, anxiety) and five factors for girls (i.e., depression, low energy, anxiety, hostility, phobic anxiety) emerged.

Delinquency. The Delinquency Checklist (DCL; Short and Nye, 1957) is a self-report inventory concerning the extent to which the adolescent engages in delinquent behaviors (e.g., aggression, truancy, running away from home, drug abuse). In the present study, the DCL was shortened to 28 items and updated to conform with current language usage with respect to various substances and activities. In taking the DCL, adolescents were asked about their delinquent behaviors during the previous year. A higher score on this scale indicates more delinquency. Factor analyses based on the data collected were conducted separately for each sex and revealed five factors for boys (i.e., heavy substance abuse, stealing, aggression, drinking and marijuana abuse, trouble with police) and five factors for girls (i.e., substance abuse, stealing, trouble with police, truancy and running away from home, aggression).

PROCEDURE

At each testing site, students completed a computer version of the self-report questionnaires described in the previous section. The entire procedure time was approximately two hours, and each student was given a check for $20.00 at the end of the session. Both parent and student consent was obtained.

Results

The results are presented in four main sections. In the first, the rates of adolescents seeking help from each type of helping resource are delineated. In the second, the relationship of the various types of help-seeking to sociodemographic characteristics, self-image, symptomatology, and delinquency is presented. In the third, differences between those adolescents who have sought help solely from informal helping agents and those adolescents who have sought help from *both* informal and formal helping agents on sociodemographic characteristics are examined. Finally, in the fourth section, differences between the two aforementioned groups on indices of self-image, symptomatology, and delinquency are identified.

RATES OF HELP-SEEKING FOR EACH HELPING RESOURCE

With regard to seeking help from formal helping agents, of the total 497 students who participated, 83 (17%) reported seeking help from a mental health professional during the past year, and 175 (35%) reported seeking help from a school counselor during the past year. With regard to seeking help from informal helping agents, 462 (93%) reported seeking help from friends, and 421 (85%) reported seeking help from parents.

ASSOCIATIONS BETWEEN TYPE OF HELPING AGENT AND SOCIODEMOGRAPHIC CHARACTERISTICS, SELF-IMAGE, SYMPTOMATOLOGY, AND DELINQUENCY

Table 1 shows the Pearson correlations between help-seeking category and demographic variables and Table 2 shows the Pearson correlations between help-seeking category, self-image, symptomatology, and delinquency. As can be seen in Table 1, positive correlations between sex and seeking help from friends ($r = .16$, $p < .05$) and sex and seeking help from mental health professionals ($r = .15$, $p < .05$) were found, indicating that females were more likely than males to report seeking help from these helping agents. Age was negatively related to seeking help from mental health professionals ($r = -.14$, $p < .05$), indicating that older adolescents were less likely than younger adolescent to seek help

TABLE 1

CORRELATIONS BETWEEN SOURCE OF HELP AND DEMOGRAPHIC VARIABLES
(SOUGHT HELP: YES = 1, NO = 0)

	Informal Helping Agents		Formal Helping Agents	
Demographic Variable	Parents	Friends	Mental Health Professionals	School Counselors
Sex (Male = 1, Female = 2)	.04	.16*	.15*	.08
Age	.04	−.08	−.14*	.09
Race (White = 1, all other = 2)	.01	−.06	−.30**	.19*
Father's Educational Level	−.06	.08	.09	−.07
Academic Achievement	.09	.04	−.11*	−.16*
Family Structure (intact = 1, reconstituted or single-parent = 2)	−.03	−.02	.10*	.10*

Note: Positive correlations indicate that higher numerical values on a specific variable are associated with *seeking help* whereas negative correlations indicate that higher numerical values on a specific variable are associated with *not seeking help*.
*$p < .05$. **$p < .01$.

TABLE 2

CORRELATIONS BETWEEN SOURCES OF HELP AND SELF-IMAGE, SYMPTOMATOLOGY,
AND DELINQUENCY (SOUGHT HELP: YES = 1, NO = 0)

	Informal Helping Agents		Formal Helping Agents	
Variable	Parents	Friends	Mental Health Professionals	School Counselors
Self-image	.23**	−.03	−.23**	−.05
Symptomatology	−.13*	.16*	.28**	.12*
Delinquency	−.11*	.01	.35**	.03

Note: Positive correlations indicate that higher numerical values on a specific variable are associated with *seeking help* whereas negative correlations indicate that higher numerical values on a specific variable are associated with *not seeking help*.
*$p < .05$. **$p < .01$.

from mental health professionals. A significant negative relationship between race and seeking help from mental health professionals was evidenced ($r = -.30$, $p < .01$), suggesting that blacks, Asians, and Hispanics were less likely than whites to seek this type of help. In contrast, a significant positive relationship between race and seeking help from school counselors was found ($r = .19$, $p < .05$), indicating that blacks, Asians, and Hispanics were more likely than whites to seek help from school counselors. No significant relationships were evidenced between father's educational level and type of helping resource.

With regard to academic achievement, those students with lower grades were more likely than youths with higher grades to seek help from mental health professionals ($r = -.11, p < .05$) and school counselors ($r = -.16, p < .05$). In addition, youths living in reconstituted or single-parent homes were more likely to seek help from mental health professionals and school counselors than were youths living in intact homes ($r = .10, p < .05$ and $r = .10, p < .05$, respectively).

As can be seen in Table 2, a more positive self-image was related to seeking the help of parents ($r = .23, p < .01$) whereas, a poorer self-image was related to seeking the help of mental health professionals ($r = -.23, p < .01$). Significant relationships between symptomatology and all help-seeking categories emerged. Specifically, students with more reported symptoms were less likely to seek help from parents ($r = -.13, p < .05$) whereas students with more reported symptoms were more likely to seek help from friends ($r = .16, p < .05$), mental health professionals ($r = .28, p < .01$) and school counselors ($r = .12, p < .05$). Finally, adolescents with higher rates of reported delinquency did not seek help from parents ($r = -.11, p < .05$) but did seek help from mental health professionals ($r = .35, p < .01$).

DEMOGRAPHIC DIFFERENCES BETWEEN ADOLESCENTS WHO HAVE SOUGHT HELP FROM INFORMAL SOURCES ONLY AND THOSE WHO HAVE SOUGHT HELP FROM BOTH INFORMAL AND FORMAL SOURCES

Overall, 275 adolescents sought help from informal resources only, and 212 sought help from *both* informal and formal helping resources. Ten adolescents did not fit into either of these two categories. Specifically, three of these ten had sought help from formal resources only, and seven had not sought any help. Because of the small number of respondents in these two categories (i.e., those who sought help from formal helping agents only, those who did not seek any type of help) their scores were not included in any subsequent analyses.

As can be seen in Table 3, males were more likely than females to seek help from informal resources only, whereas females were more likely than males to seek help from both helping resources ($\chi^2 = 8.5, p < .01$). Living in an intact versus a reconstituted or single-parent household was also related to seeking help, with those adolescents living in intact households seeking help from informal resources only and adolescents

TABLE 3
ASSOCIATIONS BETWEEN DEMOGRAPHIC VARIABLES AND HELP-SEEKING GROUP
(IN PERCENTAGES)

Demographic Variable	Informal Sources Only ($n = 275$)	Informal and Formal Sources ($n = 212$)	Significant Difference
Sex			
Male	55.3	42.0	$\chi^2(1,487) = 8.5$
Female	44.7	58.0	$p < .01$
Race			
White	56.4	48.1	ns
All Other	43.6	51.9	
Father's Educational Level			
Some High School	6.2	6.1	
High School Only	15.6	16.5	ns
Some College	70.9	66.5	
Family Structure			
Intact	66.2	49.1	$\chi^2(1,487) = 14.48$
Reconstituted or Single-Parent	33.8	50.9	$p < .001$
High School Grades			
Mostly As	15.3	8.5	$\chi^2(3,487) = 16.50$
Mostly Bs	55.7	45.7	$p < .001$
Mostly Cs	28.1	42.9	
Mostly Ds	1.1	2.8	

living in reconstituted or single-parent households seeking help from both helping resources ($\chi^2 = 14.48$, $p < .001$). Finally, students reporting higher grades sought help from informal resources only, and students reporting lower grades sought help from both types of helping agents ($\chi^2 = 16.50$, $p < .001$). No significant difference with regard to age was evidenced (Informal Only, Mean Age $= 16.90$ years; both Informal and Formal, Mean Age $= 16.91$).

DIFFERENCES IN SELF-IMAGE,
SYMPTOMATOLOGY, AND DELINQUENCY
BETWEEN ADOLESCENTS WHO HAVE SOUGHT
HELP FROM INFORMAL SOURCES ONLY AND
THOSE WHO HAVE SOUGHT HELP FROM BOTH
INFORMAL AND FORMAL SOURCES

The means and standard deviations for measures of self-image, symptomatology, and delinquency by group are presented in Table 4. A significant difference between self-image and group was evidenced with

TABLE 4
GROUP DIFFERENCES ON SELF-IMAGE, SYMPTOMATOLOGY, AND DELINQUENCY

Variable	Informal Sources Only ($n = 275$)		Informal and Formal Sources ($n = 212$)		Significant Difference
	M	SD	M	SD	
Self-Image	584.52	89.17	558.85	93.28	$t(df = 485) = 3.09$, $p < .002$
Symptomatology	21.68	12.44	27.21	14.50	$t(df = 485) = -4.52$, $p < .001$
Delinquency	55.79	5.83	58.23	8.30	$t(df = 485) = -3.79$, $p < .001$

adolescents who had sought help from informal sources only having a higher self-image than those adolescents who had sought help from both informal and formal sources ($t = 3.09$, $p < .002$). In addition, adolescents who had sought help from both informal and formal helping resources had more reported symptoms ($t = -4.52$, $p < .001$) and more reported delinquent behaviors ($t = -3.79$, $p < .001$) than did those adolescents who had sought help from informal sources only.

Discussion

This chapter describes the help-seeking behaviors of adolescents from three high schools in a midwestern community. Our findings indicate that a large percentage of adolescents reported seeking help from friends and parents, and to a lesser degree from school counselors and mental health professionals. These findings relating to adolescents' preferences for seeking help from friends and parents are in agreement with findings from previous investigations suggesting that adolescents prefer to seek help from family and friends for problems deemed "personal" (Sternlieb and Munan, 1972; Hodgson et al., 1986; Dubow et al., 1990). For example, Dubow et al. (1990) reported that 89% of the adolescents in their study consulted friends and 81% consulted family. Although peers play an increasingly important role in the lives of adolescents, our findings, along with those of Dubow et al., suggest that parents are also seen as important helpers for adolescents. Indeed, previous research indicates that the vast majority of teenagers have positive feelings toward their parents and are not continually rebelling or in a state of antagonism toward them (Douvan and Adelson, 1966; Offer, 1969; Offer and Offer,

1975; Mitchell, 1980; Offer et al., 1981, 1984; Csikszentmihalyi and Larson, 1984). Especially noteworthy from our research results is the finding that those adolescents who seek help from their parents possess a better self-image than do those adolescents who do not turn to their parents for help.

One salient finding in the literature on adult help-seeking is that users of mental health, social service and self-help groups tend to be young, white, educated, middle-class, and female; (Hollingshead and Redlich, 1958; Beck, 1961; Srole et al., 1962; Kammeyer and Bolton, 1968; Kadushin, 1969; Kravits, 1972; Sue et al., 1974; Katz and Bender, 1976; Weyerer, Meller, and Thaler, 1982). The findings of this study indicate that, among adolescents, being white and female is associated with seeking the help of a mental health professional as well as seeking the help of *both* informal and formal helping resources. In addition, whereas whites are more likely than blacks, Asians, or Hispanics to seek the help of a mental health professional, blacks, Asians, and Hispanics are more likely to seek help from school counselors. This finding has direct implications for prevention and intervention efforts especially targeted for these groups.

How do adolescents who seek help from only informal helping agents differ from those who seek help from *both* informal and formal helping agents? In the present sample, requests for assistance for emotional problems from *both* formal and informal sources tended to be female adolescents who had a lower self-image, more psychiatric symptoms, and more reported delinquent behaviors as well as lower grades in school. It may be that adolescents seeking help from both informal and formal helping agents are those who do so through their parents' initiative rather than their own. The supposition that adolescents do not come into contact with professionals on their own accord may be especially problematic for those adolescents with internalizing (e.g., depression, anxiety) rather than externalizing (e.g., conduct problems) symptomatology. Because it is during adolescence that individuals become increasingly able to conceal distress and put on an external façade (Broughton, 1981), many adolescents with internalizing symptoms may hide their real distress from their parents. Therefore, the parents may be unaware of their son's or daughter's internal states and be unable to take action toward intervention. Indeed, one could speculate that adolescents whose disturbances are outwardly manifested, such as through delinquent behaviors, would be more likely to encounter parental intervention than would adolescents whose disturbances are turned inwardly, such as depressed feelings. In contrast, it may be that those adolescents with higher rates of reported symptoms were brought to a formal helping agent due to a suicide attempt. Future efforts should attempt to determine the differences that exist between adolescents who obtain help from both informal and formal helping resources through their own volition and those who do so under parental coercion.

Future research should delineate clearly the help-seeking behaviors of adolescents and the factors that motivate them to seek help so that appropriate interventions can be designed and implemented. Indeed, before effective strategies aimed at helping adolescents in need of assistance are established, it is necessary for researchers and clinicians first to become cognizant of the specific help-seeking behaviors that adolescents employ and the variables associated with such help-seeking.

REFERENCES

Beck, D. F. (1961), Patterns of use of family agency service. Presented to the biennial meeting of the Family Service Association of America.

Broughton, J. M. (1981), The divided self in adolescence. *Human Devel.*, 24:13–32.

Brown, B. B. (1978), Social and psychological correlates of help-seeking behavior among urban adults. *Amer. J. Comm. Psychol.*, 6:425–439.

Compas, B. E. (1987). Coping with stress during childhood and adolescence. *Psychol. Bull.*, 101:393–403.

_____ & Phares, V. (1991). Stress during childhood and adolescence: Sources of risk and vulnerability. In: *Life-span Developmental Psychology*, ed. E. M. Cummings, A. L. Greene & K. H. Karraker. Hillsdale, NJ: Lawrence Erlbaum Associates, pp. 111–129.

Csikszentmihalyi, M. & Larson, R. (1984), *Being Adolescent*. New York: Basic Books.

DePaulo, B. M., Nadler, A. & Fisher, J. D., ed. (1983), *New Directions in Helping, Vol. 3*. New York: Academic Press.

Derogaitis, L. R. (1977), *SCL-90R Manual*. Baltimore, MD: Clinical Psychometrics Research Unit, Johns Hopkins School of Medicine.

Douvan, E. & Adelson, J. (1966), *The Adolescent Experience*. New York: Wiley.

Dubow, E. F., Lovko, J. & Kausch, D. F. (1990), Demographic differences in adolescents' health concerns and perceptions of helping agents. *J. Clin. Child Psychol.*, 19:44–54.

Ebata, A. T. & Moos, R. H. (1994), Personal, situational, and contextual correlates of coping in adolescence. *J. Res. Adoles.*, 4:99–125.

Feldman, W., Hodgson, C., Corber, S. & Quinn, A. (1986), Health concerns and health-related behaviors of adolescents. *Can. Med. Assn. J.*, 134:489–493.

Frydenberg, E. & Lewis, R. (1993), Boys play sport and girls turn to others: Age, gender, and ethnicity as determinants of coping. *J. Adoles.*, 16:253–266.

Hodgson, C., Feldman, W., Corber, S. & Quinn, A. (1986), Adolescent health needs II: Utilization of health care by adolescents. *Adoles.*, 21:383–390.

Hollingshead, A. & Redlich, F. (1958), *Social Class and Mental Illness*. New York: Wiley.

Kadushin, C. (1969), *Why People Go to Psychiatrists*. New York: Atherton.

Kammeyer, K. & Bolton, C. (1968), Community and family factors related to the use of a family service agency. *J. Marriage Family*, 30:488–498.

Katz, A. H. & Bender, E. I. (1976), Self-help groups in Western society: History and prospects. *J. Appl. Behav. Sci.*, 12:265–282.

Kohlberg, L., Ricks, D. & Snarey, J. (1984), Childhood development as a predictor of adaptation in adulthood. *Genet. Psychol. Monogr.*, 110:91–172.

Kravits, J. (1972), Attitudes toward and use of discretionary physician and dental services by race controlling for income and age. Unpublished doctoral dissertation, University of Chicago.

Marks, A. M., Malizio, J., Hoch, J., Brody, R. & Fisher, M. (1983), Assessment of health needs and willingness to utilize health care resources of adolescents in a suburban populations. *J. Pediat.*, 102:456–460.

Mitchell, J. R. (1980). Normality in adolescence. *Adolescent Psychiatry*, 8:201–213. Chicago: Chicago University Press.

Offer, D. (1969), *The Psychological World of the Teenager*. New York: Basic Books.

———— & Offer, J. B. (1975), *From Teenager to Young Manhood*. New York: Basic Books.

———— Ostrov, E. & Howard, K. I. (1981), The mental health professional's concept of the normal adolescent. *Arch. Gen. Psychiat.*, 38:149–152.

———— ———— & ———— (1984), *Patterns of Adolescent Self-image*. San Francisco, CA: Jossey-Bass.

_____ & Spiro, R. P. (1987), The disturbed adolescent goes to college. *J. Amer. College Health*, 35:209–214.

Radius, S. M., Dillman, T. E., Becker, M. H., Rosenstock, I. M. & Horvath, W. J. (1980), Adolescent perspectives on health and illness. *Adoles.*, 15:375–384.

Riggs, S. & Cheng, T. (1988), Adolescents' willingness to use a school-based clinic in view of expressed health concerns. *J. Adoles. Health Care*, 9:208-213.

Seiffge-Krenke, I. (1989), Problem intensity and the disposition of adolescents to take therapeutic advice. In: *Children at Risk*, ed. M. Brambring, F. Losel & H. Skowronek. New York: de Gruyter, pp. 457–477.

Short, J. F., Jr. & Nye, F. C. (1957), Reported behaviors as a criterion of deviant behavior. *Soc. Prob.*, 5:207–213.

Srole, L., Langner, T. S., Michael, S. T., Opler, M. K. & Rennie, T. A. C. (1962), *Mental Health in the Metropolis*. New York: McGraw Hill.

Sternlieb, J. J. & Munan, L. (1972), A survey of health problems, practices, and needs of youth. *Pediat.*, 49:177–186.

Sue, S., McKinney, H., Allen, D. & Hall, J. (1974), Delivery of community mental health services to Black and White clients. *J. Consult. Clin. Psychol.*, 42:794–801.

Veroff, J., Douvan, E. & Kulka, R. A. (1981), *The Inner American*. New York: Basic Books.

Weyerer, S., Meller, I. & Thaler, J. (1982), The importance of artifactual factors in the relationship between sex and mental disorders. *Internat. J. Soc. Psychol.*, 83:73-80.

Whitaker, A., Johnson, J., Shaffer, D., Rapoport, J. L., Kalikow, K., Walsh, B. T., Davies, M., Braiman, S. & Dolinsky, A. (1990), Uncommon troubles in young people. *Arch. Gen. Psychiat.*, 47:487–496.

Windle, M., Miller-Tutzauer, C., Barnes, G. M. & Welte, J. (1991), Adolescent perceptions of help-seeking resources for substance abuse. *Child Devel.*, 62:179-189.

13 ANXIETY, DEPRESSION, AND PSYCHOSOMATIC DISORDERS: DEVELOPMENTAL ARRHYTHMIAS IN ADOLESCENT MOTHERS

PAUL V. TRAD

Adolescence is a time of unprecedented physical and psychological transformation. In contrast to earlier changes in life, in adolescence, one is expected to negotiate new developmental challenges in a relatively independent fashion. Of course, adolescents will often share perceptions of maturational change with their mothers, a phenomenon especially common among teenage girls. Nonetheless, "fitting in" with and gaining the acceptance of peers, as opposed to winning the approval of the parent, assume priority during these pivotal years of advance.

The specific changes that adolescent girls experience fall into two categories—physical and psychological. Physical changes include the onset of menses and alterations in body shape. These physical alterations are mirrored by a metamorphosis in attitude that tends to influence dramatically the teenager's personality. In particular, dual psychological attitudes permeate the adolescent's behavior. Initially, the adolescent is driven to attain the acceptance and approval of peers. This desire for approval can assume numerous forms; for example, the teenager may adopt seemingly bizarre clothing or acquire an unusual manner of speech. More destructive illustrations of the need to be included in a specific clique involve abusing illegal drugs, frequent episodes of alcohol use, and experimentation with unprotected sex. A related theme that typifies the adolescent's psychology is the need to rebel from the mores of the parents. In this regard, it is not enough for the teenager to disagree with the parents or to adhere to a slightly different opinion. Instead, it is as if the adolescent must shock the parents with an extremely divergent point of view.

Most adolescents and their families endure this psychological turbulence with relatively few repercussions. In some instances, however, the teenager's sense of identity was originally somewhat tenuous; faced with the added burden of adolescent change, the teenager may succumb to a variety of psychiatric conditions. Among the most common are anxiety, depression, and psychosomatic disorder. Without treatment, these disorders can leave an indelible mark on the teenager by impeding acclimation to the developmental changes of adolescence. A teenager who becomes anxious because of a precocious separation from parental authority may carry this anxiety with her into adulthood. Depression triggered by physical development that is out of synchrony with the development of peers may also linger beyond the adolescent years. The inability to adapt psychologically to physical change may also lead to a host of psychosomatic conditions. In addition, the effects of these disorders may be exacerbated if the teenager becomes a mother. Exposure to an anxious, depressed, or psychosomatic mother may trigger in the infant distorted perceptions that culminate in dysfunctional behaviors. Treatment interventions designed to help adolescent mothers better negotiate the emotional upheaval of the teenage years may ameliorate these symptoms. A model of intervention, referred to as previewing, is described below.

Psychiatric Conditions Affecting Adolescents

Few would disagree that the teenage years are marked by significant emotional upheaval. During this time of life, the adolescent is exposed to a significant amount of stress as new information is processed at both conscious and nonconscious levels and endowed with subjective meaning (Smith, 1990). These subjective interpretations can trigger emotional responses, which, in turn, lead to cognitive, behavioral, or physiologic changes (Lipowski, 1977). In some cases, responses assume the character of a full-blown psychiatric disorder, such as anxiety or depression. In other instances, the teenager manifests an organic complaint that derives from a psychosomatic condition. Psychotherapists working with teenagers should become adept at identifying the etiology of these conditions and performing an evaluation that differentiates these diagnoses.

ANXIETY DISORDERS

Although anxiety has not been commonly reported during adolescence, the condition is known to affect youngsters in this age group. Anxiety generally manifests in one of two guises—either as an overarching, free-floating sense of dread and worry or as an exact fear of a particular object or situation that must be avoided (Steinberg, 1987). The latter form of anxiety is commonly referred to as a phobia. In addition, anxiety may exist concurrently with another psychiatric condition or psychological trauma.

The precise etiology for anxiety during the teenage years remains uncertain. It may be posited, however, that the increasing expectations and responsibilities of adolescence lead to feelings of uncertainty that spark anxiety. Pressure from peers, new school situations, and the determination to function without soliciting the advice or support of parents are all factors that may contribute to an anxiety-provoking atmosphere (Stavrakaki and Gaudet, 1989). The physical changes of puberty may also provoke anxiety if the teenager is unprepared for the dramatic transformations occurring to the body. While the teenager may know about these changes, actually undergoing them physically is unique. Especially in adolescent girls, the physical alterations associated with puberty may be unexpected and sudden. Moreover, some girls will find themselves developmentally more advanced or less advanced than their peers. At a time when one's ability to match status with peers is crucial, these discrepancies may cause extreme psychological distress manifested in the form of anxiety.

A teenager's anxiety may also stem from some previously overlooked sources. For example, anxious parents are apt to transmit a fearful attitude to the child (Eisenberg, 1958), and this attitude may become activated during times of developmental transition, such as adolescence. Temperamental vulnerability that remained dormant during childhood may ignite in the climate of uncertainty that prevails during adolescence (Thomas, Chess, and Birch, 1968; Chess, 1973). A similar response can occur with intrapsychic conflict, especially when the conflict concerns fears of abandonment, fears of mutilation, or sexual fears (Poznanski, 1973). In effect, the changes of adolescence may have a catalyzing effect on each of these conditions.

Anxiety may be awakened by the pressures of adolescent motherhood. Indeed, the adolescent mother is in a unique position. She must assert her own developmental independence and function as a caregiver to a newborn. Fulfilling the requirements of these dual roles is often difficult, causing the adolescent to experience anxiety. In turn, the teenage mother's anxious attitude may be conveyed to the infant, who begins to experience the world as a domain riddled with unpredictable experiences and events.

It is not difficult to understand why anxiety reactions may flare up during adolescence. Anxiety emerges in the form of fears or worries that are disproportionate in response to the magnitude of external stimuli (Stavrakaki and Gaudet, 1989). Viewed developmentally, fear may initially surface during infancy as a reaction to actual events in the environment. During the preschool years, fantasy enables the child to reflect on past events and to anticipate the future (Trad, 1992a). At this juncture, fears become linked to future dangers. By ages 9 to 12, as the child begins to function in a social environment, fears relating to school and social situations intensify. Ironically, the adolescent's more advanced capacity to predict future events may lead to anticipation of negative outcomes, triggering anxiety. Numerous studies have indicated that during the teenage years fears related to social relationships, worries about money, and amorphous fears about identity and adaptation become elevated (Lapouse and Monk, 1959; Maurer, 1965; Croake and Knox, 1973). Thus, childhood fears of ghosts and monsters subside with age, while fears of bodily injury and physical danger increase (Bauer, 1976). The most prevalent concerns among adolescents include fears of physical harm, bodily injury, illness and disease, personal safety, and incapacity. Second most prevalent fears relate to social behavior, including problems with gossip, reprobation, and ridicule. Females tend to express significantly more fears than males do, especially during late adolescence (Bamber, 1979).

The different incidence of anxiety in boys and girls has been confirmed by Kashani and Orvaschel (1988). According to these researchers, anxiety symptoms are encountered in 8% to 36% of boys and in 17% to 50% of girls. These researchers have also determined that 8.7% of a given adolescent sample is likely to manifest overanxious disorder. Along this spectrum, the symptoms of anxiety that have been reported in adolescents include panic attacks (Moretti et al., 1985; Ryan et al., 1985); phobias (Berg, Butler, and Hali, 1976); separation anxiety (Moretti et al., 1985; Ryan et al., 1987); excessive worrying (Moretti et al., 1985; Ryan et al., 1987); excessive concern about past behavior, marked self-consciousness, and obsessive-compulsive behavior (Rapoport et al., 1981).

DEPRESSIVE DISORDERS

A consistent theme in discussions of depression during adolescence concerns the difficulty in arriving at an accurate diagnosis. As Steinberg

(1987) points out, it is not always easy to distinguish between normal sadness and pathologic depression in an adolescent. Significantly, several studies of normal adolescent populations have indicated that many teenagers experience emotions that would be labeled as "depressive" in adults (Rutter, Tizard, and Whitmore, 1970; Trad, 1986). Moreover, adolescents sometimes respond to depressiogenic circumstances in specific ways. For example, following the death of a parent, a teenage girl might become promiscuous rather than sad. Thus, diagnosing depression in an adolescent is a challenging task (Rutter et al., 1976).

Despite diagnostic difficulties, evidence suggests that the incidence of depression increases with age. Rutter et al. (1970) found a tripling of depressive disorders from age 10 to 14 years. Kashani et al. (1987) have reported the prevalence of major depression to be 4.7% and dysthymic disorder to be 3.3% in a group of 150 adolescents, while Kaplan et al. (1984) determined that 20.8% of a group of 385 junior high and high school students administered the Beck Depression Inventory were depressed.

How can one account for this increased frequency of depression from the preschool years to adolescence? Personality development and the hierarchical advancement of defense mechanisms may partially account for the increase (Stavrakaki and Gaudet, 1989). In addition, during the transition from childhood to adolescence, a variety of biological and social influences may make a youngster more susceptible to depression. The biological, social, and psychological transformations of early adolescence may increase susceptibility to moodiness and aggression, while stimulating the urge for independence (Schoenbach, Garrison, and Kaplan, 1984). The adolescent's capacity to draw on a repository of past experience is limited. An imbalance between the environmental demands and the adolescent's psychological strength may generate perceptions of vulnerability. Finally, changes in neuroendocrine functioning during the teenage years may potentiate mood swings (Schoenbach et al., 1984). Moreover, it is relatively well established that the preponderance of depressive illness among females does not generally surface until late adolescence (Stavrakaki and Gaudet, 1989).

A variety of symptoms has been correlated with depression during the teenage years. Among the most common complaints in this age group are depressed mood (Carlson and Kashani, 1988); anhedonia (Moretti et al., 1985); self-reproach and guilt (Strober, Green, and Carlson, 1981); low self-esteem (Carlson and Kashani, 1988); suicidal ideation and suicidal

183

attempts (Ryan et al., 1987); and loss/gain of appetite or loss/gain of weight (Strober et al., 1981).

As Steinberg (1987) emphasizes, assessing depression in an adolescent is not an easy task. In particular, therapists should be alert to the following conditions. First, the possibility that the adolescent's depressed mood is an appropriate response to a particular circumstance should be investigated. For example, a teenager who fails to gain entrance to an academically elite school may experience appropriate unhappiness about educational expectations. Second, therapists should be alert to whether the adolescent is reacting in an excessively depressed manner. A teenager too easily "thrown" by circumstances or one who yields efforts too readily may be susceptible to genuine depression. Third, the possibility of genetic or familial factors influencing the teenager's mood should be explored. As an example, marital difficulties at a time when the teenager needs to experience a secure home environment may be a precipitant to depression.

PSYCHOSOMATIC DISORDERS

Psychosomatic disorders are relatively common during adolescence (Oster, 1972; Starfield et al., 1980; Rauste-von Wright and von Wright, 1981). In fact, subjective distress may be a greater predictor of adolescent physician visits than actual morbidity (Green et al., 1985). The physical and psychological upheavals of the teenage years—including the onset of puberty, pressure to rebel from the family, and the need to "fit in" with peers—may promote negative self-appraisals, elevated sensitivity to bodily changes, and somatization (Mechanic, 1983). Adolescents who experience loss, unresolved conflict, feelings of inadequacy, or other threats to their well-being may become excessively concerned with somatic sensations. Smith (1990) has observed that during adolescence psychosomatic symptoms are commonly associated with anxiety, depression, and somatization disorder. In one study, 12.8% of adolescent patients initially diagnosed with a medical condition were found to be suffering from a significant psychiatric disorder (Smith et al., 1990).

Differentiating a psychosomatic symptom from one that derives from an organic condition is not an easy task. When evaluating such symptoms, the physician should focus on the entire context in which the symptom is expressed, rather than merely examining the symptom alone (Smith, 1990). In this regard, the teenager's family circumstances are of particular significance. Therapists should attend to the relational patterns and style of communication between parent and teenager. Certain psychological attitudes—including enmeshment, overinvolvement, distance, apathy, or hostility—may provide insight into the nature of the symptoms being exhibited by the teenager.

In attempting to ascertain whether the adolescent's symptoms are organic or psychosomatic, therapists should obtain an extensive history of the primary complaint. A description of the onset of symptoms, as well as such details as the time of day when the symptoms occur, aggravating factors, and strategies that provide relief, should be obtained. Of key importance is an assessment of how the teenager's developmental status influences the symptoms. Adaptive teenage development may be divided into three stages—early, middle, and late adolescence. During the early phase of adolescence—between ages 11 and 14 years—the teenager focuses on adjusting to a new body image, acclimating to dramatic changes in physical growth, and formulating a sexual identity. Although efforts to assert independence may begin at this time, the teenager primarily concentrates upon his or her new status. Middle adolescence—spanning ages 14 to 17—inaugurates an epoch of experimentation and independence seeking. At this time, the adolescent strives to establish an identity distinct from the identity with the family. Risk-taking behavior, including drug and alcohol use and unprotected sexual activity, may be prevalent. At the inception of late adolescence— ages 17 to 21—a distinctive change is noted. The teenager is now oriented primarily toward the future, and preeminent goals include career and academic planning, the establishment of an intimate relationship with a significant other, the formulation of spiritual beliefs, and assessment of one's potential.

In approximately one decade, then, the person undergoes remarkable transformations affecting virtually every aspect of physical and psychological functioning. Given this profound metamorphosis, it is perhaps not unusual that the teenager manifests physical symptoms as a stigma of the difficulties in adjusting to developmental change. While Smith (1990) notes that virtually any organic system may be targeted for psychosomatic manifestations, the most common complaints expressed by adolescents are headache, chest pain, abdominal pain, and persistent fatigue. In one early study, Billie (1962) reported that by age 15 as many as 75% of children have experienced significant headaches. Males and females experience recurrent headaches with equal frequency until late adolescence, when females surpass males in this area (Barlow, 1984). Environmental stress, temperamental style, and superseding affective disorder tend to be common in cases of tension headache (Adler and Adler, 1987). For some adolescents, recurrent headaches may be a "symptom" of such underlying conditions as anxiety disorder or major depression. In other cases, dysfunctional families or peer problems have been encountered. Womack, Smith, and Chen (1988) used relaxation and mental imagery techniques in a group of 119 children and adolescents with tension headaches; the researchers reported that 75% of patients showed a decline in headache activity after treatment. Therapists working with adolescents should carefully rule out organic causes of the headache; and, if the pain appears to stem from the psychological changes of adolescence, psychotherapeutic treatment may be advisable.

In one study, 28% of chest pain in a sample of adolescents was attributed to anxiety (Selbst, 1985); another investigation detected hyperventilation syndrome in 20% of adolescents with such pain. Frequent episodes of chest pain may be a sign of anxiety. If the adolescent's physical exam is unremarkable, psychosomatic stressors such as sexual abuse and fear of pregnancy should be investigated (Smith, 1990). This advice is substantiated by a study in which 13% of adolescents with chest pain met the criteria for major depressive disorder (Kashani, Labadidi, and Jones, 1982). Abdominal pain, another common complaint of adolescence, accounts for 5% of teenage medical visits (Poole and Morrison, 1983). Abdominal pain is a common adolescent reaction to psychosocial stress. Finally, chronic fatigue syndrome has been reported among adolescents. One study determined that teenagers with this condition also tended to be depressed (Cooke, Warsh, and Hasey, 1989). Such teenagers and their families frequently require significant psychotherapy before they can resume normal activities.

Teenagers with a suspected psychosomatic disorder need attentive and sensitive care. Psychotherapeutic intervention is strongly urged because, in virtually all cases, the symptom is associated with psychosocial stressors that were triggered by the advent of adolescent status. Therapists should be particularly alert to a coexisting psychiatric condition such as anxiety or an affective disorder. Often the adolescent uses the psychosomatic symptom as a symbol to disguise more serious psychosocial distress.

Case Study

The following case illustrates how a psychiatric disorder, in this instance anxiety, incapacitated an adolescent mother. The teenager was initially unable to balance the requirements of her own developmental status with those of her infant.

DESCRIPTION OF MALADAPTIVE BEHAVIOR

Julianne was an 18-year-old African American adolescent with a five-month-old infant, James. A prolific speaker, the mother's tone accelerated as she related her history to the therapist during the initial interview. For much of the session her expression was harried and exhausted. Although Julianne was clean and attractive in appearance, her clothing appeared to be carelessly put on; several buttons on her sweater were undone. She had wrapped her son tightly in a blanket that kept him disguised from view. She gingerly uncovered the infant's face when the therapist asked for a better look at James. The therapist noted an expression of mixed wariness and surprise on the infant's face.

Asked to describe the factors that had motivated her entrance to treatment, Julianne spoke of an increasing inability to travel more than a few blocks from her house without experiencing panic attacks. In addition, she mentioned an escalating level of overall anxiety, with anxious or morbid fantasies concerning herself and her infant son. Julianne had a prior history of dysthymia dating back to her early teenage years. While she conceded that her fears had no basis in objective reality and believed that they had not interfered with her relationship with her son, she nonetheless dreaded the impact of her anxiety on her son as he grew older.

FAMILY HISTORY

Julianne was the oldest of three children in a middle-class family. Throughout elementary school and well into high school she had been a "quiet and studious" girl, according to her parents. When Julianne was 15 years old, her father, a school custodian, was injured at work. Thereafter, he remained home on disability leave and began to abuse alcohol. Julianne confided to the therapist during an individual session that she had become embarrassed about her father and no longer felt comfortable bringing friends home from school.

The adolescent became increasingly more self-conscious about her physical development at this time. By age 14, she had still not begun to menstruate and had told her mother of her disappointment with her "boy's body." A physical examination, including endocrine assessment, indicated that the teenager would achieve puberty later than average but was still within normal limits. Medical reassurances were of no avail in consoling Julianne, however. She became increasingly more distraught about her maturational status. Her mother believes that the teenager adopted an excessively rebellious attitude at this time to compensate for insecure feelings aroused because of rejection by peers.

Julianne was reluctant to discuss this period of her life but gradually began to disclose her feelings and concerns to the therapist. She grew to "hate" her family at this time. "My mother just complained and my father always drank, so I had to be the strong one," she said, adding that she became involved with a rough crowd at school. "We wore leather jackets and smoked a lot. Some of the boys brought knives to school and one kid threatened a teacher with a gun." In order to "hang" with the boys, the girls in the group had to "put out." "That meant we had to have sex with them whenever they wanted. And you couldn't ask them to wear a condom, because it was considered an insult to their manhood," she explained.

At the height of this rebelliousness, Julianne became ill with swollen glands and night sweats. Initially, the illness appeared to be a serious cold or the flu. After several weeks, however, the teenager's fatigue increased and she ran a low fever throughout the day. Her doctor checked her into the hospital, and eventually she was diagnosed with mononucleosis. She remained at home for almost six months, effectively isolated from friends and her social life. Because she missed so much school, she had to repeat her junior year. Her bouts of anxiety first surfaced at this time. She became increasingly uneasy about leaving home alone. Julianne explained that she overcame this fear by making sure that someone else was always with her. Constant companionship allayed her fears enough so that she could resume normal functioning.

Julianne's anxiety caused another dramatic change in her personality. Abandoning her rebellious behavior, she diligently pursued schoolwork. She also became religious and began attending a gospel church on a regular basis. Following graduation from high school, she began working as a secretary and shortly thereafter, at a church social event, met the man who would become the father of her baby. After a few dates, Julianne agreed to sleep with 19-year-old Clifford. "I pressed him about wearing a condom, but, like the other guys I've known, he didn't want to because it wasn't 'manly.'" Julianne was not overly concerned with his reaction. "Because I developed late, I always thought it would be hard for me to get pregnant." The couple dated for several months and then had a terrible fight because, Julianne explained, "Clifford wanted to date other girls and I got jealous." Soon after this change in the relationship Julianne experienced a return of the anxiety she had felt during her recovery from mononucleosis. Within a few weeks, however, this episode abated. Julianne said she was determined not to let her anxiety get in her way. "I had to accept that people weren't going to always take care of me," she said.

Shortly thereafter, her parents announced they were getting a divorce and the panic returned. This time Julianne attributed the episodes to the breakup of her parents' marriage. "My mother is a cold, bossy person, and my dad was always drunk. I didn't have much sympathy for their problems," she said. The anxiety again abated, and Julianne resumed her relationship with Clifford. A few months later she became pregnant. The couple decided to raise the child together, although they did not marry. Within several days of her infant son's birth, Julianne's anxiety level increased. Anxious fantasies about her infant's safety motivated her to seek help. "When I thought I would do something to hurt myself or the baby, I knew it was time I talked to someone," she told the therapist.

Throughout her narrative, Julianne's description of Clifford remained curiously lifeless. She reported that Clifford loved James and played with the infant when Julianne needed a break. However, Clifford was not involved in any aspect of parenting beyond playing with his son, nor did Julianne appear to expect more involvement. Since the infant's birth, Julianne said that her affection for Clifford had faded. "I just want someone who will take care of us. Sometimes I have doubts about Clifford and that's when I get scared," she said.

DYADIC MENTAL STATUS EXAMINATION

Julianne, a woman in late adolescence, possessed a reasonable degree of insight into her condition. Her concern that her anxiety could adversely affect her parenting skills was a positive sign. She denied suicidal or homicidal ideation. Her focus and concentration were occasionally impaired by anxiety, however; for example, from time to time she would "fade out" of the conversation or, withdrawing from interaction with the infant, lapse into apparently unpleasant fantasies. These reveries were of short duration, but their effect on Julianne's interpersonal abilities was powerful. Initially, she was reluctant to discuss these fantasies, saying, "I have an overactive imagination." Nonetheless, the therapist finally induced her to explore her anxious ideation. Although many of these fantasies were outlandish—for example, she envisioned objects "falling from space to crush [her or] the baby," or terrorists "kidnapping the baby at a shopping mall"— Julianne remained tense for several minutes after disclosing these fantasies.

Julianne also reported other reveries in which she imagined that the baby "threatened or criticized" her. In one persistent dream she was sitting in a bus terminal listening to announcements when a crowd approached her. "They were from my church," Julianne said, "and I knew they would accuse me of stealing." Julianne began to run away because she feared these people would beat her up. "As I ran, I suddenly realized I had left James behind. They would kill him when they found him. That's when I woke up, sweating all over," she reported.

Julianne's interaction with her infant was affectionate, but distracted. There was a palpable tension in her handling of the infant, as if she were afraid that something would spontaneously go wrong. James exerted conspicuous efforts to attract his mother's attention. His most frequently used behavior was a high-pitched squeal. At five months of age, James was a somber, watchful infant. He was able to sit on his mother's lap with support or on the floor with the therapist holding him. His reaching and grasping skills were well developed, evidently because he frequently reached for Julianne's face or hair to attract her attention. While James appeared to hear and respond to voices, he vocalized infrequently. He smiled occasionally, when his mother or the therapist played with him, but when he was by himself his mood became sober. James also displayed hesitation about confronting new stimuli or exploring new objects. Nor did he social reference his mother when confronted with a potentially dangerous stimulus.

At one point during the interview the therapist held James facing his mother. For several minutes, the baby remained sober, bouncing gently on the therapist's knee and gazing with rapt attention at his mother as she talked. Julianne, whose visual references to her son were usually brief, had an unimpeded view of James's face and gazed intermittently at the infant as she continued her conversation. After a few minutes, James hiccoughed in distress and his body stiffened. Julianne immediately addressed the baby, saying, "What's the matter sweetie?" in a gentle voice. James stared at his mother. Then his face contorted into a frown and he gave a high-pitched screech. Julianne reached for her son, whose posture was stiff, saying, "I think he wants me now." Once in his mother's arms, the infant cried loudly, waving his arms and kicking his feet. Then, as abruptly as it had begun, the crying stopped. Placed against his mother's shoulder, James became serious again. "He's not very brave about strangers yet," the mother said.

Although Julianne displayed a degree of awareness relating to her son's physical and cognitive development, she had difficulty predicting upcoming maturational changes and commented that she sometimes thought she was "missing things" in his development because of her inability to focus. She reported that she had felt great pleasure when she realized that James had begun to reach intentionally for objects but confessed uneasily that she did not remember exactly which milestones the infant had achieved.

Although this adolescent mother demonstrated some adaptive nurturing skills—for example, her rapid effort to quell the infant's distress when he cried—her unfamiliarity with developmental milestones and timetables, as well as her inability to predict imminent skills, is of concern. In addition, her history of anxiety, coupled with the nervous lapses that occurred during the interview, suggests that Julianne may not perceive or attend sufficiently to the infant's needs. In addition, various manifestations by the infant indicate that a secure attachment relationship was not necessarily evolving between this pair and that the mother was not a dependable source of guidance. In particular, the infant's somber facial expression and failure to display any incipient signs of social referencing are notable. An intervention designed to enhance the dyadic rapport, while simultaneously addressing the interpersonal deficits of this adolescent mother, was therefore recommended.

Intervention for Adolescent Mothers with Psychiatric Disorders

As indicated, certain psychiatric disorders may be more prevalent during adolescence than initially supposed. Psychiatric conditions that have been associated with the teenage years include anxiety and affective and psychosomatic disorders. These conditions often correlate with the physical and psychological changes of adolescence. If a teenager with such a condition subsequently becomes a mother, both she and her infant may suffer negative consequences.

Psychotherapeutic interventions in these cases should strive to achieve certain goals. First, the therapist needs to differentiate the psychological condition affecting the teenager from the normal developmental changes of adolescence and should ascertain, as best as possible, the etiologic factors causing the symptoms. Generally, this means that the teenager's adjustment to adolescence will need to be explored. Was puberty achieved within a typical physiologic timetable? Has the teenager acclimated to the changes in body image that accompany puberty? Equally significant, have the psychological challenges of adolescence been successfully negotiated? In this regard, the adolescent's relationships with parents and peers need to be clarified. Has the teenager found an adaptive means of asserting her independence? Once the therapist acquires an understanding of the teenager's status as an adolescent experiencing psychological difficulties, attention should shift to her role as a mother. What were the circumstances of the teenager's pregnancy? A medical and psychological history of the gestation should be obtained.

The therapist will also need to evaluate the adolescent's interaction with the infant. Are sequences of interaction rhythmic, harmonious, and attuned, or is the teenager out of synchrony with the infant's rhythms? One crucial inquiry that should be directed to the adolescent mother concerns her ability to predict imminent developmental changes that the infant may soon manifest. As noted earlier, teenagers are just beginning to explore these skills themselves and are likely to have only a tenuous ability to make predictions about their infants. One interventive technique that may assist adolescent parents in these cases is referred to as previewing, a process engaged in by adaptive caregivers (Trad, 1992a, b). The previewing process encompasses the overt manifestations of both infant and caregiver during interaction, as well as the caregiver's subjective representations of how significant developmental changes will modify the dyadic relationship. In essence, previewing captures the full texture of the caregiver's ability to make predictions about the infant's development and gradually to share these predictions with the infant as both members of the dyad traverse the developmental journey. By using the previewing process, the caregiver communicates with the infant in an intimate manner that is designed to enhance rapport in the relationship. The intimacy generated by previewing enables the caregiver simultaneously to validate past, current, and future developmental achievement for the infant.

Previewing may be defined as an interpersonal process during which the caregiver represents imminent developmental skills and then converts these representations into behaviors that introduce the infant to both the sensation of the skill and the implications the new skill will have for modifying their relationship. The previewing process comprises three key components. First is the caregiver's ability to represent or envision imminent developmental change. Representation refers to a reflective state during which past, current, and future interactions become accessible through imagery. Previewing involves not only the caregiver's awareness of the infant's current status, but also her perceptions of imminent developmental skill. As a result, caregiver representations encompass images of past memories, as well as images constructed from anticipations of the future. The second component of previewing involves the caregiver's role as an auxiliary partner for the infant. In adopting this stance, the caregiver devises behavioral exercises that introduce the infant to upcoming skills and convey to the infant that she will be available to coordinate new skills and to function as a safe haven within which the infant can practice and learn how to predict the future of their relationship. The third component of previewing is the caregiver's ability to sense when the infant has become satiated with the previewing exercise and wishes to return to a previous level of achievement. In fulfilling this role, the caregiver's sensitivity to infant cues becomes paramount.

Specific examples of previewing exercises are manifold. The caregiver who senses that her infant is ready to crawl or walk and who exercises the infant's limbs to simulate these functions is exhibiting previewing behavior, as is the parent who guides the infant's hand in grasping a small object or the mother who engages in baby talk with the infant. The developmental sequelae of previewing are diverse, but three outcomes are pertinent. First, previewing exercises focus both mother and infant on the psychological and emotional rewards derived from an interpersonal relationship in which each individual is responsive to the other. Second, previewing exercises persuade the infant that developmental challenges can be mastered; in a similar vein, the mother's confidence is bolstered through the use of intuitive skills. Finally, previewing exercises help both infant and parent predict the dimensions of upcoming change and eagerly anticipate new skills and abilities.

Although adaptive previewing behaviors are often deficient in adolescent mothers, these mothers may hone skills during intervention. Indeed, applying previewing strategies to the relationship between a teenage mother and her infant may not be difficult since previewing relies on upcoming change and, as Smith (1990) points out, during late adolescence a future orientation comes to predominate in the teenager's mind. Previewing strategies may also be beneficial for teenage mothers with superseding psychiatric conditions such as anxiety or affective or psychosomatic illness, conditions that make the adolescent highly sensitive to changes in her body. Somatic awareness may then be used to devise previewing exercises for the infant. Moreover, as the infant becomes more responsive, the adolescent mother gains confidence and the uncertainty that triggered the anxiety, depression, or psychosomatic disorder recedes.

THERAPEUTIC ALLIANCE

During this initial phase of treatment, the therapist's primary goals include establishing a bond of trust with the adolescent mother, arriving at an accurate diagnosis of the mother's condition, clarifying how the developmental factors of adolescence have contributed to the onset of the illness, communicating this diagnosis to the mother, evaluating the status of the mother–infant interaction, and formulating a strategy for improving the interaction through previewing.

In Julianne's case, the therapist conveyed to her that her efforts to seek help were commendable and that she likely could overcome anxiety and establish a more attuned rapport with her infant. The therapist displayed a supportive attitude to fortify the adolescent's sense of trust. To diagnose Julianne's psychiatric condition accurately, the therapist asked her to describe carefully an episode of anxiety, focusing on precipitating events that may have triggered the attacks.

As a result of these inquiries, Julianne was able to discern a particular pattern: her bouts of anxiety coincided with periods during which she experienced extreme uncertainty about her capabilities. These bouts of uncertainty had become more prevalent during adolescence. Julianne's recognition of the implications of the physical and psychological changes of adolescence enabled the therapist to explore the patient's perceptions of her teenage years. Certain themes were explored. For example, how had Julianne adjusted to the physical changes of puberty? Discussion of this topic disclosed her late maturational timetable. Subsequently, the therapist explored how Julianne felt about being different from her peers in the pace of her physical development. The adolescent confided that she had felt as if she could not control her body. Perceptions of body image were also discussed, as was Julianne's attitude toward her family. The teenager acknowledged that she disguised her fears by adopting a swaggering and rebellious attitude. "I did things to prove that I was one of the crowd . . . like sleeping around and getting drunk a lot," she said. The therapist reassured the adolescent mother that there would be ample time to discuss these topics in greater depth as the treatment progressed.

Another area that should be investigated early in treatment concerns the teenage mother's relationship with the infant. The therapist should perform a fairly thorough assessment of the relationship by carefully observing interactive sequences between the two. Often the mother will be hesitant about interacting with the infant in the therapist's presence. The therapist has several responses to this hesitation. First, patience is advised; most mothers will eventually become more comfortable in the therapeutic environment and begin interacting more naturally with the infant. By so doing, the therapist will be able to experience the infant's skills directly, as well as gauge the mother's reaction. During this process, the therapist should be alert to the adolescent mother's use of intuitive behaviors, manifestations parents rely on to capture the infant's attention and sustain interaction (Papousek and Papousek, 1987). Among the repertoire of intuitive behaviors are visual cuing, the parent's tendency to make direct eye contact with the infant and sustain gaze; vocal cuing, the reciprocal exchange of verbal cues; appropriate holding behavior; and appropriate feeding behavior. More general intuitive abilities extend to the provision of adequate stimulation and play activity.

After the interaction between mother and infant has been evaluated, the therapist should explain the previewing process. In this regard, it is important to measure the mother's knowledge of the infant's developmental status and to evaluate her sensitivity for predicting imminent skill. The various components of previewing should be described, and the therapist might demonstrate a specific previewing exercise for the mother. The therapist should then tell the mother that periodically she will be asked to predict and enact an imminent skill with the infant.

Once these preliminary goals have been achieved, the working-through phase of the treatment may begin.

THE WORKING-THROUGH

As the treatment progresses, patient and therapist adjust to a highly charged emotional bond. During this period of intense introspection, conflict is worked through, meaning that previously dysfunctional patterns are rigorously analyzed and interpreted. The working-through may be especially rigorous with adolescent mothers because the teenager will confront both her own intrapsychic conflict and the interpersonal conflict she encounters with the infant.

At this phase of treatment, unconscious derivatives relating to the teenager's unresolved conflict should be explored. Both the mother–therapist and mother–infant relationships now deepen in intensity.

Therapists have attributed various meanings to the working-through phase. Of significance in Julianne's case was the dream of being surrounded by a hostile crowd in the bus terminal. Significantly, in the dream Julianne leaves her infant son, James, behind. Although she feels guilt about this "inadvertent" act, the therapist also received the impression that the adolescent was unconsciously relieved of an unwanted burden.

During this phase, patients are encouraged to reevaluate their behaviors in a more objective light and to make changes in patterns of relating to others. From the inception of treatment, therapists working with adolescent mothers strive to modify interactional behaviors with the infant. Specifically, the therapist should sensitize the mother to the effect her ministrations have on the infant. The therapist may do this by having the mother interact with the infant and then asking the mother to describe the interaction, including her emotions. In effect, the therapist is encouraging the mother to become a more attuned observer of her own actions. Useful techniques for promoting these skills include videotaping and modeling by the therapist. During modeling sequences, the therapist previews a particular skill with the infant. As the previewing exercise is enacted, the therapist incorporates intuitive behaviors and establishes a sense of rhythm with the infant. By observing these episodes, the mother views interaction from the perspective of the therapist. She becomes adept at recognizing behaviors that are conducive to the emergence of new capacities, as well as behaviors that produce maladaptive responses. With the guidance of the therapist, the adolescent can begin to simulate adaptive patterns until she has relinquished virtually all her dysfunctional behaviors.

As the mother progresses through the working-through phase, she provides increasingly more intimate details about her relationship with the infant. Sessions begin to focus on how the caregiver relates to significant people in her life and maladaptive patterns are highlighted. Change becomes problematic, however, because abandoning stereotypical modes of interaction with others arouses anxiety until new skills are developed, rehearsed, and mastered. A modification in interpersonal skills necessitates experiencing new emotions, cataloging new perceptions, and learning new skills. To facilitate this process, the therapist should continue encouraging the adolescent mother to preview. In this way, the infant's development and the mother's response to maturational change become the centerpiece of discussion. These responses may be enacted through previewing exercises. For the adolescent mother, the mastery and accomplishment that emerge from these exercises provide a psychological boost in esteem that affects virtually all areas of functioning.

Regardless of progress made in treatment, teenage mothers are different from other patients largely because their own developmental attainments are in a state of flux. Adolescence is a time of transition that brings with it significant emotional upheaval. The adolescent experiences a variety of physical and psychological changes, and each change carries distinctive pitfalls. The dramatic physical changes of the teenage years involve the achievement of a sexually mature status. These alterations in the shape and appearance of the body, as well as the onset of menstruation, can cause exaggerated sensitivity in the young girl (Smith, 1990). Subjective distress is probably the greatest predictor of adolescent physician visits at this time, according to Greene et al. (1985). The onset of puberty can lead to family disruption, negative self-appraisal in the teenager, acute awareness of body change, and somatization (Mechanic, 1983).

But the physical changes of adolescence do not occur in isolation. The teenager must continue to function in society with family and peers. Perhaps the most formidable task for the adolescent at this time is the establishment of an independent identity that is separate from the identity she has enjoyed in the family. To assert this revitalized sense of self, many teenagers exhibit rebelliousness and risk-taking behaviors, as if by stretching the boundaries of acceptable conduct they can prove they are special individuals. The risk-taking and experimentation of these years can be dangerous and exert a psychological toll, however. Using a still-tenuous ability to predict future outcome, teenagers venture into areas with which they are unfamiliar. Sexual activity, drug and alcohol abuse, and truancy all have unanticipated consequences. Not unexpectedly, the frenzied behavior of the adolescent may trigger an episode of anxiety, depression, or psychosomatic illness. A similar scenario appears to have occurred with Julianne.

Successful psychotherapy helps the adolescent renegotiate the challenges posed by the teenage years in a more adaptive fashion. Previewing techniques may be used to bolster the teenager's predictive skills. For example, the adolescent might be asked to envision an upcoming event or experience of significance, such as how she might become involved in a risk-taking activity? Did she consider the outcome of the behavior before acting? During these predictive exercises, the therapist's task is continually to orient the patient to the outcome of her behavior. Previewing also teaches teenagers to perform risk–benefit analyses. As an illustration, when confronted with an opportunity to get into a car with a driver who has been drinking, the adolescent will now weigh the likelihood of an accident against the probability of an adventure. The therapist's inquiries underscore the adolescent's ability to choose positive as opposed to negative alternatives.

In cases such as Julianne's, the typical developmental transformations of adolescence are compounded by two factors. First, the teenager has a psychological disorder, and second, she is a mother. During the working-through phase, the adolescent should use previewing techniques to understand both of these phenomena. For instance, Julianne should explore why particular events in her life triggered anxiety attacks. Understanding the causes of the anxiety may not be sufficient, however; it will also be important for the teenager to devise strategies to predict future episodes of anxiety and to avoid the emotional trauma of these episodes. As a second task, the adolescent should explore the effect her psychological disorder has on the infant. To do this, the teenager's sensitivity to her own and the infant's behavioral cues should be heightened. Achieving these insights may be a slow and arduous process, but eventually the adolescent will be rewarded by the developmental accomplishments and enhanced responsivity seen in the infant.

TERMINATION OF THERAPY

As beneficial as regular psychotherapeutic sessions may be, the ultimate goal of treatment is to transform the adolescent mother into a competent caregiver who can function independently. To achieve this goal, the adolescent will need to become proficient in anticipating developmental changes that accommodate both dyadic members, as well as in enacting this strategy. Of course, it is difficult to predict with certainty the caregiver's behavior upon leaving treatment. Nonetheless, the therapist can help prepare the teenage mother for upcoming developmental changes that will most likely affect the infant. Specific skills can be anticipated, as can the mother's response to these skills.

Another facet of the termination process with an adolescent mother who has a diagnosed psychiatric condition is to insure that symptomatology remains in check. In this regard, the therapist should ask the patient how she feels about her disorder. Julianne responded by saying she believed her anxiety was under control. "I know the feelings I get when an attack is coming on," she said. She explained that she used previewing strategies to predict a more optimal outcome. "Predicting beyond the anxiety helps me," Julianne reported. She noted that interacting with James was also helpful at these times because the infant's responsivity persuaded her that she was a competent nurturer. Another area to reconcile concerns the adolescent mother's own developmental progress. Termination of treatment should not occur until the teenager has demonstrated skill in avoiding the pitfalls of the powerful maturational forces that engender impulsive and risk-taking behavior. Therapists should be scrupulous in their efforts to remind teenage mothers of the dangers of reckless behavior. Perhaps the best reminder of the consequences of risk-taking behavior is the teenager's pregnancy and subsequent motherhood.

The therapist should not underestimate the difficulty of the termination process for a teenage mother. In the figure of the therapist the adolescent has encountered, perhaps for the first time, an accepting and nonjudgmental individual. In contrast to the teenager's family and peers, the therapist acknowledges the adolescent's status as a unique person. The adolescent does not need to engage in daring or provocative behavior to capture the therapist's attention. Instead, the therapist offers unconditional acceptance. Assuming treatment has been successful, the teenage mother will have incorporated significant aspects of the therapist's perspective so that she is able to leave therapy with a secure sense of self and of her skill as a competent nurturer for her infant.

Conclusion

Adolescence is a complex developmental period fraught with significant physical and psychological change. During this crucial transition, an adolescent will be challenged to separate from her family and assert a distinctive identity. Formulating a sexual persona and acclimating to the physical changes of her body are additional challenges of this era. Given the effect these radical changes can exert, it is not surprising that many adolescents exhibit symptoms of psychological disorder during this period. Anxiety and affective and psychosomatic disorders are common, perhaps triggered by the adolescent's sense that the transformations of her body, as well as in the way in which she is treated, remain beyond her control.

The teenager's tenuous psychological state may be further compromised by pregnancy. Most frequently, the pregnancy was not planned and thus represents yet another instance of how events are beyond the adolescent's control. If the adolescent decides to give birth and raise the infant, further difficulties are likely to be encountered. For example, the relationship between the mother and infant is apt to be characterized by disharmony. Mother and infant may be oblivious to one another's behavioral cues.

One strategy that is highly beneficial in these cases is a technique referred to as previewing. Previewing, a process that involves the representation and enactment of imminent developmental milestones, enables the mother to function as an adaptive nurturing figure for the infant. Previewing rests on the foundation of predictive skills. Essentially, adolescent mothers whose predictive capacities are just emerging may be taught to anticipate imminent developmental skills in their infants and to subsequently enact these skills through rehearsal behaviors. In addition, previewing techniques may help adolescent mothers respond more adaptively to the developmental changes they themselves are undergoing. Finally, previewing strategies can help these teenagers cope better with the manifestations of their psychological distress.

REFERENCES

Adler, C. & Adler, S. (1987), Clinical and psychodynamic aspects of tension headache. In: Adler *Psychiatric Aspects of Headache*, ed. C. Adler & S. Adler. Baltimore, MD: Williams & Wilkins.

Bamber, J. (1979), *The Fears of Adolescents*. London: Academic Press.

Barlow, C. (1984), *Headaches and Migraine in Childhood*. Philadelphia: Spastics International Med. Pub.

Bauer, D. (1976), An exploratory study of developmental changes in children's fears. *J. Child Psychol. Psychiat. Allied Disciplines*, 17:69–74.

Berg, I., Butler, A. & Hali, G. (1976), The outcome of adolescent school phobia. *Brit. J. Psychiat.*, 128:80–85.

Billie, B. (1962), Migraine in school children. *Acta Paed. Scand.*, 135(1).

Carlson, G. & Kashani, J. (1988), Phenomenology of major depression from childhood through adulthood: Analysis of three studies. *Amer. J. Psychiat.*, 145:1222–1225.

Chess, S. (1973), Marked anxiety in children. *Amer. J. Psychother.*, 17:390–395.

Cooke, R., Warsh J. & Hasey, G. (1989), Epstein-Barr virus as a cause of autoimmune disease and other medical morbidity in patients with affective disorders. *Med. Hypotheses*, 29:177–185.

Croake, J. & Knox, F. (1973), The changing nature of children's fears. *Child Study J.*, 3:91–105.

Eisenberg, L. (1958), School phobia: A study in the communication of anxiety. *Amer. J. Psychiat.*, 114:712–718.

Greene, J., Walker, L., Hickson, G. et al. (1985), Stressful life events and somatic complaints in adolescents. *Pediatrics*, 75:19–22.

Kaplan, S. L., Landa, B., Weinhold, C. & Shenker, I. R. (1984), Adverse health behaviors and depressive symptomology in adolescents. *J. Amer. Acad. Child Adoles. Psychiat.*, 233:595–601.

Kashani, J., Beck, N., Hoeper, E. et al. (1987), Psychiatric disorders in a community sample of adolescents. *Amer. J. Psychiat.*, 144:585–589.

―――― Labadidi, Z. & Jones, R. (1982), Depression in children and adolescents with cardio-vascular symptomatology: The significance of chest pain. *J. Amer. Acad. Child Psychiat.*, 21, 187–189.

―――― & Orvaschel, H. (1988), Anxiety disorders in mid-adolescence: A community sample. *Amer. J. Psychiat.*, 145:960–964.

Lapouse, R. & Monk, M. (1959), Fears and worries in a representative sample of children. *Amer. J. Orthopsychiat.*, 29:803–818.

Lipowski, S. (1977), Psychosomatic medicine in the seventies: An overview. *Amer. J. Psychiat.*, 134:233–243.

Maurer, A. (1965), What children fear. *J. Gen. Psychol.*, 100:265–277.

Mechanic, D. (1983), Adolescent health and illness behavior: A review of the literature and a new hypothesis for the study of stress. *J. Human Stress*, 9:4–13.

Moretti, M., Fine, S., Haley, G. & Marriage, K. (1985), Childhood and adolescent depression: Child-report versus parent-report information. *J. Amer. Acad. Child Adoles. Psychiat.*, 24:298–302.

Oster, J. (1972), Recurrent abdominal pain, headache and limb pains in children and adolescents. *Pediat.*, 50:429–436.

Papousek, H. & Papousek, M. (1987), Intuitive parenting: A dialectic counterpart to the infant's integrative competence. In: *Handbook of Infant Development* (2nd ed.), ed. J. D. Osofsky. New York: Wiley.

Poole, S. & Morrison, I. (1983), Adolescent health care in family practice. *J. Fam. Prac.*, 16:103–109.

Poznanski, E. (1973), Children with excessive fears. *Amer. J. Orthopsychiat.*, 43:428–438.

Rapoport, J., Elkins, R., Langer, D., Sceery, W., Buchsbaum, M. S., Gillin, G. C., Murphy, D. L., Zahn, T. P., Lake, R., Ludlow, C. & Mendelson, W. (1981), Childhood obsessive-compulsive disorder. *Amer. J. Psychiat.*, 138:1545–1554.

Raust-von Wright, M. & von Wright, J. (1981), A longitudinal study of psychosomatic symptoms in healthy 11- to 18-year-old girls and boys. *J. Psychosom. Res.*, 25:525–534.

Rutter, M., Tizard, J. & Whitmore, K. (1970), Education, health and behaviour. In: *Basic Adolescent Psychiatry*, ed. D. Steinberg. Oxford: Blackwell Scientific.

Ryan, N., Puig-Antich, J., Ambrosini, P., Rabinovich, H., Robinson, D., Nelson, B., Iyengar, S. & Twomey, G. (1987), The clinical picture of major depression in children and adolescents. *Arch. Gen. Psychiat.*, 44:854–861.

Schoenbach, V., Garrison, C. & Kaplan, B. (1984), Epidemiology of adolescent depression. *Pub. Health Rev.*, 12:159–189.

Selbst, S. (1985), Chest pain in children. *Pediat.*, 75:1068–1070.

Smith, M. S. (1990), Psychosomatic symptoms in adolescence. *Adoles. Med.*, 74:1121–1134.

_____ Mitchell, J., McCauley, E. A. & Calderon, R. (1990), Screening for anxiety and depression in an adolescent clinic. *Pediat.*, 85:262–266.

Starfield, B., Gross, E., Wood, M. et al. (1980), Psychosocial and psychosomatic diagnoses in primary care of children. *Pediat.*, 66:159–167.

Stavrakaki, C. & Gaudet, M. (1989), Epidemiology of affective and anxiety disorders in children and adolescents. *Psychiat. Clin. N. Amer.*, 12:791–802.

Steinberg, D. (1987), *Basic Adolescent Psychiatry*. Oxford: Blackwell Scientific.

Strober, M., Green, J. & Carlson, G. (1981), Phenomenology and subtypes of major depressive disorder in adolescence. *J. Affective Dis.*, 3:281–290.

Thomas, A., Chess, S. & Birch, H. (1968), *Temperament and Behavior Disorders in Children*. New York: New York University Press.

Trad, P. V. (1986), *Infant Depression: Paradigms and Paradoxes*. New York: Wiley.

_____ (1992a), *Interventions with Infants and Parents: The Theory and Practice of Previewing*. New York: Wiley.

_____ (1992b), Mastering developmental transition through prospective techniques. *Internat. J. Short-Term Psychother.*, 7:59–72.

Womack, W., Smith, M. & Chen, A. (1988), Behavioral management of childhood headache: A pilot study and case history report. *Pain*, 32:279–283.

14   DISSOCIATIVE DISORDERS IN ADOLESCENCE

WILLIAM P. FLEISHER AND GERI ANDERSON

The last decade has seen an explosion of interest and controversy regarding the significance of dissociative disorders (DD) in the spectrum of psychiatric disturbances. Through exposition of the effects and sequelae of traumata and abuses, there has emerged an increasing understanding of the complex causality of such psychic injuries in the genesis of dissociative disturbances.

In the literature there exists a gap reflecting how these childhood injuries are manifest in the adolescent years. Here we review some of the child and adolescent literature, as well as some descriptive research data regarding adolescent dissociative disorders. We conclude with some principles regarding treatment, countertransference, and future issues.

Literature Review

The first reported case of childhood multiple personality disorder (MPD) was recorded in 1840 by Despine Pere. He treated an 11-year-old Swiss girl known in the literature as Estelle. She was believed to have been paralyzed by a spinal cord lesion. Later, in treatment, she was diagnosed as having a hysterical conversion disorder, which we now would refer to as a somatic dissociation. Estelle was treated with hypnotherapy and many of the current therapeutic approaches now recognized in the MPD literature.

One of the first of the more recent reports of child and adolescent MPD was by Fagan and McMahon (1984), in which four cases of

We would like to thank the child and adolescent staff, especially the M-1 South team, of St. Boniface General Hospital, Winnipeg, Manitoba, Canada, for being patient with our clinical research, Dr. Colin Ross for his mentorship and curiosity, and Ms. D. Fontaine and Mrs. D. Hill for manuscript production.

childhood MPD were described. The article was significant in two other areas. One was the development of a Behavioral Problem Checklist (BPC), which highlighted 20 behavioral signs common to child and adolescent MPD. As well, three levels of family pathology and appropriate intervention were described. Bowman, Blix, and Coons (1985) reviewed a case of MPD in a 14-and-a-half-year-old female adolescent and offered discussion regarding iatrogenesis and treatment.

Kluft (1984) presented a literature review and described five cases of childhood MPD. In two seminal books, Kluft (1985) and Braun (1986) further reviewed the literature and the familial-systemic features and factors of MPD. They also proposed treatment strategies based on anecdotal clinical experiences.

Putnam (1989) described an MPD checklist, as well as signs and symptoms of child and adolescent MPD. In a subsequent article, Putnam (1991) further identified the developmental substrates inherent to MPD and dissociative disorders.

Dell and Eisenhower (1990) reported on 11 cases of adolescent MPD and reviewed their clinical presentations. (Some of their data are presented here in the Recent Research section.) Finally, Hornstein and Tyson (1991) presented a concise review of the assessment, treatment, and management of children and adolescents in a general adolescent psychiatric facility.

Signs and Symptoms

For inexperienced practitioners, dissociative disorders may be difficult to diagnose definitively in adolescence, as many of the symptoms may appear to overlap with other diagnostic categories. Once one is conversant with dissociative phenomenology, however, the diagnostic process is simplified. The aforementioned review articles contain many checklists and symptoms clusters. They, along with the work of Reagor, Kastner, and Morell (1992), Waters (1989), and others provide us with a large selection of clinical criteria in arriving at the dissociative diagnosis. Following are a few of the symptoms and signs these authors have found to be of more substantial benefit.

1. *History of Early Childhood Trauma* — A vast majority (over 90%) of adolescents with a dissociative disorder will report a positive history of sexual, physical, severe emotional abuse, or all of these. It is common for

the abuse to have occurred early in development, to have occurred often, and that more than one perpetrator be involved.

2. *Absence of Parental Support (during the trauma)* — It is not uncommon for both parents to be perpetrators, or to be absent or passive. Given a transgenerational pattern of abuse, there is often a parallel transgenerational dissociative response for both perpetrator and victim.

3. *Absence States* — Blanking out, trancelike episodes, and excessive daydreaming occur in a large majority of cases.

4. *Amnestic/Memory Problems* — A perplexing, excessive forgetfulness occurs in virtually all MPD sufferers and includes recent events, names of close friends, and so on.

5. *Mood-State Changes* — Rapid mood swings from profound despair to elation to aggressive affectivity are extremely common and may change frequently throughout a day.

6. *Inconsistent and Unpredictable Behaviors* — This symptom is, again, virtually universally reported. The patient may dress very conservatively one moment, then seductively shortly thereafter. She or he may enjoy ice cream, yet be revolted by it next time. There are often changes in physical skills and attributes; for example, handwriting and handedness changes.

7. *Hearing Internal Voices* — These voices are associated with internal alter ego states and fragments and can be of any gender, and the content can be either helpful or demeaning. Such voices are often confused with psychosis-generated auditory hallucinations and may provide the therapist access to the alters' system.

8. *Denial of Observed Behaviors* — A very common sign. The adolescent is viewed as lying and manipulative, although his or her protestations are sincere.

9. *Somatic Complaints/Headaches/Unexplained Injuries* — It is common to have somatic correlates to abreactive memories and dissociation, and common areas of complaint are genitourinary and gastrointestinal. Headaches are extremely common, often correspond to alter switching, and are complex in nature. Persecutory alters often inflict self-mutilative wounds to promote continued secrecy and self-punishment.

10. *Inconsistent School Performance* — Adolescents will very commonly demonstrate rapid fluctuant performance, for example, from excellence to failure.

11. *Prior Diagnoses* — Adolescents are often diagnosed with a variety of disorders on the basis of the multitude of associated symptoms,

including disruptive behavior disorders (oppositional defiant disorder and conduct disorder), mood disorders, posttraumatic stress disorders, attentional and learning disorders, identity and personality disorders, eating disorders, and psychoses.

12. *Prior Treatment Failure(s)* — It is common for an adolescent to have had numerous contacts with many components of the mental health care system, to have received many treatments, and with little or no symptom resolution.

13. *Sleep Disturbances and Nightmares* — At least 75% of adolescents present with such problems, and nightmares are often associated with memory retrieval or alter intrusion.

14. *Family History of Dissociative Disorders* — In parallel to a transgenerational pattern of abuse, it is becoming increasingly evident that the sequelae of such abuses are also transgenerational in transmission.

15. *Reference to Internal Multiplicity* — An adolescent will refer to himself or herself as "we" or use third-person language to describe aspects of his or her own life.

16. *Sexualized Behaviors* — Such behaviors as early sexualized activities, inappropriate dress, poor boundary relations, and sexualized transference reactions to therapists are commonly encountered.

17. *Regressive Episodes* — Transient regressions to infantile behaviors, for example, thumbsucking, childlike language, and loss of more developed motor skills, often occur and may be associated with child alters.

18. *Self-Mutilative Behaviors* — It is very common for adolescents with dissociative disorders to engage in self-injurious and risky behaviors, and often not to recall their actions afterwards.

Recent Research

Three sets of clinical research data have been chosen to represent some of the more recent preliminary studies regarding dissociative disorders in adolescents.

DELL AND EISENHOWER (1990)

This clinical report presented 11 adolescents whom the authors assessed and followed in therapy over a four-year period and who were clinically diagnosed with MPD.

Table 1 represents the symptoms observed by the interviewers during the original diagnostic interviews with the adolescent population. Over

TABLE 1
PRESENTING SYMPTOMS

Symptoms	% (of cases positive)
1. Depression (9/11)	82%
2. Voices (9/11)	82%
3. Amnesia (9/11)	82%
4. School Problems (9/11)	82%
5. Behavioral Problems (8/11)	73%
6. Nightmares (7/11)	64%
7. Headaches (6/11)	55%
8. Drug Abuse (4/11)	36%
9. Violent (4/11)	36%
10. Self-Mutilation (3/11)	27%
11. Phobia (2/11)	18%
12. Eating Disorders (2/11)	18%

Note: From Dell and Eisenhower (1990). Adapted by permission.

70% of the adolescents displayed behavioral problems, school problems, or both; amnesia; internal voices; and depression.

The authors also reported on Fagan and McMahon's (1984) Behavior Problem Checklist (BPC), which was completed on all 11 adolescents. Although the BPC is a 20-item checklist, Table 2 represents only those items which showed a major incidence.

Dell and Eisenhower (1990) reported on the incidence of other DSM

TABLE 2
BEHAVIORAL PROBLEM CHECKLIST (BPC) SYMPTOM INCIDENCE

Symptoms	% (of patients with symptoms)
1. Schoolwork very changeable (11/11)	100%
2. Dazes, trances (10/11)	91%
3. Major forgetfulness (10/11)	91%
4. Big changes in personality (9/11)	82%
5. Lying	82%
6. Perplexes professionals (9/11)	82%
7. Discipline is ineffective (8/11)	73%
8. Suicidal (7/11)	64%
9. Stealing, destructive (7/11)	64%
10. Illness, injuries (7/11)	64%
11. Odd changes in physical skills (6/11)	55%
12. Behavior problem in school (6/11)	55%
13. Stoic in face of punishment (6/11)	55%
14. Uses more than one name (6/11)	55%
15. Aggressive/homicidal (6/11)	55%

Note: From Dell and Eisenhower (1990). Adapted by permission.

III-R conditions, including 64% with mood disorders, 55% with disruptive behavior disorders, 45% with PTSD, and 18% with borderline personality disorder. They further reported that 82% of their population eventually was positive for the diagnosis of PTSD.

FLEISHER, ANDERSON, AND ROSS (1989)

These data are based on a population of 11 adolescents who were clinically diagnosed with MPD according to DSM criteria. They all completed the Dissociative Experiences Scale (DES) (Bernstein and Putnam, 1986), a 28-item self-report scale, and the Dissociative Disorders Interview Schedule (DDIS) (Ross et al., 1989), a 131-item structured interview, which makes DSM III-R diagnoses of somatization disorder, major depression, borderline personality disorder, and all the dissociative disorders. It also inquires about histories of abuse and a number of secondary MPD features. Table 3 presents the symptom clusters for this adolescent sample.

It is worthwhile noting the high DES score, which is comparable to an average score for normal adolescents of 17.7 and for college students of 7.9 (Ross et al., 1989). Fifty-four and a half percent of the population was positive for DSM III-R substance abuse; 72.7% were positive for depression, as well as for borderline personality disorder.

The incidence of trauma was high, as expected, as shown in Table 4.

The average duration of sexual abuse at the time of diagnosis was 7.1 years; for physical abuse, 8.2 years. The average number of perpetrators was 1.6 for both the sexual- and physical-abuse groups.

TABLE 3
SYMPTOM CLUSTERS IN ADOLESCENT MPD

Symptom Cluster (maximum possible)	Average Positive
Somatic Symptoms (34)	5.4
Positive Amnesia Items (4)	3.1
Schneiderian Symptoms (11)	5.9
Secondary Features MPD (16)	8.4
Borderline Criteria (8)	5.3
ESP Experiences (6)	4.7
Suicide Attempts	2.2
DES Score	35.9

Note: From Fleisher, Anderson, and Ross (1989). Adapted by permission.

TABLE 4
TRAUMA HISTORIES

Item	% Positive
Sexual Abuse	81.8
Physical Abuse	63.6
Sexual Abuse and/or Physical Abuse	90.9

Note: From Fleisher, Anderson, and Ross (1989). Adapted by permission.

ROSS, KRONSON, AND HILDAHL (1990)

This clinical report assessed 45 adolescents referred to an adolescent treatment facility. All the participants had completed the DES and DDIS. The results of the study are shown in Table 5.

Among all the subjects, 44.4% (20/45) met criteria for a DD, whereas 55.6% were negative; 15.6% (7/45) met criteria for MPD. Interestingly, the physical abuse rate of 26.7% and sexual abuse rate of 17.8% were identical in both groups. One possibility is that some DD symptoms were mood disorder in nature. Another possibility was that the abuse histories were unknown at the time of admission.

The DD group had an average of over twice the somatic symptoms as the No DD group. Secondary MPD features were significantly higher in the DD group, as were the borderline features. The DD group had a significant three-fold increase in ESP/supernatural experiences, as well as an increased likelihood of having attempted suicide. Finally, the DES score also differentiated between the two populations. Although clinical validation studies were not done in this study, it appears that DD are common in an adolescent inpatient population.

TABLE 5
SYMPTOM CLUSTER CHARACTERISTICS OF ADOLESCENTS WITH DISSOCIATIVE DISORDERS

Symptom Cluster	DD (N = 20)	No DD (N = 25)	significance (p value)
Maximum items possible	Average number positive		
Somatic symptoms [34]	5.4	2.6	.04
Secondary Features of MPD [16]	4.3	1.4	.00001
Borderline Criteria [8]	3.6	1.6	.0004
ESP/Supernatural Experiences [6]	3.8	1.2	.0003
Suicide Attempts	1.4	0.2	.04
DES Score	20.4	13.5	.04

Note: From Ross, Kronson, and Hildahl (1990). Adapted by permission.

Treatment Principles in Working with Dissociative Adolescents

There are very little research data available to gauge the outcome of treatment techniques, and such research would be difficult to gather, given the need to "customize" treatment to any given adolescent. Earlier case reports suggested that treatment of children and adolescents might require less time than for adults. This assumption might need to be revised as more experience is gathered. Nonetheless, certain principles appear to be paramount in therapeutic work with dissociative adolescents.

1. *Trust and Rapport*—These form the key to successful treatment for all traumatized patients. Many clinicians conclude that the quality of the therapeutic alliance is more significant in treatment outcome than is the complexity of the dissociation or the severity of traumatization.

2. *Safe, Nurturing Environment*— Therapeutic intervention cannot proceed while the adolescent is still in danger of ongoing trauma. The therapy itself must be paced, and a safety monitoring system often is of great benefit to the patient–therapist relationship.

3. *Empathic yet Nonengulfing Stance*—A therapist needs to convey empathy and understanding for all personalities. This does not translate into rescuing, feeling sympathy, trying to replace the patient's parents, or attempting to please the patient through favoritism.

4. *Explicit Boundaries and Limits*—A secure, clear treatment context is needed for all personalities. Expectations and limits often benefit from explicit contracting between therapist, treatment team, and adolescent.

5. *Mapping the System*—This is an ongoing process throughout the therapy and allows the recording of the internal personalities and their relationships to one another. Mapping assists in delineating the tasks at hand and allows for ongoing monitoring of progress.

6. *"Interalter" Communication and Acceptance*—This is a central process of therapy in which the therapist accepts and spends time with all the personalities in order to facilitate the beginning of cooperation and cohesion. Nontraditional interventions (art therapy, videotaping, journaling) often are of great primary or adjunct benefit.

7. *Breaking Down Amnestic Barriers*—The development of coconsciousness among the personalities is a gradual, ongoing process and is necessary to alleviate blank spells. The barriers usually come down once memories are shared and processed and are able to be tolerated by the personalities.

8. *Memory Recovery and Abreaction*—As memories are uncovered, the associated feelings are often abreacted. Often frightening to both therapist and patient, this reexperiencing can be modulated and harnessed in the therapy to promote control and self-ownership for the patient. The presence of genuine abreaction is a potential guide to the authenticity of the content revealed.

9. *Responsibility and Blame*—The therapist must be responsible to the process of therapy and hold the client to a high standard of responsibility. Such responsibility breaks the cycle of irresponsibility of others that gives rise to the dissociation/MPD. Although a certain alter personality may have committed unacceptable acts, the whole person (including other alters) has to be held accountable so that the patient can function as a more responsible person as therapy proceeds. This is fundamental in breaking cycles of abuse.

10. *Sociofamilial Interventions*—Adolescent MPD patients can particularly benefit from systemic interventions and supports, including family, school, and friends. These interventions may range from psychoeducational to supportive to dynamically oriented in nature and may alleviate some of the isolation inherent to the disorder.

11. *Integration*—As the need for keeping secrets or sequestering memory and affects diminishes, the gradual coming together of the parts will begin, either spontaneously or with the assistance of the therapist.

12. *Postintegration*—The integrative adolescents face many new challenges, including solidifying their new gains, establishing different communications with significant others, and beginning to accept the challenges of life relevant to their developmental stage.

Countertransference Issues

Given the complexity of treatment and the often horrific nature of the endured traumata, it is not surprising that therapists react strongly to their clients' issues. Although the strict context of countertransference implies an unconscious process, a more general understanding includes conscious reactions as well. The more general meaning of countertransference is used here.

Although classic countertransference refers to an individual therapist's reactions, our belief and experience is that systemic countertransferential reactions are equally, if not more, toxic to the progress of therapy. Depending on the work setting, a systemic countertransference can occur at many system levels, including the therapeutic team, the hospital ward, the department level, the hospital administration, child and family agencies, and the governmental level. These systemic countertransferences will reflect the full gamut of responses, from those experienced by the individual therapist to the din of debate our society currently undertakes in its attempts to work through and understand such horrors.

Several authors have addressed some of these countertransference phenomena. Olson, Mayton, and Braun (1987) referred to the therapist's reactions as "secondary Posttraumatic Stress Disorder" and alluded to such reactions as numbing, problems with affect regulation, a hypervigilant societal stance, and a propensity to relive one's own trauma. Kluft (1989) referred to the rehabilitation of therapists overwhelmed by their work with dissociative patients. McCann and Pearlman (1990) used the term "vicarious traumatization" and presented a constructivist self-development theoretic paradigm to explore this area. Finally, Davies and Frawley (1992) presented a comprehensive review of dynamically based issues related to countertransference.

Our experience and observations in therapist-systemic countertransference have varied. First, there is a form of disavowal, in which the dissociative features are unattended and the therapeutic focus shifts instead to the borderline phenomenology. Second, there is often a form of identification with the aggressor in which the therapist becomes angry toward the client, often accusing him or her of being manipulative and disruptive. Third, there is a great deal of skepticism regarding the client and his or her revelations, often fueled by the failure of the system or therapist to have either protected the victim or succeeded in alleviating the pain. Finally, and of great importance, is the process of splitting, giving rise to idealization and devaluation. As a consequence, certain clients are devalued in many systems, and the therapeutic staff splits into proponents and antagonists. In hospitals, the staff will express such splitting by attributing specialness to certain patients while devaluing others. And even this process, which belongs to the system, becomes blamed (i.e., counterprojected) on the client.

In our anecdotal experience with other therapists, some countertransferential consequences appear to be more common. There are often significant problems in limit setting, and the precarious therapeutic balance between being too close versus being overly harsh and potentially rejecting is difficult to maintain. Therapists often experience periodic bouts of denial regarding the validity of their clients' reports. They often have a sense of voyeuristic curiosity in excess of therapeutic appropriateness. Finally, as the therapy progresses, and the more regressive and potentially aggressive elements surface, many therapists begin to fear for their own safety and often withdraw from the therapeutic relationship. These common countertransferences may at times significantly impede the forward progress of therapy, and require attention, which might include a peer-supervision group process, formal supervision, or the therapist's obtaining personal therapy. If the countertransference reactions are not amenable to understanding and modification, termination ot transfer of therapy must be considered.

Reporting on work with 20 MPD patients, Coons (1986) reviewed various reactions therapists experienced.

As shown in Table 6, a majority of therapists experienced exasperation (75%), anger (58%), and emotional exhaustion (50%). Desire to rescue (33%), vicarious enjoyment (17%), and fear of acting out (17%) were common, while 8% reported outside socialization, depression, lack of appointment promptness, overinvolvement, and inability to set limits.

Conclusion

As this clinical area is further studied, new nomenclature is being proposed. Ross (1989) suggested the conceptualization of a chronic trauma disorder. Herman (1992) recently proposed a subset of the posttrauma spectrum, which she called complex PTSD. Finally, Peterson (1991) summarized the history and issues of childhood MPD and argued for the creation of a diagnostic category called dissociative identity disorder.

The field of dissociative disorders in adolescence is still in its explor-

TABLE 6
COUNTERTRANSFERENCE EXPERIENCED BY THERAPISTS OF 20 PATIENTS WITH MPD

Type	Frequency %
Exasperation	75
Anger	58
Emotional Exhaustion	50
Desire to Rescue	33
Vicarious Enjoyment	17
Fear of Acting Out	8
Socialization Outside of Therapy	8
Depression	8
Late for Appointments	8
Overinvolvement	8
Inability to Set Limits	8

Note: From Coons (1986). Reprinted by permission.

atory phase, and many questions remain unanswered. The efficacy of various modalities of treatment, difficult to measure even in less complex disorders, is still unknown beyond the growing body of anecdotal clinical reporting. Although the incidence of DD in adult inpatient psychiatric patients is being explored (Ross et al., 1991), the incidence of adolescent disturbance remains unknown.

REFERENCES

Bernstein, E. M. & Putnam, F. W. (1986), Development, reliability, and validity of a dissociation scale. *J. Nerv. Ment. Dis.*, 174:727–735.

Bowman, E., Blix, S. & Coons, P. X. (1985), Multiple personality in adolescence: relationship to incestual experiences. *J. Amer. Acad. Child Psychiat.*, 24:109–114.

Braun, B. (1986), *Treatment of Multiple Personality Disorder*. Washington, DC: American Psychiatric Press.

Coons, P. N. (1986), Treatment progress in 20 patients with multiple personality disorder. *J. Nerv. Ment. Dis.*, 174:715–721.

Davies, J. M. & Frawley, M. G. (1992), Dissociative processes and transference: Countertransference paradigms in the psychoanalytically oriented treatment of adult survivors of childhood sexual abuse. *Psychoanal. Dial.*, 2:5–36.

Dell, P. & Eisenhower, J. (1990), Adolescent multiple personality disorder: a preliminary study of eleven cases. *J. Amer. Acad. Child Adoles. Psychiat.*, 29:359–366.

Fagan, J. & McMahon, P. (1984), Incipient multiple personality in children. *J. Nerv. Ment. Dis.*, 172:26–36.

Fleisher, W. P., Anderson, G. & Ross, C. A. (1989), Multiple personality disorder in adolescence and adulthood. In: *Proceedings of the Sixth International Conference on Multiple Personality/Dissociative States*, ed. B. Braun, Chicago: Rush University, p. 163.

Herman, J. L. (1992), Complex PTSD: A syndrome in survivors of prolonged and repeated trauma. *J. Traumatic Stress*, 5377–391.

Hornstein, N. & Tyson, S. (1991), Inpatient treatment of children with multiple personality/dissociative disorders and their families. *Psychiat. Clin. N. Amer.*, 14:631–647.

Kluft, R. (1984), Multiple personality in childhood. *Psychiat. Clin. N. Amer.*, 7:121–134.

_____ ed. (1985), *Childhood Antecedents of Multiple Personality*. Washington, DC: American Psychiatric Press.

_____ (1989), The rehabilitation of therapists overwhelmed by their work with multiple personality disorder patients. *Dissociation*, 2:243–249.

McCann, L. & Pearlman, L. A. (1990), Vicarious traumatization: A framework for understanding the psychological effects of working with victims. *J. Traumatic Stress*, 3:131–149.

Olson, J., Mayton, K. & Braun, B. (1987), Secondary posttraumatic stress and countertransference: Responding to victims of severe violence. *Proceedings of the Fourth International Conference on Multiple Personality/Dissociative States*, ed. B. Braun. Chicago: Rush University, p. 29.

Peterson, G. (1991), Children coping with trauma: Diagnosis of dissociation identity disorder. *Dissociation*, 4:152–164.

Putnam, F. (1989), *Diagnosis and Treatment of Multiple Personality Disorder*. New York: Guilford.

Putnam, F. (1991), Dissociative disorders in children and adolescents. *Psychiat. Clin. N. Amer.*, 14:519–531.

Reagor, P., Kasten, J. & Morelli, N. (1992), A checklist for screening dissociative disorders in children and adolescents. *Dissociation*, 8:4–19.

Ross, C. A. (1989), *Multiple Personality Disorder: Diagnosis, Clinical Features and Treatment*. New York: Wiley.

_____ Anderson, G., Fleisher, W. P. & Norton, G. R. (1991), The frequency of multiple personality disorder among psychiatric inpatients. *Amer. J. Psychiat.*, 148: 1717–1720.

_____ Heber, S., Norton, G. R., Anderson, D., Anderson, G. & Barchet, P. (1989), The dissociative disorders interview schedule: A structured interview. *Dissociation*, 2:169–189.

_____ Kronson, J. & Hildahl, K. (1990), Dissociative disorders in an adolescent psychiatric caseload. Unpublished manuscript.

_____ Ryan, L., Anderson, G., Ross, D. & Hardy, L. (1989), Dissociative experiences in adolescents and college students. *Dissociation*, 2:239–242.

Sanders, B. & Giolas, M. (1991), Dissociation and childhood trauma in psychologically disturbed adolescents. *Amer. J. Psychiat.*, 148:50–54.

Waters, F. S. (1989), Non-hypnotic therapeutic techniques of multiple personality in children. *Proceedings of the Sixth International Conference on Multiple Personality/Dissociative States*, ed. B. Braun, Chicago: Rush University, p. 165.

15 THE CHILD AND ADOLESCENT LITERATURE ABOUT THE DEATH OF A PARENT

BENJAMIN GARBER

In recent years, death, dying, and bereavement have received increasing attention from psychoanalysts and from workers in related disciplines. The rapid increase in scientific and popular publications on death suggests that there is a change underway in our attitudes about death. It appears that we are starting to examine death and dying more realistically and that we allow ourselves more empathy with the dying and the bereaved (Furman, 1974).

As more books and newspaper and magazine articles have been published on this subject, the community has made a strong demand for professional help with all situations involving death or dying. As such expectations have emerged in regard to adults, there has been a parallel increase in the demand to help children understand and deal with bereavement.

While such a demand and expectation is increasing, there is a parallel attempt to protect children from knowing and understanding the irreversibility and horrors of death. Instead of transmitting useful and honest information to children about death and dying, which would help them to cope with such crises, adults tend to pass on fairy tales, distortions, evasions, and, most important, their own anxiety about death.

The open and honest curiosity that is so natural to children is thwarted, for in response to their questions they receive denial and misinformation. The child's interest and adult's defensiveness about death is similar to earlier attitudes about sexuality; children are not only curious about where people came from but also about where they go.

All of us who study reactions to death, particularly in children, are handicapped to some extent by our cultural and individual attitudes to this troublesome topic. The traumatic impressions connected with the form of death are particularly difficult for child patients to face and are usually augmented by the tendency of surviving adults to lie about what happened. The adults are themselves so upset by the horror of the form of the death that they cannot truthfully discuss anything about it.

In recent times there has emerged a greater awareness, recognition, and appreciation of children's curiosity and concern about death and dying. Why this is so is not clear. It may well be an evolution of a natural cultural trend toward a greater openness and confrontation with the unknown. One aspect of this evolution has been a greater demand by the lay public for literature to help educate children about bereavement. This demand is in concert with an increased sophistication of psychoanalytic and developmental understanding of children's reactions to the death of a parent (Pollock, 1977; Garber, 1981; Sekaer and Katz, 1986). The result of such changes has been a proliferation of bereavement literature for grieving children.

The purpose of this chapter is to examine current trends in children's literature about the death of a parent. These trends will be correlated with children's understanding of death as a function of their level of psychosexual development. To make this examination complete, there will be a general discussion of children's literature and the concept of death as presented in children's books.

Although children may experience a variety of losses, the loss of a parent stands apart from all others as a trauma of unique proportions in scope, magnitude, and future ramifications.

Children's Stories and Fairy Tales

Children's stories and fairy tales represent various efforts to explain and deal with the phenomenon of human existence. Children's books not only express the way people think, feel, hope, desire, believe, and behave, but they also reinforce these things along idealistic lines. Children's stories satisfy and further our basic emotional needs while simultaneously trying to strengthen our faith and morality (Friedlander, 1942).

Children's literature of any given period is an important cultural and psychological interface between the world of the adult and the world of the child. The primary purpose of children's literature is to transmit our cultural heritage. Among all the media with which the child is presented, literature carries that information best from generation to generation (Heuscher, 1963).

Literature has a number of important functions during the periods of a child's development. These include the acquisition of knowledge, strengthening the capacity to fantasy, stretching the imagination, allowing temporary exercise of primary-process faculties for attainment of higher level secondary-process integration, and permitting some degree of empathic identification with a particular person, situation, or affect (Bettelheim, 1977).

As the child is presented with a story or fairy tale, he projects himself wholeheartedly into the main character of the story and identifies with the character's traumas, conflicts, and triumphs. The more direct and straightforward the character, the easier it is for the child to identify with him.

For a story truly to hold the child's attention, it must entertain him and arouse his curiosity. It must stimulate his imagination, help him develop his intellect, clarify his emotions, be attuned to his anxieties and aspirations, give full recognition to his difficulties, while at the same time giving solutions to the problems that perturb him. While this is a tall order, some component of these expectations needs to be present in every story (Peller, 1959).

A wide array of ingredients goes into the making of a good children's book. Among these are literary, artistic, and aesthetic considerations. These are beyond the range and special competence of child psychoanalysts. From the emotional perspective, however, such a book should engage the child in an experience of growth in a manner and at a pace and in areas congruent with the child's major developmental needs and capacities (Peller, 1959; Goldings, 1968).

Children's stories retain their appeal through the ages because they touch on the child's developmental conflict of that time period. Often a story's maximum effectiveness is based on its expression of the child's primary developmental fantasy. Stories dealing with loss and return may have a marked appeal to the preoedipal child. Heroic tales, especially those where a small hero overcomes terrifying giants, will appeal to the oedipal child, while stories about a group of companions or twins may be exceptionally appealing for latency children (Peller, 1959). A fear or developmental anxiety of a particular phase may become broadly visible through the child's reaction to the story. He discovers through the story that he is not the only one in the world who is struggling with such conflicting forces. While the elements of the story are retained in consciousness, the underlying meaning needs to remain unconscious; otherwise, the pleasure in the story will be diminished. This is essential so that the instinctual elements may be discharged in a manner that is ego syntonic.

Because of their touching, focusing, and expressing specific developmental conflicts, children's stories have been seen as helping children cope with the psychological problems of growing up. A child will lose interest in a particular story if the problem that it helped him cope with is replaced by another problem, or if he has progressed to the next developmental phase.

Fairy tales and stories serve the child well as they may make unbearable life worth living. Therefore, it is important for fairy tales to have a happy ending, for then the child can borrow these hopes for his own future. The fantasy has to allow a chance for recovery from the trauma, an avenue for escape, and a notion of consolation.

Although children's stories may serve as an arena for the discharge of forbidden impulses, just as often they serve as an avenue for mastery and adaptation. However interesting and enjoyable a story may be, its ultimate staying power will depend on how the story ended. In other words, it is crucial for the child to know how the hero resolved his conflict. Unless that is done in a satisfactory manner, the child will not be moved by the story's content.

Children's books and stories have always been an important element of the adult educating the child. The pleasure and knowledge that children experience from reading or having stories read to them and the pleasure that adults experience in reading to the child have remained basic ingredients of human development. Children remember favorite stories that were read to them by parents and cherish the interactions that surround the reading experience.

Since the desire for stories gives the child a chance to see what adults are doing, it is also an opportunity to see how adults handle and deal with the subject of death. Consequently, the child's awareness of, interest in, and curiosity about death has been an integral part of children's stories.

Death in Children's Stories

Death is a common occurrence in children's books and fairy tales. Almost always it is treated matter of factly in line with other events of the story. There is little meaning or significance attached to it as there is minimal mourning in children's stories. Frequently death is used as a punishment that is a natural outcome of being bad or destructive.

Often, death is made palatable in children's books. This may be accomplished by equating death with a long sleep state. The person who died may be transformed into an animal, or he may be brought back to life. The process of dying may be reversible and consequently tolerable. In those situations where death is irreversible, the child may be offered a quick replacement as a means of not dwelling on the loss. Since the consequences of the loss may be minimal, then, at best, mourning is equated with a temporary state of sadness. Active mourning rituals are seldom found in children's stories.

In children's stories death is frequently personified. This personification takes place in two ways: death is imagined as a separate person, or else death is identified with the dead (Plank and Plank, 1978).

In many stories death is rejected by children in order to be tolerated, or the finality of death is constantly being questioned. Yet the fear of death is ever-present and is most likely inborn. Since death is presented unrealistically in children's stories and since parents are reluctant to discuss death with younger children, it is not surprising that children may have great difficulty comprehending the death of someone close to them.

When death occurs in children's stories, it is a passing phenomenon that is devoid of meaning and understanding. It is treated with the same casualness as any other element of the story, so that its deeper meanings and ramifications are avoided. In spite of such avoidances, children continue to express curiosity about death and its significance. Whether it is the death of a pet or a person, children exhibit an ongoing fascination with death and a curiosity that will not be denied by adult avoidances and distortions.

Children's Books About Parent Loss

Even though the subject of death is painful and children are shielded from its impact, there are a large number and variety of children's books dealing with this subject. There are books about every type of loss that a child may experience: parent, grandparent, friend, pet, and assorted relatives. Many authors cite personal experiences with loss as stimuli for these literary efforts. The notion of literature as a vehicle of mastery is a common theme for many writers.

While a number of the books were well written, insightful, and informative, I was dismayed by how many demonstrated minimal empathy for the psychological world of the child. Many of the books were one dimensional, superficial, and embarrassingly contrived.[1]

---

[1]The material for this study was collected from 80 children's books from three libraries. All of these books were written in the last 25 years.

In examining these books it became evident that they fall into two broad and distinct categories. Books in the larger group tell a story about a loss and are geared to elicit an emotional response. A smaller group of books imparts information about death and dying. A few books made a valiant attempt to integrate both goals by presenting brief clinical vignettes with accompanying explanations. It is most useful to view both categories of books as complementing each other depending on the particular needs of the child.

The books that tell a story about the death of a parent are diverse in that they pick up the process at different points in time. Most of the stories were well written and richly illustrated. Although the stories differed in content, they shared certain commonalities. These books touched on developmental conflicts and their interplay with the child's reaction to the loss.

Most stories begin in a setting in which a parent is dead or dying, and adults attempt to hide the truth from the child. This is similar to parental secretiveness about sexuality because its presence is not acknowledged. However, the child discovers the truth, which makes the adults appear foolish in their evasiveness and secretiveness. Just as primal-scene discovery is denied, so is the reality of death. Consequently, the child's reality-testing equipment may become compromised. Bowlby (1960) was explicit about the long-term danger for the child when facts about a death are hidden, distorted, or denied. Avoidance of the truth is more common with younger children, for adults have an overwhelming need to shield younger children from the experience of death.

With older children, such protectiveness diminishes, and they are informed within a reasonable time, albeit with evasiveness and delay. The necessity of telling children the truth no matter what their age is a common theme that permeates many writings. The idea that falsehood, deceptions, and distortion interfere with mourning is a commonplace in the literature.

In most books, the hero of the story is an only child. While this makes for a cleaner story line, it is an unrealistic situation and not conducive to adaptation to the loss. Such a family constellation is rife for oedipal victory fantasies with the child replacing the dead parent. The child's sleeping in the parental bed and displaying hypermature behavior contributes to massive identifications that interfere with mourning. The reversal of roles is another potential outcome in such a familial constellation.

The importance and usefulness of siblings is not recognized or appreciated in the literature. For an older sibling to assume a temporary parental role in the eyes of a grieving child is potentially helpful in adapting to the loss. While pathological adaptations may occur in any familial constellation, the variety of possibilities and their potential outcomes are not adequately addressed in the literature.

The preloss situations were evenly divided between the idealized and the conflictual. For younger children, the preloss parent possessed admirable qualities that were not recognized or appreciated till after the death. The parent was seen as wise, kind, giving, and understanding. These qualities were discovered while the parent was dying in a courageous manner. The parent's flaws in the preloss relationship did not exist, or they were minor. Such an idealization is developmentally appropriate, yet it may also interfere with the child's anger toward the lost object. While the child is angry at the parent for having died, there is also a need to be angry for parental shortcomings while alive. Such a need is seldom recognized in the literature, so that anger is an uncommon affect.

For older children and preadolescents, the parent–child relationship was more conflictual. There was a conflict between the child and the surviving parent, which was resolved before the end of the story. The dichotomy may be related to the authors' accurate perceptions that younger children have a greater need to idealize both parents. The children in these stories displayed an uncommonly narrow range of affective reactions in response to the loss. The most common affective state portrayed is longing and sadness. All the youngsters experienced massive doses of sadness. This is appropriate, as sadness is the most prominent affective state. It is easiest to identify and the easiest for adults to empathize with. In many stories there are flashes of anger. These are transient and directed at the person who died for having died. The anger is also at the unfairness and injustice of it all. I have yet to read a story in which anger is directed at the lost object for being deficient while alive. The lack of anger is plausible as it is the most difficult affect for adults to admit toward the dead. Children are much freer with their anger toward the dead, but, then, these stories were not written by children.

Anxiety is a prominent and pervasive affect in most stories. The anxiety is about the surviving parent's dying or the child's dying (or both). Clinical experience has shown that children may experience a fear or dread that the dead will come back to haunt the living. There may also be anxiety about having wished the parent to die and the anticipated retaliation, as well as guilt from an oedipal victory. None of these issues

223

dealing with anxiety as a derivative of rage were addressed in the stories. Current or past anger toward the dead was played down and diminished in importance.

One of the commonest affects of mourning was neglected in most stories about younger children. The shame and embarrassment about having lost a parent and being different from others was not addressed except in stories about adolescents. The associated embarrassment about being deficient and lacking and being thrust in the spotlight is a common affective reaction in bereaved children. Apparently embarrassment in younger children is neither recognized nor fully appreciated.

All the stories lacked the recognition and appreciation of acute grief that is akin to a somatic response. The sense of pain and tearing away that one may experience as a physical sensation in one's chest or abdomen is completely ignored. It is the episodic grief response that sets the mourning process in motion.

A conclusion from these stories is that the authors lack an appreciation of the richness of children's affective experience in dealing with loss.

One of the main strengths of many books is the emphasis on remembering as an integral part of mourning. Several books made remembering their primary focus. The emphasis on older children's remembering through recalling mutual experiences and younger children's repeating activities that were done with the lost parent are essential for mourning to occur. Remembering as a means of maintaining a connection and continuity with the lost object's strengths and deficits are basic elements of the mourning process. However, the overdetermined preoccupation with memories, that are devoid of significant affects and repeated in a stereotyped manner, may be used defensively by children who are incapable of progressing in the process (Garber, 1981). In such instances the remembering becomes a major defense seldom appreciated by adults. The singular place of remembering as a focus of mourning, however, is a pervasive theme in most stories. While the authors appreciate the importance of memories for mourning, it is likely that memories make for a more interesting story.

The adults in most stories are perceived as helpful to the grieving child, perhaps not perfectly empathic and at times stumbling in their responses; nevertheless, the adults make repeated efforts to help the child. In several stories the adults were depicted as cold, aloof, unempathic, and hostile vis-à-vis the mourning child. The stories where the adult seemed unhelpful came across as exceptionally contrived. There were instances where the adults were depicted as overly sweet, helpful, empathic, and understanding, so much so that one would wonder whether such portrayals defended against underlying anger, competitiveness, and blaming the child for the loss. Envy of the child who has many years ahead of him while the surviving parent does not may have also been defended in such portrayals.

While there are many books about the loss of a parent, two stand out that are exceptionally insightful. Even though *Charlotte's Web* by E. B. White (1952) was written 40 years ago, it is a classic tale about the meaning and significance of loss. This book does not deal with the death of a parent, nor does it deal with human loss. It approaches the subject of loss in a manner that is experience near and yet appropriately distant.

It is a beautiful story of animals assuming human characteristics in which a close bond develops between a pig and a spider. The spider becomes a parent substitute and protects the pig from being slaughtered. The pig is portrayed as selfish and needy, not unlike younger children who want to know who will take care of them before the dead parent is buried. Ultimately the pig's success is enhanced by the spider, who dies of old age. The story has a happy ending, however, as the spider leaves a sac of eggs that hatches many spiders who keep the pig company for the rest of his life.

The story has a fairy-tale quality and deals with the subject of loss in a highly intelligent and emotional manner. Yet it allows a detachment and distance that is appropriate for children's stories. It offers pearls of wisdom about interactions between people and animals without moralizing or seeming contrived. It is an ideal story about loss for children and for the child within the adult who has lost someone important.

Another useful book dealing with loss is *How It Feels When a Parent Dies* by Jill Krementz (1981). This book has moving accounts by children who lost a parent. Each one of the 18 children talks in the first person about his or her loss. Their experiences are accompanied by photographs. The children's stories are detailed and personal. One is moved by these youngsters' accounts about themselves, the death, and the lost parent. One can sense the grief, the sadness, and, at times, the anger.

Unfortunately, some of the accounts sound as if they are those of older children, as their words were edited to sound mature. While grieving youngsters mature too quickly, it is doubtful that they can express themselves as fluently and maturely as the author portrays. This book underlines a significant developmental conflict for a grieving child. Children who experience parental loss are expected to grow up too quickly. The leisurely to-and-fro rhythm of development becomes accelerated as the child is expected to shoulder heavier responsibilities. He is constantly urged to grow up, which dovetails with the latency child's inherent tendency to comply. The net result is a child who is uneven developmentally. Such a youngster may experience the tension that accompanies uneven developmental states. Consequently, he may do well during times of crisis but may decompensate during periods of stability.

Nevertheless, this is a useful book because it allows the child to identify with the affects and experiences of others in similar circumstances. The book also addresses his adaptive capacities, for it shows how others have dealt with and adapted to a trauma of monumental proportions.

Upon reflection about commonalities of the various children's books about loss, there emerged several recurrent themes. These themes illustrate essential points about the mourning process in children.

The child needs to learn from the book that death is irreversible. Once people have died, they are gone and will not come back. Where they are and how they got there is a function of one's personal philosophy. Nevertheless, they are gone and will not return as we knew them.

The child needs to recognize that he will experience a variety of powerful affects in response to the loss. Some will be obvious while others may be subtle and complex. While these affects may influence his behavior, they should be allowed to emerge and they will diminish with the passage of time.

Remembering is an essential component of mourning. One needs to remember the good and the bad even though it may be painful. Ultimately, remembering will help the child come to terms with the loss.

The child needs to come away with the impression that most adults are helpful in dealing with loss. While the surviving parent or others may not always be empathic to his pain or may be clumsy in their efforts, nevertheless, it is with the help of significant adults that the child has the best chance of mastering the trauma.

Children's Informational Books About Loss

Since mourning in children has been equated with an affective experience, and since therapists work within an affective frame of reference in dealing with loss, then the information-oriented books about death and dying may be seen as of limited value and lesser appeal. The cognitively oriented books deal with facts rather than feelings. Consequently, they offer a grieving child and parent the appropriate words to attach to the catastrophic events. Such an offering may elicit a mixed reaction. At first glance it is inherently practical and useful, but then it may be used for defensive ends.

The cognitively oriented informative books approach the subject with a missionary zeal in an attempt to educate and inform children about this mysterious subject called death. They rail against a society that hides and sanitizes a normal function of living. The approach is reminiscent of how the early manuals on sex education dealt with their subject. It is assumed that adults withhold information about death just as they withhold information about sex from the curious child. These manuals present useful information about the causes of death, life-saving procedures, funeral homes, funerals, and cemeteries. They quote facts and figures that relate loss to a set of numbers. They offer cross-cultural comparisons that are interesting and informative.

The informational books cater to the defenses of rationalization and intellectualization in a way that may obscure and interfere with the discharge of significant affects. For neurotic children, such offerings may interfere with affect discharge; however, for more disturbed youngsters the bolstering of intellectualized defenses may not only be useful but necessary.

Whereas the early informative books were strictly factual, the current ones include clinical vignettes to illustrate their points. It is the appreciation of the clinical component that has made the recent books interesting. A proper balance between the intellectual and the affective is paramount to every therapeutic encounter.

Nevertheless, children and adults are forced to learn meaningful facts about death since it is repressed, denied, and avoided in one's daily encounters. As people are born in hospitals and usually die in hospitals, just how one deals with death is unknown until confronted in one's own experience. In that regard these books offer useful information about a subject whose existence is ignored until the moment of personal impact.

The usefulness of therapy to help the child is dealt with in a shallow and superficial manner. Therapy is recommended for any and all situations in an idealized manner. The possibilities and pitfalls of psychotherapy are not presented in balanced fashion. This approach may result from the fact that many of the writers are educators.

Among the reviewed informational books, one stands out as the most popular and useful, *Learning To Say Goodbye*, by Eda LeShan. This book was written by a professional who is familiar with the subject of loss. The writing style is clear and lucid, facts are well presented, and sections flow effortlessly from topic to topic. One of the book's strengths is that it is thorough and complete. A section dealing with therapy is well presented.

The book does, however, have flaws. The main flaw is that it presents a sugar-coated version of mourning. For every question there is a simple answer; for every conflict there is an easy solution. The author makes erroneous assumptions about how children mourn. For example, in two cases where the children did not mourn after the loss she speculates that they mourned before the parent died. Clinical experience has demonstrated that anticipatory mourning is of limited value (Samuels, 1988). There is also the assumption that dealing with the loss causes magical changes in the child's personality. That just does not happen. Children mourn along a developmental spectrum. While some children may engage in an adultlike mourning experiences, others may be incapable of dealing with the loss. In between the two extremes are various gradations of a partial mourning process (Garber, 1981). Such possibilities and complexities are ignored by the author.

I approached the informationally oriented books about death and dying with reserve and skepticism. My reason for this approach is an awareness that parents and therapists may find it easy to throw a book of facts in the child's direction as a means of disposing of a painful subject. This overly intellectualization has been a commonplace with sex education, so that death education may be approached similarly. While I do recommend these books and find them educational, I also recommend them with caution and a footnote of self-awareness.

Adolescents' Books About Parent Loss

Books for adolescents about parental loss were thoughtful and well written. As for younger children, the books were divided between telling a story and imparting information.

The story books for adolescents, just like those for their younger counterparts, fall into definite patterns. In every story there is an only child in conflict with the dying or surviving parent. The conflicts revolve around the developmental issues of adolescence: autonomy versus dependence, separation-individuation, and sexuality. The youngsters in these stories are exceptionally mature in understanding their situation. In the midst of crisis, they pontificate about life and the human condition. Invariably, they are the ones wronged and treated unjustly by the adults, while the adults are self-absorbed, insensitive, and underestimate the adolescents' awareness. Eventually, the adults come to realize the errors of their misperceptions.

The authors identify with the adolescent's conflicts with adults by demonstrating instances in which the adolescent has been mistreated and victimized. The adolescent's usual response is hurt, isolation, and withdrawal. The adolescent's dependency needs are denied as the youngsters are shown to be competent and comfortable in their aloneness and self-sufficiency.

Some books deal with a situation in which a lonely, isolated youngster is left to struggle with his feelings and questions about the loss. The adults are preoccupied with their own problems. There may be an occasional friend that is helpful; nevertheless, these stories point up the clinical impression that a child without familial or community resources is a lonely mourner indeed.

The adolescents are depicted as exceptionally sensitive, perceptive, and empathic to the adults. The adolescent is presented as more empathic to the surviving parent's distress than other adults are. In assuming that position, the adolescent is idealized and becomes a more worthy competitor for the surviving parent's affections. That the adolescent is seen as wise and sensitive beyond his years emphasizes the notions of hypermaturity and role reversal.

Most of the youngsters appear hypermature, which is appealing, yet emerges as a major clinical problem. With the parental loss, they are expected to act and behave in a manner beyond their years. They are hurried through developmental periods by greater demands and higher expectations. Consequently, the normal leisurely developmental rhythm becomes obliterated. Current functioning is sacrificed at the expense of future psychopathology. The authors of these books do not appreciate this subtle but significant clinical point. They also become seduced by the hypermature adolescent at the expense of a sophisticated story line.

The competitiveness between the adolescent and same sex parent is not uncommon. The parent may regress to the adolescent's level. The parent's sexual needs and longings are hinted at but never made explicit. Since the adolescent is an only child, the triangular elements of the situation are accentuated.

The parental need for the adolescent to assume the dead parent's place is a common occurrence. This is often resolved with the adolescent's moving out or going off to college.

Just as with the younger child, the grieving adolescent is idealized. This idealization assumes the form of the adolescent's being more empathic and sensitive to the dying parent than the spouse is. Such an occurrence makes for arresting drama but is not a reflection of reality. Adolescents tend to become more self-absorbed during the parent's illness as a way of avoiding overpowering affects.

Most of the books for adolescents were good to excellent in addressing loss and the surrounding conflicts. In every situation there was a palpable struggle between parent and child before the loss or subsequently. The best book for this age is *Endings* by Benett Bradley. I was challenged by this book because it posed thoughtful questions about what it feels like to experience various losses.

The high quality of the books implies that it is easier to write for a more sophisticated and thoughtful audience, or perhaps this group of authors just happened to be in touch with their own adolescence.

The "how to" books dealing with death for adolescents are exceptionally well written. They might as well be labeled "everything you ever wanted to know about death and dying but were afraid to ask." These books are thorough and readable because they present the facts in a variety of formats. Some are presented as question-and-answer sessions, while others are written as a discussion between the knowledgeable educator and eager students.

They all purport to have the same mission, and that is to demystify the forbidden subject and bring it out of hiding. At times, such presentations border on a crusade to inform and to instruct. The author's appeal to the reader is based on an identification with the wronged adolescent from whom important information is withheld by the secretive (i.e., bad) parent and other adults.

The one pervasive criticism is that every conflict about death is resolved in a direct, neat, and simple manner. Every question has an answer, and every dilemma has a resolution. Ambiguities and ambivalences do not exist as the books address the adolescent's need for closure and resolution. Developmental dilemmas do not exist as every conflict leads to progress. This approach betrays the authors' perceptual split of adolescents' intellectual capabilities. While, on one hand, there is insistence on the adolescent's ability to comprehend death and what it means, there is a lack of appreciation of the adolescent's capacity to comprehend dilemmas and ambiguities.

Developmental Considerations in Books Dealing with Parent Loss

There has always been controversy in the psychoanalytic literature about children's ability to mourn (Fleming and Altschul, 1963; Wolfenstein, 1966; Miller, 1971). In recent years, there has emerged a consensus about children's ability to deal with loss (Pollock, 1972, 1977, 1978; Furman, 1974; Garber, 1981; Sekaer and Katz, 1986). Children are seen to mourn along a developmental line. Some children may engage in an adultlike mourning process (Furman, 1974; Lopez and Kliman, 1979), while others are incapable of dealing with the loss. Most children fall on a spectrum between the two extremes. They may engage in some type of partial mourning activity, given a host of internal and external factors. Children will mourn to the degree that their cognitive equipment, emotional maturity, and environmental factors will allow. A mourning process may begin; however, it may become attenuated, derailed, or pushed underground and then reemerge when the child is further along in his development, external conditions permitting. Consequently, children may demonstrate various elements of the mourning process; yet one may get a sense that the work is not completed. Instead, the child may become stuck in a kind of stereotyped repetitive way of dealing with the loss in a manner that precludes further progress.

Children's books about loss address the basic elements of the child's mourning. There is an emphasis on not excluding the child from the knowledge about the loss or from the activities and rituals surrounding the death. There is also an emphasis on honesty and the reality that the person who died will not return. Consequently, distortions of reality are minimized.

Discharging affects and remembering the lost object are equally valid in facilitating the work of mourning. Because the helpfulness of adults in assisting children with the trauma is recognized and supported, these books focus children appropriately on the loss experience.

Nevertheless, developmental considerations are minimal as it is assumed that all children are capable of engaging in an adultlike mourning process. The mourning model for adults is held up as an ideal and expectation; consequently, the bereaved child is deemed a failure if he does not measure up. The authors do not recognize the individuality of the child's experience and that children do mourn but they do so differently from adults. Consequently, the authors do not recognize that children may mourn piecemeal at different points in their development or not at all. It is important for the authors to appreciate that even though children may not be capable of engaging in a mourning process, they should be afforded the chance and the opportunity to do so — because the exposure may become the baseline for a mourning process that is to follow.

The degree to which a child's mourning depends on the permission and the model of the surviving parent is also not considered. The surviving parent needs to mourn, to give the child permission, and to be more or less in phase with the child in order for the child's mourning to proceed. If these parental elements are not present, then the child's mourning will be aborted no matter how capable the child may be in engaging in the process.

An important point that these books do not present is that development is not necessarily continuous (Kagan, 1971). With regard to mourning, it means that if the child is incapable of dealing with his loss at the present time and under the present circumstances, he may be able to do so at some later point in his development. For the oedipal and latency child, one would anticipate an engagement in the work of mourning with the expectation that the elements of the loss may be pursued at some time in the future. Such an accomplishment is not necessarily a failure but rather the beginning of a lifetime process.

In addressing the mourning process of adolescents, most authors recognize the pivotal issues of adolescent development. There is an emphasis on dependence versus independence and autonomy, as well as the sexual competitiveness between adolescent and parent. The issues of adolescent loneliness, shame, and embarrassment about the loss are also highlighted.

There is, however, a marked lack of awareness of how adolescents mourn. Their mourning is quite diverse and does not follow any prescribed pattern (Garber, 1985). While adolescents experience a mourning process that is similar to that of the adult, it is variable and disguised. It is essential to recognize that since adolescents are overly concerned about being different, they are constantly at odds with their feelings about the loss. They are concerned that the intensity and variety of affects will set them apart from their peers. Consequently, they are always questioning and measuring their feelings about the loss. They are wondering about the degree of normality and concerned whether they feel what they should. Thus, while adolescents may be overwhelmed with powerful affects about the loss, there is a tendency to hide, to modulate, and to diminish those feelings because it would make them different. The result is pervasive embarrassment about what they feel, loneliness, and isolation because of a reluctance to discuss appropriateness. The most common method for adolescents to mourn is in a state of aloneness.

This is one more illustration of the authors' inability to appreciate developmental distinctions as they expect the adolescent to conform to the adult model of mourning.

Conclusions

Having read many children's books about loss, one may wonder whether these books have the power to heal. I think that under the proper circumstances, the appropriate book presented by an empathic adult can be helpful to a child dealing with loss. While a book may not be a significant instrument in the process of working through, it can be a stimulus for feeling, thinking, and raising questions about an experience that confronts us all. Exactly how this occurs I do not know — but we may consider some possibilities.

The book and its bearer give the child permission to think about what happened. It becomes an avenue for confronting painful issues through a distancing vehicle that the child can accept or reject. Since children become easily overwhelmed by powerful affects, books give them the means of experiencing strong feelings in small doses. Any potentially overpowering reaction can be stopped by the turn of a page. Books are convenient in that they allow us to taste and to feel within a controlled and controllable framework. Thus a book offers a means of abreacting in a manageable manner.

Identification with the story's central character is another method by which a book may help. In identifying, we unconsciously borrow and try on the experiences and strengths of others and make them part of our own personality. Doing gives a child a sense that, as others have done it before, so can he — perhaps not exactly like the other, perhaps not as completely, but close enough to make it workable.

Finally, a book stimulates interaction between parent and child and facilitates a dialogue about what happened and what it feels like. After all, that is what therapy is all about.

Having reviewed a number of children's books dealing with all types of losses, I would like to offer a favorite piece of literature about loss. It is a poem in the fore of a book called *The Missing Piece* by Shel Silverstein (1976). I was introduced to it by a seven-year-old patient whose mother died when he was two. Over the years, I have found it useful in helping children put their loss and adaptation in a proper perspective (Garber, 1988).

This is a poem about a thing that was missing a piece. It was not happy, and it set off in search of its missing piece. The thing encountered various adventures in this search. It found various missing pieces along the way, but none of them seemed to fit or work out. They were either too big, too small, too square, too thin, or too sharp.

This poem deals with loss as well as various attempts at resolution which may or may not be effective. There may be an attempt to resolve the loss prematurely, to find a replacement too quickly, or to bring closure inappropriately. This poem hints that mourning is not a one-time event but a lifetime process that permeates every developmental phase.

> And then one day it came upon
> another piece that seemed
> to be just right.
>
> . . . .
> It fit!
> It fit perfectly!
> At last! at last! And away it rolled
> and because it was
> now complete,
> it rolled faster and faster!
> Faster than it had ever rolled before!
> So fast it could not stop to talk to a worm
> or smell a flower
>
> . . . .
> Oh my, now that it was complete it could not sing at all.
> "Aha" it thought.
> "So *that's* how it is!"
> So it stopped rolling. . . .
> And it set the piece down gently,
> and slowly rolled away
> and as it rolled it softly sang—
> "Oh I'm lookin' for my missin' piece.
> I'm lookin' for my missin' piece."
>
> (Silverstein, 1976)

I have yet to read a story that expresses the nature of loss more eloquently than that.

References

Bettelheim, B. (1977), *The Use of Enchantment: The Meaning and Importance of Fairy Tales*. New York: Vintage Books.

Bowlby, J. (1960), Grief and mourning in infancy and early childhood. *The Psychoanalytic Study of the Child*, 15:9–52. New York: International Universities Press.

Bradley, B. (1987), *Endings*. New York: Lippincott.

Fleming, J. & Altschul, S. (1963), Activation of mourning and growth by psychoanalysis. *Internat. J. Psycho-Anal.*, 44:419–432.

Friedlander, L. (1942), Children's books and their function in latency and prepuberty. *Amer. Imago*, 3:129–150.

Furman, E. (1974), *A Child's Parent Dies*. New Haven, CT: Yale University Press.

Furman, R. (1964), Death and the young child: Some preliminary considerations. *The Psychoanalytic Study of the Child*, 19:377–397. New York: International Universities Press.

Garber, B. (1981), Mourning in children: Toward a theoretical synthesis. *The Annual of Psychoanalysis*, 9:9–19. New York: International Universities Press.

—— (1985), Mourning in adolescence: Normal and pathological. *Adolescent Psychiatry*, 12: 371–387. Chicago: University of Chicago Press.

—— (1988), Construction and reconstruction in a case of parent loss. In: *Childhood Bereavement and Its Aftermath*, ed. S. Altschul. Madison, CT: International Universities Press.

Goldings, C. R. (1968), Some new trends in children's literature from the perspective of a child psychiatrist. *J. Amer. Acad. Child. Psychiat.*, 7:377–397.

Heuscher, J. (1963), *A Psychiatric Study of Fairy Tales*. Springfield, IL: Charles C. Thomas.

Kagan, J. (1971), *Change and Continuity in Infancy*. New York: Wiley.

Krementz, J. (1981), *How It Feels When a Parent Dies*. New York: Knopf.

LeShan, E. (1976), *Learning To Say Goodbye When a Parent Dies*. New York: Macmillan.

Lopez, T. & Kliman, G. (1979), Memory, reconstruction and mourning in the analysis of a four-year-old child. *The Psychoanalytic Study of the Child*, 34:235–271. New Haven, CT: Yale University Press.

Miller, J. (1971), Reactions to the death of a parent: A review of the psychoanalytic literature. *J. Amer. Psychoanal. Assn.*, 19:697–719.

Peller, L. J. (1959), Daydreams and children's favorite books. *The Psychoanalytic Study of the Child*, 4:414–433. New York: International Universities Press.

Plank, E. & Plank, R. (1978), Children and death: As seen through art and autobiographies. *The Psychoanalytic Study of the Child*, 33:593–621. New Haven, CT: Yale University Press.

Pollock, G. (1972), On mourning and anniversaries: The relationship of culturally constituted defensive systems to intrapsychic adaptive process. *Israel Annual of Psychiatry*, 10:9–40.

_____ (1977), The mourning process and creative organizational change. *J. Amer. Psychoanal. Assn.*, 25:30–34.

_____ (1978), Process and affect: Mourning and grief. *Internat. J. Psycho-Anal.*, 59:255–276.

Samuels, A. (1988), Parental death in childhood. In: *Childhood Bereavement and Its Aftermath*, ed. S. Altschul. Madison, CT: International Universities Press, pp. 19–37.

Sekaer, C. & Katz, S. (1986), On the concept of mourning in childhood. *The Psychoanalytic Study of the Child*, 41:287–314. New Haven, CT: Yale University Press.

Silverstein, S. (1976), *The Missing Piece*. New York: Harper & Row.

White, E. B. (1952), *Charlotte's Web*. New York: Harper & Row.

Wolfenstein, M. (1966), How is mourning possible? *The Psychoanalytic Study of the Child*, 21:93–123. New York: International Universities Press.

16 DIAGNOSTIC ASSESSMENT AND THERAPEUTIC APPROACHES TO BORDERLINE DISORDERS IN ADOLESCENTS

DEREK MILLER

It appears certain that if borderline pathology is to stand in a diagnostic category in its own right, it will have to throw light on aspects of normal development, as the neuroses and psychoses did [Ross, 1976, p. 305].

There has been considerable argument as to whether, in adolescence, the borderline syndrome really exists. It has been thought to be a convenient diagnosis to describe an intractably difficult child who may be over-dependent, be overdemanding, and have little in the way of social inhibitions.

Borderline syndrome, borderline personality, borderline, and border-line diathesis have all been used descriptively; this paper will attempt to clarify those instances when an adolescent who suffers from a borderline syndrome is also a borderline personality. I will discuss the significance of this differential diagnosis in the treatment of disturbed adolescents. A particular emphasis placed on the underlying etiology of the symptoms, as well as the importance of containing these, helps diagnostic differentiation. This is important in the therapeutic prognosis because of the way symptoms distort therapeutic intervention. The borderline syndrome significantly impairs psychological development and creates a situation in which the individual becomes postpubertal but does not become adolescent.

Young people who are prone to overwhelming anxiety, impulsive behavior, a profound sense of being persecuted by authority figures, and disorganization of their personalities under perceived stress are often diagnosed as suffering from a borderline syndrome. The perception of stress, depending on the balance between psychosocial stress and support, is based not just on reality. It also depends on personality distortion due to developmental trauma, genetic biological vulnerability, and biopsychosocial insults due to chronic illness or injury. Those symptoms can exist in other personality disorders, and so they are, in a sense, nonspecific.

The term "borderline syndrome" was first used in 1953 to describe patients who presented themselves with ill-defined symptoms and complaints (Knight, 1953). During the period of disintegration, those suffering with such a syndrome typically show magical thinking and grandiosity. They are likely to feel, beneath this, worthless and unlovable.

Case Examples

CASE EXAMPLE 1

Karen was a 16-year-old girl with a two-and-a-half-year history that included a period of self-starvation and bulimia; self-mutilation by wrist cutting; drug abuse, which included bouts of marijuana smoking, cocaine sniffing, hits of lysergic acid (LSD), crack-cocaine; and alcohol abuse. She had made a number of suicide attempts, although she denied that she was suicidal. Referral was precipitated by an overdose of Fiorinal because of an intractable headache that followed her falling out of bed while "stoned" on marijuana. She was sexually promiscuous, having had six or seven sexual partners following her first intercourse at age 14 with a 22-year-old man. Her relationship with her parents was such that they claimed no knowledge of any of her behavior.

In the borderline syndrome, therapists are often made the victims of a destructive projection, and the therapist may then feel as much a nonperson as the patients feel themselves to be.

Karen had been in psychotherapy for years with different psychiatrists. She had been briefly hospitalized at age 15, and it was following this that she had been sent to a boarding school. She was referred by a previous therapist, and it was explained to her and her parents that she could be seen for a diagnostic assessment preliminary to making treatment recommendations. The assessment included a number of clinical interviews, a physical examination, biological tests for mood disorders, and projective testing. In her second interview, she told the psychiatrist that she knew one of his former patients. "I suppose you think you helped her," she said. "She was worse after you saw her and my teacher at school agrees." After a third interview she had her mother call yet another psychiatrist whom a friend of the patient recommended. She said, "I do not want to be mean, but I did not like you the moment I walked into your office."

Karen's attitude toward adults was that they were either wonderful or useless. She despised her mother, was constantly enraged by her, and worshipped her distant, uninvolved, businessman-father, who thought her "high spirited." She had consistently lied to both parents, who did not see her as particularly disturbed. Karen was overtly depressed, complaining of constant boredom. She did not feel sad but felt better on drugs and sex and when she was cuddled. She had no self-soothing mechanisms; she had never sucked her thumb nor had she ever masturbated.

The description of the symptomatic clusters of the borderline syndrome, even when the person is also a borderline personality, can be ascribed to a variety of stress responses with different etiologies. They could be descriptions of those who suffer from biologically based affective disorders. In addition, these patients respond to their internal world of fantasy as if it were real (Klein, 1975). In these young people, when the stress is removed, reality testing is restored, although they then tend to establish highly clinging, overdependent relationships. Easily disappointed, they may then quickly resort to symptomatic behavior.

On the basis of the symptomatic clusters, Kernberg (1972) has attempted to differentiate borderline personality in those who suffer from a borderline syndrome. A borderline syndrome appears as a nonspecific ego defect, apparent when a teenager responds to stress with regression, poor reality perception, low frustration tolerance, and poor impulse control. It particularly appears when young people, because of the psychosocial deficiencies that become manifest around the time of puberty, are unable to master this developmental phase to become early adolescent. Such youngsters become fixated in an emotional response in which they become easily overwhelmed with rage. Although they may be inappropriately grandiose, they maintain an intense, negative dependence on one or both parents, usually, but not always, their mothers. They seem to respond to every parental action and inaction with rage.

There is no doubt that Karen could be considered to be suffering from a borderline syndrome. She had previously been labeled as an "eating disorder," a drug abuser, and a histrionic personality. Karen also showed splitting, projection, primitive idealization, denial, omnipotence, and projective identification. These are thought to be the specific symptoms of a borderline personality.

All this would imply that, although Karen suffered from a borderline syndrome, she was also a borderline personality. The latter diagnosis is meaningful only if the prognosis is different from that of a borderline syndrome. Even with the differentiation of ego defect into specific and nonspecific, however, the differentiation between a borderline syndrome and a borderline personality on the basis of a description of symptoms is inadequate. All these symptoms can appear in youngsters who suffer from a transient borderline syndrome.

CASE EXAMPLE 2

Anna was a 15-year-old girl who was first seen when she was in intensive medical care following a serious suicide attempt. She had bought large quantities of over-the-counter sedatives from a local pharmacy. Prior to taking the pills, she called her "boyfriend" and announced that she was going to kill herself. After thinking about this for an hour or so, the young man called her mother, who found her daughter unconscious on her bed. She had vomited but, fortunately, had not inhaled the vomitus. She was rushed to the hospital comatose. Anna had been previously diagnosed as bulimic and had been briefly hospital-ized in an eating disorders program some months before. After she regained consciousness, she was furious to discover she was still alive because, she said, "I decided I was going to kill myself."

She was in the hospital for three weeks in an adolescent program and was diagnosed as suffering from a borderline syndrome with intermittent bingeing and vomiting, marijuana abuse, and school failure. Projection was manifest: she was enraged at her mother who, in her daughter's eyes, could do nothing right; she blamed teachers for her school failure and her parents for her suicidal attempts, and she took no responsibility for herself. Her new psychiatrist was "wonderful; her parents were useless."

Thus, Anna, too showed primitive idealization, projection, projective identification, denial, and omnipotence. On the basis of specific symp-tomatology, she, like Karen, could have been diagnosed as a borderline personality. Both girls showed a superficial capacity to make relation-ships. Although splitting was marked in both of them, the intensity and outcome of treatment was quite different.

Karen was in intensive individual therapy three times weekly along with family work with the parents. She was in treatment for three years before any significant improvement could be considered firm. Anna stopped abusing marijuana and alcohol after five outpatient sessions. She became involved in drama classes, her school work improved, and, one year later, she was asymptomatic and goal directed toward entering a university. She had retained one boyfriend for the year and had made a whole new circle of friends. She was seen once weekly for four months and then would occasionally have an appointment to discuss her career plans, and so on. Her father was supportive of her therapy, provided he did not have to be involved. Her mother had an occasional session with a social worker to help her cope with her initially verbally defiant daughter and her rather passive husband.

These two patients with equally disturbed initial presentations seem to demonstrate that the symptomatic presentation in a borderline syndrome does not indicate whether or not a borderline personality is present.

The Diagnosis of Borderline Personality

Although there is confusion in the literature, the label of borderline syndrome is sometimes used as if it always includes a borderline personality. It has been theorized (Kernberg, 1972) that the fixation peculiar to borderline syndrome occurs in the developmental stage between five and twelve months of age, when there still persists a dissociation of good- and bad-self representations. It is my thesis that such a syndrome should best be described as a "borderline personality." There is then also a failure of attachment (Bowlby, 1980). Failure at this developmental level is due to genetic and constitutional etiology in the child, the mother's emotional unavailability to her infant, or both.

The differential diagnosis from a borderline syndrome that does not also subsume a borderline personality depends on when developmental failure occurs. When the developmental failure occurs in the first two years of life, a borderline personality is created, and treatment is long, difficult, and often in vain. Later developmental failure, the result of a failure to receive or be provided with emotional supplies at puberty, for example, produces a similar clinical picture with a quite different prognosis. The failure in infancy leads to an immense difficulty for the patient in establishing a therapeutic alliance; if the developmental failure is later, this is not so.

The different outcome and intensity of treatment with Karen and Anna depended on when the developmental failure occurred.

Karen's developmental history was as follows. She was the second of three girls. She was a wanted child, but the mother was diagnosed as suffering from *placenta previa*. An emergency cesarean section was necessary, and the infant was in intensive care for the first five days of her life. The mother, a fashionable socialite, did not see her baby until the child was six days old. The baby returned home after the mother did and was two weeks of age when she came home. She was bottle fed as the mother thought that breast feeding was "disgusting." In the first year of her life, she was looked after by the mother, a nanny, and an *au pair* girl. Then a succession of *au pair* girls acted as babysitters for varying periods of time until she started school.

Anna, on the other hand, had a normal birth and delivery. There was evidence of a satisfactory attachment between mother and child. The mother remembered her first contact with the baby, and she was the primary caretaker for the first five years of the child's life. Anna did not respond well to her mother's going to work when she was seven, and she became fretful and "difficult." The parents had difficulty finding consistent caregivers when the mother was not able to stay home with the child. There was also increasing tension between the parents. When Anna was 12 years of age, the family moved and changed neighborhoods. This necessitated a change of school. The new neighborhood was extremely affluent, and a general attitude among the local youth was that they were entitled to be gratified. In junior high school, Anna initially felt extremely isolated. Only when she developed an eating disorder did she find a group of like-minded peers. She got involved then with alcohol and marijuana and became sexually provocative. She was perpetually enraged with her mother, who handled this by emotional withdrawal. Anna then began to binge and vomit, and a succession of self-mutilating behaviors was followed by a serious suicide attempt. She was grandiose, arbitrary, and highly impulsive, and projected the source of all difficulties.

Both girls showed symptoms that would fit the diagnosis of a "borderline syndrome" with a "borderline personality," but Karen had the latter. Neither had yet become adolescent (Miller, 1968). Symptomatically there appeared to be little difference between them, and both showed an apparent fixity of personality organization, disturbed interpersonal relationships, disturbances in the sense of reality, excessive and intense anxiety, impulsive behavior, and fleeting neurotic-like symptoms (Petti and Vela, 1990). On psychological tests (Masterson and Rinsley, 1975), these youngsters both responded with an open demonstration of their conflicts.

The developmental insult to Karen took place in the first year of life. With Anna, problems did not appear until latency, major developmental trauma having appeared at puberty. When she lost relationships with a stable peer group, there were no available significant extraparental adults. Not only did she lose the stability of the larger social system in which she had lived for twelve years, she moved to a new neighborhood that was filled with young people of a different socioeconomic group.

Those who suffer from borderline personality disorders show a more fixed inability to learn from experience and a greater inability to adapt to new situations. Because of their early deprivation, they find it harder to relate in therapy. Such adolescents have been described as showing poor personal hygiene, but this seems more typical of a schizotypal personality disorder, and neither of the two patients demonstrated this behavior. Unless the youngster also suffers from pervasive low self-esteem, this symptom seems unusual in most borderline personalities.

A person with borderline personality is thus one in whom the developmental defect occurred in the first year of life. The developmental defect is intrafamilial. If the patient suffers only from a borderline syndrome, the developmental defect is likely to occur later and may be significantly extrafamilial. This latter concept is based on the idea that personality development does not just depend on relationships within the nuclear family, but also involves significant emotional involvement with a peer group and extraparental adults, along with involvement with the way of life of the social system within which the child lives. In the second patient, Anna, this was clearly the issue.

When an early adolescent's personality development is disturbed because of either long- or short-term inadequate parental attachments (Bowlby, 1980), the teenager becomes overdependent on peer involvement. When, for a variety of reasons, this may be traumatically withdrawn, the vulnerable child may feel overwhelmingly rejected and present with a borderline syndrome.

The diagnostic issue that differentiates the borderline syndrome from a borderline personality is based on when the developmental insult occurs. In the United States, because of the social organization of the junior high and high school systems, the loss of peer support is particularly common, especially when it occurs because of a family move that takes place when the child is pubertal. The adolescent, whose positive parental attachments are then under stress, may appear with an acute deprivation depression (Miller, 1986) that may show itself as a borderline syndrome. This is then likely to produce further social isolation, often with school failure, parental coercion, or rejection and a further regression. When, in such students, peer relationships are threatened, the adolescent may attempt to gain a sense of self by

243

identifying with pathological peer groups. An adolescent suffering from a borderline syndrome may appear with an eating disorder, antisocial behavior, drug and alcohol abuse, or suicidal ideology. In large cities in the United States, emotionally vulnerable children who suffer from a borderline syndrome are very likely to join youth gangs. The structure of the gang organization, with its rigidity and its permission to express either aggressive or regressive impulses, offers a haven for such young people. The behavior that is instinctually gratifying may then become learned.

The therapy of borderline adolescents who present themselves with a combination of these symptoms is extremely difficult. If the attachments to parents become transiently tenuous and the missing peer and extra-parental attachments become replaced, seriously disturbed "borderline" youngsters may improve with very little therapy and be returned to a developmental track. When there is no consistency between early bonding and dependence and there is a history of early abuse, neglect, maternal rejection, and multiple caretakers, the capacity to trust others is developmentally impaired. Prior to puberty, a child — even with this type of early history — can, if the environment becomes "good enough," accept emotional support from its family with consequent reduction of tension. When puberty, with its inevitable struggles, arises (Miller, 1986), young teenagers with early experiences such as these may appear for treatment after having made suicidal attempts or gestures or because of violent behavior toward others, drug abusive behavior, eating disorders, or other behavioral disturbances. Psychologically, these youngsters show splitting, with devaluation of themselves and others. They are manipulative, impulsive, and greedy for gratification. Failing psychologically to separate-individuate (Leightman and Nathan, 1983), they live in a world filled with malevolent objects. With little capacity to invest in others in a non-needgratifying way, they tend to attribute motivation to others in an oversimplified, illogical, and idiosyncratic manner (Kestenbaum, 1983).

As these young people move from a disturbed infancy through childhood to puberty, they show increasingly serious disturbances in their ability to form meaningfully positive interpersonal relationships. They adapt to situations but do not involve themselves in a genuine way. The dynamic move from the psychological responses to the physical changes of puberty to development into adolescence implies the capacity to be ambivalent and to retain a basic emotional investment in the internal image of parents. The developmental lag that is inevitable in those suffering from either a borderline syndrome or a borderline personality organization interferes with the psychological factors that make adolescence possible (Masterson, 1972).

Like all the clusters of psychological syndrome complexes, the borderline syndrome may have different etiologies — some biological, some psychological, and some social. In the borderline personality, the etiology is also biopsychosocial, but social factors are relevant only insofar as family and social pathology influence the mother–child relationship. It is noteworthy that psychosocial support for the mothers of infants who might otherwise become borderline personalities offers a most helpful preventive intervention.

The borderline syndrome, unless a borderline personality is also present, does not necessarily represent extensive psychopathology, although symptomatically the situation may look equally deleterious. The borderline syndrome does not necessarily imply a failure in the capacity to make positive interpersonal relationships with others. High-quality psychotherapeutic intervention is always necessary. The need for sophisticated long-term intervention is always present if the problems produced by a borderline personality are to be resolved. Therapy of the borderline syndrome fails, however, if the short-term management of acute symptoms is accompanied by repeated changes of therapists. Such changes repeat one aspect of extrafamilial pathology: an instability of parental and significant extraparental adult relationships. It also repeats the experience of rejection that, in the borderline syndrome, is highly significant in the etiology of the disorder.

Therapeutic Problems

A pessimistic attitude by therapists as well as by parents concerning the outcome of therapy with young patients labeled as suffering from a borderline syndrome may produce a self-fulfilling prophecy. Historically, this has also been the case with those labeled schizophrenic. In institutionally based treatment driven by cost considerations, borderline adolescents are likely to be inadequately treated. As their symptomatic behavior becomes learned, a justification for only behavioral intervention can be said to exist. Such young people are often placed in residential treatment centers that take a single theoretical approach. Or, when they behave antisocially, are deemed delinquent, and placed in correctional centers, they are rarely offered effective intervention. If the youngster suffers from a borderline syndrome due to developmental failure at puberty, residential treatment, whatever its theoretical approaches, may produce positive results as relationships with extraparental adults and peers are provided. The environment, by its very nature, becomes "good enough," and the person returns to a developmental track.

When adolescents are inadequately treated, their personality distortion and developmental failure are likely to becomes chronic and unresponsive to the care they receive. The youngster may begin to suffer from a chronic deteriorating syndrome. Adolescents labeled borderline are often treated in psychiatric hospitals with techniques that are highly socially aberrant, using isolation devices and physical and chemical restraints. A further complication is that those who experience identity confusion, an inevitable consequence of borderline disturbances, tend to identify with the label they are given. Further, if diagnostic labels that carry a doubtful prognosis are told to parents, their level of anxiety increases the developmental stress their children experience.

An intractably difficult borderline adolescent who has not responded either to situational interventions, or to an appropriate biopsychosocial intervention is overdependent, overdemanding, and socially destructive (Westen and Rudolph, 1990). Such young people may continue to retain this type of behavior for a variety of reasons; it may be instinctually gratifying (Kernberg, 1982) or become a learned response to stress even if any dynamic issues have been resolved. Further, it may come to be expected by the social system in which the child lives. Institutional symptoms can develop in any type of residential setting as well as in the community at large. If the built environment in which the child lives is impoverished and withholding, it seems to invite the very behavior for which help is being sought.

Biological Etiology of the Borderline Syndrome

About one third of children and adolescents with a borderline syndrome or personality disorder have abnormal EEGs (Rosenfeld and Sprince, 1965). It is unclear how many have diagnosable mood disorders, just as it is unclear how many use drugs, alcohol, and varieties of antisocial behavior to deal with psychic pain. At least one third of adolescents in correctional centers in the United States, many of whom would carry a borderline diagnosis, also have diagnosable mood disorders.

The symptoms of mood disorder should be inquired about in all adolescents who present themselves to treatment with the behavioral disturbances of which the borderline syndrome is an example. The symptoms that should be looked for are rapid mood fluctuations, disturbed sleep patterns, poor appetite early in the day, and an irritability that occurs at about the same time every day. Often, this cluster of symptoms is cyclical in nature. Also common in these syndromes are learning disabilities. Recent studies indicate that they occur in 52% of such patients; attention deficit disorders are also strikingly common (Weigeland, 1975). A history of maternal separation prior to the age of five has an incidence that is statistically greater in a group of children and adolescents with a diagnosis of borderline personality than those with other labels (Bradley, 1979).

Like so many symptom complexes in psychiatry in which a variety of behaviors are complementary, there is little evidence that there is a specific biopsychosocial etiology in the borderline syndrome, and not all those who show developmental deprivation in infancy become borderline personalities. Similarly, not all who show developmental deprivation in later childhood or at puberty have a borderline syndrome.

Behavioral symptoms have prognostic indications. Insofar as they impair physical health, the teenager's ability to make a positive emotional involvement with others and retain a positive emotional cathexis with the parent, therapy becomes more difficult (Chethik, 1986). If symptomatic experiences can be attenuated or temporarily contained, the evidence seems to be that the outcome can be more satisfactory. If symptomatic control cannot be altered, there is considerable evidence that borderline adolescents grow into borderline adults (Ekstein and Wallerstein, 1956). In addition, neuropsychological handicaps or psychotic responses have an impact on the failure to develop core aspects of higher functioning and result in maladaptive coping mechanisms (Pine, 1986).

Problems of Treatment

The adequate therapy of those with a borderline syndrome for whom treatment is sought involves planning a therapeutic environment, either in the community or in psychiatric or educational settings. Such an environment involves biopsychosocial treatment that both deals with the specific etiological causes and nonspecifically provides for the generalized developmental needs of young people (Knesper and Miller, 1976).

If the biological etiology of a borderline syndrome is a major mood disorder, without appropriate psychopharmacological intervention, psychosocial interventions alone will tend to be less valuable. On the other hand, if the therapeutic intervention removes the child from all possibility of continuing family relationships (Bettelheim and Sylvester, 1948) or demands institutional conformity to a socially aberrant way of life, thus putting the adolescent under further developmental stress, medication is less likely to be effective. If the etiology of the syndrome is a psychological trauma without current evidence of biological dysfunction, psychotherapeutic intervention may lead to failure if symptomatic behavior is allowed to continue. Antisocial behavior offers pathological instinctual gratification and makes it difficult for the youngster to develop any motivation to change or become an ally of the therapeutic process. Children whose etiological illness produces a symptomatic presentation of the borderline syndrome are likely to create around themselves an environment that is persecutory, coercive, and rejecting. Parents may eventually find their children's disturbed responses to stress intolerable, as may therapeutic and educational staff.

Working with borderline young people is intensely difficult because they project into involved adults intense emotional turmoil as well as the experience of helplessness. This may be one reason why the staff of adolescent programs in psychiatric hospitals often withdraw from patients in a variety of subtle ways. Techniques of isolation may be used more because the staff want relief from persecutory responses produced in them by the patients than because of any overt disturbed behavior on the part of the patients. In behavioral programs, staff may spend time with each other, assessing levels of behavior, rather than with the patients. The use of television and video games on some adolescent programs may produce an excuse for staff–patient withdrawal. Apart from the problems these patients create for residential treatment centers, including hospitals, there are particular psychotherapeutic problems.

These patients make many therapists uncomfortable with their professional identity. The patients' provocative attitude is a manifestation of their basic pathology (Giovacchini, 1972), but it can produce a situation in which therapists find the patients almost intolerable. In the second diagnostic interview, Karen said, "I don't want to be mean, but I don't like you. l know you think you helped Anna, but I know her and she is no better. As a matter of fact, I think she is worse. I have asked my mother to contact Dr. B, who a friend of mine sees; she says he is very nice and warm and understanding."

Psychotherapists may become angry with these young people and may reject them because of their failure to respond satisfactorily. The therapists may imply an unwillingness on the part of the patient to improve. Therapists who feel helpless may, with a variety of rational-izations, then pass these young people onto other therapists. Thus, many adolescents sent to treatment because of a borderline response to stress seem to go from therapist to therapist and placement to placement. Ultimately, they are likely to develop a profound distrust of adults, whom they come to perceive as unreliable and rejecting. In her first interview, Karen said, "I have had eight psychiatrists; I liked some of them, but I don't think any of them changed anything. If I don't want to be different, I won't be. . . . I will say anything but only I know if I mean it."

Young people with a borderline syndrome do not develop a sense of autonomy. Their dependence is, however, highly negative. This is an exaggeration of the normative experience of early adolescence in which parents are often felt as uncaring and critical. The anger of the early adolescent is ambivalent; however, the anger of borderline postpubertal youngsters is split off from loving experiences; and the experience is one of hostile dependence.

Their intense feelings of persecution make the development of a therapeutic alliance with borderline young people difficult. When sepa-ration from the "hated" parent takes place, massive regression is not uncommon. In the initial stages of therapy, the therapist needs to empathize with the adolescent's beliefs (Bradley, 1979), rather than agreeing with their validity. Confrontation about dishonesty is relatively valueless; it is far more useful to look upon all communication as indicating something of the patient's fantasy life rather than to be preoccupied with the patient's "honesty." Basically, the goal of the therapist is to become an "auxiliary ego" to help contain the patient's tension (Masterson, 1972). A holding environment is created that maximally absorbs the patient's tension and returns a feeling of security. The therapist's intent is to help the patient assess reality, thus modifying the negative responses to environmental events (Giovacchini, 1972). The therapist's aim is to help clarify limits and monitor the expression of feeling, thus helping the patient establish the difference between reality and fantasy. One initial goal is to correct cognitive misperceptions (Kernberg, 1972). Another issue for the therapist while the patient is involved in this type of supportive therapy is to engage in "cognitive marking" and thus help him or her expand his or her knowledge of the world.

Therapy is enormously difficult. Even when there is an indication for skilled specific psychopharmacologic interventions, there is no justification to modify the adolescent's perception of the world by giving non-specific sedatives and tranquilizers. The goal should be for the adolescent's ego functions to be as much in contact with reality as possible.

Summary

Not all young people who present with a borderline syndrome are equally vulnerable. Clinical manifestations appear along a spectrum that varies from an apparently less severely disturbed psychoneurotic to those who appear with almost total ego fragmentation (Giovacchini, 1964).

When the syndrome appears as a result of social system trauma in early adolescence, adequate diagnosis and appropriate intervention can make for speedy recovery. A typical scenario is the absence of a peer group that is developmentally needed, along with the family tension and social system turbulence produced by a change of location, school, or cultural environment. When executives move with their families, for example, their adolescent children are likely to react with at least depression, with at worst a borderline syndrome.

The therapy of disturbed borderline young people is likely to be successful only in an environment that optimally meets developmental needs with skilled intervention in biological, psychological, and social fields. The latter should include work with the family in which the individual psychopathology of the parents, their marital relationships, and the strengths and weaknesses of the family system are all assessed.

REFERENCES

Bettelheim, B. & Sylvester, A. (1948), A therapeutic milieu. *Amer. J. Orthopsychiat.*, 18:191–206.

Bowlby, J. (1980), *Attachment and Loss*, Vol. III. New York: Basic Books.

Bradley, S. J. (1979), The relationship of early maternal separation to borderline personality in children and adolescents. A pilot study. *Amer. J. Psychiat.*, 136:424–426.

Chethik, M. (1986), Levels of borderline functioning in children: etiological and treatment considerations. *Amer. J. Orthopsychiat.*, 56:109–119.

Ekstein, R. & Wallerstein, J. (1956), Observations on the psychotherapy of borderline and psychotic children. *The Psychoanalytic Study of the*

Child, 11:303–311. New York: International Universities Press.

Giovacchini, P. L. (1964), The submerged ego. *J. Amer. Acad. Child Psychiat.*, 3:430–442.

_____ (1972), Technical difficulties in treating some characterological disorders: Countertransference problems. *Internat. J. Psychoanal. Psychother.*, 1:112–127.

Kernberg, O. (1972), Early ego-integration and object relations. *Ann. Amer. Acad. Sci.*, 193:233–247.

_____ (1987), Borderline personality organization. *J. Amer. Psychiat. Assn.*, 15:661–685.

Kernberg, P. F. (1982), Borderline conditions: childhood and adolescent aspects. In: *The Borderline Child*, ed. K. S. Robson. New York: McGraw-Hill, pp. 101–120.

Kestenbaum, C. J. (1982), The borderline child at risk for major psychiatric disorders in adult life. In: *The Borderline Child*, ed. K. S. Robson. New York: McGraw-Hill, pp. 49–55.

Klein, D. F. (1975), Psychopharmacology and the borderline patient. In: *Borderline States in Psychiatry*, ed. J. E. Mack. New York: Grune & Stratton, pp. 75–91.

Knesper, D. & Miller, D. (1976), Treatment plans for mental health care. *Amer. J. Psychiat.*, 133:65–80.

Knight, R. (1953), Borderline patients. *Bull. Menn. Clin.*, 19:1–12.

Leightman, M. & Nathan, S. (1982), A clinical approach to the psychological testing of borderline children. In: *The Borderline Child*, ed. K. S. Robson. New York: McGraw-Hill, pp. 121–128.

Masterson, J. F. (1972), *The Treatment of the Borderline Adolescent*. New York: Wiley.

_____ & Rinsley, D. B. (1975), The borderline syndrome: The role of the mother in genesis and psychic structure of the borderline personality. *Internat. J. Psycho-Anal.*, 56:163–177.

Miller, D. (1986), *Attack on the Self*. Northvale, NJ: Aronson.

Petti, F. A. & Vela, R. M. (1990), Borderline disorders of childhood: an overview. *J. Amer. Acad. Child Adoles. Psychiat.*, 29:327–337.

Pine, F. (1986), On the development of the borderline child to be. *Amer. J. Orthopsychiat.*, 56:450–457.

Rosenfeld, S. & Sprince, M. (1965), Some thoughts on the technical handling of borderline children. *The Psychoanalytic Study of the Child*, 20:495–517. New York: International Universities Press.

Ross, M. (1976), The borderline diathesis. *Internat. Rev. Psychoanal.*, 3:305–321.

Weigeland, H. (1975), A follow-up study of twenty borderline psychotic children: Fifty years after discharge. *Acta Psychiat. Scand.*, 60:465–476.

Westen, D. & Rudolph, P. (1990), Object relations in borderline adolescents. *J. Amer. Acad. Child Adoles. Psychiat.*, 29:338–348.

17 PARADISE LOST—BULIMIA, A CLOSET NARCISSISTIC PERSONALITY DISORDER: A DEVELOPMENTAL, SELF, AND OBJECT RELATIONS APPROACH

JAMES F. MASTERSON

Reading this book reflects the reader's pursuit of his or her own vital narcissistic professional interests. The recent emphasis on narcissism as being mainly pathologic has, however, given the term a bad reputation. That it is essential for life has been overlooked. The key distinction is between being centered in the self, which includes consideration of others, and being exclusively self-centered, excluding others. For example, if I am writing this paper as a reflection of my own grandiosity and see you the reader as existing only as a source of mirroring, that grandiosity is pathologic narcissism. On the other hand, if I perceive it as an interest by my colleagues in my work, and I acknowledge their interest, that is healthy narcissism.

The development of healthy narcissism can leave some residual feelings of "paradise lost" in all of us. In early life within the matrix of the symbiotic, grandiose, self-omnipotent object representation of the dual mother–child unit, we all had the feeling that "the world was our oyster." Later, however, during the rapprochement phase, the phase-appropriate frustration of the grandiosity and omnipotence brought our self- and object representations into accord with the world of reality, and we lost those images of grandiosity and omnipotence. Despite this change, or as a result of it, there can remain a residue of nostalgia in all of us for that lost paradise when we felt the world was our oyster. This residual feeling-state can sometimes induce a countertransference of envy evoked by a narcissistic patient who still seems to retain that paradise that we lost. Of course, when the countertransference envy is evoked, we have also to join the narcissistic patient in denial of the reality price paid for the persistence of infantile grandiosity. Beyond that, this denial can then produce blocks in understanding the severity of the impairments caused by pathologic narcissism. My hope is that bringing this issue to your attention at the beginning of a chapter on narcissism and "Paradise Lost" may help you to identify and defuse whatever nostalgia remains and therefore clear away any blocks to reading on.

This paper presents a subcategory of a closet narcissistic personality disorder (Kohut, 1968; Kernberg, 1974; Meissner, 1979; Masterson, 1981, 1985, 1988, 1993) whose central psychodynamic theme could be described as "paradise lost."

Theory

In normal development during the separation-individuation stage, the mother supports the child's individuation or self-activation, reinforces the separation and emergence of the child's real self into the world of reality, and defuses the child's grandiosity and omnipotence. In patients with a narcissistic disorder this does not occur. Instead the mother— having a narcissistic disorder herself—is unable to support the child's individuation and instead idealizes the child's grandiosity to shape the child to her needs. The child experiences disappointment, rage, and depression (abandonment depression) at the failure to have her real self supported. The child defends against these painful affects associated with this immature, inadequate, unsupported sense of self by identifying with the mother's idealization of the grandiose self, and it is therefore reinforced rather than defused. The child emerges from this stage with an exhibitionistic, narcissistic personality disorder and feels unique, ad-mired, and adored through the pursuit of perfect mirroring. Later in development, however, owing to a series of developmental traumas, this exhibitionism is severely shattered; and, unable to tolerate the depression and the loss of the exhibitionism, the patient withdraws her narcissism into the closet because it is so painful to leave the grandiose self exposed. To defend against the loss and to restore the grandiose sense of self, the patient changes from seeking mirroring of her own grandiosity by others to idealizing others and basking in their glow, thus developing a closet narcissistic disorder.

The intensive psychoanalytically oriented psychotherapy focuses on mirroring interpretations of the idealizing defense and then exploration of the underlying narcissistic vulnerability, for example, "It is so painful for you to focus on your self that you turn to others as a guide to protect yourself" (Masterson, 1988). These interpretations overcome the patient's transferential acting out of the idealization defense, help to establish a therapeutic alliance, give the patient access to what the idealization is a defense against, for example, the inadequate self and the abandonment depression that allows the patient to work through these painful affects, which, in turn, allows the real self to emerge.

Differential Diagnosis

Although self psychology identified this group as narcissistic disorders with an idealizing selfobject transference (Kohut, 1968), it is highly unlikely that one would diagnose these patients as having narcissistic disorders using DSM III since they do not conform to the criteria that emphasize almost exclusively exhibitionistic narcissistic features, for example, entitlement, grandiosity, exhibitionism, and so on. Patients with closet narcissistic disorders are not exhibitionistic or obviously entitled since they maintain their grandiose sense of self through idealizing and mirroring the object representation, which is projected onto others, and then "basking in the glow" of the object's mirroring responses. The grandiose self that is maintained in this way, however, is not overt but is hidden.

The mirroring behavior, as well as their proneness to experiencing depression—unlike their exhibitionistic brothers and sisters, who are intolerant of depression—can often create the initial clinical impression that these patients have a borderline personality disorder. Thus it is difficult to differentiate between a closet narcissistic personality disorder and a borderline personality disorder. The key to the difference is seen in the intrapsychic structure. In the narcissistic personality disorder, self- and object representations are fused, while the borderline's are split and separate. The narcissistic personality disorder seeks perfection and entitlement; the borderline personality disorder will settle for mere approval. The narcissistic personality disorder resists confrontation but responds to interpretations of narcissistic vulnerability, while the borderline personality disorder responds to confrontation and regresses when offered interpretations of narcissistic vulnerability before a therapeutic alliance has been established.

Case History

Jane, 22, a single college senior, was referred for consultation from out of town with a diagnosis of borderline personality disorder. Her chief complaint was: "I have trouble controlling myself. I'm in a cage and I can't get out. I explode when frustrated, and I hit my hand against the wall. I had bulimia for six years, although I don't have it any longer. I was hospitalized for four months two years ago for bulimia and at the time was extremely suicidal and depressed. I can't seem to do anything right. I have to be a workaholic, and I have to always get A's or people will laugh at me if I'm not perfect. I am now living with a man that I expect to marry. I have been working with my current therapist once a week since the hospitalization. She was my psychology instructor. She's a wonderful person, seems to like me a lot. We talked mostly about day-to-day issues, my bulimia subsided, but I got more and more depressed. She felt I needed more intensive psychotherapy for the depression."

The present illness, which began when Jane was in the fourth grade, age 9, had three precipitating stresses: the father was hospitalized for depression; the mother became increasingly depressed and withdrew; and the patient, having previously been extremely attractive — a point of great emphasis in the family — began to grow and change in size, her shoulders broadened, and she began to put on weight. She had to stop swimming, her favorite activity, because of recurrent infections, and her weight ballooned. This change in size and weight was further aggravated by feminine body development at age 13. Her mother ignored her femininity and continued to dress her as a boy. Her "paradise lost" feeling-state at the time was later reported in the working-through phase of treatment as follows:

"I felt depressed, fat, ugly and hated myself. At age 8 or 9, when I lost my attractiveness and gained weight, I got ugly. I couldn't handle the loss. When I was little I had everything. I could do no wrong. I was perfect. I had lost my perfection, my beauty. I was devastated, and that's when I started to eat and throw up in order to get rid of the weight.

"I had been spontaneous until age 8 or 9, but I became cold and mechanical and the diet and the treadmill started, but I felt no one liked me. I just wasn't good enough.

"I endured this as long as I could and then slowly, at about age 13, I began to get on the treadmill. I became a workaholic at school and a tennis-aholic after school, and the bad feelings about myself went underground. At the same time I also became bulimic and started to throw up four or five times a day. Despite the fact that I was throwing up daily, neither my mother nor my father had the least awareness that something was wrong. I ended up being president of my senior class and having a wonderful façade and feeling miserable underneath."

FAMILY HISTORY

Father, wealthy, alcoholic, obese, a manic–depressive, had a severe automobile accident two years ago and may have brain damage. The father was a severe alcoholic throughout the patient's childhood, was rarely home, and used his money to bribe the patient to remain infantile. He was not available for her efforts toward self-activation and adaptation. The mother, probably a closet narcissistic disorder herself, was an extremely obese, milder alcoholic. She had had a successful career on her own, which she gave up at marriage at her husband's insistence. The mother saw the patient as the carrier of her disappointed and unfulfilled narcissistic wishes. Seeing the patient as having "unique special abilities" she projected an idealized fantasy onto the patient and thereby reinforced the patient's grandiosity and pressured the patient to live up to these special abilities. At the same time, in reality, she literally ignored her daughter and palmed her off on governesses. She also, however, rewarded the patient's infantile regressive behavior. "I did not have to to anything for myself as a child; my mother did it for me."

Two brothers, six years and four years older than the patient, envied, resented, abused, attacked, terrorized, and perhaps sexually abused her throughout her childhood. "They used to hold me under the water until I couldn't breathe—from age five to ten they used to hit me and pinch me—chase me around the house. I used to stay alone in my room to avoid them." When she sought protection from her mother, she was ignored or placated. Thus there was physical abuse, but no known sexual abuse.

PAST HISTORY

The youngest of three and "a beautiful child," she recalled herself in the early years as "feeling special, being perfect, not having to do anything" for herself until the time of her father's hospitalization when she was age eight or nine. Throughout these years, however, her mother simultaneously idealized her and ignored her and left her to her own devices. Jane recalled long periods of playing alone in her room with Barbie dolls and having grandiose fantasies of being an Olympic swimming champion. As she got older, these fantasies were replaced by fantasies of marrying famous, wealthy men who would admire and love her. At the same time, throughout these early years, she had repetitive, fearful dreams, of being attacked: "A dream—I was in bed—I woke up trying to scream and nothing came out of my mouth. I was frightened. Usually it's related to someone in the bedroom trying to kill me. Makes me think of my brothers' abuse, which hurts me to think about." When frightened, she would regularly sleep with her parents in their bed.

At the time of her father's hospitalization and her mother's depression, she became depressed and reflected her rage back onto herself, hating herself. Throughout her childhood, both parents denied and placated her loneliness, her self-hate, and her brothers' abuse.

In grammar school, although she was bright, the same problems infiltrated her relationships with peers. She was dependent on her girlfriends and intimidated by them and would frequently be upset at their rejections and come home crying. Her mother would permit her to stay at home. As she moved from junior high school to high school, she lost weight and became attractive to boys. She moved more and more into her perfectionism and became an "A" student, a top tennis player, and president of her class. Under this surface of perfectionism, her bulimia and depression deepened. She had suicidal thoughts of hanging herself or cutting her wrists.

She managed to finish high school successfully and went away to college. Separation stress, however, brought on severe depression and increased bulimia, and now drinking and sexual acting out were added to the depression. She was attracted to narcissistic men who devalued her as she tried to please them. She had brief sexual affairs that the men usually ended. She dropped out of college at the end of the first year but enrolled in a college near her home, where she did a little better; but the depression, sexual acting out, and drinking continued.

Emotional detachment and withdrawal and deeper suicidal preoccupation ensued. She had several episodes of psychotherapy or counseling once a week without much improvement. About a year prior to beginning treatment with me, she had been hospitalized for depression and suicidal thoughts for four months, during which time there was family treatment as well as individual therapy. Throughout this time, the need to be perfect in the eyes of her parents was not touched on at all. Upon discharge, she went to live with her cousin. She took a job, where she met her boyfriend, Bob, lived with him for awhile, and now is planning to marry him. Bob is 27, a successful engineer who supports her but tends to be overprotective, reinforcing her need to lean on him. She reported that their sexual relationship was adequate but that she had difficulty achieving orgasm. She continued in outpatient psychotherapy once a week and although the bulimia subsided, the depression, rage, and difficulties activating herself to finish college continued.

Differential Diagnosis

That there was no thinking disorder and the patient's symptoms were more or less lifelong, not limited to episodes of illness, and impaired her functioning suggested a personality disorder. Despite the family history, the patient did not appear to have an affective disorder. Her depression seemed related to separation stresses and was not cyclical; there were no vegetative symptoms; and she had had many trials of antidepressant drugs without success.

She met all the *DSM-III* criteria for bulimia.

The history of panic attacks with frightening dreams in childhood and at the beginning of psychotherapy, along with the history of physical and perhaps sexual abuse, indicated a possible posttraumatic stress disorder. Beyond that, in the course of the psychotherapy, the patient developed a severe phobic state.

The personality disorder differentiation was between borderline personality disorder and closet narcissistic personality disorder. The mirroring, grandiosity, and perfectionism all pointed to a closet narcissistic personality disorder.

DIAGNOSTIC IMPRESSIONS

(1) Bulimia (Meissner, 1979; Mitchell, 1991; Fairburn and Hay, 1992; Hartmann, Herzog, and Drinkman, 1992; Schwartz, 1992; Yager, 1992; Steiger et al., 1993; Fairburn et al., 1993; Randall, 1993)

(2) Closet narcissistic personality disorder

(3) Posttraumatic stress disorder

(4) Phobia

I recommended that she move to New York City to have intensive psychotherapy three times a week.

COURSE OF PSYCHOTHERAPY

Jane began the psychotherapy with regressive narcissistic acting out defenses mirroring her mother, Bob, and me and expecting "to be taken care of." Rage at empathy failures of the mother were acted out on Bob and me. Once she banged her hand against the wall so hard that she had a small fracture and needed a cast. She was depressed and slept a lot, and there was no continuity from session to session. When I did not take over for her in interviews, but instead expected her to take responsibility for reporting her feelings, she responded with anger and helplessness.

259

Investigation of the anger and helplessness led to the idealizing defense against her difficulty activating and focusing on her self: "I never thought of thinking about myself. I hated myself."

This first bit of self-activation or support released a panic about being attacked, a panic whose content differed markedly from her later separation panics at self-activation. This reflected the anxiety seen in posttraumatic stress disorder, rather than that seen in separation anxiety about lack of empathy for the self. It was expressed in dreams and in waking up in a panic with hypnagogic illusions of "someone there."

The panic led to exploration of the physical abuse by her brothers and the lack of protection by the parents throughout childhood. No history of sexual abuse emerged at this time. The panic then subsided, her self-activation was reinforced by her getting a part-time job as a salesgirl, and she turned in the interviews to further exploration of her narcissistic vulnerability: "Why didn't I support self — afraid not to please mother — had to be perfect for her. Frightened to be without her, but don't know who I am or what I want to be."

I interpreted that it was so painful for her to focus on the bad feelings about her self that to restore her sense of self, she invested emotion in others and tried to be perfect in their eyes. She acknowledged and then elaborated on her extreme sensitivity to others and the need to be perfect in their eyes. This unleashed anger and depression, however, which were defended against by blocking, helplessness, and acting out with Bob. Interpretations of these defenses against narcissistic vulnerability led to further exploration. "Parents didn't believe I was sick. Should have protected me. I was mother's little girl, couldn't tell her."

After nine months of psychotherapy, the patient returned to school part-time. Further exploration of her idealizing defenses, what she came to call the perfectionistic treadmill, led to further investigation of her narcissistic vulnerability and to memories and some working through of the loss of paradise at age nine. She recalled that she had given up on herself and turned to being perfect in the eyes of others to restore the grandiose self. I was able to interpret that she tried to restore the loss of paradise by turning from her self, trying to be perfect in the eyes of the object, and her feelings of depression, anger, and hate were expressed by the bulimia. This led to more memories of depression and loss in the sessions and more self-activation in her life.

Parallel with these events in psychotherapy, her wedding was approaching, and her mother, in her usual fashion, was coopting all the plans. Jane's separation anxiety mounted. She again regressed, acting out with Bob, and threatened to call off the wedding. "I'll be leaving the only security I've known. . . . Even though they ignored me, they were always there"; that is, both mother and father overindulged her dependency needs. I interpreted that her anxiety about the wedding was the same as her anxiety about treatment; that is, she was anxious about growing up, giving up the perfectionist treadmill, and supporting herself.

Subsequently, she asserted herself with her mother and took over the planning, thus reinforcing her emerging self. However, my vacation occurred at the same time as the wedding, and she became anxious that without therapeutic support, she would regress under family pressure when she returned home for the wedding. Nevertheless, she managed the wedding well and returned to report: "Amazing what I've conquered. I feel so proud. But I'm still anxious about giving up the little girl and feel trapped by marriage, school, treatment."

She now began to explore and work through her separation anxiety and the underlying rage and depression of her fragmented self: "I have no confidence in my self. I can't do it on my own — afraid to go out into the world. I feel hurt, angry, devastated by 20 years of rejection — parents, brothers and classmates. Parents were attentive when I was little, or sick, or perfect. Mother constantly told me I was 'gifted, special, unique.' I had only to show it. I felt guilty and deserted."

She returned to the losses of age nine to thirteen, but then her memories went further back to age three to five, when she felt deserted by both mother and father, and attacked by brothers. Mother was involved in her own social activities. These memories led to further resistance, whose interpretation led to a clarification of her struggle between the grandiose self and her emerging real self. The perfectionistic treadmill was reinforced by school. She panicked about tests, studied obsessively, and meanwhile felt trapped: "I can't be perfect." Flaws and difficulties in her work evoked narcissistic rage at her self. I interpreted that the issue was not so much school but the perfectionist treadmill to deal with her bad feelings about herself. This interpretation would impel her to forego the perfectionism and be guided in her work by her real self, and this would create separation anxiety, anger, and depression, which led to further working through of the relationship with the mother. "Mother stressed my special gifts. If I didn't get an 'A,' I was letting her down. I had to study all the time and play tennis as bulimia got worse and worse. I dreaded going away to college and was miserable there — talked to mother every night on the phone — dated boys to find a replacement for mother."

Separation anxiety and rage at her self-activation emerged and were expressed against herself. She again pounded the wall and this time injured her hand. Depressed and confused, she said: "Don't know where I'm at. How do I handle self without perfection? What else is there? Afraid of letting go of perfection. Want to kill self or run away. Who am I? Angry at self or mother and father. Can't get angry at mother, she didn't mean it." I interpreted that she had invested so much emotion in the good image of her parents that she couldn't acknowledge any flaws, and the anger had no place to go but to be reflected back on her. This led to more self-activation: "I did what I wanted over the weekend rather than study all the time and felt good about myself. Then I panicked, started throwing up, and attacked myself for not being perfect. In the panic my thoughts turned to Mother. Why do I have to get anxious? Felt like screaming, leave me alone. I don't want to do it. Want to do what I want to do."

I interpreted that the perfectionistic treadmill was a way of dealing with her anxiety about herself. "Everything I did had to be approved by mother, or I was wrong."

After these sessions, the patient felt "I had a choice. I did what I wanted with less anxiety. I studied enough, got through finals without the treadmill, visited home without regression."

As the patient moved back and forth between affect and working through and resistance, a pattern emerged of bursts of painful affects and memories, followed by resistance, so that there was no deepening of the momentum of the working through. The patient was on a plateau. My interpretation—that it was so painful for her to focus on her bad feelings about her self that she protected herself by retreating to the perfectionistic treadmill—brought to center stage her mirroring transference-acting-out in the sessions that had blocked further progress; my therapeutic neutrality evoked the rage and disappointment at her mother's lack of support for her individuation. Rather than express these feelings, she defended against them with me as she had with the mother, by mirroring her idea of my expectations.

She exploded: "I don't like you. I feel like I am talking to a wall. You are not interested in me. You never seem friendly. You put me down. But I don't say anything about these feelings and don't question, I just go along with you as I did with them."

I questioned why she hadn't brought this up before and pointed out certain paradoxes. She felt I wasn't interested, yet she had improved from the work. I then interpreted her mirroring defense against the feelings of rejection impelled by my therapeutic neutrality and pointed out how it blocked progress. The patient responded that the problem was not her but "this kind" of therapy, where the patient had to "talk to a wall." This issue of her transference-acting-out defense was only initially touched on at this time and had to be repeatedly worked through later.

The details of the first two years of psychotherapy have been emphasized to illustrate the establishing of a therapeutic alliance and the beginning of the working-through phase. The extraordinary course of the last two years of treatment is summarized in the following pages, and a brief follow-up two years after termination is presented.

The momentum of the working-through process was complicated by the onset of a severe panic state as Jane became more and more self-activated. Her fear of going out or being alone reached such proportions that a nurse was required to stay with her when her husband was at work.

The panic state seemed to be caused by a combination of physiological and psychological forces: a dysfunction of the locus ceruleus and separation anxiety, each reinforcing the other. Medication (Xanax) was used for the former, and psychotherapy dealt with the latter. At one point, desensitization techniques were tried with a behavior therapist.

As if this were not enough, concurrently the patient developed a severe Epstein-Barr syndrome: severe headaches and dizziness, great lethargy, recurrent joint pains, and throat and kidney infections. She would spend days in bed and be unable to attend sessions. Consultations with medical experts confirmed this diagnosis, and the suggestion was made that the stress of psychotherapy was overwhelming a marginal stress-response system. Frequency of interviews was reduced to twice a week.

It was unclear how much of her symptomatology was emotional, but with increasing reservations, I attempted to maintain the momentum of the working-through process. There were, of course, periods of regressive resistance as her physical symptoms took over the clinical picture, and at these times, the working through stopped, and I refrained from putting her under therapeutic pressure. But each time she got better control of her physical state, it was possible to return to working through.

The physical picture dominated the third year of treatment and gradually waned and disappeared in the fourth year as her functioning returned and the momentum of the working through was restored. In the middle of the fourth year, she became pregnant, and her husband got a job offer in another city that he could not refuse. I felt that the patient was in the latter part of the working-through phase and needed more time to complete it before termination. She, however, decided to leave, and there was a short termination phase. By the time she left, the panic and the Epstein-Barr were gone; she had a much better sense of self and was looking forward to having the baby. I felt that despite her progress, the abandonment depression had not been sufficiently worked through and might cause trouble later. I referred her to a therapist in the local area.

Two years after termination, I received the following letter from her therapist: "The patient came in a week ago for her last session before her second baby was to be delivered. She mentioned that you had written and how surprised she was that you were writing about her. She thought that she 'was pretty ordinary, compared to other patients.' At the same time she talked about how you changed her life; that she can't believe how far she has come. When I asked what it was about her work with you that had made such change possible, she said it was your utter predictability. She said you were always there for her, that you always responded in the same way, and that she got to the point where she could predict your response. Still when she's troubled, she knows what you would say if she talked to you and she uses that to comfort herself. It also meant a lot to her that you shared some common interests and skills. I have been intrigued by the fact that she has done well in therapy with both of us, although our styles are different. The patient definitely feels that if she were to become deeply disturbed again, she would want to work with you. She trusted you on a deeper level and still mourns the premature termination of her therapy with you."

Discussion

It is impossible in a brief paper to include accurately all the subtle shifts in affect, theme, and the interventions that take place. Although, there obviously were other interventions, such as clarifications, confrontations, and communicative matching, the main emphasis was on narcissistic vulnerability, for example, how painful it was for the patient to focus on herself and her need for idealizing defenses against it—the perfectionist treadmill. This focus in and out of the transference acting out led to her recapturing the memory affect of the abandonment depression associated with the loss of grandiose self, which, in turn, led to the perfectionist focus on the object with the onset of bulimia. Working through some of this depression and anger led to further emergence of her real self in her life; for example, her life became more adaptive, and simultaneously there was some working through beyond the "paradise lost" phenomenon to the origins of the grandiose self defense in the first three years of life. The uncovering of these memories led to resistance expressed in her transference-acting-out which was then interpreted.

The advantage of the developmental self- and object relations approach is not that it is easy to grasp, but that, once grasped, it opens the doors to many of the mysteries of psychotherapy with the narcissistic personality disorder and enables the therapist to keep the reins of therapy firmly in his or her hands. When it is pursued faithfully, it more than justifies the effort, providing, as it does, a life preserver to rescue and sustain the deprived and abandoned in their struggle and eventually a beacon to guide them to overcome their developmental trauma, reconstruct their psyche, and rejoin the mainstream of life. These objectives — a fulfillment of both the therapist's and the patient's deepest wishes — enhance the mutual struggle and endow it with a vitality and nobility that gives the work its enduring satisfaction and significance.

REFERENCES

Fairburn, C. G. & Hay, P. J. (1992), The treatment of bulimia nervosa, special section: Eating disorders. *Ann. Med.*, 24:297-302.

———— Jones, R., Peveler, R. C., Hope, R. A. et al. (1993), Psychotherapy and bulimia nervosa: Longer-term effects of interpersonal psychotherapy, behavior therapy and cognitive behavioral therapy. *Arch. Gen. Psychiat.*, 50:419-428.

Hartmann, A., Herzog, T. & Drinkman, A. (1992), Psychotherapy of bulimia nervosa. What is effective? A metaanalysis. *J. Psychosom. Res.*, 36:159-167.

Kernberg, O. (1974), Contrasting viewpoints regarding the nature and psycho-analytic treatment of narcissistic personalities: A preliminary communication. *Amer. J. Psychoanal. Assn.*, 22:255-267.

Kohut, H. (1968), Psychoanalytic treatment of narcissistic personality disorder: Outline of a systematic approach. *The Psychoanalytic Study of the Child*, 23:86-113. New Haven, CT: Yale University Press.

Masterson, J. F. (1981), *Narcissistic and Borderline Disorders*. New York: Brunner/Mazel.

———— (1985), *The Real Self*. New York: Brunner/Mazel.

_____ (1988), *Psychotherapy of the Disorders of the Self—The Masterson Approach*, ed. R. Klein. New York: Brunner/Mazel.

_____ (1993), *The Emerging Self—A Developmental, Self, and Object Relations Approach to the Treatment of the Closet Narcissistic Disorders of the Self*. New York: Brunner/Mazel.

Meissner, W. (1979), Differential diagnosis of narcissistic personalities from borderline conditions. Presented at annual meeting of the American Psychoanalytic Association, Chicago.

Mitchell, J. E. (1991), A review of the controlled trials of psychotherapy for bulimia nervosa. *J. Psychosom. Res.*, 35(Suppl. 1):23–31.

Randall, L. (1993), Abnormal grief and eating disorders within a mother–son dyad. *Brit. J. Med. Psychol.*, 66:89–96.

Schwartz, H. J. (1992), Psychoanalytic psychotherapy for a woman with diagnoses of kleptomania and bulimia. *Hosp. Comm. Psychiat.*, 43:109–110.

Steiger, H., Leung, F., Thibaudeau, J. & Houle, L. (1993), Prognostic utility of subcomponents of the borderline personality construct in bulimia nervosa. *Brit. J. Clin. Psychol.*, 32:187–197.

Yager, J. (1992), Psychotherapeutic strategies for bulimia nervosa. *J. Psychother. Pract. Res.*, 1:91–102.

18 A REVIEW OF EATING DISORDERS IN ADOLESCENTS

LYNN E. PONTON

In his historical papers that have reviewed the development of the field of eating disorders, Lucas (1981) underscores the need for an integrative approach. He describes six eras wherein controversial data have led to polarized and dogmatic positions. The first, 1868–1914, marks the discovery and acknowledgment of eating disorders in the literature and is titled "the descriptive era." It is perhaps best described by a student of Charcot's, who comments:

> The diagnosis of mental anorexia is extremely simple. It merely requires thought . . . the history guides you, and every time you find the patient has gone upon a restricted diet, either voluntarily or from some emotional causes, and this has been followed by a loss of psychic ideas of appetite, you can safely assume the existence of mental anorexia, either pure and simple or associated with something [Lucas, 1981, p. 255].

The biological era followed in 1914, when Simmond, a pathologist, described "pituitary cachexia" (cited in Lucas, 1981). The etiology developed from the autopsy of a young woman who died of cachexia with pituitary failure. Lucas describes the third era, 1930–1961, as a period of rediscovery. It included the end of Simmond's disease when extensive pathological reports did not substantiate the diagnosis. This era also sparked the recognition of a certain psychopathological component in patients with eating disorders. The fourth era, that of the psycho-analytic perspective, followed the period of rediscovery. The lingering effect of Helene Deutsch's work (1944, 1981), characterized by descriptions of fears of impregnation and delayed adolescent sexuality, still hovers over the field. Lucas (1981) describes the fifth era of eating

267

disorders, 1961–1980, and highlights the importance of the work of Hilde Bruch, a clinical theoretician who worked to define the diagnoses, develop clinical strategies, and educate patients and their families. Crediting the biopsychosocial model and the importance of a developmental approach, Lucas introduces the sixth era in the study of eating disorders. He details the complex interactions and genetic determinants that lead to a variable degree of biologic vulnerability in persons who are at risk for experiencing the illnesses. He states:

> Anorexia nervosa is the ideal paradigm for the study of these interacting factors, and such a model is herein proposed. . . . Specific early experiences and family influences may create intrapsychic conflicts that determine a psychologic predisposition. Societal influences and expectations play their role in setting the social climate that is conductive to the development of the disease. The biologic factors may be mediated by pubertal endocrine changes that initiate the disorder. Psychologic conflicts lead to personality and behavioral changes that promote and support the dieting. Social factors, such as the cultural obsession with thinness, tend to reinforce the psychologic motivation. Each of these factors has greater or less importance for the person in whom the disease may manifest itself in degrees of severity [p. 259].

Although Lucas is one of the great theoretical and clinical integrationalists in the field of eating disorders, much has happened since he wrote his thoughtful and predictive descriptions. Recognition and diagnosis of the disorders has significantly increased during the past 10 years; the diagnostic categories of anorexia nervosa, bulimia nervosa, and obesity are better understood and the process of subcategorization has begun; the combined role of the media and social pressure in promoting thinness among females is far better understood; and educational efforts have enlightened both the general public and the mental health community. In summary, this has been a decade of heightened awareness and education, but it has served to highlight the magnitude of this category of illnesses. Simultaneously, in the United States, money from medical health insurance has been regularly denied persons suffering from eating disorders, with a consequent result in increased awareness but decreased opportunity for treatment.

The Diagnosis of Eating Disorders

Two disorders, anorexia nervosa and bulimia nervosa, are defined in the *DSM-III-R* (American Psychiatric Association, 1987) and are discussed here with specific attention to diagnostic criteria. Obesity is not listed as a diagnostic syndrome in the DSM-III-R but is a serious health concern with adolescents and is discussed following this section. In this chapter, the term eating disorder refers to anorexia nervosa and bulimia nervosa. The diagnostic criteria for anorexia nervosa as defined by DSM-III-R are: (1) refusal to maintain body weight over a minimal normal weight for age and height or failure to make expected weight gain during a period of growth; (2) intense fear of becoming fat even though underweight; (3) body or shape distortion ("feels fat even if thin"); (4) in females, the absence of at least three consecutive menstrual cycles that would otherwise be expected to occur; and (5) considerable crossover between the two diagnoses, and they can be diagnosed concurrently. Forty-seven percent of patients with anorexia nervosa demonstrate bulimic behaviors, and 30–80% of patients with bulimia have a history of anorexia nervosa (American Psychiatric Association, 1987).

The diagnostic criteria for bulimia nervosa as defined by the DSM-III-R are: (1) recurrent episodes of binge eating; (2) a feeling of lack of control over eating behavior during the eating binges; (3) engaging in a method to prevent weight gain (self-induced vomiting, laxatives, diuretics, dieting, or exercise); (4) a minimum of two binge eating episodes a week for at least three months; and (5) persistent overconcern with body shape and weight.

Persons with anorexia nervosa and bulimia nervosa may experience weight loss, but it is more severe ($> 15\%$ below minimum body weight) in anorexia nervosa and may be life-threatening. Six percent of patients with anorexia nervosa are reported to die with the illness (American Psychiatric Association, 1987).

Obesity

Thinness is much admired in western cultures, including among adolescents (Stunkard et al., 1972), and obese adolescents are frequently stigmatized (Tobias and Gordon, 1980). Obese adolescents may be discriminated against, both in school and in employment (Canning and

269

Meyer, 1966, 1967). Using a definition of a triceps fat fold thickness greater than the 95th percentile, a 10-state nutrition survey studied the prevalence of obesity in the pediatric population and documented a prevalence of obesity in 6–13% of all adolescents (Kleinman, 1987).

The etiology of obesity is complex and contains psychological, social, and biological factors. Disease is rare as a cause for obesity. There are, however, several syndromes with associated obesity, including the acquired syndromes: Frohlich's syndrome, characterized by hypothalamic tumors; Cushing's syndrome, defined by adrenal cortical hyperplasia and pituitary tumors; and myelodysplasia, marked by spinal defects and hydrocephaly. The congenital syndromes associated with obesity include Alstrom's syndrome, which presents with manifestations of hypogonadism and retinal degeneration; Biemond's syndrome, which has colomboma, hypogonadism, polydactyly, and mental retardation; Carpenter's syndrome, with acrocephalosyndactyly, mental retardation and hypogonadism; Kallman's syndrome, with anosmia, hypogonadism, and cleft palate; Klinefelter's syndrome, characterized by a male phenotype with more than one X chromosome and hypogonadism; Lawrence-Moon-Bardet-Biedl syndrome, with retinitis pigmentosa, hypogonadism, and mental retardation; and Prader-Willi syndrome, with infantile hypotonia, mental retardation, and short stature (Kleinman, 1987).

Obesity is believed to be connected most strongly with environmental factors, particularly diet, lack of physical activity, and family patterns of feeding. Psychological explanations were formulated by Hilde Bruch (1974), who stated that feeding becomes a substitute for other sources of satisfaction. Most notably, obese children who are heavily stigmatized exhibit a greater sensitivity to criticism and lower self-esteem (Kalucy, 1976).

The treatment of obesity should include an integrated approach employing behavior techniques, skill-building, nutritional counseling, family and group counseling that deals with problems related to dieting and self-esteem, and group approaches with other adolescents (Melon, 1992).

Theories Addressing the Etiology of Eating Disorders

There is no single theory that explains the development of eating disorders, but integrating theoretical contributions from different perspectives is extremely useful in promoting clinical understanding. There are many dynamic theories that help explicate the pathology of people with eating disorders. Perhaps best known is Bruch's (1982) description of the pathological relationships between patients with anorexia nervosa and their mothers. Bruch describes a developmental dysfunction in the mother's ability to perceive and respond to the needs of her child; the child is then unable to differentiate between her own needs and those imposed from outside. These patients' perceptions of their bodily experiences are often disturbed; and they do not trust, nor can they identify, their own feelings. Bruch describes this disorder as being primarily related to deficits in the sense of self and the development of autonomy. Bruch's theories employed psychoanalytic principles but countered earlier psychoanalytic formulations that emphasized the importance of conflicts over sexuality in patients with eating disorders. Much earlier, Helene Deutsche (1944), describing patients' fantasies and fear of oral impregnation, highlighted the internal conflicts of patients with these disorders.

Social theories also play an important part in the understanding of eating disorders. Eating disorders are commonly found in young women from the upper middle class, although it appears that the prevalence of these disorders is increasing for young women among all social classes and with diverse ethnic backgrounds (Yates, 1989). For these young women, thinness and scrupulousness regarding food, eating, and exercise become primary goals about which they may organize their lives. In western society in general, persons with more endomorphic body patterns are devalued (Chisholm, 1978). Much of this pressure is targeted at adolescent girls and young women and gives them a clear message that thin is best.

Theories regarding the role of the family in these illnesses have also aided understanding. A decade ago destructive forces within the family were thought to produce and perpetuate anorexia nervosa. This assumption was based on family studies conducted by Minuchin, Rosman, and Baker (1980), but these studies lacked controls and did not take into account a variety of factors. There is some credence, however, that can be given to the descriptions of these families. The anorexic is often the identified patient in a family that can accurately be described as enmeshing, overprotecting, and rigid. Families such as these have difficulties resolving conflict.

Bulimic patients describe their families differently than do anorectics. They experience greater neglect, rejection, and blame (Humphrey, 1988). The mothers of bulimics appear emotionally distant from, rather than enmeshed with, their daughters. Families of bulimic patients are reported

271

to have high expectations but significantly greater overt conflict and negativity (Johnson, Lewis, and Hagman, 1984). Despite the profusion of literature in this area, the contribution of families to eating disorders is not clear. Family comorbidity, genetic contributions, stress, and social factors may play important roles.

In the arena of psychological theories, there have been contributions from several areas, including examination of personality, body image, and a number of other factors. Garfinkel and Kaplan (1985) report that cognitive styles should be examined in bulimic and anorectic patients. They highlight how the cognitive style and personality of bulimics differ from those of anorectics, and they report that women who binge and purge are more likely to have a history of childhood maladjustment. The four personality features that are consistently found in bulimic patients are self-regulatory problems, social discomfort, sensitivity to reflection, and high academic expectations for which the pursuit of thinness becomes a vehicle of expression (Johnson and Conners, 1987; Casper, Hedeker, and McClough, 1992).

Bruch (1982) has written more on body distortions than perhaps anyone in the field. Credit must be given to her for promoting under-standing around mother–daughter representation and underscoring shared difficulties that mothers and daughters have in separating and feeling comfortable with their bodies. Eating can be used to express the earliest conflicts over loving and being loved, loving and hating, attacking and being attacked, and punishing and being punished. The work that has been done in this particular area represents a whole spectrum of interesting ideas.

Following the work of Bruch, most authors have continued to emphasize the anoretic patient's intense neediness, onto which she superimposes a search for identity, separateness, and autonomy. Using this theoretical perspective, an eating disorder represents both a wish for and the fear of passive gratification. Regardless of the importance of this theoretical component, it does reflect the words of patients who echo that they cannot be gratified. Chatoor (1989) postulates that individuals with eating disorders share a common disturbance in somatopsycholo-gical differentiation, defined as an inability to separate physiological sensations of hunger and fullness from emotional feelings. Chatour believes that somatopsychological differentiation is a developmental process that is achieved in the first two years of life, a process that can be affected by parental, infant, or environmental factors. She postulates that infantile, adolescent, and adult-onset eating disorders all include a disturbance in somatopsychological functioning.

Biological theories are most frequently based on studies that have been conducted on persons maintained on semistarvation diets. They report that starving persons undergo sleep disturbance, impaired concentration, indecisiveness, withdrawal, mood lability, anxiety, and depression (Garfinkel and Kaplan, 1985). There is a host of abnormal neuroendocrine axes in anorexic patients who are self-starved, and, in fact, the whole endocrine access is very much affected by the starvation process. In starvation, the hypothalamus secretes a larger amount of corticotropin-releasing factor, which stimulates the adrenal cortex. The degree of elevation of corticotropin-releasing hormone in the cerebral spinal fluid of anoretic patients correlates with the degree of their depression (Gold and Rubinow, 1987).

Kaye and colleagues (1982) demonstrate that endogenous opiates are elevated in the CSF of anorectics, although certain beta endorphins are reported to be within the normal limits. Through the disruption of the endocrine axis, beta endorphins could possibly be implicated in these disorders, creating the inhibition of central nervous system catecholamine that is characteristic of anorexia. Underweight anorectic women also have low levels of another neurotransmitter, serotonin. Serotonin is important in the regulation of sleep, pain, appetite, and mood. All these factors indicate the important role that the biological aspects play in the maintenance of this illness.

Physiological Changes with Eating Disorders

Physiological changes with eating disorders are well summarized in the review articles by Herzog and Copeland (1985), Halmi (1983), and Yates (1990). I will highlight some of the areas important to focus on clinically. First, anorexia nervosa in many ways parallels other "starvation states." There are many changes consistent with this, including differences in total sodium, potassium loss, and decreased T_3 and T_4. Decreased production of blood cells of all types is a frequent phenomenon (Halmi, 1983). Anemia, leukopenia, and thrombocytopenia are associated with changes in the bone marrow. The anemia may contribute to fatigue (Yates, 1990). In patients with bulimia nervosa, hypokalemic alkalosis is one of the most serious physical problems. Careful monitoring of serum creatinine and BUN is important. Also quite serious are EKG changes increased by electrolyte abnormalities. Most remarkable are flattening of the T wave, ST segment depression, and lengthening of the QT interval. Long-term presence of anorexia nervosa may lead to cardiac changes, including thinning of the wall of the left ventricle. EEG changes are also notable, revealing moderate to marked slowing. Vomiting is more significant in patients with EEG changes, indicating that it might reflect cerebral spinal fluid changes. For bulimics, many gastrointestinal abnormalities—tears from vomiting, erosion of dental enamel, and gastric dilatation with the risk of rupture—present significant risk. Renal changes that reflect dehydration and a reduced glomerular filtration rate may also be present. The incidence of renal calculi is increased.

Hormonal abnormalities are also found with these disorders. If amenorrhea, one of the diagnostic criteria for anorexia nervosa, is present, it may appear associated with hypothalamic abnormalities even before weight loss. Amenorrhea in anorexia nervosa is associated with a reversion of gonadotropin secretion to the prepubertal pattern (Boyer, Katz, and Finkelstein, 1974). Specifically, there is a decrease in the pattern of gonadotropin pulsations and the development of what is quite similar to a prepubertal pattern. Gonadotropin secretion is decreased in both male and female adolescents. Other hormonal changes include a change in growth hormone, which is elevated in response to the decreased levels of somatomedin C.V., and abnormal temperature regulations that occur regularly secondary to the loss of body fat or a hypothalamic defect. The complexity of physiological changes in adolescent patients with eating disorders necessitates that the treating therapist be informed about the condition and either be fully trained or work with someone who is fully trained in the medical aspects of these illnesses.

Treatment

Although there is a whole spectrum of severity, from mild to severe, in patients presenting with these disorders, many of the patients with anorexia nervosa and bulimia are extremely difficult to treat and respond best to combined modalities of treatment. And, although many papers are written about treating adults with eating disorders, Wachsmuth and Garfinkel (1983) underscore the point that there is only a limited number of articles available on the treatment of adolescents. They emphasize the importance of the treating physicians or therapist's being able to set and prioritize clear treatment goals for this age group.

The goals they outline include establishing and maintaining a treatment alliance; weight restoration or a cessation of bingeing, vomiting, or other unhealthy weight reduction methods; improvement in eating behavior; and improvement in social behavior.

Outpatient treatment is the most frequent option and its choice is determined by severity of symptoms (Ponton, 1993). It should be individualized but may include a protocol approach for symptom control. Individual psychotherapy is the most common treatment modality, used within a multimodality approach outpatient treatment. Bruch (1982) describes a style of therapy in which the therapist pays close attention to the patient and assists with identification, clarification, and understanding of feelings.

Inpatient treatment is determined by the presence of specific criteria, which Herzog and Copeland (1985) define as weight loss greater than 30% over a three-month period; metabolic disturbances manifested by vital sign changes, or changes in the potassium or bound urea nitrogen; suicidal risk; severe purging with a risk of aspiration; or the presence of psychosis and the existence of a family crisis that puts the adolescent's physical health or safety in jeopardy. A combined methodologic approach to inpatient treatment should be adopted, including the implementation of an eating-disorder protocol to restore eating and a combined approach utilizing individual family, group, and biological therapy. The inpatient hospitalization might begin with a behavioral modification plan that reinforces weight gain by offering a levels system with increasing responsibility and privilege. Nasogastric feeding is also frequently employed if the severity of weight loss mandates it (Larocca and Goodner, 1986). The inpatient unit also offers an opportunity for intensive education about faulty eating behaviors and can use group, milieu, family, and individual therapy; diet and exercise counseling; and psychoeducational material to promote changes in eating and social behavior.

Family therapy may be an important component of both inpatient and outpatient treatment. It is particularly important in the treatment of adolescents. In a randomized study of discharged inpatients with eating disorders (Russell, Szmukler, and Dare, 1987) family therapy was found to be most effective with patients whose illness was not chronic and where the onset of the illness had occurred at 19 years or younger. Family therapy appears to be particularly helpful if the patient needs to attain autonomy from the family.

Psychotropic therapy may be an important component but should be carefully integrated with the use of other therapies. Anorectic patients who are depressed have lowered urinary excretion of 3-methoxy-4-hydroxy phenylglycol, which suggests a greater responsiveness to norepinephrine-reuptake blockers such as imipramine or desipramine (Herzog and Copeland, 1985). There are, however, to date no published controlled trials of the use of tricyclic antidepressants in adolescents with eating disorders (Wachsmuth and Garfinkel, 1983). Imipramine and phenelzine have been found to be superior to placebos in reducing depressive and bulimic symptoms in the treatment of bulimia (Bond, Crabbes, and Sanders, 1986), but more controlled studies are needed in the pharmacotherapy of eating disorders.

In general, restrictor anorectics experience more side effects than bulimics with medications. Therefore, careful attention to the side effect profile must occur when treating that population.

Medications that have some utility in treating patients with eating disorders include antidepressants, phenothiazines, anxiolytics, cyproheptadine marketed as periactin, clonidine, naloxone, and lithium.

Tricyclics and other newer antidepressant agents are frequently used in the treatment of bulimia nervosa and are recommended in the treatment of anorexia nervosa when an affective disorder has been diagnosed concomitantly. Treating adolescents diagnosed with anorexia nervosa with tricyclic medication necessitates a careful monitoring of cardiac function with serial EKGs. Adolescents' greater proclivity for cardiac changes makes the consideration of alternatives to tricyclic antidepressants such as Fluoxetine important.

The use of Fluoxetine and other serotinergic agents is also important in patients with bulimia nervosa, where they have been shown to decrease bingeing and associated cravings. Fluoxetine is believed to accomplish this by increasing serotonin levels in the brain. Patients who respond successfully claim that they get full faster and crave binge foods less. It is important to note that antidepressant medication may decrease either depressive symptoms or binging patterns. Current understanding indicates that there is an independent relationship between the two factors, so that one, both, or neither may improve.

Phenothiazines are occasionally used in the treatment of low-weight patients with anorexia nervosa who also present with symptoms of severe anxiety or delusional material. Attention to side-effect profile is crucial and lowered dosage administered because the patients are quite sensitive to medications. Pimazide (Vandereycken and Pierloot, 1982) has been shown to be slightly better than placebo at increasing weight gain. Occasionally patients with anorexia nervosa who are in the hospital on bedrest may benefit from mild anxiolytics to decrease anxiety prior to meals. Xanax has been used for that purpose.

Cyproheptadine (Periactin) is an antihistamine and antiserotonergic agent that competes with histamine and serotonin for receptor sites. This blockage of serotonin supposedly leads to an increased appetite, helping the patients to eat. The medication is manufactured in 4-mg. capsules and given 4–20 mg. per day (Mitchell, 1987; Yates, 1990).

Other agents that have demonstrated some utility include Clonidine (Catapres), which is an adrenergic potentiator that may act centrally to assist patients with strong binge cravings during the withdrawal period. The common dosage is 0.1 mg. bid, but the dose range may be as high as 0.2 to 0.8 mg.

Naloxone hydrochloride is a narcotic antagonist, a synthetic congener of oxymorphone. It is also supposed to decrease cravings in doses of .4 to 2 mg. per day possibly acting through stimulation of beta endorphins.

Lithium carbonate is the treatment of choice for patients codiagnosed with an eating disorder and bipolar affective disorder. Caution must be exercised in using this medication with either bulimic or anorectic patients because of the risks associated with neurological and cardiac toxicity in the population (Bond et al., 1986).

Outcome

The outcome in patients with anorexia nervosa remains guarded. Hsu (1980) found that 50% of hospital-treated patients relapsed within a 12-month period. Studies conducted in Great Britain (Hawley, 1985; Bryant-Waugh, Knibbs, and Fosson, 1988) examining early- to mid-adolescent-onset eating disordered girls found that 65% to 76% percent of the girls were within 15% of ideal body weight at greater than five-year follow-up; however, regular menses were found in only 50%. There appears to be the continued presence of psychosocial difficulties and eating disturbance. The outcome research in bulimia nervosa focuses on different factors in changed eating behavior. Norman and Herzog (1986) note a reduction in core symptoms, somatic complaints, and depressive symptoms in their study examining treatment versus nontreatment groups. Several studies (Brotman, Herzog, and Hamburg, 1988; Wozniak and Herzog, 1993) document high rates of both relapse and recovery.

Better understanding of the chronicity of the illness and promoting the use of terms such as "relapse" and "remission" instead of "cure" promote clinical understanding and further prevention. Understanding the wide range of severity included within the spectrum of eating disordered patients is crucial.

Epidemiology Including Subgroups as Increased Risk

Specific subgroups of patients with eating disorders deserve special attention. The first is prepubertal children (latency age to early adolescent, approximately 8–13 years). The second group is patients who present with eating disorders and another psychiatric diagnosis concomitantly; most commonly this is an affective, personality, substance abuse, or anxiety disorder. A third group is males presenting with the disorder.

Very little is known about the prevention of eating disorders in latency-age children (Singer et al., 1992). Certain characteristics have been found more commonly in this population when diagnosed with anorexia nervosa or bulimia nervosa (Irwin, 1984; Jemerin and Ponton, 1987). These include a more frequent association at the time of onset with a physical illness; the failure to make expected height and weight gain rather than a weight loss; a dramatic decrease in fluid intake; and a clinical picture that frequently shows a battery of other symptoms, including depression and anxiety. Jaffe and Singer (1989) propose that these children have a specific syndrome and do not fall into either diagnostic category. Singer and colleagues (1992) propose that eating disorders in prepubertal children can be conceptualized as food phobias, and they suggest a cognitive behavioral model of treatment that examines the patient's and family's behaviors and beliefs. A combined therapeutic approach using individual and family therapy is particularly important with this younger age group.

First-degree relatives of individuals with anorexia and bulimia nervosa are reported to have an increased frequency of affective disorders (American Psychiatric Association, 1987). Vanderheyden and Boland (1987) emphasize, however, that neither anorexia nervosa nor bulimia nervosa should be considered as a variant of affective illness. Although there is clearly an association between affective illness and eating disorders, the relationship between these diagnostic categories still is not well understood, and to identify eating disorders as subtypes or variants of affective disorder would be premature. The diagnoses can be made concomitantly, and the comorbidity of these two categories of illness is a growing area of study (Herzog et al., 1992).

Patients with comorbidity demand a carefully conducted assessment phase of treatment. Major depression is the most commonly diagnosed comorbid disorder (Herzog et al., 1992; Hoffman and Halmi, 1993). Patients diagnosed with both anorexia nervosa and bulimia nervosa exhibited the most chronicity and psychiatric comorbidity (Herzog et al., 1992).

This pattern suggests a subgroup at high risk that should be treated with attention to their high rate of severity. Early detection and appropriate treatment of comorbid disorders increase the likelihood of a good prognosis.

Bulimia nervosa has also been linked to alcohol use (Bulik, 1987) and substance abuse (Lipscomb, 1987). Using the Diagnostic Interview for Borderlines, Pope and colleagues (1987) failed to find a correlation between bulimia nervosa and borderline personality disorder, but other investigators have found comorbidity (Herzog et al., 1992). Garner, Garfinkel, and O'Shaughnessy (1985), and Herzog and colleagues (1992) have further subdivided and defined the diagnoses of anorexia nervosa and bulimia nervosa. They have supported the development of three broad categories with specific features including the two major diagnostic groups and a third diagnostic subgroup that carries both diagnoses. Better definition and understanding of specific subgroups might lead to more specific treatments.

There are varying reports of the prevalence of anorexia nervosa in the adolescent female population (ages 12 to 18 years) from one in 100 females to one in 800 (American Psychiatric Association, 1987). Pyle and colleagues (1983) reported that 4.5% of freshman college students met the diagnostic criteria for bulimia nervosa. Herzog and colleagues (1984) reported that 90% to 95% of the anorectic and bulimic population is female. In the past, most anorectic and bulimia patients were white and from middle-class or upper middle-class families. There are now reports of eating disorders in African-Americans (Pumareiga, Edwards, and Mitchell, 1984), in Asians (Kope and Sack, 1987), and in cultures that are increasingly exposed to western society's influence on both the female's role in society and her physical appearance (Pate et al., 1992).

Although clinicians and researchers tend to agree that eating disorders have increased dramatically over the past two decades, many prevalence surveys indicate that anorexia is to be found in approximately one case per 100 adolescent girls, with women of the highest social classes at greater risk. The incidence of eating disorders, specifically anorexia nervosa, is reported to have doubled in the past 20 years (Jones et al., 1980; Willi and Grossmann, 1983). A study from Great Britain attributes part of the increased incidence to the larger number of young women in the population (Williams and King, 1987). Cultural factors, however, are believed to play the dominant role (Yates, 1989). The pressure of high achievement seems to increase the risk of developing an eating disorder. Herzog and Copeland (1985) report that 15% of all women medical students have a lifelong history of an eating disorder. Eating-disordered patients may rely excessively on the environment for their sense of self-worth, which makes them extremely vulnerable to cultural pressures. Although many women in our culture are preoccupied with weight, anorectic patients can be differentiated on the basis of their sense of ineffectiveness, lack of introspective awareness, interpersonal distress, and fears of maturity.

Males are said to constitute 5–10% of all anorexia nervosa patients. Overall, the presentation, history, and family dynamics of male and female eating-disordered patients are remarkably similar. Lerner, Orlas, and Knapp (1976) found that physical attractiveness predicts self-concept and self-esteem in adolescent girls, whereas physical effectiveness predicts self-concept in boys. Therefore, it is not surprising that male patients with eating disorders present with unconventional psychosexual development and gender identity issues. Male anorexia nervosa patients are reported to be more extroverted and score superfeminine on many of the personality scales. Yeager and colleagues (1988) found a high prevalence of binge eating problems, terror of being fat, and diuretic use in homosexual male college students, indicating a male group at higher risk for eating disorders.

The changing cross-cultural patterns reported by Pate and colleagues (1992) are also reflected in clinical practice. What does appear to be associated with eating disorders, regardless of cultural background, is loss, as reported in the studies by Kope and Sack (1987) on Asian adolescents and by Pumareiga and colleagues (1984) with a population of African-American adolescents. A second feature is displacement or upward mobility, often reported when a subgroup of minority patients with eating disorders are studied. Kope and Sack (1987) also noted in their study of Asian adolescents that compulsive, perfectionistic Asian girls were more likely to present with the diagnosis of anorexia nervosa.

Summary

Many review articles address the diverse and rapidly developing field of eating disorders, but there are far fewer articles addressing the specific population of adolescents. The social contributors (desire for thinness amplified by the media) to these illnesses are considerable and affect all adolescent and latency-age girls to some degree. Understanding the full range of behavior and those at high risk to develop pathology is important. Developing prevention programs that target adolescent girls and their families, schools, and the relevant media is also important. Prevention has been a much-neglected area within the field of eating disorders.

The chronic nature of eating disorders characterized by remission and relapse bears further study. Attention to the factors that provoke a symptomatic period is crucial. Along with relapse and remission are shifts between diagnostic categories within the field of eating disorders and comorbid illnesses. A better understanding of the factors that cause these shifts to occur would be quite valuable.

Outcome and prospective studies would provide valuable information about the course of the illnesses and further identify the individuals at high risk. Certain groups are known to be at high risk, such as girls involved in specific athletics (e.g., gymnastics) or career activities, but recent investigations have indicated that girls involved in what was previously believed to be a low risk activity, such as swimming, may also be at risk (Benson et al., 1990). Further investigation of these factors is crucial.

Cultural factors play a role in these illnesses, and cross-cultural studies provide crucial information. We must also continue to explore the biological and psychological correlates of these illnesses and further define the complex and heterogenous etiology of these illnesses. Their study still promises to yield exciting challenges.

Increased public awareness regarding the need for treatment of these illnesses is a high priority. If untreated, chronicity appears inevitable. Examination and study of the most cost effective methods of treatment are very important.

REFERENCES

American Psychiatric Association (1987), *Diagnostic and Statistical Manual of Mental Disorders III-Rev.* (DSM-III-R). Washington, DC: American Psychiatric Press.

Benson, J. E., Allemann, Y., Theintz, G. E. & Howard, H. (1990), Eating problems and caloric intake levels in Swiss adolescent athletes. *Internat. J. Sports Med.*, 11:249–252.

Bond, W. C., Crabbes, E. C. & Sanders, M. C. (1986), Pharmacotherapy of eating disorders: A critical review. *Drug Intel. Clin. Pharm.*, 20:659–662.

Boyer, R. M., Katz, J. & Finkelstein, J. W. (1974), Anorexia nervosa: Immaturity of the 24-hour luteinizing hormone secretory pattern. *New Eng. J. Med.*, 291:861–865.

Brotman, A. W., Herzog, D. B. & Hamburg, P. (1988), Long-term course in fourteen bulimic patients treated with psychotherapy. *J. Clin. Psychiat.*, 49:157.

Bruch, H. (1982), Anorexia nervosa: Therapy and theory. *Amer. J. Psychiat.*, 139:1531–1538.

Bryant-Waugh, R., Knibbs, J. & Fosson, A. (1988), Long-term follow-up of patients with early onset anorexia nervosa. *Arch. Dis. Children*, 63:5–9.

Bulik, C. M. (1987), Alcohol use and depression in women with bulimia. *Amer. J. Drug Alc. Abuse*, 13:343–355.

Canning, H. & Meyer, J. (1966), Obesity: Its possible effect on college acceptance. *New Eng. J. Med.*, 285:1407.

_____ & _____ (1967), Obesity: An influence on high school performance. *Amer. J. Clin. Nutrition*, 20:352–354.

Casper, R. C., Hedeker, R. C. & McClough, J. F. (1992), Personality dimensions in eating disorders and their relevance for sub-typing. *J. Amer. Acad. Child Adoles. Psychiat.*, 31:830–840.

Chatoor, I. (1989), Infantile anorexia nervosa: A developmental disorder of separation and individuation. *J. Amer. Acad. Psychoanal.*, 17:43–64.

Chisholm, D. (1978), Obesity in adolescence. *J. Adoles.*, 1:177–194.

Deutsch, H. (1944), *The Psychology of Women*, Vol. I. New York: Grune & Stratton.

_____ (1981), Anorexia nervosa. *Bull. Menninger Clin.*, 45:499–511.

Garfinkel, P. E. & Kaplan, A. S. (1985), Starvation based perpetuating mechanism in anorexia nervosa and bulimia. *Internat. J. Eating Dis.*, 4:661–665.

Garner, D. M., Garfinkel, P. E. & O'Shaughnessy, M. (1985), The validity of the distinction between bulimia with and without anorexia nervosa. *Amer. J. Psychiat.*, 142:581–587.

Gold, D. W. & Rubinow, D. R. (1987), Neuropeptide function in affective illness. In: *Psychopharmacology*, ed. H. W. Meltzer. New York: Raven Press.

Halmi, K. (1983), Anorexia nervosa and bulimia. *Psychosom.*, 24:111-129.

Hawley, R. M. (1985), The outcome of anorexia nervosa in younger subjects. *Brit. J. Psychiat.*, 146:657.

Herzog, D. B. & Copeland, P. M. (1985), Eating disorders (a review). *New Eng. J. Med.*, 313:295-303.

_____ Norman, D. K., Gordon, C. & Pepose, M. (1984), Sexual conflict and eating disorders in 27 males. *Amer. J. Psychiat.*, 141:989-990.

_____ Keller, M. B., Sacks, M. R., Yeh, C. J., & Lavore, P. W. (1992), Psychiatric co-morbidity in treatment- seeking anorexics and bulimics. *J. Amer. Acad. Child Adoles. Psychiat.*, 31:810-818.

Hoffman, L. & Halmi, K. (1993), Co-morbidity and course of anorexia nervosa. In: *Child and Adolescent Clinics of North America*, ed. M. Lewis & J. L. Woolston. Philadelphia, PA: Saunders, pp. 129-145.

Hsu, K. L. (1980), Outcome of anorexia nervosa: A review of the literature (1954-1978). *Arch. Gen. Psychiat.*, 37:1041-1046.

Humphrey, L. L. (1988), Relationships within subgroups of anorexics, bulimics and normal families. *J. Amer. Acad. Child Adoles. Psychiat.*, 27:544-551.

Irwin, M. (1984), Early onset anorexia nervosa. *South. Med. J.*, 77:611-614.

Jaffe, A. & Singer, L. (1989), Atypical eating disorders in young children. *Internat. J. Eating Dis.*, 8:575-582.

Jemerin, J. & Ponton, L. (1987), Eating disorders in children. Presented at Child Grand Rounds, Langley Porter Psychiatric Institute, San Francisco.

Johnson, C., Lewis, C. & Hagman, S. (1984), The syndrome of bulimia: Review and Synthesis. *Psychiat. Clin. N. Amer.,* 7:247-273.

_____ Conners, M. E. (1987), *The Etiology and Treatment of Bulimia Nervosa*. New York: Basic Books.

Jones, D. J., Fox, M. M., Babigian, H. M. & Hutton, H. E. (1980), Epidemiology of anorexia nervosa in Monroe County, New York: 1960-76. *Psychosom. Med.*, 42:551-558.

Kalucy, R. (1976), Obesity: An attempt to find a common ground among some of the biological, psychological and sociological phenomena of the obesity/overeating syndrome. In: *Modern Trends in Psychosomatic Medicine*, Vol. 3, ed. O. Hill. London: Butterworths, pp. 404-429.

Kaye, W. H., Picker, D. M., Naber, D. & Ebert, M. H. (1982),

Cerebrospinal fluid opioid activity in anorexia nervosa. *Amer. J. Psychiat.*, 139:643–645.

Kleinman, R. E. (1987), Obesity. *Pediatrics*, 18:205–208.

Kope, T. M. & Sack, W. H. (1987), Anorexia nervosa in Southeast Asian refugees: A report on three cases. *J. Amer. Acad. Child Adoles. Psychiat.*, 26:795–797.

Larocca, F. E. & Goodner, S. A. (1986), Tube feeding: Is it ever necessary? *New Directions Ment. Health Serv.*, 31:87.

Lerner, R. M., Orlos, J. B. & Knapp, J. R. (1976), Physical attractiveness, physical effectiveness and self-concept in late adolescents. *Adolescence*, 11:313–316.

Lipscomb, P. A. (1987), Bulimia: Diagnosis and management in the primary care setting. *J. Fam. Pract.*, 24:187–194.

Lucas, A. R. (1981), Toward the understanding of anorexia nervosa as a disease entity. *Mayo Clin. Proc.*, 56:254–264.

Melon, L. (1992), Eating disorders. Lecture given to medical students at University of California, San Francisco.

Minuchin, S., Rosman, B. & Baker, L. (1980), *Psychosomatic Families: Anorexia Nervosa in Context.* Cambridge, MA: Harvard University Press.

Mitchell, J. E. (1987), Pharmacology of anorexia nervosa. In: *Psychopharmacology*, ed. H. Y. Meltzer. New York: Raven Press.

Norman, D. K. & Herzog, D. B. (1986), A three-year outcome study of normal weight bulimics: Assessment of psycho-social functioning and eating attitudes. *Psychiat. Res.*, 19:199–207.

Pate, J. D., Pumareiga, A. J., Hester, C. & Garner, D. M. (1992), Cross-cultural patterns in eating disorders: A review. *J. Amer. Acad. Child Adoles. Psychiat.*, 31:802–809.

Ponton, L. (1993). Issues unique to psychotherapy with adolescent girls. *Amer. J. Psychother*, 47:353–372.

Pope, H. G., Frankenburg, F. R., Hudson, J. I., Jonas, J. M. & Yurgelun, T. D. (1987), Is bulimia associated with borderline personality disorder? *J. Clin. Psychiat.*, 8:181–184 (May).

Pumareiga, A. J., Edwards, P. & Mitchell, C. B. (1984), Anorexia nervosa in black adolescents. *J. Amer. Acad. Child Adoles. Psychiat.*, 23:111–114.

Pyle, R. L., Mitchell, J. E., Eckert, E. D., Haluorson, P. A., Newman, P. A. & Goff, G. M. (1983), The incidence of bulimia in freshman college students. *Internat. J. Eating Dis.*, 2:75–85.

Russell, G. F. F., Szmukler, G. L. & Dare, C. (1987), An evaluation of family therapy in anorexia and bulimia nervosa. *Arch. Gen. Psychiat.*, 44:1047.

Singer, L. T., Ambuel, B., Wade, S. & Jaffe, A. C. (1992), Cognitive behavioral treatment of health-impairing food phobias in children. *J. Amer. Acad. Child Adoles. Psychiat.*, 31:847–852.

Stunkard, A., d'Aquilie, E., Fox, S. & Filion, R. (1972), Influence of social class on obesity and thinness in children. *J. Amer. Med. Assn.*, 221:579–584.

Tobias, A. & Gordon, J. (1980), Social consequences of obesity. *J. Amer. Diet. Assoc.*, 76:338–342.

Vandereycken, W. & Pierloot, R. (1982), Pimazide combined with behavior therapy in the short-term treatment of anorexia nervosa. *Acta. Psychiat. Scand.*, 66:445–450.

Vanderheyden, D. A. & Boland, F. J. (1987), A comparison of normals, mild, moderate and severe binge eaters and binge vomiters using discriminant functional analysis. *Internat. J. Eating Dis.*, 6:331–337.

Wachsmuth, J. R. & Garfinkel, P. E. (1993), The treatment of anorexia nervosa in young adolescents. In: *Child and Adolescent Psychiatric Clinics of North America*, ed. M. Lewis & J. L. Woolston. Philadelphia: Saunders, pp. 145–160.

Willi, J. & Grossmann, S. (1983), Epidemiology of anorexia nervosa in a defined region of Switzerland. *Amer. J. Psychiat.*, 140:564–567.

Williams, P. & King, M. (1987), The "epidemic" of anorexia nervosa: Another medical myth? *Lancet*, 7:205–207 (January 24).

Wozniak, J. & Herzog, D. B. (1993), The course and outcome of bulimia nervosa. In: *Child and Adolescent Psychiatric Clinics of North America*, ed. M. Lewis & J. L. Woolston. Philadelphia, PA: Saunders, pp. 109–127.

Yates, A. (1989), Current perspectives on the eating disorders: I. History, psychological and biological aspects. *J. Amer. Acad. Child Adoles. Psychiat.*, 28:813–828.

_____ (1990), Current perspectives on the eating disorders: II. Treatment, outcome and research directions. *J. Amer. Acad. Child Adoles. Psychiat.*, 29:1–9.

Yeager, J., Kurtzman, F., Landsverk, J. & Wiesmeier, E. (1988), Behaviors and attitudes related to eating disorders in homosexual male college studies. *Amer. J. Psychiat.*, 145:495–497.

PART V

TREATMENT MODALITIES

The crux of any compendium about adolescence is the consideration of treatment, and Volume 20 is rich with treatment perspectives. Baroness Ghislaine Godenne begins with a fundamental issue, establishing a therapeutic alliance with a teenager, and Bertram Slaff speculates about the usefulness of short-term, even single-session, psychotherapy with adolescents. This theme is further elaborated by two leaders of the distinguished Toronto clinical research group, Harvey Golombek and Marshall Korenblum, when they present their recommendations about time-limited psychotherapy with teenagers.

Specific clinical situations require modified or special approaches. Philip Katz discusses the critical issues of treating the suicidal adolescent. From years of devoted experience, Irving Berkovitz can write with authority about psychiatric interventions in the adolescent's school life. A more complicated treatment intervention, family therapy with personality disorders, is discussed by Claude Villeneuve and Normand Roux. Considerations of more restrictive interventions conclude this section: partial hospitalization by Dennis Grygotis and Eitan Schwarz, and residential treatment by Jacquelyn Seevak Sanders.

We do not consider psychiatric hospitalization in this volume—its indications and use have changed dramatically in the past few years. Certainly we will return to this modality in the near future.

19 FORMING A THERAPEUTIC ALLIANCE WITH TEENAGERS

BARONESS GHISLAINE D. GODENNE

In this essay on therapeutic alliance, I illustrate how, I, after 30 some years of treating adolescents, have (in my own idiosyncratic way) developed a technique for establishing a therapeutic alliance even with teenagers reluctant to therapy.

Kaplan and Sadock (1991) define therapeutic alliance as a

> conscious contractual relationship between therapist and patient in which each implicitly agrees that they need to work together to help the patient with his or her problems; involves a therapeutic splitting of the patient's ego into observing and experiencing parts. A good therapeutic alliance is especially necessary for the continuation of treatment during phases of strong negative transference [p. 185].

Although I was trained in a Freudian psychoanalytic institute, my work with teenagers is mostly "eclectic," borrowing from a number of therapeutic methods that not only fit my own personality but also, at any given time in therapy, might help in my work with an adolescent. To duplicate blindly what works for one therapist might, however, produce few results with a different therapist. Doctor Otto Allen Will, a well-known psychoanalyst, would get patients to "open up" by his simple question, "What ails you?" When, as a young resident I tried to emulate him by asking the same question, the patient angrily responded, "Where in the earth did you learn to speak English?"

I believe that, regardless of the psychiatric discipline to which one adheres, the establishment of a therapeutic alliance follows the same general principles. To quote Sandor Lorand (1961): "Success in establishing a therapeutic relationship with the patient depends to a large extent on the therapist's personality, ease, self-assurance and patience, and especially on flexibility in using all types of psychotherapy" (p. 241). There are, however, situations outside of our control that might help or hinder the establishment of a working alliance. A very aggressive patient, for instance, not only refused to talk to a couple of psychiatrists who had been sent to evaluate her but also attempted to attack them, stating that only God had a right to know what was on her mind. I was the next psychiatric resident to assume emergency room duties and thus proceeded to try to evaluate her. When, to my surprise, she was most cooperative, easy to deal with, and informative, I asked her about her sudden change of behavior. She answered, "Because you are Doctor God. It's written on your pocket." Indeed the end of my name, Godenne was being covered by my left arm so that my name read "Doctor God"!! Indeed a fortuitous circumstance!!

It is essential not to confuse a "therapeutic alliance," which is a conscious alliance, with an essentially unconscious "positive transference." A positive transference without a working alliance may result in a "flight into health," a "transference cure" that is a result of strong transferential feelings toward the therapist; but it is not a working through of the problems that brought the patient to seek help. In addition, if a teenager relates to the therapist as he or she would relate to a "best friend," for fear of losing the therapist friendship, the therapist might not hear the aspects of the patient's life of which he or she not only is afraid might be disapproved but also might be ashamed.

One's first contact with an adolescent patient sets the stage for the therapy, and so it is crucial to handle it with the utmost care, especially when the teenager denies having any problems needing attention or admits to having problems but has no trust in the therapist's ability to help. Teenagers often deny that they need to see a "shrink." They have little or no insight into their problems and cannot define what is troubling them. Worse, they are often sent, despite their objections, to see a therapist chosen by a parent, teacher, or some other adult in their lives—the very same people with whom they have difficulties. They are striving for independence, eager to move away from their parents' influence, and here they are, brought to the office of a complete stranger in whom they are expected to confide. Our first efforts should therefore be to reassure adolescents that we are not their parents' agents, but doctors specializing in their age group, that we are interested in assessing if, indeed, they need help, and, if they do, we will do our very best to be useful to them.

With that in mind, I choose to know *nothing* about the adolescent I am about to see. I do not read referral notes or school reports, and I ask that the person who calls me to make the appointment refrain from giving me any information about what precipitated the referral. I explain to the referring adult that not knowing in advance why I am seeing the adolescent facilitates my first contact with him or her. I assure the adult, however, that in the course of my evaluation I will set time aside to see him or her. If inadvertently I do learn the reason for the consultation, I will inform the teenager as soon as I see him or her of what transpired during the referral phone call, as I do not want to be in a position to ask a question for which I already know the answer.

It is under those circumstances that I first meet my patient, to whom I can honestly say I know nothing about the reason I am seeing him or her. Sometimes adolescents don't believe me and make such comments as, "You must know. What did my parents tell you when they called?" or "The school said they were going to send you a report." I tell the teenagers that I had asked their parents not to tell me anything about the problem(s) the youngsters are having, as I want to hear from him or her first what is going on in their lives. I might acknowledge that I did indeed receive a letter from the school; it's on my desk but I did not read it, and I will read it only at the end of the appointment. If the teenager still won't tell me why he or she was sent to me, I drop the issue and continue taking his or her history. The history taking has to flow naturally to avoid having the adolescent build up more defenses. I usually go from finding out about parents, siblings, pets, friends (of same and different sex) to ask about school, the youngster's goals in life, recreation activities and so on.

I am careful not to appear more interested in one area or another, as patients sometimes tell us what they believe we want to hear. Years ago a patient with whom I had been working for a couple of years was interviewed by a medical student. She confided in him that she had had many sexual experiences but had kept that information from me. I did nothing with this important piece of information until a few weeks later when the patient came to my office and said she felt so guilty about her interview with the medical student that she wanted to get it off her chest. Indeed, she had never had sex (she was only 15 years old), but the student had appeared so eager to hear her sexual history — when she admitted having sex, he wanted to know how many times, with how many partners and so on.. To please him she made up an exciting history of sexual orgies in a cabin behind her home in Texas. Patients do sometimes go to great lengths to entertain their therapists.

Once I have completed the history, if I still do not know the reason for the referral, I might say something like "Peter, I still have no idea why I am seeing you! Could you help clarify that question?" By such a remark, I confirm once more my lack of knowledge of the situation and also give the patient reassurance that I, for one, don't see him as "crazy" (which is why so many adolescents believe they are sent to psychiatrists). A few years ago, a patient was referred for me to sign a commitment paper on him. He was most uncooperative during the appointment until I told him that I had been asked to commit him to a psychiatric facility because of recent "crazy behavior" at home, but I had trouble evaluating the situation as he did not talk. His response was, "I thought you had decided to put me away so why talk." I answered, "How can I commit you without hearing from you what happened?" He then told me the whole story, which led me to conclude that not only did he not belong in a hospital, but he did not even need psychotherapy. I saw his parents, and their story coincided with his. They were young and inexperienced and had overreacted to typical adolescent behavior. We discussed more appropriate ways to deal with teenagers, and they all left relieved by my evaluation. They advertised me in their neighborhood as the psychiatrist who in one visit could cure a teenager sent her for commitment papers! My reputation seemed made until I was referred all the psychopaths of the area!

Finally, before the appointment with the adolescent comes to an end, I ask him or her to draw (tree, house, person and person of the opposite sex), and as he or she is drawing I ask if it's OK that I read the report the school sent me about him or her. As I read it, if I run into any information he or she did not share with me, I report it to the patient in a very matter-of-fact way so he or she will know what I know and have the opportunity to comment on it or ignore it.

As the adolescent is about to leave my office, if I have determined that I should see him or her again, I don't ask if he or she would agree to return to see me; but I say, in a very assured tone of voice, that I will make an appointment with the parents to bring him or her back the following week. Asking teenagers if they are willing to come back is placing them in the awkward position of admitting that they need psychiatric help. It is also not a genuine question because, regardless of their answer, I will schedule another appointment to see them. A note of caution: if more than a week elapses between the first and the next appointment, one risks losing whatever little headway one might have gained in establishing a therapeutic alliance.

Despite legitimate concern that by seeing the parents one compromises the establishment of a working alliance, as teenagers might feel that we are "ganging up" on them, it is essential not only to hear from the parents their concerns concerning their adolescent but also to get from them a complete developmental history, family history, and the like. To minimize any negative effect my appointment with the parents might have on the therapeutic alliance, I ask the teenager if it's OK if I talk with his or her parents. Thus once more I clearly state my position: I am the adolescent's private therapist; he is the one who is my patient and can choose if I see or do not see the parents. In the rare instance when a patient refuses permission, I will postpone my visit with the parents until, in the course of subsequent appointments, I obtain consent.

When I do meet with the parents, I invite the adolescent to remain in the office while I see them, although I do mention that parents often feel more comfortable talking in the absence of the teenager. Rarely do adolescents insist on remaining in the office; they are usually only too happy to be spared a confrontation with their parents. Once they have agreed to let me talk to their parents, I ask the adolescents to bring them from the waiting room to my office, again reinforcing my role as *the adolescent's therapist* and not an agent of his or her parents. I also make it clear to both the adolescent and the parents that I will not divulge anything the adolescent tells me, unless he or she is a danger to himself or herself or to others, although I will feel free to relate to my patient any information I gather from his or her parents.

Occasionally, I learn from the parents a very important aspect of the adolescent's behavior that he or she neglected to tell me. In those instances, I make a point to see the adolescent for a few minutes before he or she leaves the building in order to let him or her know that his or her parents informed me of a problem that I understand was probably too hard for him or her to tell me. Only when he or she is ready to talk about it can we try to understand it. If I neglect this last step, the patient who suspects that the parents have related to me all aspects of his or her behavior might be so fearful of my reaction to the information just reported that he or she will refuse to return to see me. His or her anxiety, however, will be relieved by seeing that I am unchanged by the disclosure.

A good first appointment does not assure the formation of a solid working alliance, but it does play a very important role in obtaining it. As adolescents return to see us, they want to know more about us and often feel it is unfair that we get answers to our questions but they don't have the opportunity to find out about us. I tell them that, indeed, it seems unfair but that, on the last day of their therapy, I will answer all their questions. I have never had to do so. One patient told me on the last day of his analysis, "I could know the answers to all my questions today, but I no longer need to, I know you pretty well as my analyst and that is enough."

Psychotherapy with adolescents is full of roadblocks. Indeed, adolescents who are striving for independence and have little faith in adults are going to have to accept a certain degree of dependence on their therapist and learn to trust his or her motives. They will, we hope, come to see us as people more reliable than those in their everyday environment. In addition, adolescents want quick results, but they will have to come to terms with the fact that therapy is a slow process and that the road to achieving the final goal may at times be arduous. These obstacles to treatment force us to concentrate our efforts on keeping reluctant adolescents in treatment long enough to establish a therapeutic alliance. Losing adolescents to therapy is often due to the fact that from the very beginning our role is not clear to them. Early in treatment, we should spend time explaining to our patients the process of therapy: that they might become somewhat dependent on us initially but that by the end of therapy they will be more independent than they were when they first started; and that it will be hard at times to tell us what is on their minds, but that is the only way we together can find out what is at the root of their problems.

While discussing how the unconscious can play tricks on one, it is often reassuring to give examples from our own lives so they do not feel that we place ourselves above them. I explain to them, for instance, how at times when I am angry and can't express it, I get a headache. Although we belong to a different generation, we must convey to our adolescent patients that we are eager to understand their world and that we do indeed share some of their interests. At all times, however, we have to remain their therapist and not become a "buddy," because teenagers will see that latter role as "phony." Even though they might enjoy hearing us talk their language, use their curse words, speak their slang, they will not readily form a therapeutic alliance with a person who "plays a role." Sharing interests, on the other hand, and showing our knowledge in an area important to them will help them see us as allies.

For example, one day John told me that he had nothing more to tell me because I was not interested in the things he loved. I asked him to give me a chance to prove myself, and he said, "You know nothing about cars." I said that I probably knew more than he expected me to, and he challenged me in a game in which each of us would give the make of a car and the last one to come up with one would win. We played, I won, and John left the appointment saying, "My mother won't let me talk about cars. She says she is not interested in them. It's boy stuff." The test, however, was not quite over. The next week John wanted to play the car game again, and I noticed under his coat that he had brought in a car magazine. We played. He lasted longer than the week before, but I ended up by winning because I knew the makes of many European cars. This cemented our relationship: I was trustworthy, I was able to talk about kid stuff, and so maybe he could start sharing with me some of his hidden world.

Sometimes, it is through a pet that one reaches an adolescent. I always inquire if they have pets and often share with them my interest in animals. Before a solid working alliance has been established, talking about a pet's feelings is at times as close as one can get to the feelings poignantly transferred to their pet. (Admittedly, when the pet is a fish, the job is not that easy!) As the therapeutic alliance solidifies, the patient is slowly able to admit that he or she is experiencing the same feelings as those with which he or she endowed the pet.

To obtain a therapeutic alliance, we have to see ourselves as the adolescent's advocate and ally but not fall into the trap of becoming his or her accomplice. For acting-out patients, a very thin line can be drawn between both roles, and at times one feels that one is dangerously dangling on a tightrope. Indeed, we want to have patients share with us their thoughts and feelings, but what do we do when they inform us of some delinquent act they are about to commit or their plans to run away from home? In these instances should we make exceptions to the rule of confidence that governs treatment and by doing so seriously threaten the therapeutic alliance? As therapists for adolescents we must allow a certain amount of acting out, but, equally important, we must know when to step in. Unlike Aichhorn (1935), who was a master at forming working alliances with wayward youth, we do not have the luxury of time or of a controlled and secure environment in which to treat them.

In the course of treatment we are likely to run into a period (or periods) of negative transference in which the patient declares that he or she just can't talk to us, that he or she does not like us, that our personalities aren't a good fit, and he or she wants to quit therapy. Very often such comments carry the following messages: "You really do not care about me; you just want my parents' money" or "You are just like my parents; you don't want to let me go, to let me grow up." I usually handle such a situation by telling the adolescent that if he or she does not feel that he or she can work with me, although I do not agree that it is the case, I will refer him or her to another psychiatrist because he or she still has problems that need attending to. I do not recall any patient's leaving under such circumstances, as my offer to transfer him or her in order to finish the work we started together reassures him or her that my primary concern is his or her welfare.

But let us return to the parents who are left outside of the therapeutic work. If I feel they are very needy of support, I will refer them to another therapist with whom I work closely and who has views similar to mine on how to work with adolescents. Most parents, if one has taken time to explain to them how one best works with teenagers, will accept, albeit reluctantly, one's modus operandi. I explain to them that for the time being my relationship with their adolescent has to remain a one-to-one relationship and to bring them into the psychotherapy will compromise my work. I tell them, however, to feel free to get in touch with me if some important event happens in their teenager's life and they are not sure how to handle it. I add that they should inform their adolescent of the call because I will mention it when I see him or her. If at any time during therapy, my patient, I, or both of us feel a need for me to meet with the parents to straighten out some misunderstanding or to improve their handling of a particular situation, I will schedule an appointment with them but only after having thoroughly discussed with the patient what I plan to share with them. I saw Paul's mother once because, although she had referred Paul to me because he was abusing alcohol, Paul told me that his mother was the one who bought the alcohol for him. Mrs. X explained that indeed it was so because Paul was not of age to buy alcohol legally and she was protecting him from the police.

Sometimes, my patient instructs me about what I should say. Occasionally, a family meeting is advisable, so that the adolescent and the parents can, in the presence of a third party, exchange their views about a given situation or event. During those family meetings, one often feels like one is walking on eggshells—one wants to remain the patient's ally but at the same time be of some support to the parents, who after all have the final word about the child's remaining in therapy. Soon after a tumultuous family meeting, I try to schedule a session with my patient to straighten out any misunderstanding that could threaten our therapeutic alliance.

With suicidal adolescents the working alliance may be stretched to the limit. It is advisable to deal with suicide threats before the crisis by informing the patient that any suicide attempt will bring about a reconsideration of our work. If the positive transference is strong enough, such a threat to terminate treatment usually keeps the patient from making a suicide attempt. Once more, it conveys the message that I am interested in working with them but not if they sabotage treatment by hurting themselves.

Provocative adolescents too often test our patience to the limit. A good sense of humor is helpful in such circumstances, for it allows us not to become the adversary against whom the youngsters have to fight, but one who understands their game. Going along with it takes the wind out of their sails. The completely silent adolescent is not any easier. For them not to feel under pressure to talk, which would tend to increase their defenses, I try to keep busy, by leafing through a magazine, playing solitaire, or doing whatever I feel comfortable doing. My dogs often serve as cotherapists; they have helped many shy, angry, anxious teenagers to open up.

The only adolescents I have learned never to treat are children of friends! Indeed, not only does treating them frequently lead to losing my friends (as I have to curtail all contacts with them as long as the child is in therapy with me), but also it may interfere with their adolescent's treatment as he or she might feel he or she never can quite trust me not to be influenced through my friendship with the parents.

This essay focuses on the therapeutic alliance and thus only tangentially addresses psychotherapeutic work with adolescents. I would be remiss, however, if I did not mention that once the working alliance is consolidated, one's technique in the therapy proper may undergo changes. Such change will not be detrimental to the therapy if the therapist explains to the adolescent that now that he or she understands what they together are working toward, the therapist might, for instance, be less active in the sessions. Failing to acknowledge a change in our technique might make the adolescent wonder if he or she has done something wrong, if we have lost interest, or even if we are angry at him or her or whatever else he or she might fantasy.

In summary, as we work with adolescents, we have to concentrate our efforts very early in treatment to establish a therapeutic alliance. Once it is established, we have to work at maintaining it despite situations in which it might be threatened. For it is, indeed, most of the time, only a "fragile alliance" (Meeks, 1971).

REFERENCES

Aichhorn, A. (1935), *Wayward Youth*. New York: Viking Press.

Kaplan, H. I. & Sadock, B. J. (1991), *Comprehensive Glossary of Psychiatry and Psychology*. Baltimore, MD: Williams & Wilkins.

Lorand, S. (1961), Treatment of adolescents. In: *Adolescents: Psychoanalytic Approach to Problems and Therapy*, ed. S. Lorand & H. Schneer. New York: Paul B. Hoeber, pp. 238–250.

Meeks, J. E. (1971), *The Fragile Alliance*. Baltimore, MD: Williams & Wilkins.

20 THOUGHTS ON SHORT-TERM AND SINGLE-SESSION THERAPY

BERTRAM SLAFF

Ernest Jones (1955), in his biography of Freud, gives an early example of single-session therapy. In the summer of 1910 Freud was on holiday in the Netherlands when he received an urgent telegram from Gustav Mahler, the composer, asking for an appointment. Jones states that Mahler was greatly distressed about his relationship with his wife. Though loath to interrupt his vacation, Freud responded affirmatively to Mahler's request. Then he received another telegram cancelling the appointment.

> Soon there came another request, with the same result. Mahler suffered from the *folie de doute* of his obsessional neurosis and repeated this performance three times. Finally Freud had to tell him that his last chance of seeing him was before the end of August, since he was planning to leave then for Sicily. So they met in an hotel in Leyden and then spent four hours strolling through the town and conducting a sort of psychoanalysis. Although Mahler had had no previous contact with psychoanalysis, Freud said he had never met anyone who seemed to understand it so swiftly. . . .This analytic talk evidently produced an effect, since Mahler recovered his potency and the marriage was a happy one until his death, which unfortunately took place only a year later [pp. 79–80].

A number of years ago, a 35-year-old woman consulted me because of a severe state of depression that began, she said, shortly after her younger daughter's birthday three months earlier. She could provide no explanation for the profound dysphoria. Relationships with her parents, her husband, and two daughters, now 12 and 14, were described as good.

A detailed medical history was obtained. Mrs. K mentioned that she had had a breast removed because of a tumor, subsequently reported as malignant. To avoid alarming her children, who were then seven and nine, she had told them that she had had a cyst removed from her breast and forcefully maintained a cheerful response to the surgery. When she was asked when the procedure had taken place, she replied that it was shortly after her younger daughter's birthday.

I was aware that often women with breast cancer are told that if they survive five years, they can then consider themselves out of the danger of recurrence. For five years Mrs. K had maintained a bold façade denying a major worry so as not to alarm her young children. Mrs. K now felt that she was well. Was it possible, I asked, that the apprehension and anxiety over a possible recurrence had been hidden for five years and had now surfaced as depression when she felt safe and when her children were now adolescent? An appointment was made for the following week.

On the weekend Mrs. K called to report some dramatic events. She had discussed the session with her husband, and he had supported her in revealing the facts of her cancer operation to their daughters. There was a great deal of emotional upheaval and weeping among all the family members with strong evidence of love and support; and the depression had lifted! Mrs. K thanked me for what she called my great help and cancelled the next session, saying that the problem was over. Recognizing the possibility of a "flight-into-health" defensive maneuver, I asked her to keep me informed as to how she was feeling. A month later, and again three months afterward, she called to say that she was continuing to feel well.

In 1969 a distinguished professor of theology called to express his concern about his 15-year-old son, who, he felt, was behaving disrespectfully to his parents and might be in need of help. At issue was the boy's recent refusal to wear a tie and jacket at the family dinner each evening. After one session with him, it was my impression that this was not a psychiatrically troubled youth. There did seem to be an intergenerational conflict between the boy, an only child, and his somewhat older parents (mother, age 50; father, age 60), who had rigid and perhaps old-fashioned expectations. I alerted the parents to the student rebellions that had recently taken place at Columbia University, at Harvard University, and in the French university settings and raised the possibility that their son's behavior might not be a manifestation of disrespect but rather a response to his generation's desire to resist adult formalisms. I expressed confidence in the basic health of their son. The parents reacted favorably to my intervention. Follow-up calls indicated a satisfactory resolution of the difficulty.

A 16 year-old, 6′ 7″ high school basketball player consulted me because of an obsessive and haunting conviction that he was a "phony"; he knew he was tall, but he felt "small." When others commented on his height and his excellent athletic prowess, he was inwardly overwhelmed with feelings of dishonesty, which he kept to himself. He was fully aware of the facts, but he could not harmonize and integrate the knowing he was tall, yet feeling he was small.

He was the youngest of three boys. He reported that his mother had often said to him that, no matter what, he was her youngest child and would always be her baby. I speculated that he may have dealt with this comment concretely: babies were small; if he would always be her baby, perhaps that was taken to mean he would always be small, a fixed perception that left no room for actual growth.

He was highly excited by what I said. He felt that this made his ruminating less "crazy" and more comprehensible. He continued to see me for a short time, but with the conviction, which lasted, that the mystery was on the way to being solved and that he could now see his way clear to getting over the obsessive preoccupation with his being "small" and a "phony."

David Malan (1976) remarks:

> Anyone who practices long-term psychotherapy occasionally meets a type of patient who may be described as a 'ripe plum,' ready for picking. . . . This is often a basically healthy patient suffering from symptoms due to an acute conflict, whose unconscious is very close to the surface, and who responds dramatically to a simple piece of insight that, to an experienced psychotherapist, is utterly obvious. Robert Knight quotes a typical example: "a farmer suffering from weakness of his right arm, which was very clearly a conversion symptom designed to prevent him from being able to express his wish to hit people. . . relieved almost immediately by what amounted to a single interpretation" [p. 349].

Moshe Talmon (1990) believes that for many professionals, single-session encounters might be considered as no treatment at all or as intake or consultation at best. He asks, how could they be called therapy, if therapy implies deep and long-term changes of personality. He reports that he was trained to see therapy as a relatively long process. Single sessions often suggested "no-show" for the second appointment, "dropout," "premature termination," "failure," and other negative evaluations. Talmon learned about the frequency of the single-session therapy phenomenon while working in the Department of Psychiatry at the Kaiser Permanente Medical Center in Hayward, California. There he discovered that the most frequent length of contact for every one of the therapists employed there was a single session and that 30% of all patients chose to come for only one session in a period of one year. Though many were offered another appointment, with no fee or a very small one, they chose not to keep their second appointment or to seek therapy elsewhere. He later studied 100,000 scheduled outpatient appointments during a five-year period (1983–1988) and found the frequency of single-session contacts to be extremely consistent.

An extensive review of the literature reveals that this finding has been well documented over a period of more than 30 years in a variety of settings. In a follow-up study by Talmon of 200 patients he had seen just once, 78% said that they had gotten what they wanted out of the single session and felt better or much better about the problem that had led them to seek therapy. A "blind" postdoctoral student interviewed a sample of Talmon's single-session therapy (SST) patients; her interviews did not evoke significantly more positive or negative outcomes than Talmon's own had.

After studying dropouts in a community mental health center, Silverman and Beech (1979) concluded that the notion that dropouts represent failure by the client or the intervention system is clearly untenable. They reported that almost 80% of the clients interviewed said that their problems had been solved, 70% acknowledged satisfaction with the services rendered, and the majority of client expectations of the center were met.

Basing his findings on research at the Tavistock Clinic in London, Malan and his associates (1975) advise that psychiatrists who undertake consultations should not automatically assign patients to long-term psychotherapy or even to brief psychotherapy, but should consider the possibility that a single dynamic interview may be all that is needed.

Cummings and Follette (1976) reported that being seen for only one session of psychotherapy resulted in a significant decline in the patients' overall utilization of medical facilities. This was evident over a five-year period. "The finding that one session only, with no repeat psychological visits, could reduce medical utilization by 60% over the following five years was surprising and totally unexpected" (p. 167).

People who initiate a call to a mental health provider often feel themselves to be in a state of crisis, sometimes subsumed under the rubric of adjustment disorders. Crisis-intervention techniques are then called for. At present, great attention is being paid to the redesign of the health delivery system in the United States. Cost containment is a major focus of political interest, and governmental and insurance company support for long-term psychotherapies is under serious challenge. The concept of single-session therapy may prove to be a timely one.

Talmon (1990) states, "The single-session therapy approach is offered to patients and therapist who are ready and motivated to take care of business *now*, and it leaves the door open to what has become known as intermittent therapy throughout the life cycle" (p. xvi). The goal is to promote substantial changes in patients' lives. Efforts are made to provide guidance on how to use time differently, how to foster readiness and motivation, and how to combine the necessary intake-diagnostic process with that of prompting change.

The therapist's attitude toward the phenomenon of SST in general is of prime importance. He must be more inclined to see a single session as potentially valuable rather than as a dropout failure. Eric Berne (1966) says approvingly:

> The patient has a built-in drive to health, mental as well as physical. His mental development and emotional development have been obstructed, and the therapist has only to remove the obstructions for the patient to grow naturally in his own direction. . . .The therapist does not cure anyone, he only treats him to the best of his ability, being careful not to injure, and waiting for nature to take its healing course [p. 63].

Two traditional ways of perceiving the first session are seen as potential resistances to SST: using the session primarily for history-taking, assessment, and diagnosis; and using the session to establish rapport, avoiding issues that might be sensed as disturbingly confrontational. Presession inquiry is seen as part of the therapeutic process. A person might be asked to keep a detailed diary of the disturbing events prior to the session. Identification of significant others in the person's constellation may be sought, and these persons might be invited to share in the session.

The multiple challenges of SST include how to address the questions of how to start and end therapy in one session; how to create a focus when there is so much information to sort out; how to open up toward patients' strengths rather than pathology; how to use the first session to practice solutions; how to leave enough time to attend to last-minute issues; what to include in the final feedback; and how to leave an open door for further change or therapeutic contacts.

SST is not psychoanalytic psychotherapy reduced and concentrated into one session. It is not predicated on the examination of transference and countertransference issues. It does not call for the reliving of meaningful early experiences in one's childhood. It does not focus on resistances. It is a response to readiness to change, which is conceptualized by Talmon (1990) as

> a state of immediate preparedness and willingness in which various conditions are near a threshold and can, with recognition and skillful facilitation, be assisted and potentiated into actuality. Readiness may occur when old mental constructs have either decayed "spontaneously" (through disuse or maturation) or have been actively proved untenable or unworkable, resulting in a crisis with its attendant combination of emotional pain and growth opportunity. . . . Creating readiness for action and change is crucial for the success of SST [pp. 36–37].

Certain people are thought of as unsuitable candidates for SST. These include those who might require inpatient psychiatric care, such as suicidal or psychotic persons; individuals suffering from conditions that suggest strong genetic, biological, or chemical components, such as manic-depression and schizophrenia; persons with organic manifestations, such as Alzheimer's; and those, often including mental health professionals, who request long-term therapy up front. Some borderline patients, people involved in difficulties with the law, and persons involved in compensation struggles are not considered good choices for SST.

Persons who might gain from SST include those who come to solve a specific problem; the "worried well," who come for a mental health check-up, essentially to ask whether they are "normal"; those who can identify, perhaps with the therapist's assistance, helpful solutions and past successes; patients who have a particular "stuck" feeling, such as anger, guilt, or grief over past events; persons who come for evaluation and need referral for medication, medical examinations, or other nonpsychotherapy services; persons who would be better off without any treatment, such as individuals going through the normative crises of living; and patients faced with a truly unsolvable problem. "Acknowledging the impossibility of change and aiding patients to cease useless or compulsive attempts to solve the impossible may help them attain a measure of equanimity and acceptance by letting go of further attempts for 'cure'" (Talmon, 1990, p. 31).

Conclusions

Jerome Frank (1990) stresses that most outpatients may have considerable powers of spontaneous recuperation as well as the ability to resolve their problems. It is up to the therapist to mobilize these potentials in single-session therapy by encouraging the patient, through understanding and empathic responsiveness, to explore alternative solutions. The complexity of the therapeutic encounter is acknowledged and recognition given to the anticipatory phase, the session itself, and the mulling over that follows indefinitely.

This approach, of course, challenges powerfully the traditional role of the therapist as a patient observer, awaiting the gradual exposure of the layers of defenses the patient has acquired through a troubled lifetime. It is hoped that, through the reliving of these difficulties in the transference, newer and more effective techniques for living might be discovered. Instead the emphasis is on the "here-and-now," the approach is that of "crisis intervention," the time frame of reference is not long term but immediate. The therapist must be energized from passive waiting into forceful creative leadership. That there is a risk of inadequately trained therapists' "acting out" destructively in this newer role must be conceded and guarded against.

Malan and Osimo (1992) state that the field of brief psychotherapy has for many years suffered from the "hypothesis of superficiality," that only superficially ill patients can be treated by a superficial technique and with only superficial therapeutic results. The authors consider this hypothesis to be based on preconception and prejudice. They believe that evidence currently available leads to the opposite conclusion: that therapeutic benefits that are wide ranging, deep seated, and long lasting may occur even in patients with relatively severe disturbances.

Psychiatrists who work with adolescents know that many referrals arise out of conflicts between teenagers and their parents. The therapists are aware that the young people are in a rapid-growth phase, physically and emotionally, and that apparent disturbances may be temporary and may be outgrown over the course of continuing growth and development. "Crisis intervention" techniques may be quite sufficient.

REFERENCES

Berne, E. (1966), *Principles of Group Treatment*. New York: Oxford University Press.

Cummings, N. & Follette, W. (1976), Brief psychotherapy and medical utilization. In: *The Professional Psychologist Today*, ed. H. Dörken, R. Bent, N. Cummings, J. Dinorin, W. Follette, D. Jacobs, D. Rodgers, A. Shapiro, J. Whiting & S.Wiggins. San Francisco: Jossey-Bass.

Frank, J. (1990), Foreword. In Talmon, M., *Single-Session Therapy*. San Francisco: Jossey-Bass, pp. xi–xiii.

Jones, E. (1955), *The Life and Work of Sigmund Freud, Volume 2* . New York: Basic Books.

Malan, D. (1976), *The Frontier of Brief Psychotherapy*. New York: Plenum Press.

_____ Heath, E., Bacal, H. & Balfour, F. (1975), Psychodynamic changes in untreated neurotic patients, II: Apparently genuine improvements. *Arch. Gen. Psychiat.*, 32:110–126.

_____ & Osimo, F. (1992), *Psychodynamics, Training, and Outcome in Brief Psychotherapy*. London: Butterworth-Heineman.

Silverman, W. & Beech, R. (1979), Are dropouts, dropouts? *J. Comm. Psychol.*, 7:236–242.

Talmon, M. (1990), *Single-Session Therapy*. San Francisco: Jossey-Bass.

21 BRIEF PSYCHOANALYTIC PSYCHOTHERAPY WITH ADOLESCENTS

HARVEY GOLOMBEK AND MARSHALL KORENBLUM

Conducting psychotherapy with adolescents is often exciting, stimulating, and thought provoking. It can also be challenging, frustrating, confrontational, and disarmingly honest. To maintain equilibrium the therapist must bring to the therapeutic journey some background in normal psychological development, that is an understanding of the early, middle, and late stages of adolescence; an understanding of changes in symptoms and clinical presentation that vary with stage; an understanding of the characteristic patterns of transference and countertransference that vary with stage; and some appreciation of cognitive functioning during adolescence, most importantly with regard to abstract thinking and time perspective (Offer, 1969; Golombek & Marton, 1992).

Empirical developmental research and clinical studies have demonstrated a progression of conflictual themes throughout the course of adolescence. During early adolescence, teenagers present with exaggerated feelings of dependency and neediness; during middle adolescence, with exaggerated feelings of independence and self-sufficiency; in late adolescence, with exaggerated longings for intimacy and closeness (Golombek and Kutcher, 1990). Associated with these thematic changes are changes in the predominant transference reactions. Early adolescents tend to experience a therapist as a frustrating provider. Middle adolescents tend to experience their therapists as a challenging and controlling authority figure, while late adolescents tend to experience therapists as intimate, idealized confidants. As central intrapsychic conflictual themes are experienced in the therapeutic relationship, the transference often becomes an important arena for the development of emotional insight into maladaptive, stage-specific, exaggerated personality patterns. The patterns that appear clearly in the transference are presented most often by patients in relation to difficulties with current interpersonal relationships. Reference to genetic formulations are frequently presented in the therapy but are generally experienced by patients to be of less emotional importance, particularly with early and middle adolescents.

Adolescents either come voluntarily or are directed to therapy by parents or other authority figures because of specific concerns related to particular problems. Unlike adults, they seldom present with a recognition of pervasive personality difficulties requiring extensive change. When interested in psychotherapy, they indicate a wish to proceed with focus and direction and seek assurance that help can be received within a reasonable time. Since most adolescents experience major conflicts surrounding dependence–independence, the prospect of entering a close relationship with an adult that has a predetermined time limit feels safer and more comfortable than agreeing to become involved in a time-unlimited therapy, which suggests continued and prolonged dependency.

Work with adolescents requires that the therapist be realistic about what changes are possible within a developmental stage and within a specific time frame. The therapist must give up fantasies of therapeutic perfectionism and help the patient make small but significant changes in major areas of conflicted functioning. Helping an adolescent grow in personality functioning, which will allow movement into a more mature phase, often represents the most realistic goal that can be achieved. Psychotherapy with adolescents should be conceived as a method of helping them get back onto the developmental track rather than as an attempt at accomplishing a total personality overhaul.

The purpose of this chapter is to illustrate that brief psychodynamic psychotherapy is an effective tool particularly well suited to the adolescent age group. A case example is described to demonstrate the use of a specific model of brief therapy.

Brief Psychodynamic Psychotherapy with Adolescents: A Rationale

Adolescents not only present with symptoms of psychiatric disorder but also with conflicts surrounding developmental tasks. Foremost among these are (1) psychological separation and individuation; (2) achieving a balance between independence and dependence; and (3) forming a cohesive identity—sexual, vocational, recreational, and religious. Fears of psychological regression and identity diffusion, together with wishes for autonomy and authenticity, necessitate a psychotherapeutic approach emphasizing activity, clarity, defined goals, and empowerment. Brief psychodynamic therapy encompasses such qualities.

In brief therapy, the therapist is active. The emphasis is on the here-and-now. A finite time limit (or a finite number of sessions) is chosen, which minimizes regression. Having a fixed endpoint highlights issues of attachment and detachment and the need to "move on" in life. Termination of therapy mirrors the termination of childhood, and therefore useful grief work associated with the loss of primary love objects can be accomplished. The beginning, middle, and end phases of brief psychotherapy parallel, in telescoped fashion, the early, middle, and late phases of adolescence, with their corresponding issues of dependence, autonomy, and intimacy.

In brief psychotherapy, a clearly defined focus is chosen, mutually agreed upon, and adhered to. This process models boundary settings, negotiation, and persistence in the pursuit of goals. Requiring agreement between the therapist and patient on the choice of focus conveys respect for the adolescent's decision-making capabilities and ownership of the process and outcome.

Peer problems, conflicts with parents and teachers, and confusion in relationships with significant others are common for teenagers. Since interpersonal foci are preferred in brief therapy, this modality is particularly appropriate for adolescents. Developmental fixations such as unresolved oedipal conflicts are also appropriate issues to address.

We have selected 16 weeks as a suitable duration of therapy. Four months corresponds roughly to a school term or semester and thus fits the sociocultural schedule of most teenagers. Furthermore, outcome studies of psychotherapy with adults demonstrate that about two-thirds of patients reach significant improvement by the 16th session, lending empirical support for this time period. It is long enough to establish a therapeutic alliance, but not so long that strong dependence, the bane of an adolescent's psychological existence, is fostered. In this age group, developmental fluidity and characterological openness allows for greater therapeutic impact in a shorter period of time.

The goals of brief therapy with adolescents include a reduction in symptoms, attainment of emotional and intellectual insight, the removal of blocks to healthy personality development, improved interpersonal functioning, and consolidation of identity formation by connecting thoughts, feelings, and behavior with underling wishes.

The Core Conflictual Relationship Theme Method (CCRT)

There are several models of brief psychodynamic psychotherapy. The models of Sifneos, Davenloo, and Malan have been described elsewhere (Bauer & Kobos, 1987). In their current work with adolescents, the authors have adapted the Core Conflictual Relationship Theme (CCRT) method of Lestor Luborsky (1984). This model was selected because it emphasizes interpersonal conflicts and can be formulated and conveyed to teenage patients with clarity and simplicity. It incorporates both supportive and expressive approaches and is designed for use in both open-ended and time-limited therapies.

The CCRT is derived from "relationship episodes," which are narratives spontaneously reported by the patient about interactions with significant others, that is, parents, peers, authority figures, and the therapist. The themes that emerge most frequently in the relationship episodes are divided into three components: (1) wishes or intentions toward significant others (w); (2) the expected responses of others (actual or imagined) (ERO); and (3) the expected response of the self (actual or imagined) (ERS). The presenting symptoms are generally viewed as components of the expected responses of the self and are understood within the context of the CCRT. The wishes may be progressive or regressive, and the expected responses of the self and others may be adaptive or maladaptive. In our usual formulation of the CCRT, we focus on the positive, progressive, and growth-enhancing wishes and on the negative, maladaptive, and dysfunctional expected responses of the self and the other (i.e., those expected responses which interfere with the realization of positive wishes).

During the assessment phase, the therapist gathers enough data from the relationship episodes to formulate a CCRT. The CCRT then becomes the focus of the therapy. Its meaningfulness is established by trial interpretations, and it is explicitly shared with the patient. Patient and therapist agree together that the CCRT that has been developed during the assessment will become the focus of the therapy. The goal of therapy will become the modification of the negative responses of the self and others. The positive wishes usually remain intact and unchanged. The essence of the CCRT as a conceptual framework for understanding the patient's interpersonal difficulties usually remains constant over the course of the therapy, but its finer details are elaborated or modified as insight is developed by both partners in the treatment process.

Case Example: Maria

The patient is a 19-year-old college sophomore pursuing a degree in architecture. She lives with her father, age 46, a successful dentist and her mother, age 42, unemployed but well known in Eastern Europe as a political activist. Also living in the home is a younger sister, age 17, attending high school.

The patient presented for therapy because of feelings of boredom, insecurity, and unhappiness experienced over the past year. She felt troubled by continuous high tension in the family; she always felt in conflict with one or another family member. She was concerned with being underweight and had difficulty sustaining a nutritious diet. She was anxious about her inability to "get close to boys" either emotionally or physically.

Maria felt she had become more concerned about her problems since changing colleges during the past year. Before college, until age 17, she had felt regimented by her parents and always tried to be a good girl who pleased. Enrolling in college was initially motivated by a desire to please, but she was surprised by her subsequent enjoyment of the work. At the assessment, she expressed concern about whether she would have enough talent to pursue a professional career.

Although she felt able to socialize easily with girls, she had always had difficulties getting close to boys. In her dating experience, she seldom advanced beyond a third date. She felt that boys initially found her clever but intimidating. When they showed continued interest, she would inevitably become frightened of sexual advances and would seek to break the relationship. She feared the boy was not genuinely interested in her but just wanted to use her and then reject her. Anticipating this pattern, she would repetitively become cool and aloof and discourage further contact.

The patient was born in England, where her parents had emigrated from Eastern Europe so that father could pursue postgraduate dental training. After the move, father was busy, active, and happy while mother felt isolated, lonely, miserable, and displaced. Having left a successful political career behind, she felt she would be happier if she had a child. The patient was born without complications soon after emigration.

When the patient was two, the family moved to Canada to further father's career, and another child was conceived in an attempt to help mother deal with unhappy feelings associated with again being displaced.

The patient's happiest family memories are from between ages two to six. She felt close to dad. There was a lot of affection between them, with much hugging, kissing, and sitting on his lap. She remembers mother at this time appearing depressed, withdrawn, and sitting alone for long periods. Little affection was observed between the parents.

When the patient was six, the family moved to another city. With this transition, conflicts between the parents intensified, and the patient remembers "falling out of love" with her father and identifying with her mother. She feels she has disliked father ever since.

When the patient was 11 years old, the family became aware that father was having an affair with a hygienist with whom he worked. Mother became seriously depressed and was treated with antidepressants. She recovered after several months.

At age 17, the patient left home to attend college. At first she felt insecure and anxious and lost 10 pounds. She was criticized heavily by the mother who called her a "skinny runt." The patient had anticipated feeling better living away from home, but instead she initially felt depressed, inactive, and ashamed. Mother called the patient a "whore" for leaving home, living alone, and not being available to support her in the family. During this period, the patient felt isolated and lonely but after four months began to feel somewhat better. She became more outgoing and began to make friends, party, and drink socially. She felt happier and gained weight, but her grades deteriorated.

When she was 18, the parents insisted that she return home. She enrolled at the local school of architecture and returned to living at home. Her academic work improved, but soon she began again to feel sad and lonely. The family noticed her severe unhappiness, and the patient was referred to one of us (M.K.) after father had made inquiries with professional colleagues.

Maria describes herself as having been a serious and cerebral high school student. Intellectually she was competitive, and she soon discovered that she could dominate both male and female friends with her brain. She was never able to get close to a boy. In the senior year of high school, she began to feel gauche, naive, insecure, and uncomfortable around boys. She repeatedly felt rejected by boys she was attracted to and quickly rejected any boy who was attracted to her.

Maria presented as an attractive, well-groomed, well-made-up late adolescent dressed in fashionable clothing, which successfully disguised her thin physique. She was cooperative, engaging, and psychologically observant and appeared motivated to change. She was moderately anxious and very sad. She seemed very intelligent, and there was no evidence of a psychotic or organic disorder. She was preoccupied with a poor self-concept and described inconsistent self-esteem. Her feelings about herself could fluctuate from feeling worthless to feeling superior to others, whom she could experience as silly, without ambition, and intellectually inferior.

She was diagnosed as having a depressive disorder N.O.S. and showing traits of an avoidant personality disorder.

Following assessment, the information gathered was reviewed with the patient; we noted how conflicted she felt and thought about herself and others. She expressed concern about her persistent sad and anxious feelings. She was interested in pursuing psychotherapy to try to effect some changes in her symptoms and to try to alter her disturbed relationship patterns.

In choosing a focus for therapy, she gave priority to her wish to be able to get involved in a stable and close relationship with a boy. From a review of her repetitive maladaptive pattern of involvement with boys, an initial working "core conflictual relationship theme" (CCRT) was formulated. The wish was stated as follows: "I wish to become involved in a close relationship with a boy, both physical and emotional." The expected response of the other was stated as follows: "Initially the boy will regard me as attractive, smart, desirable and strong, but soon he will discover that I am ugly and weak and will reject me for somebody more pleasing." The expected response of the self was stated as follows: "In a relationship with a boy I will initially feel strong, superior, and attractive, but inevitably, by the third date, I fear that I will feel ugly and will wish to withdraw."

I recommended a course of brief psychotherapy that would extend for 16 sessions, one session per week. Each session would be of 50 minutes' duration. While keeping in mind her presenting symptoms of boredom, insecurity, and unhappiness, we would focus on the CCRT we had established together. Our goal would be to try to effect a small change in this very important area.

The patient was instructed that during the sessions she should try to say what she was thinking and feeling. I would listen, try to understand, explore, and make clarifications. I would also share understanding when I thought this would augment her own efforts at self-understanding.

Maria agreed with the recommendations. She concurred with the method and agreed to work within the focus we had defined. With regard to the length of treatment, she did ask, "What if I need further treatment?" to which I replied, "After our sessions are finished, we will schedule a three-month follow-up session. We should see how it goes without treatment for a while, and we will review the need for further treatment if that seems necessary at the time of follow-up." She seemed comfortable with this arrangement.

The patient entered therapy with motivation and interest. She attended regularly and talked readily about her conflicts in relation to family members and peers. She worked mainly at trying to understand problems in the here-and-now. Whenever I attempted to focus on transference material, however, that is, to point out how a conflictual pattern under examination might be presenting itself in the therapeutic relationship, she would agree half-heartedly and intellectually, but it did not seem meaningful to her.

In sessions one through nine, the patient began to appreciate the strength of her CCRT. She recognized how pervasive this pattern was within her personality structure and how her repetitive distortions of self and others were persistent and maladaptive. She made a concerted effort to make some changes in the way she related to others and began to be more open to meeting boys and dating.

Some excerpts from sessions 10 and 11 illustrate how the patient participated in therapy and how I (M.K.) responded within the framework of the supportive expressive, time-limited model. Since all the sessions were audiotaped, this material comes from transcripts.

SESSION 10

Pt. Remember the last time when I was in here I was talking about this guy Eric that I had met?

Dr. Uh huh.

Pt. Well he's going back to New York Saturday and. . . . I don't know after that time we got together he invited me to come to a party with him and we went and things were O.K. but there were some awkward moments . . . but last night we went out for dinner and then we went out for coffee and then he came back to my place. Everything was going really well and after my parents went to sleep and then it was just Eric and I and everything went kind of funny. I think it was me who turned everything funny because there was all this tension, and yet in the back of my mind he was going. I had the TV on and the videos were just going and he just turned to me and said "Are you going to watch videos all night or what?" He said, "I can't decide what to do." I said "Why?" and he said, "Well I can't decide whether I should run away and go home or whether I should kiss you and run away and go home?" So I said "Am I supposed to make the decision here?" and he said, "No, no you're not. I have to make that decision." So he kissed me, and then I just totally overreacted to it. I started shaking, so then I was completely embarrassed and so I had to admit to him that I was nervous because there was no way not to admit it. He was laughing at first, and he said, "You're worse than me." But then, I didn't know, there was just something really weird happening.

All night I was waiting for him to kiss me, and then when he did I couldn't handle it. He started kissing me and I was just like shaking and I just couldn't believe it and my whole body went cold. I just felt so frustrated and stupid and I don't think he could understand what happened to me and I couldn't explain to him how I was actually so attracted to him and how I liked him so much and how I felt, how he made me nervous because I was actually so attracted to him and how uncomfortable I am with that and also on top of everything there was a little part of me saying he was going away and this was stupid and. . . .

He said something about, I don't know what I'm doing here and do you know what I mean. I didn't really know what he meant. I didn't want to let him go. I was in the situation that I didn't want him to leave. But I didn't want him to stay either. And so I said to him, "I feel like a real jerk," and he said, "I don't think you are," and I said, "Would you tell me if I really was?" He said, "Yes, I would." So he sat with me for awhile and I think he was waiting for me to come around and I never did and finally he said, "Well, I'm gonna go home." It wasn't the way I visualized the end of the night. I wanted things to be a lot friendlier between us. I said I would like us to write after you leave to New York. I hated myself for being such a suck, but I couldn't stop it. He doesn't even know that it is because I like him so much, you know; it just scared me so much, like how intensely I felt. So he just went to the door and he hugged me. It was so awkward then at the door, so I just said to him, "I'll miss you" and he said, "I'll miss you too." And then he said something very odd, he said, "Actually I thought about you a lot after we met the other night." I thought that was a strange thing to say when he's going out the door, and he's never said anything like that to me before. He never said I find you attractive or I like you then or I liked you now.

Dr. You are saying that you were feeling very close and attracted to him and felt that he was interested in and clearly attracted to you. And things were going the way you wished them to go and then for reasons that aren't clear — you and I will have to try to understand — you became frightened, you were trembling. This closeness that you want, when it happened and he made an advance toward you, you became frightened.

Pt. I remember that I was so afraid of revealing myself to him because I felt stupid, foolish, and totally wrong to like him so much, and so soon and, on top of that, that he's going away. And I felt this is wrong; this is stupid and I don't want him to know I'm being this silly and that I like him this much.

Dr. You were fearful of showing the intensity of your feelings, just how much you cared for him. You experienced your feelings as silly, inappropriate, unrealistic, and all those kind of things. You were on the verge of showing your true feelings, which you felt would be ridiculed.

The core conflictual relationship theme emanating from this session was understood as follows: "I wish to become close and involved with a boy. In a developing relationship, I will ultimately reveal my true feelings and will appear as stupid, silly, inappropriate, ridiculous, and weak. The boy will experience me as stupid and weak and will reject me."

SESSION 11

Dr. Driving was bad?
Pt. Yea, it's really slow out there.
Dr. We said we would meet for 16 sessions, and we have had 10. There are six more, including today. We should keep that in mind.
Pt. I know you said that it was goal oriented. Are we doing that?
Dr. I think we have come to understand a particular pattern. How do you feel?
Pt. I feel there has been a lot of recurring themes. I think we are talking about the same kind of feelings and situations. I guess what I'm worried about is the completion of our goal. I don't see the answers miraculously appearing in the next few sessions. Are we going to

reassess at that point or what, because there is definitely insight coming in but—do you know what I mean? I'm not sure that we have achieved our full goal.

Dr. The goal, as far as I can see, would be for you to understand something about the pattern that you bring into a situation, that you would understand it. What use can you make of that understanding when new situations come up or you encounter problems. What is emerging in my mind—and you can tell me if we are on the same track—is that, in terms of a major theme or major pattern, what seems to be most central now is that you want to get close to a boy. When you are in a situation where you feel close and the boy seems to show some interest in you, you find yourself feeling frightened.

I thought it was very interesting what you said last day, that what was going through your head part of the time you were with Eric was that this is silly, because he is going to be leaving soon. In your mind, what was going on was he's going to be leaving soon, and I think those are related. You think, I want to get close, but when I do get close I find myself getting anxious and I feel that the other person is really not reliable and I can't count on him.

All of that seems to be understandable given your background. I think that the stuff you told me about your family, your earlier experiences were, I think, very similar to what you were an observer of, or a participant in, in your family, in regard to your mother and father's relationship. You can get close to a man, but you can really get burned. He's not really trustworthy. I think that's what comes flooding back to you. The anxiety comes not from this particular person you are sitting with but from the meaning of the situation. That's the pattern that's emerging in my mind. Do you feel that, or do you see some more to it?

Pt. Yeah, I can see how my past interferes, but I think also that I myself have to take a large part of the responsibility for my behavior. I think there's something in me that just naturally is very, very afraid, apart from my life experiences. There's something in me that's just very. . . . I'm not really sure what it is, but I think part of it is linked to an unreasonable amount of pride or something, because I'm just so much more afraid of being shunned or rejected or anything, than trying to establish the contact at all. Even though, as you say, I'm caught in a dichotomous situation, part of me is dying to be that close to somebody, but the sort of rational, cool, calm

317

side that I imagine I have just couldn't stomach being that close to somebody and then having that person leave. Up until the point that my father had an affair, my mother never felt insecure at all and I was going to say I didn't know if that fit, because they never seemed to feel insecure about themselves. But I do remember after that happened my mom went through a period of complete self-loathing.

Dr. That's exactly, I think, similar to what goes on inside you, because the sequel to "I want to get close to somebody; and, if I get close to somebody, I really can't trust that person because they are going to reject me" is, I think, "They are rejecting me because I'm ugly, and unattractive."

Pt. Yea, in fact I'm not even sure if it follows. I think it is always there. That sentiment is always there, and it's just like when I told you, if for some reason I get a genuine feeling from someone, that they do like me or are attracted to me, I always feel like I've pulled something off. I genuinely always think that the only reason you like me is because you haven't seen the real person I am, and maybe I have that real fear of getting close to somebody because eventually they're going to find out. Maybe I could fool them the first time we meet or the second time, but the third time they are going to notice a) that I'm too thin, b) that I'm not beautiful, c) that I'm really mean.

Dr. I think there is an intermediate step there that I don't think you are always aware of. You want to get close, and then what comes up is the feeling that this person is inevitably going to reject you. As a way of trying to explain to yourself, how come you feel like whoever you meet is going to reject you, you say to yourself, "I'm thin, I'm ugly, I'm mean, I'm cruel, I'm distant, I'm intellectual, I have an air of superiority."

Pt. But that's sort of the way it's always going to be with me, isn't it? That kind of rationale. Because it's in my subconscious and I really have no idea of how to get rid of that kind of mind set because as we've discussed before it's almost like my bodyguard. Nobody really wants to be defenseless. I can see there actually being a real hesitance on my part to give up that kind of thinking. Even though I want to, I mean I really do. Even the last time when I was talking to you about Eric, with a little bit of hindsight l realized there were times when I didn't feel that way; there were times when I felt good in his presence because he made me feel that way, because I just never got this feedback from him like you're ugly, you're thin, you're mean. . . . There were times when that didn't happen at all, which was amazing to me.

Dr. I think that shows that you have some flexibility, you're not just cemented into this pattern. That, in fact, you did meet him and you did see him a few times. Then you did put yourself in a situation of having him come back to your house and spending time with him. For you, I think, that was not so easy. I think you are fighting these things. I recognize how hard it is, but I can see that you're just not sitting still with your bodyguards.

The core conflictual relationship theme developed in this session was formulated as follows: "I want to get close to a boy. When I get close I feel frightened and fear that I cannot trust him. I feel transparent and worry that I will be discovered to be ugly and mean. The boy will inevitably reject me and leave me." This central theme appeared repeatedly with variations over the remaining five sessions. Exploring the central theme remained our agreed-upon focus, and through continued exploration, the patient was able to work through her newly acquired insight. She recognized that this central pattern contained distortions of herself and of others and that these distorted representations interfered with her intense wishes for heterosexual intimacy and closeness. In the termination phase of the brief therapy, she began to appreciate the repetitious disturbances in her interpersonal relationships. Changes started to appear in her expected responses of self and others. An excerpt from the last session (number 16) illustrates the changes in thoughts, feelings, and attitudes that were observed at termination.

SESSION 16 (CONCLUDING SESSION)

Pt. Eric's been gone six weeks now I guess and like the first week he was gone I really felt bad, I really missed him and stuff. It's not like I don't now, but it's OK. I'm fine that he's not here. The first week I was angry. I thought, I meet somebody I really like and I make a jerk of myself and I don't even get a chance to ameliorate the situation because he's gone. It seems like a long time ago already that he was here and we spent some time together, even though it wasn't. I just realized it's OK. He's a great guy. If he comes back, if he wants to see me, great. I'm not hung up on this. People have said to me, "Did you write him yet?" I said no because I've been extremely busy at architectural college.

Dr. That's a change for you, because my sense is that in the past you would have held yourself back from getting involved with someone because you'd say if I get involved with him again I'm just going to get really hurt and I don't want any part of it, forget it. Wipe him out of my mind because of the feeling that any separation or independence on another person's part can overwhelm me and I can become highly emotional and I can't stand it. I sense that is part of your past pattern. Now I sense a difference. You're more understanding of it and not as threatened by it. So we could get together, so we could be close, so it might end or he might have other people to see or other things to do. That's not going to destroy me.

Pt. I just started to realize that I have to take chances in life. Everybody is out on a limb. I think I've always felt like, because of my own deep insecurity, that it's a greater chance for me to take than anybody else, but it's not. I think it's hard for everybody but you've got to put yourself in an uncomfortable situation to get something you want. And, like we've said, I want to have a relationship and if I want to have one, I have to put myself out somewhere. No one's going to knock on the door and say, "Hi, I'm here." It's not that way for anything. Like I've said, I have a tendency to just lay back in all aspects of my life because I'm afraid to explore and I'm afraid to fail. I've done it for a long time; I've just sort of hidden myself in books in school and not really tried to go out there and get what I want.

But now I just decided to get moving. Even this year I was feeling like I don't want to apply for jobs and this is the time to do it for summer jobs and who's gonna hire me. But now I'm sending applications, I've got to try. I'm taking things less like it's such a deep personal failure. People fail at things all the time, and sometimes there's nothing you can do. You can't look at everything like, oh my god I screwed up again. That's my mentality, and I'm starting to realize that it's wrong and I'm coming out of it. I feel a lot calmer, which I'm really happy about. Not saying I never get angry and I don't fear rejection; I'm still me. But I also feel a lot more centered now.

Discussion

The case presented illustrates how a particular type of brief psychotherapy can be applied in the treatment of an adolescent. The therapeutic approach taken was developed by Luborsky (1984) and is described as supportive expressive psychodynamic psychotherapy (time limited). It focuses on a formulation of a central neurotic pattern designated as the CCRT (Core Conflictual Relationship Theme), which is constructed from patient narratives called relationship episodes. During therapy the therapist listens, understands, formulates and interprets various aspects of the central conflict in such a way that it can be emotionally understood and psychologically worked through. Usually the wish remains unchanged throughout the course of the treatment, but modifications occur in the mental representations of the self and of the other. Negative representations become more positive as neurotic distortions are somewhat unravelled. The aim is to promote a small change in the internal intrapsychic world of the patient in an area of major psychological importance. Small changes in self-image and in the perception of significant others can lead to more adaptive and satisfying emotional, cognitive, and behavioral responses.

In the patient presented, the strong wish to become involved emotionally and physically with a boy persisted throughout therapy. After the fifth week of treatment, the patient ambivalently decided to pursue a relationship with a boy where she had recognized mutual interest. By the 12th session she had acknowledged clearly that when she got close to someone she liked she automatically expected rejection. She expected that the boy would discover her competitiveness (which she regarded as meanness) and also her thinness (which she regarded as symbolic of her essential unattractiveness).

She appreciated the genetic determinants of the CCRT in relation to her early childhood relationships with her parents. Throughout her life she had felt that she was valued by her mother principally as a source for narcissistic gratification. Independence was regarded as a display of cruelty and meanness. Although she experienced considerable angry feelings toward mother, she also strongly identified with her and with her conflictual relationship toward the father. She felt, like mother, that men are untrustworthy and self-centered and would leave her for someone better when they discovered her deficiencies and weaknesses. Like mother, she tended to feel that she had an attractive public self but an embarrassing, flawed, and weak private self. When she found herself alone with Eric, about to kiss, she felt overwhelmed with anxiety. She felt her private self was about to become exposed and that Eric would quickly reject her. She was surprised when he told her that he liked her a lot, had thought about her during the previous weeks, and wished to continue the relationship.

321

As therapy progressed, Maria felt that her wish to get close to a boy was realistic and that a relationship would develop in the near future. She felt determined to continue in her efforts to meet boys and was optimistic that she would become increasingly comfortable with closeness. She became more intensely involved in her academic work and actively pursued finding a summer job. She recognized that she had projected many of her fears onto Eric and that she had been inclined to interpret his behavior as signifying rejection based on her presumption that he had discovered her unattractiveness and weakness. At the end of treatment she felt calmer and happier within herself and could better appreciate her talents and appealing qualities.

Throughout the therapy, the patient was able to work actively within two aspects of the triangle of insight, that is, within the area of current relationships and within the genetic perspective. She found it helpful to reconstruct how her core conflictual relationship theme arose from the internalization of powerful experiences in childhood. Over the course of the four months of therapy, she recognized how many of her self-representations were bound up in her identification with her mother and how many of her feared expected responses from boys were related to her internal representation of father as cruel, rejecting, and critical. Much as the therapist tried, the patient was not able to examine the CCRT within the context of the transference. During the termination phase, the patient repeatedly expressed anxiety that the goals of treatment might not be accomplished within the 16-week time frame. The therapist felt, in part, that some of the anxiety about ending stemmed from an unconscious fantasy that the termination was a rejection, that is, that she felt that the therapist was ending treatment because he wanted to get involved with a new patient or because he was experiencing her as unattractive and weak. All attempts to explore this possibility were resisted. She tenaciously held to a positive transference within a positive treatment alliance.

Conclusion

John Meeks (1986) has written:

Psychotherapy contracts with adolescents tend to be unnecessarily prolonged. This may result in a blunting of the developmental thrust towards independence, which partially nullifies the positive impact of the therapy. Individuation, the goal of adolescent development, is best served by assisting the adolescent towards a workable character synthesis and then quickly moving aside so that the adolescent's strengths propel him towards real and available objects outside of the therapy office [p. 266].

We have here presented the advantages and efficacy of time-limited brief psychodynamic psychotherapy for the adolescent age group. Activity, clarity, and consensus all facilitate engagement. Choosing a relationships focus, fundamental to the CCRT method, is a therapeutic approach that is user friendly for teenage patients.

Establishing an effective therapeutic alliance with the teenager is essential for psychotherapy. Limiting both the goals and the duration of therapy discourages regressive dependency and enhances the formation of a positive working alliance. Concentrating on a central focus allows for a significant, small psychological change to occur in an important area of functioning within a short time frame.

Brief psychotherapy is not a panacea. Further study is needed to help refine indications, contraindications, and selection criteria. Davanloo (1980) has estimated that only one third of adult outpatients are suitable for brief therapy. Outcome comparisons between open-ended, long-term therapy and time-limited, short-term therapy need careful investigation.

At present, time-limited psychodynamic psychotherapy seems most applicable for nonpsychotic, depressed, or anxious adolescents who are capable, with the help of a therapist, of delineating a single focus and who possess sufficient motivation to sustain a four-month contract. The CCRT method encompasses both supportive and expressive techniques and can be used in combination with such other approaches as pharmacotherapy and family or group psychotherapy. Brief psychotherapy should be considered as an additional effective tool in our overall treatment armamentarium.

REFERENCES

Bauer, G. P. & Kobos, J. C. (1987), *Brief Therapy*. Northvale, NJ: Jason Aronson.

Davanloo, H. (1980), *Short Term Dynamic Psychotherapy*. New York: Aronson.

Golombek, H. & Kutcher, S. (1990), Feeling states during adolescence. *Psychiat. Clin. N. Amer.*, 13(3):443–454.

_____ & Marton, P. (1992), Adolescents over time: A longitudinal study of personality development. *Adolescent. Psychiatry*, 18:213–283. Chicago: University of Chicago Press.

Luborsky, L. (1984), *Principles of Psychoanalytic Psychotherapy*. New York: Basic Books.

Meeks, J. (1986), *The Fragile Alliance*, 3rd ed. Malibar, FL: R. E. Kreiger.

Offer, D. (1969), *The Psychological World of the Teenager*. New York: Basic Books.

22 THE PSYCHOTHERAPEUTIC TREATMENT OF SUICIDAL ADOLESCENTS

PHILIP KATZ

In recent years there has been a substantial number of articles on suicidal adolescents, primarily from the viewpoints of epidemiology and assessment of suicidal risk. The literature on the understanding and treatment of the suicidal adolescent is sparse but growing. Hendin (1991) wrote that the current revival of interest in the psychodynamics of suicide derives, in part, from the increasing realization that assigning to a patient a diagnosis that carries a high risk of suicide is not in itself an explanation for suicide.

Menninger (1938) said that society accepts superficial reasons for suicide but that there is a whole murder-story industry that has grown up because of the general disbelief in superficial motives for murder. He believed that people are unwilling to explore the deeper motivations for suicidal behavior.

Epidemiology

The epidemiology of adolescent suicides is striking, illuminating the importance of the prevention of suicide through understanding and treating the suicidality. Esman (1992) quotes Harkovy that 60% of all adolescents experience suicidal thoughts, and that in one-third of that number, that is, 20% of all adolescents, suicidal thoughts are persistent. A Gallup poll reported that 6% of all adolescents have attempted suicide and that 15% have come close to attempting suicide. It is generally assumed that the official statistics of adolescent suicides are unreliable, since suicides are frequently listed as accidents, and that suicide is far more common at younger ages than is stated. According to the Suicide Prevention Center in Los Angeles (Toolan, 1968), 50% of suicides among children and adolescents are reported as accidents. Miller (1981) claimed that there are five times as many suicides and ten times as many parasuicides (suicide attempts) as reported, and Toolan (1968) asserted that many accidents in children and adolescents are really attempts at suicide. At any rate, using official figures we do know that in the age group of 15 to 25 suicide is the second leading cause of death in Canada (accidents are the first) and the third leading cause of death in the USA (accidents first, homicides second). Offer (1992) reported that 90% of all adolescents who commit suicide have seen a mental health professional in the previous six months.

Preparation of the Therapist

As the literature on assessment of suicidal risk is abundant and well known, I shall jump ahead, past the assessment, to the point where the patient is seeing the psychiatrist for psychotherapy, either in hospital or in the office. The therapist knows, that even in hospital, a patient may attempt suicide at any time. The therapist has to try to find out what interventions must be made and what psychodynamic constellations must be worked through to relieve the pressure within the patient to commit suicide. It is a very high-pressured situation, and it is necessary, therefore, to focus first on the mind of the therapist and its preparation for this challenge, both emotionally and intellectually.

To begin the study of the mind-set of the psychiatrist, I would like to share a searing experience that I had during my training in child and adolescent psychiatry:

Leon was a bright 14-year-old who was admitted to our hospital's adolescent unit after an attempted suicide. His father was a rather sadistic bank guard, who, when he came up to see Leon in hospital for the first time, refused to hand over his guns before going on the ward and created quite a scene before leaving without seeing the boy. Leon's mother was an extremely compulsive woman who throughout her married life had seven menus, one for each day of the week, and they had not varied in all the years. The patient had made a number of attempts to get away from his parents and be placed somewhere else.

During his four-month hospital stay I saw Leon twice a week in psychotherapy. Responding well, he returned home and continued his therapy twice a week, working through his educational difficulties and some of the problems in his social life. He began, however, to become increasingly depressed and talked more and more about suicide. I could not pick up what was going on with him, and my orthodox Freudian supervisor, who was convinced that the problems were oedipal, had me firing oedipal interpretations at the boy. Leon then stole one of his father's revolvers, took off from home, and began phoning me two to four times a day to discuss whether or not he should shoot himself. He would not come to see me because he was afraid that I would hospitalize him. He felt that he really needed to kill himself but wanted to give me a chance to talk him out of it. After about four weeks of this, I was becoming pretty frantic and consulted with several other faculty members about the case, all of whom had different ideas about what was going on and had different suggestions or interpretations, none of which worked. What was troubling me the most was the feeling that we were inexorably moving toward the youngster's suicide.

Finally, I consulted another supervisor, who pointed out how I had been coerced by the youngster, was being blackmailed by him, and was so fearful of his suicide that I could not deal with the issues and with my anger at what he was doing to me. He pointed out that I had been missing the essential conflict, which was that the youngster had been developing a homosexual transference—which he was fighting—and that every time I was giving to him or was friendly and generally nice to him, it made the situation more and more seductive. At the same time, the youngster could not handle my being hostile, or rejecting, or ungiving to him, because of his dependency needs. We came to the decision that the only choice I had was to tell all this to the youngster over the phone and discuss his homosexual fears of our relationship, and his fears of rejection by me, and the bind that this put him in. I was to tell him that the only way to work it out was for him to come twice a week to see me at the office and that I would take no more phone calls from him. Leon hung up on me.

Throughout the next month I checked the newspapers daily, looking for reports of his body's being found. His parents heard nothing from him, and I heard nothing. A month after that last phone call, Leon phoned to ask for an appointment, and we then began to work on these problems.

I learned that it was essential not to be vulnerable to coercion. One could only be invulnerable if one was prepared to accept failure, to accept that some suicidal patients will commit suicide. I was reminded of the opening day of my entry into medical school. On the first day of first-year medicine, the Dean of the University of Manitoba Medical College spoke to us and told us that we should be prepared for failure, that in the end all doctors fail always because the struggle of a physician is to preserve life and in the end everyone dies. It was a pretty shocking statement to hear at that time, but it did help to prepare us for the inevitable experiences in medical school and as interns, when we struggled to preserve life and failed. This acceptance of failure, the acceptance of the death of a patient, is particular to the medical profession and is a major explanation of why nonmedical professionals refer so many suicidal patients to psychiatrists. The therapist of a suicidal patient must not withdraw from the patient because of fear of failure, for that might well precipitate the suicide.

The Role of the Therapist

In dealing with suicidal adolescents, a therapist must take an active role; he or she cannot be a blank, passive, noninterventionist therapist. It is absolutely essential that the therapist throw a lifeline to the patient, that he give the patient hope. Hope is the key ingredient that prevents suicide. The therapist has to have a perception of himself or herself as a rescuer. Most suicidal adolescents are in a state of desperation; they believe that they are trapped in inescapable pain, the pain of shame, of embarrassment, of degradation, of guilt, or of loss. Hendin (1991) says that despair or hopelessness are not accurate descriptions of the state of suicidal adolescents, because those words imply a resignation to the youngsters sad lot in life, as they see it. Desperation implies that they cannot go on with their present situation. They must have hope of something better, or they *will* commit suicide.

The active role for the therapist requires that he be prepared to talk openly about the suicidal ideation, the perception of suicide, and the plans for it—because if you don't talk about it, the implication is that you don't feel you can do anything about it, and that makes the situation more hopeless yet for the adolescent. Aware of the adolescent's state of desperation, the therapist must engage in an immediate and concerned exploration of why the patient feels so inescapably trapped and do a quick, but gentle, reality testing of the factors concerned, trying to discover whether or not the adolescent really is trapped. If more is required, there has to be an offer of concrete help, an intervention by the therapist with the school, the workplace, the family, the courts, whatever is required to bring some hope into the life of the patient. A connection must be made.

CASE EXAMPLE

I still remember the anxiety and discomfort that I felt as my first interview with Jerry went from bad to worse. He was 14 and openly planning to commit suicide; he had several guns hidden away. His parents had forced him to come see me, so he was cold and hostile as we began the interview. It seemed that no matter what I said, it evolved into something confrontational. Jerry became more hostile, and I became more anxious as I saw the hoped-for alliance drifting farther and farther away and the risk of Jerry's committing suicide increasing rapidly. After about 15 minutes of painful struggle, I stood up and said, "I don't like the way this interview is going! It's no good! Come with me!" My office is a converted apartment. I took Jerry into the kitchenette, asked him what soft drink he would like from the assortment in the refrigerator, and took one myself. We stood there in the kitchenette, drinking our soft drinks, close and far more casual, and chatted about the office. There was a table hockey game in there. He started to twirl the controls, I took the other side, and a hockey game broke out. When the game ended, we were on friendly terms and were able to form a relationship that allowed us to work through his suicidality and that became the foundation of the therapeutic alliance for the next several years of psychotherapy.

In many cases, if a therapist is to intervene successfully, the psychodynamic constellations that lead to suicidal urges have to be uncovered and worked out. Therefore, the therapist must be aware of an array of possible psychodynamic constellations that could cause a patient to be suicidal. This knowledge will facilitate the search for the patient's specific situation and assist the therapist in coping with his own anxieties about being faced with a suicidal patient he does not understand. The therapist has to know how the various factors that predict a likely suicide play their role, for example, how does a suicide of a family member lead to suicide among others?

Etiology of Suicidal Behavior

Suicide can be seen as the final common pathway for a number of psychodynamic, developmental, and biological determinants.

INTRAPSYCHIC REACTIONS

1. REUNION FANTASIES

Suicide attempts may be the expression of a strong wish to join a dead relative or friend. These wishes may have been operative for a long time, interfering with the establishment of other relationships and thus decreasing the supports for the patient.

2. REBIRTH FANTASIES

Some suicidal adolescents have the fantasy that if they kill themselves they will be reborn into a better and a happier life.

3. REWARD FANTASIES

Some suicidal adolescents believe that they will be compensated for their miserable life on earth with a happier afterlife.

4. REVENGEFUL FANTASIES

Many adolescents enjoy the fantasy of how sorry family, relatives, and friends will be if they commit suicide. Those who attempt suicide often have the fantasy that they will see and be witness to everyone being sorry.

5. REVENGE

Freud (1917) wrote that suicide expressed a repressed wish to kill an introjected, ambivalently regarded, lost love object, an act of revenge. Normal mourning had not occurred.

6. ATTACK ON THE PARENT-OWNED BODY

Laufer (1968) wrote that some adolescents do not take over the ownership of their body from their mother. They may seek to vent their anger at their mother by attacking "her body."

7. IDENTIFICATION WITH A SUICIDE

An adolescent who has identified with someone who has committed suicide— a family member, relative, or friend—may feel that he or she must do the same.

8. REACTIONS TO TRAUMATIC EXPERIENCES

Patients who have experienced such traumas as rape, sexual abuse, or severe physical abuse feel degraded and fear the repetition of the trauma. If they are unable to master the fear of its repetition, they become desperate and may try to escape by committing suicide.

9. COUNTERPHOBIC TO THE FEAR OF DEATH

Adolescents and children who are fearful of death may not be able to tolerate the anxiety about it and may attempt suicide to end the anxiety or to prove to themselves that they will not die. This dynamic is at the root of many risk-taking behaviors.

For example, I worked with Danny, a little boy who had just turned five and who had been admitted to hospital because he was throwing himself out of windows and in front of cars. He openly expressed a wish to die. He had not seen his mother since he was ten months old, when she became psychotic. She had been hospitalized ever since. His father abandoned him when he was 18 months old, and he had not seen his father or his siblings since then. He was placed in a convent for a year, then in three different foster homes. The suicidal behavior began in the third foster home.

The first clue to Danny's suicidal behavior came during play therapy when the baby figure was hit by a car and taken to hospital in an ambulance, where it met up with the mother figure. I explained that mother would not be in any hospital he wound up in, but that I would find his mother, and as soon as she was well enough, I would take him to see her. He was pleased, but his pleasure did not diminish the suicidal behavior.

Some weeks later we were playing ball on the hospital grounds when he stopped to stare at a big tree. I went over and kneeled beside him. He said, "The tree is big. When is it going to die?" I said not for a long while and that I'd like to tell him a story for him to finish. "Once upon a time there was a little boy and he grew up to be a big man." "He died!" I tried again. "Once upon a time there was a little boy who grew up to be a great big strong man." "He died!" My supervisor and I decided that this was the key to Danny's troubles. All the grownups he had ever known had disappeared — to him they had died. Yet, all alone in the world, he had to be big and strong and grownup. He was always jumping on tables and saying, "Look how big I am!" Yet being big meant dying; therefore the counterphobic need to test death. When next he jumped up on a table with me and exclaimed how big he was, I said no, he wasn't big and didn't need to be, as the staff and I would take care of him for a long time. After ascertaining that we would look after him for a long, long, long time, he gave me a hug, and the suicidal behavior ended.

10. GUILT

Adolescents sometimes blame themselves for specific incidents, such as the breakdown of their parents' marriage, accidents, or deaths, and seek to expiate their guilt by suicide.

11. ESCAPE FROM A HARSH SUPEREGO

A harsh, rigid superego can make patients feel guilty about everything they do, making their lives miserable, and leading them to seek escape in death.

12. FEAR OF PAINFUL EGO DISINTEGRATION

Fragile patients, such as schizophrenics or borderlines, fear ego disintegration due to stress or the loss of empathic supports and will seek to avoid the pain by suicide.

13. FEAR OF OVERWHELMING RAGE

Some adolescents struggle with overwhelming rage due to sexual or physical abuse or narcissistic wounding. They fear ego disintegration, fragmentation of the self, or loss of control with horrifying and disastrous results. Suicide may be a way out for these patients. Hendin (1991) noted that "suicide can be a form of control exercised by people who feel torn apart by rage and violence" (p. 1151).

14. REACTIONS TO THE LOSS OF ROMANTIC ATTACHMENTS

Neurotic patients may find that the loss of a close opposite–sex friendship leaves them with only their parents as libidinal objects. The guilt is painful and intolerable, and suicide is an escape. Narcissistic patients may not be able to tolerate the loss of an alter-ego/twinship relationship and the resulting fragmentation of the self.

One of my patients, James was 18 when he plunged into an intense romance with Diana, who, like him, was an avid basketball player, very good looking, and very bright. When she dropped him after two weeks, he was absolutely devastated, could not function, became depressed, and talked about suicide. He felt terrible, as if he had lost part of himself. He found my interpretation of his losing his female twin, the kind of girl he would like to be if he were a girl, to be very helpful. It enabled him to have some perspective on his situation and gain mastery over it, and to understand why he felt that he had lost part of himself.

15. REACTIONS TO ACUTE OR CHRONIC DISEASE

Patients with acute or chronic disease often feel that they are defective and abnormal and that therefore they will not be able to make friends. They are often embarrassed about their dependence on their parents and may seek escape from these painful situations in suicide.

16. PROJECTIVE IDENTIFICATION

The patient may project his bad feelings about himself, believing that others, such as his parents or his therapist, may see him to be as badly off as he sees himself. He finds this situation intolerably destructive.

INTERPERSONAL SITUATIONS

1. FAMILY HISTORY OF SUICIDE

When a family member has committed suicide, the adolescent may read the family's response as an acceptance of suicide as a way out of life's difficulties.

2. FAMILY HOPELESSNESS

If the family feels hopeless about an unacceptable life situation, they may convey that feeling to the adolescent and suicide becomes the only way out.

3. FAILURE TO ACHIEVE FAMILY STANDARDS

When a family has set high standards of achievement that the patient cannot reach, the patient may feel humiliated and that he or she is a failure, becoming full of self-hatred and eventually suicidal.

4. FAMILY SCAPEGOATING

Families may choose one member on whom to blame everything and extrude him or her from the family and the world.

5. PARENTAL DEATH WISHES

One or both parents may have death wishes toward a child with which the child/adolescent tries to comply by a suicide attempt, often in the form of an "accident."

Mark was referred to me at 13, soon after his father's death. He was depressed, self-destructive, confused, and although very bright, doing badly in school. He became involved in the drug scene, barely graduated high school, worked at a variety of jobs where he was frequently injured, and took several years of university but did not graduate. Throughout a 17-year period of once- or twice-a-week psychotherapy, we struggled with a continuous feeling of doom and an ever-present consideration of suicide. There was a strong positive transference that played a major role in keeping him alive.

In the course of a session, in the 17th year of treatment, Mark asked me how come he never saw me angry. Didn't I ever get angry in the course of my professional work? I said that the incident that stuck out in my mind involved a 12-year-old boy. When we started he was schizophrenic and had ulcerative colitis. I was strongly influenced by the work of Melitta Sperling, who said that ulcerative colitis in childhood was the child's compliance with parental death wishes. This young patient turned out to be aware of his parents' death wishes toward him, and, with my and his internist's support, he slowly improved — his colitis became much better, ceased hallucinating, and became less withdrawn and much happier. After some two years of treatment, on the day after I left on a two-week vacation, the parents, with no warning to either of us, took the boy to the Mayo Clinic for an "assessment." The Mayo Clinic surgeons thought that now, when he was in remission, was a good time to operate and remove the diseased bowel. They ignored the psychiatric history. My young patient folded up and died, postoperatively, which was what I would have predicted. I now told Mark that I was furious with the parents for "killing the boy."

Mark burst into tears and sobbed for a long time. He did not know why he was so affected, and so I asked if he felt there were parental death wishes toward him. That was when he began to remember the subtle death wishes from his father when Mark was a child and frequently sick in hospital. He had not remembered them before this, and I had no clue that they existed. We talked about his feeling a need to go along with his father's death wishes, and over the next couple of hectic weeks I helped him to turn against those wishes. He then became free of his suicidal preoccupation, went back to university and finished his degree, and is now happily married.

6. ANGER AT THE FAILURE OF A PREVIOUS ATTEMPT

If a youngster has made a suicide attempt and the family, agencies, hospitals, and the like have ignored it, the youngster may be very angry and make an even more serious suicide attempt.

PHILIP KATZ

7. DESPERATION ABOUT THEIR LIFE SITUATION

An intolerable life situation may exist in the area of family, school, workplace, social life, the law. The suicide attempt may be a cry for help, a coercive act to force help, or a desperate attempt to escape from an unbearable life situation.

I saw a four-year old North American Indian boy whose 11-year-old brother had hung himself. The 11-year-old had been a very bright, intellectual, artistic, and gentle boy who constantly was beaten up, ridiculed, and taunted by the more aggressive school and neighborhood kids for his gentle, scholarly ways. His suicide note read, "I can't stand this poverty any more."

Suicide fantasies may be a self-soothing mechanism for fears of being helpless and of being trapped. Nietzsche (1982) wrote: "The thought of suicide is a great consolation: with the help of it one has got through many a bad night" (IV, p. 157).

8. MAJOR FAMILY MOVE

If a move occurs during a critical period of an adolescent's development, it can rupture peer relationships. It is often difficult for adolescents to enter a new peer group, and they wind up feeling isolated and incomplete—quite painful feelings. Adolescents also need their peer group for their sense of self, of belonging to, and of sameness with the human race.

9. SEPARATION/DIVORCE OF THE PARENTS

A suicide attempt in this situation may be a coercive attempt to force a reconciliation; or an attempt to escape the painful shame and embarrassment that the adolescent feels about the parental breakup and its accompanying loss of friends and relatives; or it may be an angry attack on the parents. Hendin (1991) wrote, "For most suicidal patients, a rejection of life usually includes a rejection of the parents from whom it originated. The patient is likely to feel that he/she was abandoned first."

10. CONTAGION

There have been a number of reports of situations, especially on North American Native reservations, but also in middle- and upper-class areas, in which after one adolescent commits suicide, a number of his friends follow (e.g., Rodgers, 1981). The first one to commit suicide is usually an idealized leader who, because of his own low self-esteem, feels doomed

335

to failure, dreads the resultant embarrassment, and can not bear the resultant anxiety. After his suicide, his admiring peers feel that there is no hope for them, and they follow his lead.

PSYCHOPATHOLOGICAL DISORDERS

DEPRESSION

Depression (unipolar, bipolar, and reactive) is thought to be at the root of about 30% of adolescent suicides. Dubovsky (1992) reports that in a psychotic depression the risk of suicide is six times that in nonpsychotic depressions and that the majority of adolescents who are clinically depressed are psychotically depressed; one needs to look for the psychosis.

These patients may have hallucinations telling them how bad they are and leading them to the conclusion that their situation is hopeless and that they must kill themselves. Characteristic of these severe depressions are anhedonia, self-loathing, and anger at the self. Antidepressant medication is indicated, along with supportive psychotherapy. Depressed adolescents need a therapeutic program to deal with their fears of recurrence. Reactive depressions usually require exploratory psychotherapy to determine why the youngsters are so angry with themselves.

MANIC COMEDOWN

Patients coming down from a manic episode are notoriously at risk for suicide. They fear embarrassment and recurrences of the manic attacks, which are often quite painful, and they fear dropping into a depression. Lithium medication and supportive psychotherapy are indicated.

SCHIZOPHRENIA

Schizophrenic patients may have paranoid delusions that cause them to feel hopelessly trapped, or they may have auditory hallucinations telling them to kill themselves. Antipsychotic medication is indicated, along with supportive psychotherapy.

BORDERLINE STATES

Patients with borderline states often attempt suicide to escape from their painful lives, the lack of pleasure, the emptiness, the anxiety, and the tortured nature of their relationships. Medication, hospitalization, and long-term psychotherapy may be indicated.

NARCISSISTIC PERSONALITY DISORDERS

The grandiose fantasies of patients with narcissistic personality disorders are particularly vulnerable to the painful blows of reality, causing them to be enraged at themselves for not being "marvelous" and exposing them to the feelings of worthlessness and degradation that the grandiose fantasies defended against. The world just doesn't suit them, and they may decide to try to leave it or coerce it into shape. Many of these patients are anhedonic, feeling flat and unemotional. Their grandiosity deprives them of the normal satisfactions and joys of everyday life. "Of course I got an A+." "Of course she likes me." Anything less than perfection is seen as an attack on their grandiose self-concept.

These patients also fear their murderous narcissistic rages; they dread what they might do and hate the world because they cannot get what they feel they are entitled to. Their frequent abuse of drugs and alcohol adds to their problems by causing confusion.

Therapists need to be aware that some of these patients have fantasies of being immortal and do not believe they will die. They may freely use suicide attempts as a manipulation.

ALCOHOL AND DRUG ABUSE

Patients may despair about beating their alcohol or drug addiction and seek to end their painful lives. The depressant effects of alcohol and drugs contribute to this gloomy outlook. So, too, does the frequent finding that alcohol abuse and drug abuse interfere with the patients' interpersonal relationships, thus depriving them of emotional support. Also, often these patients are members of antisocial groups, which leads to a decreased expectation of help from society.

IDENTITY CONFUSION

Adolescents who are uncertain about their identity are often unable to make decisions. They find that situation intolerable and potentially very painful and seek to escape the trap they are in by attempting suicide.

Tony was 15 when he told me that "acid" had saved his life. He had been placed in a group home run by a priest when he was 14 because of some delinquent behavior on his part. He became obsessed with the fear that the priest would want him homosexually. He felt that he could not tolerate a homosexual involvement, but at the same time he felt that he would not be able to say no. The obsession became so severe that he was unable to bathe or shower, or even go to the bathroom without great fear. Yet he knew that the priest had never made any overtures to any of the boys in the group home and had done nothing to rouse his suspicious. He decided he could not go on like this, that not being able to say no to many things was impossible to live with. On his way to jump off a bridge, he ran into a friend who, when he heard about Tony's dilemma, told him that LSD would solve his problems and gave him some LSD. Tony took the "acid" and afterward felt much better. "Now that I was an acidhead, I could say no." Once he had an identity, he could assert himself.

If the therapist is knowledgeable about these possible causes of suicidality, it will make the information he obtains more meaningful, thus reducing his own fear and helplessness and enabling him to feel more confident, which, in turn, helps his patients to have hope of escaping from the trap in which they find themselves.

The Internal Environment of the Adolescent

These suicide-inducing situations involve adolescents, whose internal and external milieus are almost invariably in a state of upheaval. The developmental changes of adolescence challenge the stability of the adolescent psyche. The growth spurts outrace the body image, leading to a lack of coordination and clumsiness, with a resultant loss of confidence and self-esteem. Deviations from growth norms cause anxiety or panic and self-loathing. The tidal waves of sexuality can cause an adolescent to feel that his body is out of control and can drive him to defend himself against incestuous involvements, thereby disrupting relationships with the parents and other family members. The parents, along with various societal structures, are deidealized. The deidealization of the parents is in itself depressing, and the accompanying questioning of parental values leads to confusion about values and ethics and malfunctioning of the decision-making system.

The External Environment of the Adolescent

At the same time, in the midst of all this stress, the adolescent is struggling with society's expectation that he will reduce his dependence on his parents and family and start realizing his potential. But society's supports are being steadily pulled out from under the adolescent, adults with whom the adolescent can have meaningful, supportive relationships are being removed, a very significant loss. The high incidence of separation and divorce means that many youngsters have only one parent to relate to and frequently only one extended family. The high rate of mobility (every year one family in five moves) means that often there is no extended family at all in the city in which the adolescent lives. Even in two-parent families, as economic pressures increase, both parents have to work, and they come home tired and irritable, lacking the necessary energy for nurturing and supporting the adolescent.

Since the patterns of recreational activity move along the lines of age-related groups, family visiting family has become a rarity. Their parents' friends are relative strangers. The social lives of the children center around their peers. The teacher in the little red school house who taught a student for several years and knew his siblings and parents has been replaced by a different teacher for each class who often does not even know the names of the 250 or so students he or she teaches each day. The policeman on the neighborhood beat now drives around in a big car, remote and feared. The clergy are not as prominent as they used to be and are seen as being out of touch with the adolescents. Significant adults have indeed disappeared from the world of the adolescent. Communities no longer have the cohesion they used to have, and societal institutions are seen to be impersonal or even hostile.

Many adolescents today have only their tired parents to talk to if they want adult explanations and viewpoints, and the thunderous din of their peer group beats out an alienating message. The suicidal adolescent needs a relationship with an adult therapist and, in my experience, almost invariably welcomes it. The adolescent's psychiatrist must prepare himself to accept the burden of his patient's need.

Hospitalization

There are times during the treatment of a suicidal adolescent when hospitalization has to be considered. If the patient becomes seriously suicidal, hospitalization may buy time in which to work on the problems while the patient is protected and the therapist has some relief from the pressure. During even a brief hospital stay, an adolescent's depression may improve, a crisis may fade, and the adolescent may develop new skills or gain new perspectives. Hospitalization should not be seen as evidence of a failure; it is a useful therapeutic stratagem to derail a growing suicidal momentum, to increase ego strength, and to enhance the observing ego.

Summary

The therapeutic work with a suicidal adolescent begins with the therapist's recognition that there are a multitude of causes for suicidal behavior and that the risk of a serious suicide attempt lies in the patient's feeling of desperation about his situation, the feeling that he faces intolerable pain due to shame or embarrassment, degradation, guilt or loss. The patient can not assess whether his view of his situation is realistic or not, and he is unable to conceive of alternative solutions. The therapist must throw the patient a lifeline to give him hope of escaping from his belief that he is trapped in a world of unending pain. That lifeline may be an active intervention in the life of a patient, reality testing of the patient's perceptions that he is trapped, or both. The choice of interventions is based on an exploration of the psychodynamic and psychopathological constellations that have caused the patient to feel so trapped. Patients, in their anguish, will resort to extremes of coercion and manipulation; the therapist must be able to tolerate and work with these behaviors. The therapist must maintain his belief that he can find ways to help the patient, while accepting the possibility that some day he might fail. He can succeed only if he is prepared to fail.

Meeks (1984) summed up his article on suicidal adolescents in the following way:

> Success in the therapy of these youngsters does not depend on brilliant insights as much as on persistence, patience, and a sustained hope for the future. The treatment process may become a demonstrated proof that the therapist can stand to feel the patient's feelings and live the patient's painful existence, without giving up on life or the patient [p. 5].

REFERENCES

Dubovsky, S. (1992), The interaction between mood and character. Lecture presented to the University of Manitoba Department of Psychiatry, Winnipeg, Man., Canada.

Esman, A. (1992), Suicidal behavior. Lecture presented to the Review Course in Adolescent Psychiatry, American Society for Adolescent Psychiatry, San Diego, CA.

Freud, S. (1917), Mourning and melancholia. *Standard Edition*, 14:243–258. London: Hogarth Press, 1957.

Hendin, H. (1991), Psychodynamics of suicide, with particular reference to the young. *Amer. J. Psychiat.*, 148:1150–1158.

Laufer, M. (1968), The body image, the function of masturbation, and adolescence, *The Psychoanalytic Study of the Child*, 23:114–137. New York: International Universities Press.

Meeks. J. (1984), The suicidal adolescent. In: *Clinical Update Adolescent Psychiatry*, Vol. 23. Princeton, NJ: Nassau.

Menninger, K. (1938), *Man Against Himself.* New York: Harcourt, Brace & World.

Miller, D. (1981), Adolescent suicide: Etiology and treatment. *Adolescent Psychiatry*, 9:327–341. Chicago: University of Chicago Press.

Nietzsche, F. D. (1982), *Thus Spake Zarathustra*, trans. T. Common. New York: Modern Lib.

Offer, D. (1992), Help-seeking behavior in depressed adolescents. Presented to the Minnesota Society for Adolescent Psychiatry, St. Paul.

Rodgers, D. D. (1981), Suicide in the Canadian Northwest Territories. In: *Circumpolar Health*, ed. B. Harrald & H. Hansen. Nordic Council for Arctic Medical Research Report Series 33, pp. 492–495.

Toolan, J. (1968), Suicide in children and adolescents. In: *Suicidal Behaviors*, ed. H. L. P. Resnik. Boston: Little, Brown, pp. 220–227.

23 THE ADOLESCENT IN THE SCHOOLS: A THERAPEUTIC GUIDE

IRVING H. BERKOVITZ

Despite the diminishing finances of many public school systems, many resources are still available to help in advancing the development of the individual adolescent, especially the adolescent who is receiving psychotherapy. Often therapists and/or parents are not aware of these resources. This chapter will consider resources available in most school districts, including programs for adolescents diagnosed as seriously emotionally disturbed (SED) according to Public Law 94–142 (and its recent successor, P. L. 101–476).

Importance of School to Children and Adolescents

Next to the family, schools are the most influential areas of learning and development for the majority of children. Experience in schools can help younger and older children develop 1) cognitive abilities, 2) social skills with peers, 3) lessening attachment to and dependence on family, and 4) ability to relate to adults, other than parents and relatives (Berlin, 1975). In addition, many public and private secondary schools have programs that try to provide adolescents with help in career choices, college selection, sex and family life education, drug and alcohol abuse reduction, child care, suicide/depression prevention, health enhancement, and anti-gang education, among others. Private schools may have smaller classes, more resources, and more parent participation than is often available in public schools.

History of School Consultation

Assistance to teachers and other school personnel in regard to the mental health of children in schools probably began soon after the first

Thanks for editorial assistance from Max Sugar and Alice Healy-Sesno.

schools were established. The earliest published report in the United States by a mental health professional was by Witmer (1896), a psychologist. He consulted with a teacher on the classroom management of a mentally retarded child. Anna Freud (1930), herself a teacher before becoming a psychoanalyst, consulted with teachers in Vienna in the 1920s.

After World War II, the community psychiatry movement emphasized mental health consultation to all agencies, including schools, as a way of reducing mental health casualties and admissions to hospitals and clinics. Caplan (1970) defined mental health consultation as a "process of interaction between two professional persons—the consultant who is a specialist, and the consultee, who invokes the consultant's help in regards to a current work problem" (p. 19). Originally he proposed that the consultant accept no direct responsibility for implementing remedial action. Nonetheless, many consultative programs did include direct service to children.

In the 1980s and 1990s, the implementation of P. L. 94–142 increased the number of psychiatrists consulting to programs for emotionally and mentally disturbed children. These children and adolescents have been estimated to comprise about 15% to 30% of the school population, but only 1% to 2% are considered eligible for the programs in P. L. 94–142. Because medical diagnosis, medication, and family treatment are often necessary with this group, more psychiatrists are directly evaluating and treating these children, as well as consulting to the school personnel who are educating and counseling them. As a result, school psychological services, as well as more general consultative services to the 90% of the school system containing the nondisabled students, unfortunately have decreased markedly with this concentration of funding for special education.

Case Management

Child and adolescent psychiatrists should find it useful to relate with school personnel, in one way or another, around the treatment of each young patient they are seeing in their offices. In the case of students diagnosed attention-deficit hyperactivity disorder (ADHD) requiring medication, it is especially necessary. Many therapists, however, focus productively on the intrapsychic and familial aspects of the young patient's symptomatology without any special attention to the school sphere. For many patients this may pose no serious detriment, but the therapist risks overlooking important contributions and needs in some youth's peer relations and cognitive spheres.

Learning of the youth's functioning in these spheres can be accomplished at various levels of engagement with school personnel:

1) A letter or phone call to the school (with permission of parent and teenager), requesting information about school grades, teacher evaluations, descriptions of behavior, psychological test results, and reports of home visits, if these have been done. School records and personnel often have data that can be useful to the therapy.

CASE EXAMPLE 1

A 20-year-old male student became gradually more withdrawn in his second year at an out-of-town college, to the point of not attending classes. Asked to leave school, he entered psychotherapy and began to explore the origins of his problem. In examining the record of his elementary school years, obtained from the school district, he was first startled and then pleased that he existed officially in school records. He was helped by the records to be reminded of specific teachers and classes. He saw more clearly that his withdrawal from the school process had begun at age 9 to 10, in the fourth grade, the year his parents divorced. He was stimulated to recall that in sixth grade his mother had not supported his remaining in a class for gifted students, whereas his father had. Because he was living with mother, who prejudiced him against father, he was less influenced by father's opinions. In retrospect, he felt that with encouragement he could have succeeded in the gifted class. His discussion of these elementary school years produced in him more animation than did other sessions. Also, one or two teachers had recorded positive comments about him, which pleased and surprised him and led into a discussion of the positive qualities he had shown in those years. Some of these events had been discussed in previous sessions. Thanks to the records, he had a more concrete and vivid framework for remembering and reconstructing the events.

2) If the young person's problem involves school behavior and/or performance, a visit to confer with involved staff may be in order, but only if parents and the adolescent are willing. Certainly the intrapsychic focus is crucial in providing psychotherapy, but the school personnel's reactions to the patient's negative behavior may interfere with recogni-

tion of positive changes in the teen patient. A conference with involved school personnel, when done judiciously and with respect for the student's and the school staff's feelings, can be helpful to the course of the treatment. This will often be easier in a small private school than in a large public secondary school. The private school staff and students may be more accustomed to a therapist's visits. If the therapist does make a visit, the student may wish the therapist to ignore him or her during the visit. Successful interventions using meetings with school personnel in elementary schools have been reported (Aponte, 1976).

CASE EXAMPLE 2

The following is an example where intervention might have been helpful. A 13-year-old boy enrolled in the seventh grade of a prestigious private school had alienated the faculty and administration by his provocativeness, poor academic performance, and fights with other students. After a few weeks, therapy helped him to see that he was angry at his parents, especially their high expectations of him, their favoring a younger brother and sister, and his mother's critical attitude toward him. With therapy, he was beginning to show less anger at school and better academic performance; however, several faculty were unforgivingly negative about him. At the end of the semester he was expelled from the school, despite his parents' protests and efforts on his behalf by some faculty. The shame and negative self-image that he suffered clouded his next few years in public school and required reparative efforts in therapy. Had the treating psychiatrist been able to arrange a meeting with some of the faculty and help the angry members to express their feelings before the decision had become final, the boy might have been helped to continue in the school, and this ego-damaging rejection might have been averted.

3) In secondary schools, a visit to an adolescent's classroom could be useful but may be difficult because the student usually has five or six classes per day. A meeting with involved teachers and counselors may be more helpful, and some insurance plans provide for this. Both student and teacher, however, may be uncomfortable about the visit. The degree of the teenager's embarrassment and shame at letting teacher and peers know that he/she is seeing a psychiatrist has to be considered. In the smaller classes typical of special education (described later), there may be less shame because of a greater acceptance of mental health factors.

There can be great value in seeing first-hand the quality of peer and teacher interaction with one's patient.

4) In some cases, the parents are willing for the teacher to come to the office to discuss the adolescent and his or her behavior in school. Although this can be of value, there is the risk that the teacher may then develop a special attitude toward this student, positive or negative, that may influence their interaction unduly or arouse peer envy and hostility.

Relating to School Personnel

In both consultation and case management, certain operating principles need to be kept in mind. The first is to realize that most school personnel have ambivalent feelings about a mental health professional entering the school domain. There can be a mixture of awe, overexpectation, resentment, fear, envy and at times, even disdain. The mental health person is on the educator's turf, so to speak, and needs to act considerately as "a guest" in the school. The mental health person may also be initially unfamiliar with educational jargon or practices.

Educators, for the most part, pay more attention to achievement and the coping parts of a child's behavior and thinking than to the pathology. The term "therapy" is avoided in favor of the term "counseling." Many teachers would want the disturbed/disturbing student to be removed from their class, rather than to be repaired. Today's public school teachers are stressed by greater numbers of disturbed/disturbing children. Fortunately, many experienced teachers, and especially those in special education, feel less disturbed by a symptomatic child and accept the challenge in trying to help such a child, providing there are not too many in the same classroom.

Behavioral Intervention

Behaviorally oriented investigators have demonstrated the relationship of students' discipline problems to mutually aversive interactions between problem students and their teachers. Following baseline data collection, a "problem" female junior high school student was given instruction in the dispensation of contingent social reinforcement. The authors demonstrated that training the student to show approval of her teachers verbally and nonverbally "led to increased verbal and nonverbal reinforcement of the student by three of her four teachers and a decrease in disapproval for all four" (Polirstok and Greer, 1977).

347

Attitude of Mental Health Professional

On the other side of the interaction, some mental health personnel may have conscious (or unconscious) disrespectful or depreciatory attitudes toward public education and educators. Most educators are sensitive to such prejudices and will withdraw from, or become hostile to, such attitudes openly or covertly. The consultant will need to exercise self-scrutiny to eliminate such attitudes. As much as possible a coequal relation should prevail, in which there is mutual respect for each other's expertise. Most educators are conscientious and hardworking, despite the too frequent lack of societal appreciation or adequate financing. Managing interpersonal events in a classroom of many children requires skills different from those required for doing psychotherapy, where one is relating individually or in small groups. To consider the teacher as primarily a therapist is inappropriate, although many beneficial therapeutic interactions can, and do, take place in classrooms. Unfortunately, some harmful interactions occur as well.

To give advice or recommendations to a teacher or other educator on the phone, or even in a letter, may result in misunderstanding, frustration, or confusion and no benefit to the student-patient. For example, to recommend to a teacher that one's patient needs more individualized, nurturing attention and positive support may increase the resentment and/or guilt of an already overtaxed teacher, who may feel that he/she is already giving too much attention to the child. Yet, at times, the detection and correction of a teacher–student conflict can reduce or interrupt a student's increasing disability.

Categories of School Personnel

It is important for the therapist to have a knowledge of the several different categories of school personnel in order to relate to a school milieu. The schematic organization of a typical school district is illustrated in Figure 1. Each category will have different functions and responsibilities. The regular teacher is primary, possibly with classroom aides. In special education there is the special education teacher and the resource-room specialist teacher. In the elementary school the principal is the gatekeeper and needs to be contacted before a therapist can enter a school. The secondary school is larger and the principal's approval may be not necessary or even obtainable. In the secondary school of more than 800 students, the principal usually has a staff of an assistant

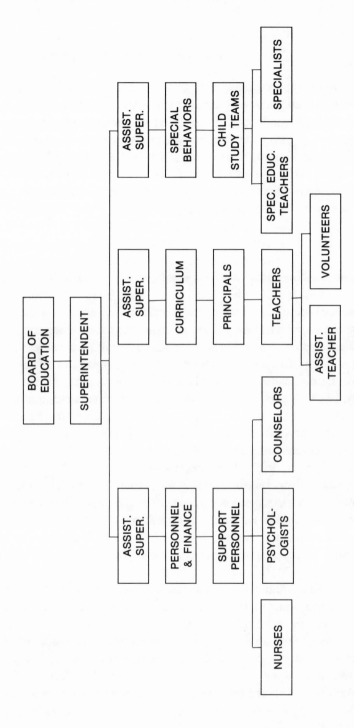

Fig. 1 — Schematic Chart of a School District

principal, one or two deans, a head counselor, two or three other counselors, a psychologist (full-time or part-time), and a nurse. Usually the counselor or nurse is most informed about students who are having difficulties, and possibly about one's patient. Some districts have school physicians, home–school coordinators, and/or social workers. The superintendent and assistant superintendents of the school district will usually be uninvolved unless the case is of such magnitude or trouble that one advises the parent to seek assistance at that level.

Secondary Schools

The size of secondary schools may make effective intervention more difficult. Middle/junior high schools range from 800 to 2000 students. Middle schools contain grades six to eight, while junior highs contain grades seven to nine. These students are experiencing prepubertal or pubertal development and all the physical concomitants, namely high physical mobility, twitchiness, rapid mood alternations, and difficulties concentrating on academics. They have been referred to as "hormones with legs." School personnel have great difficulty managing and educating students of this age. Surprisingly, many school personnel have not received sufficient staff development training about the vicissitudes of pubertal changes and adolescent defiance.

High schools range in size from 800 to 4000, grades 10 to 12 or 9 to 12. In the secondary schools the teacher may meet the class of 35 to 50 students five 50-minute periods per week. The class load of the average teacher is five to six such classes per day, or a total of 150 to 250 individual students per teacher. As a result, the teacher may not be familiar with each student, except for the high achieving or the very troublesome.

High-school-age students are usually less twitchy than younger adolescents but are still in the throes of developing identity, exhibiting confusion and impulsive attempts at independence from adults. High school personnel have special stresses with the community's demands for academic achievement, high SAT scores, no dropouts, and college acceptances. Additionally, schools are often expected to decrease drug and alcohol abuse and teenage pregnancy, to reduce suicide attempts and completions, and to endure gang problems and violence on campus (Jellinek, 1990).

The counselor at times can be a coordinating person who will help a therapist's intervention about a student. However, counselors often are hard pressed to care for their average load of 300–500 students. Here too the "squeaking wheels" will get the attention. When a psychiatrist does call, the counselor may then take extra interest or, at times, resent the added responsibility. Often he or she is the first, after the teacher, to talk with students showing behavior problems, unless the deans or assistant principals have been called upon to do this. In some schools, unfortunately, I have found several of the counselors to have been unknowing and ill at ease to deal with emotional problems and were unsure about the type of intervention needed, especially when suicide threats were involved. The nurse or psychologist is often more expert with mental health issues and can be a valuable ally in helping the student's adjustment in the school. These personnel are also overloaded and are becoming less prevalent in many schools. Athletic coaches may be of assistance if they are interested in providing developmental benefits for all students and not bent only on producing winning teams. Activity teachers (e.g., drama, school magazine, marching band) may know the strengths and weaknesses of students in their groups and how to improve self-esteem and skills.

Ideally, in a face-to-face meeting the therapist can evaluate the sophistication or biases of the particular teacher or counselor and decide on how best to present a recommendation without wounding the educator's self-esteem or increasing guilt. Parents, and some insurance plans, will often reimburse for such meetings. A teacher or counselor can often provide data about an adolescent's peer relations, judgment, social skills or deficits, and coping skills. This may advance the psychotherapy.

Levels of School Intervention During Therapy

The levels of use of the school milieu for the adolescent patient vary from minimal to moderate to highly interventive, depending on the type of school and degree of pathology in the young patient. A moderate level could involve telephone conversations and/or visits with involved school personnel, without classroom visitation. The highly interventive level can include classroom visitation, attendance at IEPs (individualized education plan) and even advocacy at administrative levels for change in program or other measures.

The *minimal* level involves requesting school records, hearing about school issues from parents, and listening to the patient talk about the school academic and social scene. If the therapist is knowledgeable from treatment of other youths from the same school, he or she can make inquiries and explore the patient's relations and feelings about the different student groups and activities. At times, suggestions for possible experimentation with a change of group membership may be indicated.

CASE EXAMPLE 3

A 16-year-old adopted Anglo boy in the 11th grade had turned against his Anglo peer group and associated mainly with Latino gang members on campus. This aroused concern in his parents and confusion among his former Anglo associates. He had achieved his goal of being "jumped in" as a member of this gang and was on the verge of increased involvement in more violent gang activities. Whether this act of being accepted or the fear of further violence was responsible, almost immediately he resumed his pregang activity of spending hours perfecting his skateboarding skills. As a result, he spent less time with the gang members. The following school year he enrolled in a smaller, private school and no longer associated with his Latino friends.

Despite occasional anxiety, the therapist had never joined the parents in expressing disapproval of his gang associations but had explored his attitudes about the other groups on campus and had empathized with his pleasure from the respect given him by the gang group. Most of the gang members lived in families more dysfunctional than his. In addition, he gained in self-esteem from being able to give academic help to some of the less accomplished gang-member peers. This year of closer bonding with peers who were emotionally more expressive than his parents and more divergent culturally and economically seemed to help his self-esteem and development. Luckily there was no legal or other damage. The therapist's acceptance of and empathy with the social needs on a large high school campus may have helped the patient lessen whatever needs were present to defy his parents by his choice of associates.

Many campuses (depending on size) have several distinct social groupings. A few of these may be listed as follows (names used may differ in each locality): 1) "squares," those doing well academically and avoiding difficulties. This group may include those termed "nerds"; 2) the "soshes" or popular ones, those who are personally attractive, often with outstanding social and political skills, liked by students and staff; 3) "dopers," known to use or abuse drugs and/or alcohol; 4) "jocks" (and in coastal cities "surfers"), those with physical skills. Some may be members of the school's athletic teams; 5) loners; 6) gang members or "wannabees," those pretending or aspiring to gang affiliations. A visit to any large high school campus by a therapist may be educational and vividly demonstrate this range of identities.

A second level of assistance can be termed *advisory*. For this the therapist needs to know the range of extracurricular activities available on the campus of the patient's school. Although fiscal considerations are reducing the available list, many schools still offer a wide array. Among these may be dramatics, chorus, debating club, newspaper, yearbook, orchestra, marching band, student government, community service, and many others. If the student has a modicum of athletic ability, team sports can promote positive attitudes and behavior, including self-discipline, responsibility, a sense of pride and self-esteem, and an increase of friendships. Some coaches do appreciate the value of providing developmental benefit for all team members, as well as having a winning team. For less academically skilled youths, important mentor relationships can develop with empathic coaches, as well as teachers.

Consulting the school newspaper, perusing the bulletin board in the principal's office, or talking to a counselor may provide fuller information about programs in a particular school. In discussing the patient's interests and activities this knowledge can be very useful. Encouraging the youth's seeking out those available in the school milieu can be an additional empowering part of the therapy. Some districts offer special counseling opportunities for gay and lesbian students.

In addition to knowing what to suggest in school social and interest activities, it can be useful to know that school units are available in a particular district that can provide a smaller group educational context. So often the heavily populated large high school is psychologically noxious to the vulnerable teenager. In many districts, especially the larger ones, there are specialized interest (magnet) schools, for example, for performing arts, business, fashion, science, computers, the gifted, and the highly gifted. These magnet schools are often at the junior and senior high level and usually contain only 200 to 300 students. Parents need to make an application, but spaces may be limited. Alternative schools, containing kindergarten to grade twelve and usually 200 to 300 students, similarly offer a smaller, more intimate school experience, often with parent participation.

At the other end of the achievement spectrum are continuation high schools, containing 50 to 400 students, with each student often receiving individualized instruction and learning at his or her own pace. These students often had difficulties in the larger high school or difficulties with legal agencies, or they need to work and therefore have a shortened day at school. Pregnant adolescents may be provided a separate school or class in some districts, where prenatal health care and parenting training are taught. Some high schools will provide infant care while the mother attends class and then baby-care classes as part of the curriculum. Knowing of this gamut of educational and social units can help a therapist to advise teen and/or parents about what to seek in the local schools. Positive, satisfying group experiences can improve the health, as well as the therapy, of many adolescents.

If a teen is more severely disturbed, lacking in social skills, or showing behavior problems, some therapeutic opportunities do exist in many schools, even with today's more limited resources. First is individual counseling, which is rare but still available, and provided by some motivated counselors or school psychologists. More prevalent is group counseling (Berkovitz, 1987). Usually this is provided by counselors or school psychologists in once-per-week, one-hour sessions with six to eight members. Occasionally a nurse, teacher, administrator, or outside agency professional may be the leader. A school behavior and/or performance focus will usually prevail, but often family and personal problems will receive attention and some help (Kaplan, 1975). Before suggesting such a group to one's patient it may be well to meet the leader and try to determine his or her expertise and type of group.

Peer counseling is becoming more common in many secondary schools. Here students in upper high school grades will receive training to counsel younger students having minor problems. The training may extend over one or two semesters. Screening of potential peer counselors/counselees and later supervision of the counseling will be provided by a counselor or school psychologist. Often the training period provides useful therapy for the trainees. Training may occur in a class context with academic credit, or before or after school without academic credits. The opportunity to help others is therapeutic for many teens. A specialized type of peer counseling is mediation peer counseling, in which peers are trained to mediate interstudent conflicts. The following example shows the types of psychological problems that may be uncovered and helped in such procedures.

CASE EXAMPLE 4

Three girls in a junior high school who were close friends were having a difference with each other that they brought to peer mediation. Two student peer mediators were present with an adult monitor, who happened to be a trained social worker. The girls objected to each having become a critical "mother" to the others. In the context of a heated discussion, one girl mentioned having been molested by her father and uncle. A second girl then told of having been raped at age 10 and then needing an abortion. The boy's mother had arranged the abortion and sworn her to silence. The girl's own mother still did not know of it. The two student mediators were shocked by all this unexpected, disturbing revelation. The adult monitor stressed the need for confidentiality about these revelations and provided support to the trainees. She then began the process of providing help to the two traumatized girls. Legal requirements to report the offenses to the proper authorities were observed.

Also increasingly prevalent in the United States, mostly in high schools but also in some junior high and even elementary schools, are school-based clinics (SBC). There were 300 to 400 in operation in 1992, staffed by medical and nursing personnel to deal mainly with adolescent physical health problems. Proper care of physical health is certainly an important part of adolescent self-esteem and reality awareness. Some clinics report that 20% of referrals are for mental health problems. Some clinics do budget for mental health staff, but many rely on volunteer services. Thus, mental health problems do receive some attention, whether with psychotherapy or guidance around medical, sexual, and other issues (Adelman and Taylor, 1991; Lear et al., 1991).

Special Education Programs

If the teen patient is not helped sufficiently by these minimal and moderate interventive measures, referral to the special education section of the school district may be needed. These are mandated services required in the United States by federal law. In the 1990s more than 4 million children are being educated under several special education laws. Public Law 94–142 was first passed by Congress in 1975 and mandated services to all exceptionalities — blind, deaf, aphasic, mentally retarded, autistic, orthopedically handicapped, learning disabled (LD), and seriously emotionally disturbed (SED). These 4 million children in the United States comprise approximately 10% of the school population. Mental health factors are relevant to all of them, but specifically about 10% of these are classified LD or SED, and comprise 1% to 2% of the total school population.

The numbers of identified children differ from state to state, depending on classification criteria and fiscal provisions. These students may be receiving 1 to 2 hours per day in a special class termed the resource specialist program (RSP) but spending most of the day in their regular class. Or some students may need to be in a special class for the entire day, termed special day class (SDC). This is especially so for those classified SED. Those students who cannot be provided with necessary services in these locations can be placed in nonpublic schools (NPS), including residential schools, if indicated. This is often paid for by the student's home school district, occasionally with costs shared by other agencies, such as mental health, probation, or welfare. Public Law 99–457, passed in 1986, extended the benefits of this service to handicapped infants and toddlers, from birth through age 2. P.L. 101–476, passed in 1990, amended P.L. 94–142. It used the word "disabled" for "handicapped" and added autism and traumatic disabilities as covered diagnoses. It also added rehabilitation counseling and social work services, and mandated that schools help disabled students plan for when they leave school.

These laws have improved school services for all disabled children, but especially for the approximately 400,000 SED children in American schools. Unfortunately, it has reduced the finances available for psychological assistance to the other 36 million less disabled children in regular education classes, of whom 10% to 15% also need services. Owing to the rising costs for the care of these SED children, many school districts are trying to provide preventive measures that may reduce the severity of symptoms in at-risk children so that they might not require special education (Knitzer, Steinberg, and Fleisch, 1990).

One of the dilemmas in referring children or adolescents to these programs is that what the clinician will consider "severely disturbed" is not always what school personnel will call SED or "seriously disturbed," because school criteria are more narrow. The latter try to exclude conduct or behavior disorder and ADHD, even though these diagnoses do often involve underlying depression. Still, many conduct/behavior disordered and ADHD children are enrolled in the classes. School criteria for SED are defined as a) an inability to achieve adequate academic progress that cannot be explained by intellectual, sensory, or health factors; b) an inability to build or maintain satisfactory interpersonal relationships with peers and teachers; c) inappropriate types of behavior or feelings under normal circumstances; d) a general pervasive mood of unhappiness or depression; or e) a tendency to develop physical symptoms or fears associated with personal or school problems. *DSM III-R* (or *IV*) diagnoses are not relevant for school purposes. Mention of behavior or conduct disorder without stressing the above criteria may often be used in some districts to exclude a student from the program.

In an individualized education plan (IEP) a meeting with the school psychological personnel, with or without outside professional consultation, will determine the status and eligibility of the child and prescribe a program within the school system, if available. There may be a variety of programs available. The minimum is 1 to 2 hours in a resource room for tutoring or even group counseling, with the student in his or her regular class the rest of the day. If this is not of sufficient help, the next step is a special class. Learning disability classes contain up to 14 students with one teacher and one aide. If the student's behavior cannot be contained in this class, the next step may be entry to an SED class where there are only eight to nine students with one teacher and two aides. Although many of the special education teachers in these classes are very concerned and altruistic, for the most part, they are hard pressed to deal with the more disturbed, especially aggressive, children. Psychiatric and social work consultants are provided in some districts to help the teacher understand the children's behavior, as well as their own feelings of frustration and failure. Some programs offer family therapy as well.

A therapist who is treating an adolescent needing one of these programs can inform the parent to apply to the school psychologist or principal of the child's school. This should begin the prescribed timeline for evaluation leading to the IEP and special services. When parents are in disagreement with the school authorities about the appropriate program for the child, arbitration, or a fair hearing, may be indicated. Here a more legalistic procedure may ensue with the entry of advocates for the child and/or outside experts, including the therapist. The psychiatrist may need to testify to represent the needs of the child.

Often the smaller SED class may be a therapeutic location for a disturbed adolescent, depending on the skills of the teacher and the kinds of behavior in the other students. The parent or possibly also the therapist should visit the classes to determine their appropriateness for the patient. Too often the majority of the students may consist of a number of aggressive boys. Usually only one or two girls are referred to each class. This will require special attention for the provision of contact with other girls to help reinforce feminine identities, especially for girls

357

at menarche. Some programs will pay special attention to "mainstreaming" the students, that is, providing attendance for part of the day in regular classes.

Mainstreaming can reinforce the student's ability and self-control to stay in larger class groups, help him or her find friends on the campus, and maintain or teach social skills. In some cases an aide may have to accompany the student to lessen loss of control and possible disruption to the mainstream class. Too few schools provide students in mainstream classes with programs about avoiding stereotyping and providing a more tolerant acceptance of deviant individuals. A consulting mental health professional often can help a school or class provide this.

Often the SED class is housed in a room or bungalow separate from the main part of the school. This may provide a separateness that shelters the other classes from the occasional loud friction or noise of SED children, but it also sets up an implication of difference that may lead other children to stigmatize them. Occasionally other teachers will not wish to have the disruptive SED children mainstreamed to their class, even for part of the day. Teachers in SED classes often have to curry favor with other teachers to facilitate this exchange. Some SED teachers arrange for reverse mainstreaming, where nondisabled children come into the SED class for part of the day (e.g., for art instruction).

Hopefully, most children will not need to stay in these segregated classes for more than two years. If by then benefit has not occurred, some states (e.g., California) have legislated that the student may be referred to a clinical unit where more traditional mental health services may be used, especially family therapy, as a supplement to the SED class. Unfortunately, some do stay longer than two years. Some districts are planning on total mainstreaming of special education students with special support given to the classroom teacher for management of the more difficult children. This may prove to be a loss for many of the children and an additional burden for many teachers.

Many children do gain from the advantage of a smaller group sheltered experience, with a higher ratio of concerned personnel.

CASE EXAMPLE 5

Jessica, a 14-year-old eighth grader and victim of child abuse, has been in special education classes since third grade. Her father tried to abort her and she was born prematurely. She was neglected as an infant. She had no friends, partly owing to poor hygiene. She would not clean or groom herself. According to the school personnel her mother was like that too, but two younger siblings were more clean. Jessica raised mice, at home and if one died she showed no compassion. She was felt to be above average in intelligence but would not make eye contact. The other eight students in the SED class were boys, one of whom terrorized Jessica with his aggressive outbursts. The woman teacher and one female aide took a special interest in Jessica, helping her with grooming and self-esteem, including providing her with books on grooming. Five months later she had shown some improvement in grooming and was less offensive to peers and adults. She was slightly more assertive with the aggressive boys, and was acting as a learning assistant in a remedial class of younger children, which improved her self-esteem. She was being mainstreamed to adaptive physical education and typing. Unfortunately, she was to be out of school for the summer and could well lose some of her gains. Despite the preponderance of aggressive boys, however, the smaller classroom allowed empathic, nurturing attention from the female staff. This kind of attention was not available in her own family. Whether the staff will remain intact long enough so that Jessica can internalize more of a positive self-image is unfortunately never guaranteed in a public school setting. Also, she is approaching the age when it may be necessary to promote her to high school. The challenge may be therapeutic, but there may not be a comparable nurturing group of personnel available. Ultimately, referral to a nonpublic school may be necessary. There a more dependable therapeutic program may be possible.

The boys referred to SED classes, usually manifesting aggressive behavior problems, are often more difficult to help. Many live in dysfunctional families, which also have difficulties with them. Parenting instruction, if available, may be of help.

CASE EXAMPLE 6

Edward, a 14-year-old in eighth grade, was defiant and belligerent, pretended to stab peers with scissors, and terrified Jessica. He brought a slingshot to school and hit peers with berries. He had matches at school, cut class frequently, and was absent 30 times this past year. His academic work deteriorated, and he did no homework. Yet he seemed to like responsibility—for example, doing errands, working (for pay) in his uncle's garage. Though he showed mechanical abilities, he refused to work on a bicycle provided for him in class. He refused to ride the special education bus and paid for his own public bus transportation to school. He seemed to be of average intelligence. His mother is non-English speaking. His father, who is 30 years old, will talk to the teacher on the phone but refuses to come to school to see her. A younger sibling is intelligent and Edward often embarrasses him. Edward has been referred to a behavioral intervention program and then nonpublic school. Although Edward is seen to have some assets, it is felt that the public school program has been ineffective.

Some school districts have a behavioral modification unit, to which the student may be assigned for a brief period (e. g., 3 weeks). There a behavioral program will be developed that can be continued when the student returns to the SED class. A consultant from the unit will visit the SED class to help the teacher maintain the program.

Some male students may experience important positive growth in an SED class, such as occured with Jessica.

CASE EXAMPLE 7

Bobbie, age 12, a "bright" seventh grader, was diagnosed as having ADHD. Ritalin was prescribed and then cylert (pemoline). Without medication, he was considered "crazy." Once he had grabbed the teacher from behind playfully. He made no true eye contact, was overweight, and peers made fun of him. He lived with his mother, who was on disability subsistence. He called his father "an SOB, he left us." He is an only child and is considered immature socially. After 5 months in the class, he was considered a "model student" but was beginning to show more sexual preoccupation. His pubertal development will need specific attention. He is considered ready for mainstreaming to regular classes, which he refuses. So far this is not being strongly urged upon him. Despite the prevalence of the other more aggressive boys, the smaller class does seem protective and nurturing for him and he does receive some counseling. Unfortunately, the minimal counseling being provided by the school psychologist has not yet helped his social skills sufficiently. Also, a helpful adult male in his life has not yet been available, at home or in the SED program.

If some youngsters need a longer period of a remedial milieu, a specialized therapeutic nonpublic school may need to be considered. Approval for this may be available in some districts and contested in others. The district, in some cases conjointly with other agencies, will have to subsidize the NPS or even residential program. This can be located nearby or occasionally even in a distant community. At times, the legal recourse of a fair hearing may be necessary to help the school district agree to provide such a program. A recent publication describes in greater detail how to maximize the potentials of these programs for SED children (Fritz et al., 1993).

Reentry

At times consultation with teachers or counselors is essential for an optimum reentry of a patient into regular classes from special school or hospital care.

CASE EXAMPLE

A 14-year-old girl who had been hospitalized for anorexia was reluctant to return to her former school. She feared questions from her classmates who would then label her as "crazy." A consultant in the school was able to explain anorexia to the teachers and the principal in a way that avoided the stigma of "craziness." The discussion focused on specific difficulties this girl would have in getting back to the primary task of learning because of continued preoccupation with food. Special approaches were devised by the teachers themselves, stimulated by the consultation. As a result, the reentry was accomplished smoothly. In contrast, another patient with anorexia returned to a school that did not receive this assistance. Within 3 weeks she reported that she felt the teachers "don't understand me, and I think they hate me." She refused to return to the school and had to be transferred to two additional schools before resuming her education (Newman, 1980, personal communication).

Conclusions

This brief survey of the therapeutic potentials in American secondary schools may have omitted some resources available since each school and district will have its own characteristics and financial exigencies. I hope I have stressed that knowing what is available in local schools can be of assistance in helping young persons enrolled in those schools. Many school personnel, despite the stressful demands on today's schools and educators, are altruistically motivated and often can become allies for the therapist in helping young patients. Mutual respect and appropriate, discreet sharing of information can facilitate such efforts.

Knowing the roles of the different categories of school personnel and the nature of the stresses affecting the larger secondary schools can be helpful. There are a variety of activities and groups in the average high and middle school that can reinforce ego development and healthy identity formation. In the cases of less well functioning adolescents, there are often more therapeutic and individualized settings available, such as group counseling, peer counseling, magnet schools, continuation schools, alternative schools, private schools, and the smaller classes of special education, stipulated by Public Laws 94–142 and 101–476. These laws will at times provide for special nonpublic schools, even in residential settings.

REFERENCES

Adelman, H. S. & Taylor, L. (1991), Mental health facets of the school-based health center movement: Need and opportunity for research and development. *J. Mental Health Admin.*, 18:272–283.

Aponte, H. J. (1976), The family school interview: An ecostructural approach. *Family Process*, 15:303–312.

Berkovitz, I. H. (1977), Mental health consultation for school administrators. In: *The Principles and Techniques of Mental Health Consultation*, ed. S. C. Plog & P. I. Ahmed. New York: Plenum, pp. 93–118.

_____ (1980), School interventions: Case management and school mental health consultation. In: *Treatment of Emotional Disorders in Children and Adolescents*, ed. G. P. Sholevar, R. M. Benson & B. J. Blinder. New York: Spectrum, pp. 501–520.

_____ (1985), The adolescent, schools and schooling. *Adolescent Psychiatry*, 12:162–176. Chicago: University of Chicago Press.

_____ (1987), Value of group counseling in secondary schools. *Adolescent Psychiatry*, 14:522–545. Chicago: University of Chicago Press.

_____ & Seliger, J. S., eds. (1985), *Expanding Mental Health Interventions in Schools*. Dubuque, IA: Kendall/Hunt.

Berlin I. N. (1975), Psychiatry and the school. In: *Comprehensive Textbook of Psychiatry II*, ed. A. M. Freedman, H. I. Kaplan & B. J. Sadow, 2nd ed. Baltimore, MD: Williams & Wilkins, pp. 2253–2255.

Caplan, G. (1970), *The Theory and Practice of Mental Health Consultation*. New York: Basic Books.

Freud, A. (1930), The relation between psychoanalysis and education. In: *The Writings of Anna Freud*, 1:121–133. New York: International Universities Press.

Fritz, G. K., Mattison, R. E., Nurcombe, B. & Spirito, A. (1993), *Child and Adolescent Mental Health Consultation in Hospitals, Schools and Courts*. Washington, DC: American Psychiatric Press.

Jellinek, M. S. (1990), School consultation: evolving issues. *J. Amer. Acad. Child Adoles. Psychiat.*, 29:311–314.

Kandler, H. O. (1979), Comprehensive mental health consultation in high schools. *Adolescent Psychiatry*, 7:85–111. Chicago: University of Chicago Press.

Kaplan, C. (1975), Evaluation: Twenty-seven agency-school counseling groups in junior and senior high schools. In: *When Schools Care*, ed. I. H. Berkovitz. New York: Brunner/Mazel, pp. 226–238.

Knitzer, J., Steinberg, Z. & Fleisch, B. (1990), *At the Schoolhouse Door*. New York: Bank Street College of Education.

Lear, J. G., Gleicher, B. H., St. Germaine, A. & Porter, R. J. (1991), Reorganizing health care for adolescents: The experience of the school-based adolescent health care program. *J. Adoles. Health*, 12:450–458.

Polirstok, S. R. & Greer, R. D. (1977), Remediation of mutually aversive interactions between a problem student and four teachers by training the student in reinforcement techniques. *J. Appl. Behav. Anal.*, 10:707–716.

Witmer, L. (1896), Practical work in psychology. *Pediatrics*, 2:462–471.

24 FAMILY THERAPY AND SOME PERSONALITY DISORDERS IN ADOLESCENCE

CLAUDE VILLENEUVE AND NORMAND ROUX

The treatment of personality-disordered adolescents remains a therapeutic challenge. These adolescents manifest behaviors that cause significant impairment in social and occupational functioning or subjective distress (American Psychiatric Association, 1987). As for other adolescent psychopathology, there is no single psychotherapeutic method that is suitable to all. These problem children are still in great need of parental support, and the difficulties of their family are important and intermingled with their own individual problems. A multilevel approach, including family therapy, appears to be indicated.

The purpose of this chapter is to present an approach used with some personality disordered adolescents in which the family is brought to a central position. The approach is described for adolescents living at home, still in need of continuing care from their parents, but who are not suited to psychoanalytic or explorative psychotherapy. They may lack motivation, show unworkable individual transference, or demonstrate limited capacity for introspection. The intervention may follow a brief hospitalization and the family has to replace the inpatient staff for support and structure. The adolescent and his family must, however, show enough strength and control so that the intervention is feasible on an outpatient basis. The approach may be applicable to other types of personality disorders in adolescence but is described here for adolescents who are borderline or immature narcissistic.

The approach, which has been used for the last five years with over 20 adolescents, fits the current tendency to maximize the ambulatory treatment of psychiatric patients and reduce hospitalization. The intervention also remains congruent with the widely accepted notion that individual treatment of ill adolescents is of prime importance. The modality described may be the first step toward an individual approach. Before the intervention is presented, a description of the families and of the current psychiatric treatment of personality-disordered adolescents is summarized.

The Family of the Personality-Disordered Adolescent

Understanding the families of these adolescents is essential for understanding some of their otherwise unexplainable and incongruous behaviors. Clinicians usually agree about the severity of the family psychopathology in most cases of personality disorder. There are usually chronic unresolved problems, often ending up in conflictual and never completed separation. Blurred boundaries between parents and child are often present, leading to coalitions, triangulations, and idiosyncratic roles assigned to children. The presence of significant psychopathology among the parents led Vaillant (1977) to conclude that the development of a personality disorder is associated with day-to-day contact with chronically disturbed parents. The parenting is poor, there is no parental alliance, and one of the parents may overtly or covertly encourage the child to rebel against the other parent. Inconsistent discipline and confusion then ensue. Chronic feelings of mutual alienation, loss, and guilt, which may be both primary and secondary to the adolescent's psychopathology, are also often present. Even though these characteristics are not specific to families of personality-disordered adolescents, their severity and frequency are striking here.

In the families of immature adolescents, the family structural defect often involves a symbiotic type of relationship between the index adolescent and one of the parents, usually the mother. This pathological parent–child bond can sometimes be traced back to an early trauma that was often accompanied by the withdrawal of the other parent. The overinvolved parent's neediness is then met by this child, who becomes a provider of emotions. The child is kept in a dependent and infantilized position. Overprotection and intrusiveness by one parent are frequently accompanied by a strained relationship between the child and the peripheral parent. The latter often abdicates this parental role toward that child.

The child's ego development is thus prevented. His lack of autonomy and initiative, which has been fitting more or less the family, may become intolerable in adolescence. The immature adolescent presents infantile patterns of behavior and feelings and has limited social relations (Kugelmass, 1973). Owing to the lack of parental alliance, the child may be in a position of power and out of control. He usually feels helpless, though, facing the demands of the external world and often gives up, unable to struggle. Depression, school refusal, and violence toward the mother are frequent.

The Family of the Borderline Adolescent

Many psychopathological features of borderline patients are assumed to be related to their parents (Masterson, 1972; Zinner and Shapiro, 1972) or to their family disturbances (Mandelbaum, 1977; Egan, 1988). Drawing on the psychoanalytic developmental theory of Mahler (1968), Zinner and Shapiro (1972) implicate a basic problem around separation-individuation. A re-creation of the failure of early parenting is postulated in which the parents see the adolescent either as ruthlessly independent or as ravenously demanding and dependent (Shapiro et al., 1977). The parents then withdraw and resort to pathological defensive operations that are also used by the borderline adolescent. Some other authors, Masterson and Rinsley (1975) in particular, also consider individuation under the threat of abandonment a central issue. These families apparently cannot tolerate change. They shift from extreme rigidity to explosive outbursts when there is a change in the family functioning, such as when the adolescent tries to leave home.

It is also assumed that many borderline patients were submitted to abuse, neglect, and loss during their childhood. The family relations are usually chaotic. The patient may be caught in a web of contradictory and unintegrated affects and fantasies, leading to confusion. He may, in turn, contribute to the chaos. According to Kernberg (1979), the borderline patient engenders family dysfunction. Because of his emotional instability, his primitive defenses and his inability to make trusting relationships, he instills strong emotions in others. At the time of the referral, there is an impasse; both the adolescent and his parents are locked into angry and sad feelings. The parents are unable to set limits and to contain the adolescent's rage, which could possibly lead to splitting. The patient may also feel that nobody is attuned to his experience. Some of his symptoms may then appear as quasi-logical phenomena when happening within the family.

367

The Psychiatric Treatment of the Personality-Disordered Adolescent

There is a general feeling of pessimism regarding the psychiatric treatment of personality disorders. Even though these patients form a very large group of the psychiatric population, they end up getting minimal treatment (Gunderson et al., 1989). There seems to be a consensus that regressive transference is often not constructive, so that the focus is on a supportive, reality-oriented approach based on confrontation and limit setting. The treatment of the personality-disordered adolescent follows the same trend and is implemented through various treatment modalities including individual psychotherapy and group, inpatient, or residential treatment. Concurrent family therapy has been recommended (Williams, 1975).

The literature on the family treatment of personality-disordered adolescents focuses mostly on specific groups (see Tolan, Cromwell, and Brasswell, 1986, for delinquents; Textor, 1987, for drug-abusing adolescents). Only a few studies provide a formal description of family therapy with borderline adolescents (see in particular Shapiro et al., 1977; Shapiro, 1982; Egan, 1988), while reports about family therapy with immature adolescents are anecdotal. Within a psychoanalytic frame of reference, Shapiro et al. (1977) concomitantly use individual, couple, and family therapy with borderline adolescents. Their intervention with these families focuses on pathological projective identification, and interpretation is the main therapeutic tool.

Even though family therapy is indicated with adolescents who are still immersed in the family system and have difficulty separating — borderline and immature adolescents — reports on the process and on the modalities of intervention with their family are lacking.

Family Intervention

Taking into account the severity of their pathology, intervention with these families is a tremendous task requiring a theoretical and empirical background. The approach has to be flexible and based on the policy that the choice of the therapy has to suit the characteristics of the adolescent as well as the status of the family (Offer and Vanderstoep, 1974).

The adolescents studied here can be treated on an ambulatory basis but are not candidates for psychoanalytic psychotherapy; a family intervention, therefore, becomes almost a necessity. Counseling the parents could be an alternative. That modality is effective when the parents follow the therapist's recommendations, but this is rarely the case. Moreover, the authoritative, advice-giving style used in some counseling can augment parents' feeling too dependent and undermine their sense of competence. The proposed intervention is centered on the family while keeping a developmental perspective. The ultimate goal is geared toward the adolescent's individuation and to helping take from the family the positive aspects and to be able to extricate from the pathogenic part. Using a systemic framework, the separation-individuation process is conceptualized here as a family task. An organizational change within the family system, with the resolution of the deeply ingrained chronic marital problem, may not be a realistic goal. Following McKinney's (1970) model for multideficit families, the growth potential of the adolescent is emphasized as well as parental competence and their healing capacities. The approach is based on the same premises used in the other treatment modalities of personality-disordered adolescents. Emphasis is on structure through limit-setting and on support.

Working with these families implies the use of possibly more than one therapeutic modality so as to maximize the therapeutic alliance with both the family and the adolescent. The work may have to be done with the most receptive members for a while, which is often the case with the family of an immature adolescent. Meetings with the adolescent alone or with the parents separately or together may be used as stepping stones. These sessions may help to unblock resistances that are usually massive and to reaffirm alliance. A systemic way of conceptualizing change, however, is maintained that is not defined by the number of people present in any given session. As intensive individual treatment is not done, the adolescent and her family are treated by the same therapist thus preventing the conflict this type of patient and the family bring when the treatment is split.

In terms of family approaches, the intervention is systemic and can be described as structural first, then communication focused, while using a psychoanalytic understanding of the subjective reality of individual family members. The approach necessitates a very active participation from the therapist.

THE THERAPIST'S ROLE

With personality-disordered adolescents, the holding environment (Winnicott, 1960) required for ego organization is broken and needs assistance (Shapiro, 1982). The family treatment, which borrows from the inpatient treatment of borderline adolescents (Masterson, 1972), must promote the development of a firm family structure. The therapist provides, at the onset of the intervention in particular, a containing structure for the family, so that the family can become again the holding structure for the disturbed adolescent. The therapist provides that structure as he bears and metabolizes the painful, distorted, and acted-out affects and helps the family to deal with loss and rage. Internalization leading to greater separation from other family members is thus promoted. The therapist joins the system and assumes a strong leadership role. He becomes a benevolent authority figure, able to confront, to set ground rules, and to prevent the family's frozen patterns of functioning. The therapist works toward restructuring with the parents at the top before leading the family to deal with basic issues such as improving communications. He also helps the family realize that there are alternative solutions to separation other than abandonment.

In essence, the therapist lends his reality to the family, so that the group will become more cohesive. The therapist can do it only through empathy since entry in the system may cause crises and threaten to break strong bonds. This phenomenon may occur with the dysfunctional family of the borderline patient as well as with the boundary-problem family of the immature adolescent. In this regard, the therapist empathically has to make sure that each family member's sense of self is maintained. He has to be particularly sensitive to the adolescent especially when confronting the youngster's omnipotence defenses; the adolescent may then feel overwhelmed by depression and despair. Empathy allows the exploration of the family's inner experience and may reveal unexpected avenues for change. The therapy of a family with a borderline girl illustrates the therapist's role.

Family therapy was used as the main therapeutic modality with the Martin family when Kim, 15 years old, refused to continue in individual psychotherapy. Hospitalization had been thought of but was postponed as the family engaged in treatment. Kim was isolating herself and was perceived as bizarre by her teacher. She had been taking drugs for a year to alleviate her feelings of isolation and anxiety. She had problems mastering affects. Her mood shifted from apathy, with feelings of emptiness, to intense outbursts of anger. She was showing identity problems, with uncertainty about self, values, and long-term goals. Her mother got hold of unmailed letters addressed to an older man, in which Kim expressed a mixture of erotic and aggressive feelings.

The younger of two girls, Kim had been a model child, sacrificing her autonomy partly to fulfill her parents' needs. She had not been a source of worry until she reached adolescence. She then started to show long-repressed resentment toward her parents, but could not express it clearly. Kim had been dominated by infantile patterns of feelings and behavior and was still giving a great deal of emotional power to her parents even though she perceived them as uncaring. The father was minimally involved in the family, keeping himself at work every night, while the mother remained frustrated at home. The parents could not tolerate each other, and Kim became the target of their dissension. They blamed each other over minor details, and Kim was always in the middle. The arguments usually ended with the father's withdrawal, leaving Kim more confused. Mr. Martin had refused any involvement in the treatment, as he felt his wife was exaggerating Kim's problems and that she was herself a psychiatric case. He was seen alone many times before he agreed to come to family sessions. The family relations were detrimental to Kim's already shaky personality organization. She was a prisoner of the family's functioning but was unable to extirpate herself from it.

Owing to the severity of Kim's and her family's psychopathology, the therapists had to be very active in the first phase. They had to contain Kim's instinctual outbursts as well as the family regression and hypersensitivity. They modulated and validated, through empathy, the subjective experience of each member that was disavowed by the others and helped them tolerate pain. To prevent chaos and help the members to take some distance, the therapists had to be flexible and use various modalities. For example, they often worked with family subsystems. The parents were seen alone for part of many sessions by one therapist so as to promote parenting alliance. The other therapist, in the meantime, met with the two girls together or separately. Video playback and a one-way mirror were also used as distancing devices. Slowly, much of Kim's behavior emerged as difficulty separating and fear of abandonment, while the family's efforts at discouraging separation were highlighted. As their mutual alliance improved, the parents regained some control over the family and Kim's behavior became more predictable.

THE PARENTING ALLIANCE

At the time of the referral, the parents are often overwhelmed by their problematic adolescent. It is usually possible, then, to get their cooperation and involvement in the treatment. First of all, the therapist must promote the development of a parenting alliance, which is of prime importance in the treatment of disturbed young people. A power hierarchy, which is almost implicit in normal families, has to be reaffirmed here with the parents at the top. They are encouraged to set rules and to use power constructively so as to acquaint their children with the consequences of their defenses and with the external reality. The therapist strengthens the parental subsystem when allied with the two parents and emphatically tries to understand their individual points of view. He thus helps each parent to acknowledge and respect the parenting role of the partner. He also instills mutual support, which is strongly needed as doubts and frustration related to the reawakening of the parents' unresolved conflicts with their own parents resurface. These conflicts are usually bound to their inability to contain their child or to promote separation.

The therapist serves as a model for the overburdened parents. Being calm, while remaining emotionally available, the therapist makes the parents learn to remain empathic and holding even when the adolescent is difficult or has difficulty separating. Hope is instilled where pessimism has long prevailed. The structure provided by the parents helps strengthen the adolescent's ego and promote internalization. The adolescent may then be able to tolerate and control affects, such as separation anxiety or rage, which could have been overwhelming before. In brief, the parenting alliance becomes an essential element of the holding environment. The treatment of the Roberts family illustrates the necessity of the parenting alliance.

Jane, 14, the oldest of three, had been diagnosed as borderline. She was labile in mood, intense but unstable in her relationships, and impulsive, as manifested by compulsive stealing, uncontrollable outbursts of anger, and minor self-mutilation. She was in psychotherapy for one year but had not improved significantly. The mother was also followed in psychotherapy, while the father had been seen only once and, for an obscure reason, had not been involved in the treatment. Jane's behavior became worrisome for her therapist. She was tyrannizing the family, checking the whereabouts of all members, and imposing her decisions. Recently, she had put a knife to her mother's throat during their never-ending arguments.

The mother–child relationship had always been tumultuous and intense, with difficulty separating. There was overinvolvement by the mother but also distancing. The father was peripheral, participating in a lot of sports when not working. He was taking a stoical stance vis-à-vis Jane's behavior. He was observing without intervening, in the belief that all her behavior was due to her illness and that he could not do anything about it. During the family sessions, he took sides against his wife, who did not seem to acknowledge his presence. The parental void had led to Jane's control over the family, feeding her omnipotence.

The mother–daughter interactions left the therapists feeling overwhelmed and frightened. As a defense against painful subjective experiences, both mother and daughter communicated through projective identification and action discharge. They were locked into concern with survival issues. For both, any difference or opposing thought was perceived as rejection. Because their relationship was at a standstill, the father was used as a pivot for change.

The parents were seen alone for part of each interview, and the father was encouraged to set limits. He started within sessions, with the support of one of the therapists to confront Jane, while the mother was prevented from intervening negatively. Mrs. Roberts then realized that her husband could be of some help, as opposed to the way her father was in her own family. She let Mr. Roberts take a greater role, and a parenting alliance was slowly developed. Jane's feelings seemed then to be contained. She progressively gave up her omnipotent stance, and her capacity for repression seemed to increase. These changes paved the way to working on the family's distorted communications.

WORKING ON COMMUNICATIONS

Strengthening the family structure decreases the confusion, harnesses the forces, and makes improving communications possible. As the communications are worked on at the interpersonal, intrafamily level, the family members as real objects are both participants and therapists, and their interactions are used as a therapeutic lever. Clarification and confrontation used by the family or the therapist become powerful tools against distortions and pathological defense mechanisms underlying serious character pathology. Similar to the way the staff, in milieu therapy, deals with an adolescent's pathological defenses (Meeks and Cahill, 1988), family members can also contribute to changing these pathological mechanisms. Denial, projection, displacement, and perceptions not based on external reality are then tackled. The work starts at the interpersonal level but is geared toward the intrapsychic. The move is from the outside toward the inside to reach the needs, affects, and subjective experiences of individual family members. The therapist uses the here-and-now to facilitate the emotional interchanges. He modulates the process by allowing an optimal dosage of emotional expression so as to make the experience positive for the family. Verbal exchanges between some family members are encouraged while the therapist and the other family members may be observers. A discussion follows in which feedback is given. The parents' own childhood experiences and memories, charged with feelings of loss, grief, and rage, may resurface. The therapist can also use reframing and interpretation to help family members decode the intrafamily communications and learn to metacommunicate.

With the Roberts family, the work on communication was focused on the mother–Jane relationship. Their separation difficulties and the activated abandonment depression came to the fore. In the presence of the rest of the family, they were closely monitored by one of the therapists to work through that painful state. Jane's defiant behavior was seen as an effort to separate and an unconscious wish to reunite. She slowly learned to separate without feeling rejected or ashamed. The distorting effect of mother's and daughter's primitive defense mechanisms was also tackled. Their massive use of splitting of the self and of the object whenever they were angry was slowly replaced by a reconciliation and fusion of the good and the bad. They came to acknowledge that they had been projecting some parts of the self they had found unacceptable. The work had to be done cautiously, though. Both mother and daughter constantly scrutinized the other for any sign of rejection. Slowly, the fantasized other was finally replaced by the real one. As they learned to communicate their affects in words, they solved some of their problems and operated at a more symbolic level. The family was seen steadily over a two-year period.

In the Martin family, Kim was full of resentment against her parents but could not express it in a meaningful way. Her 20-year-old sister, Jackie, was most helpful in verbalizing for her what she thought Kim was experiencing; Jackie had earlier lived some of the same difficulties. Kim then realized that her rage could be put into words and would not destroy her parents and threaten her relationship to them. She realized that her "good girl" behavior had been prompted by her fear of losing her parents or their love. In her moments of apathy, Kim felt nobody cared, and she withdrew, denying her neediness. Within the holding environment provided by the therapy, her parents challenged her denial, insisting that they cared about her, and made her understand that discussing could be more fruitful for her than withdrawing. Even though Kim did not seem to be moved by these confrontations, in the long run they had a positive effect. Her self and object representations changed slowly, and her apathy decreased.

When the therapy deepens, the chronic marital problems that were detoured by the index adolescent often come to the surface. The idea of reestablishing a closer marital bond may be very frightening for the parents. If they decide to work on their marital problems, the adolescent may be present as an observer for a few sessions. Kim's distortions related to her parents' problems could then be shaken up.

As expected, the treatment did not change the Martin's marital problems that had developed over 20 years of marriage. The intervention appeared, however, to help the parents accommodate to each other. Mrs. Martin realized that she was too heavily invested in her husband for self-fulfillment. She found a job as a secretary, which also helped her separate from her daughter.

COUNTERTRANSFERENCE ISSUES

The family of the personality-disordered adolescent requires an important affective and cognitive investment from the therapist, and this type of family raises intense negative feelings. It is of no surprise that not many of these families are taken into treatment. The enormous conscious and unconscious family needs and the morbid family atmosphere, such as an invading depression or a barely controlled violence, are a source of overwhelming feelings and fatigue for the therapist. As he "joins" the family, the therapist feels the family members' anguish and misery. He may also reexperience his own unresolved conflicts around separation in particular. He may tend to overidentify with one or the other party, being the adolescent or the parents against the other. The therapist may also face massive resistances. One of the parents, for example, may be opposed to any kind of involvement that would mean a questioning of his or her position in the family. Facing these difficulties, the therapist may become overinvolved or may withdraw. To prevent these reactions, the therapist must continuously acknowledge his own feelings so as to remain empathic to all members, including sometimes inadequate parents or indifferent adolescents.

The use of a cotherapist is helpful with these families as a way to cope with countertransference reactions and to prevent being swallowed up by the system. Cotherapy can help in understanding countertransference issues and the confusion that sometimes surrounds the treatment. The necessity to modify the techniques continuously with these families is also facilitated by cotherapy. Besides supporting each other, the cotherapists together can more easily master family resistances. One of the therapists may, for example, interpret the resistance, while the other supports a resistant member. The following treatment of a very immature adolescent illustrates some countertransference issues.

Paul Lewis was a very obese adolescent living with his two parents. He had had school problems all along and had repeated one grade. He was referred at 14, though, when he did not follow the medical treatment for his obesity and refused to attend school. The boy was called "Fatty" by his schoolmates, and he could not fend for himself. At home, he was violent toward his mother when she refused him anything. He loudly expressed his need for more freedom but remained quite dependent and self-centered.

When Paul was two years old, his mother was seriously hurt in a car accident and remained partially disabled. She withdrew from social activities and developed a regressive type of relationship with Paul. The excluded father stayed away from the dyad and became more involved with his older son and with issues outside of the home. Paul's psychological development became seriously curtailed. The family had always been at war. At the time of the referral, the parents were barely speaking to each other, and the situation had recently gotten worse as the father took an anticipated retreat from work.

Paul was not motivated to get any help. He had acquired some power in the family, a privilege that he was not ready to give up. He refused individual help and barely came to family sessions, in which he did not participate actively for many months. He managed to have his parents carry all the feelings and the responsibilities for his misbehavior. The parents had been fighting over their attitudes toward their son, which meant, in effect, who was going to serve him.

During the sessions, Mrs. Lewis bitterly complained about the two other members, but the weak father could not match the mother's attacks. Paul was then continuously triangulated into a web of painful feelings, attack, and confusion. During those recurrent periods of intense feelings expressed by the mother, Paul was quite moved. During similar episodes in the past, his mother had made threats to leave home or kill herself. Exploration of the interactions surrounding these episodes was met with strong parental resistance. The Lewises often ended the sessions by blaming the therapists.

These pathological interactions were of great annoyance to the therapists. As a way to break the pattern, one of them dealt with the mother alone over three long sessions while the rest of the family observed. Mrs. Lewis had become a person from whom everybody but Paul stayed away. Through the therapist's patience and empathy, her defenses went down, and she showed sad feelings. The therapist was then able to model for the father an appropriate response. The mother felt that she was being listened to and came to realize that her own attitudes contributed to the others' behavior toward her. The father was progressively reintroduced, while Paul was kept aside.

Detriangulating Paul was very threatening for the parents, especially for the mother. The emotional return of the father meant for her possible emotional closeness to him. She did not want to be submitted again to the disappointments and pain she had experienced years before. Both parents desperately tried to bring Paul back into the discussion. The experience was therapeutic for Paul, though, who came to realize that he was not responsible for all the family's misery.

Through painstaking hours of family progression and regression, Paul's autonomy was worked out. An agreement was finally reached to leave him in charge of his diet and his school work. In return, he was given rewards leading to more autonomy, such as getting his driver's permit. Paul was finally sent to a boarding school close to his home. The family treatment continued for another year, and the boy was seen alone on demand, as he was having a very difficult time at school. Now, two years later, he is back home and is still obese. Some of his preoedipal fixations being removed, he has, however, reached the stage of being a separate person with relative autonomy. His feeling of omnipotence has been replaced by a realistic pride about himself concerning a part-time job and his new ability to make friends.

Summary

To prevent an endless debate between those supporting an intrinsic deficit versus an environmental deficit, the adolescent's problem has been seen here as both an individual problem and the metaphorical expression of a family problem. The intricacy of this two-faceted problem appears vividly with borderline and immature adolescents. Both the adolescent and family have, among other problems, difficulty separating. The approach described here focuses on that particular aspect; each therapeutic step is geared toward the adolescent's separation-individuation. Concerning the course of therapy, restructuring is perceived as the first therapeutic step and a prerequisite to work on such issues as delineating personal and family problems and improving communications. The approach is not, though, a panacea for the treatment of all personality disorders in adolescence and should not preempt the use of other approaches. As reported by Esman (1989) in regard to borderline adolescents, there is enough variation in the syndrome to allow the use of a variety of treatment approaches. Involving the family may not be feasible, and the adolescent sometimes must be removed from a detrimental family situation.

The family of the immature or borderline adolescent is often seen as untreatable but what the therapist wants to accomplish and is ready to share often paves the way to effective intervention (Offer and Vanderstoep, 1974). The therapist must be ready to struggle with the family and with himself. The therapist has to be courageous, patient, and optimistic. The intervention is usually done on a middle-term basis with encouragement to the family to consult again if needed. The approach may thus appear obsolete at a time of a "quick-fix" culture. Family therapy can be a powerful tool with very disturbed, personality-disordered adolescents. The family approach must be flexible and based on a psychodynamic understanding of the problems. As so many of these cases fail to respond to the usual treatment and make therapists and institutions feel powerless, looking at the intervention from another angle can be refreshing.

The experience can be rewarding for the adolescent, as she is becoming emancipated from the family, and for the parents, who facilitate the process. Working with these families is difficult but can also be rewarding for the clinician. Hours spent with them gives access to the subjective experiential reality that makes the substance of behavior and may allow the exploration of shadowy areas of the human condition. Family therapy becomes, then, a journey full of pain, uncertainties, and wonder for both the family and the clinician.

REFERENCES

American Psychiatric Association (1987), *Diagnostic and Statistical Manual of Mental Disorders (DSM-III-R)*. Washington, DC: American Psychiatric Press.

Egan, J. (1988), Treatment of borderline conditions in adolescents. *J. Clin. Psychiat.*, 49(suppl.):32–35.

Esman, A. H. (1989), Borderline personality disorder in adolescents: Current concepts. *Adolescent Psychiatry*, 16:319–336. Chicago: University of Chicago Press.

Gunderson, J. G., Franck, A. F., Ronningstam, E. F., Wachter, S., Lynch, V. S. & Wolf, P. J. (1989), Early discontinuance of borderline patients from psychotherapy. *J. Nerv. Ment. Dis.*, 177:38–42.

Kernberg, O. (1979), Psychoanalytic psychotherapy with borderline adolescents. *Adolescent Psychiatry*, 7:294–321. Chicago: University of Chicago Press.

Kugelmass, J. N. (1973), *Adolescent Immaturity*. Springfield, IL: Charles C Thomas.

Mahler, M. (1969), *On Human Symbiosis and the Vicissitudes of Individuation*, Vol. 1. New York: International Universities Press.

Mandelbaum, A. (1977), The family treatment of the borderline patient. In: *Borderline Personality Disorders*, ed. P. Hartocollis. New York: International Universities Press, pp. 423–438.

Masterson, J. F. (1972), *Treatment of the Borderline Adolescent: A Developmental Approach*. New York: Wiley-Interscience.

_____ & Rinsley, D. B. (1975), The borderline syndrome: The role of the mother in the genesis and psychic structure of the borderline personality. *Internat. J. Psycho-Anal.*, 56:163–177.

McKinney, G. E. (1970), Adapting family therapy to multideficit families. *Soc. Casework*, 51:327–333.

Meeks, J. E. & Cahill, A. J. (1988), Therapy of adolescents with severe behavior problems. *Adolescent Psychiatry*, 15:475–486. Chicago: University of Chicago Press.

Offer, D. & Vanderstoep, E. (1974), Indications and contraindications for family therapy. *Adolescent Psychiatry*, 3:249–262. New York: Basic Books.

Shapiro, E. R. (1982), The holding environment and family therapy with acting-out adolescents. *Internat. J. Psychoanal. Psychother.*, 9:209–226.

_____ Shapiro, R. L., Zinner, J. & Berkowitz, D. A. (1977), The borderline ego and the working alliance: Indications for family and individual treatment in adolescence. *Internat. J. Psycho-Anal.*, 58:77–87.

Textor, M. R. (1987), Family therapy with drug addicts: An integrated approach. *Amer. J. Orthopsychiat.*, 57:495–507.

Tolan, P. H., Cromwell, R. E. & Brasswell, M. (1986), Family therapy with delinquents: A critical review of the literature. *Fam. Proc.*, 25:619–650.

Vaillant, G. E. (1977), *Adaptation to Life*. Boston: Little, Brown.

Williams, F. (1975), Family therapy: Its role in adolescent psychiatry. In: *The Adolescent in Group and Family Therapy*, ed. M. Sugar. New York: Brunner/Mazel, pp. 178–193.

Winnicott, D. W. (1960), The theory of the parent–infant relationship. In: *The Maturational Process and the Facilitating Environment*. New York: International Universities Press, pp. 37–55, 1965.

Zinner, J. & Shapiro, R. L. (1972), Projective identification as a mode of perception and behavior in families of adolescents. *Internat. J. Psycho-Anal.*, 53:523–530.

25 ADOLESCENT PARTIAL HOSPITALIZATION: A DEVELOPMENTAL PERSPECTIVE

DENNIS C. GRYGOTIS AND EITAN D. SCHWARZ

The purpose of this chapter is to examine the structure and function of partial hospitalization programs in the context of adolescent development. Partial hospitalization is a treatment modality that is gaining increasing attention as a cost-effective alternative to full hospitalization. In such programs, an adolescent usually spends a major part of each day or evening receiving mental health and educational services but continues to live in his usual environment. A conceptual basis for psychosocial development is elaborated here and then employed to clarify the design and implementation of adolescent partial hospitalization programs. We hope that a developmental perspective will remain the conceptual framework for design of programs and evaluation of patients even at this time of cost-driven experimentation with health care delivery systems.

Conceptual Background: The Development Trajectory

When clinicians diagnose psychiatric disorders or assess psychological wellness, they essentially sum the relative condition of a set of developmentally achieved processes. They visualize how such processes evolve and interact with each other over time in a unique biopsycho-social environment to provide the individual with more integrated, resilient, and adaptive functioning. Using psychoanalytic conceptualizations, Anna Freud (1965) described a number of such processes as developmental lines. Broadening this conceptualization, we distinguish here developmental processes especially important to clinicians working with adolescents. These include 1) sensorimotor development, dependent on physical maturation, nutrition, sleep, health, adequate physical activity, self-care, and freedom from physical violence (Schwarz and

Perry, 1994); 2) psychological development, including separation-individuation, object relations, identity formation, affect regulation, impulse control, and psychosexual development; 3) cognitive development and educational progress; and 4) social development, including family and peer relationships, a sense of belonging to the community and the world at large, and moral and spiritual development.

Each of these processes interacts with the others and with biological predispositions and social factors. Each can be clinically evaluated, however, according to its type (what it is), its relative intensity (how much it dominates or pulls the overall process of development), and its directionality (where it is heading with respect to age-appropriateness). At any point in time, each of these evolving processes contributes to the overall progression of development and age-appropriate functioning. Thus, each process can be conceptualized as a force and visualized as a vector with directionality and intensity.

Optimal development implies an integrated and balanced progression of developmental influences acting in concert and evolving over time. Thus, the many vectors representing developmental forces can be visualized in multidimensional space as pulling on a point that depicts the overall state of development and functioning of the individual. As this process moves through time, the point describes the "developmental trajectory." A developmental trajectory is thus conceptualized here as a curve over time describing the sum of vectors of the discrete developmental processes. The developmental trajectory gives a quick view of progress toward optimal biopsychosocial functioning. Experienced clinicians all have in mind an optimal "normal" curve describing a progression of age-appropriate functioning. Adolescence can be conceptualized as referring to a segment of this trajectory.

Adolescents who present for psychiatric assessment and treatment exhibit dysfunction or distortion in one or more aspects of their development caused by interacting biopsychosocial factors. Diagnostic and treatment interventions with adolescents aim at correcting developmental trajectories. Clinicians are especially interested in identifying processes that cause deviations in the developmental trajectories and can be corrected. Deviations can occur when a discrete process exerts too large or too small a pull relative to other processes, causing the developmental curve to be pulled away from optimal direction. Such pulls can be driven primarily by biological, psychological, or social factors. Assessment usually includes evaluation of the degree, nature, and direction of deviation from optimal curve and an analysis of the vectors operating at the time, including healthy forces, as well as those pulling the curve away from optimum. With varying degrees of completeness, clinicians evaluating adolescents attempt to discover the individual processes, or vectors, acting at the present; understand how they have evolved and interacted in the past; and predict the course of the general curve into the future.

The Developmental Trajectory and the Continuum of Clinical Interventions

Once they identify and assess psychopathology in terms of deviant developmental processes, clinicians develop treatment plans that aim at correcting the deviation and thereby restoring the developmental trajectory to more optimal correlation with the ideal normal curve. Even disorders that are deemed primarily biological in origin exist in a developmental context. Practical clinical issues such as insight and compliance with medication treatment are embedded in this context. Treatment options include decisions about the therapeutic structures within which to place the adolescent. Such therapeutic structures can take many forms, best deriving from the developmental needs of the adolescent. The type, direction, and intensity of a deviant process determines the nature and setting of treatment. For example, at one extreme is inpatient hospitalization, where 24-hour care is provided to the adolescent outside of his family, school, and community. At the other extreme, a mild deviation in cognitive development, exerting a small pull on the developmental trajectory, may require only consultation and educational remediation.

If the degree of developmental deviation is extreme—for example, severe disruption of the developmental trajectory posed by life threat by suicide, abuse, or a severe eating disorder—the therapeutic response must be sufficient to provide safety and enable immediate and intense treatment. Severe deviations may include significant biologically driven affective dysregulation, disturbances in object relations and identity formation, threats to physical or psychic integrity deriving from violence or abuse, disruptions of physical functioning (such as eating disorders, pseudoseizures, management of chronic diseases), and impairment of reality testing. Clinically, such deviations may be manifested by serious maladaptive or harmful symptoms, such as suicidal, runaway, or homicidal behavior; psychotic or affective disorders; substance abuse; or school refusal.

Inpatient hospitalization can best be seen as a protective holding environment for adolescents who present with severe temporary or permanent deviations in their developmental trajectories. The therapeutic structure of the inpatient setting is optimally geared to protecting the adolescent from internal or external harm, providing assessment, initiating biopsychosocial treatment, stabilizing, and discharge planning through its intensive holding environment and multimodal treatment. In today's atmosphere, discharge is usually planned to a less restrictive environment immediately upon admission. Regardless of the length of hospitalization, however, the developmental trajectory must be sufficiently, albeit partially, restored so that the adolescent integrates the current precipitating stressor affectively, cognitively, and socially to pose a danger no longer to himself or others. Removal from the demands and supports of the adolescent's usual environment, on the other hand, may have adverse effects on his developmental trajectory, including lowered self-esteem and perception of self as defective. Excessive encouragement of his adaptation to the synthetic inpatient environment is not necessarily equivalent to promoting the adolescent's development. Therefore, during the course of an inpatient hospitalization, an ongoing awareness of the developmental trajectory and the best use of the setting must be continually maintained to assure optimal functioning of the adolescent in his family, school, and community settings.

At the other extreme of the treatment continuum lie outpatient services. Such services provide therapeutic opportunities for the adolescent and his family that catalyze ongoing development within the natural setting. However, the adolescent's affective, cognitive, and social resources must be sufficient to promote development and assure safety. Midway on the continuum is the public or private full-day school program with some therapeutic features. Such programs vary in their relative emphasis on developing the therapeutic space versus providing an educational setting.

A comprehensive approach to adolescent development also considers clusters of other issues. These include pregnancy, sexuality, sexual orientation, and sexually transmitted diseases; drug, tobacco, and alcohol use; addictive and eating disorders; peer relations, sports, and gangs; violence, high-risk behaviors, and abuse; attempted or threatened suicide; vocational and career planning; and living with chronic nonpsychiatric or psychiatric illness. Preventive attention to these areas constitutes a cost-effective intervention.

The Developmental Trajectory and Design of Partial Hospitalization Programs

The remainder of this chapter explores how such programs can be structured to restore or correct the developmental trajectory. In contrast to inpatient hospitalization and outpatient treatments, partial hospitalization programs can provide a therapeutic opportunity that supplements the environment rather than replaces or merely catalyzes the developmental needs of the adolescent and his family.

Focusing on partial hospitalization programs in greater detail, we will examine actual programs with the goal of assisting the reader in refining existing efforts or planning new programs. We will scrutinize two particular designs to illustrate how structural components promote progress toward the goal of restoring the developmental trajectory. To illustrate, we will refer to two programs with which we are intimately familiar. While Program A is set in a full-service, private psychiatric hospital and Program B in a general hospital, they are more similar than different. In both programs, psychiatric interventions, including treatments with medication and individual psychotherapy, are provided by a psychiatrist specializing in the care of adolescents who looks to the programs to provide a psychosocial context for his efforts.

Assessment

Thorough diagnostic assessment is crucial to rational treatment planning. The assessment setting must integrate the family, school, and elements of the community into the assessment process. Areas of special concern in assessing an adolescent's developmental trajectory include the impact of current disorder on the development of identity, cognitive style, and social competence. Identity formation includes differentiation of the adolescent's values from those of the family while integrating them into a societal context. The adolescent experiments with and develops his own unique, individual, publicly and privately expressed self in such matters as personal taste in clothes, music, and intellectual and creative pursuits. Adolescents may also need to develop a self concept that adaptively integrates biopsychological traits, such as proneness to mood or anxiety disorders, the schizophrenic spectrum disorders, or addictions, such as substance abuse and eating disorders. Cognitive development during adolescence aims at achieving formal operations (Piaget and

385

Inhelder, 1958) and comfort with the particular profile of talents and deficits. Social competence includes the development of such qualities as empathy, compassion, altruism; the refinement of skills in relationship to peers of both sexes; development of skills in relating to non-parental adults in a variety of contexts (e.g. work place, school, social situations); and awareness of larger community and world events and socioeconomic and cultural issues. These concerns must be reviewed for each adolescent in addition to specific behavioral or psychopathological problems because they are influenced by and in turn influence the course of such disorders.

PROGRAM A

In Program A, patients are usually referred from inpatient programs and less frequently from schools or community practitioners. Admission criteria are not precisely spelled out but include the adolescent's ability to form therapeutic alliances and the family's agreement in writing to fully participate in required activities. Patients are excluded at admission or discharged later if they are unable to meet these requirements.

In addition to the standard psychiatric nursing assessments, the adolescent receives a sensorimotor and leisure time assessment by the occupational therapy department. The teacher performs an educational assessment to determine the functional grade level of the adolescent and, more importantly, to rule out learning disability. In order to integrate the family system into the milieu structure, an emphasis is placed on observing the family system. The dietician performs a nutritional and dietary assessment of the adolescent and the family. In addition, specific attention is directed toward the adolescent's need for further education in sex education/sex abuse, alcohol/substance abuse and adoptions, divorce, and reconstituted families.

Soon after admission, the dietitian, the occupational therapist, or both observe the family during a mealtime. Mealtimes offer excellent opportunities to view the family's set of values and rules (Grossman, Poznanski and Banegas, 1983). Family mealtimes can also be seen as a microcosm of a family's dynamics, communication patterns, role identification, and vocalization patterns. The mealtime can offer staff an excellent opportunity to perform comprehensive assessments for eating disorders, as well as other psychiatric disorders, and to model more adaptive eating behaviors and communication patterns for the adolescents and their parents and families.

These assessments focus on the patient's strengths and competencies as well as on developmental deviations. At the initial staffing, led by the patient's attending psychiatrist, all evaluations are summarized in writing and an initial master treatment plan is developed for the adolescent and his or her family. A short list of goals and objectives is compiled from the most disabling and maladaptive area of the adolescent's and family's functioning. This list identifies deviations in the developmental trajectory and plans for restoring the process. This assessment is reviewed regularly.

PROGRAM B

In Program B, referral sources and admission criteria and procedures are similar to those of Program A. Here intake emphasizes assessment and diagnosis of the adolescent and his or her family. The staff makes an initial screening assessment by reviewing available records and obtaining studies from or communicating with the attending physician, schools, or hospitals. The prospective patient's and family's treatability in the program's present patient mix are evaluated, as is the prospective patient's influence on the milieu. If appropriate, the staff interviews the adolescent and family and decides whether to admit. The staff then integrates these data with recorded observational data gathered in the initial week from program teachers and therapists, who observe the adolescent individually, in groups, and with his family. The family itself is observed in several meetings, as well as in a multiple family group, during the first week. Rating scales are used to determine levels of depression (Beck et al., 1961), substance abuse, or other symptoms.

Together with psychiatric assessment by the attending physician, this information is then reported verbally but systematically in a diagnostic staffing to a senior child and adolescent psychiatrist medical director, who integrates it together with the staff and writes a detailed, developmentally organized clinical note that includes a problem list and treatment plan. The treatment plan is reviewed and updated periodically according to clinical needs using the same format. In contrast to Program A, which formally surveys the entire life space of the adolescent and his family from multiple perspectives, Program B relies on the skills of a senior child and adolescent psychiatrist to integrate the clinical information and provide a sound, comprehensive, clinical and developmental assessment.

Treatment of the Adolescent

Even if the current disorder is biologically driven and requires biological intervention, a multimodal approach must address the effects of the disorder on the patient's developmental trajectory. Optimal treatment requires a therapeutic structure or a therapeutic space. This concept refers not only to an actual physical space staffed by professionals serving patients, but to the full subjective sensorimotor and psychosocial experience of an adolescent and his family interacting with a milieu of physical space and staff. Winnicott's (1953) "holding environment" is a description of such a space promoting development. Additionally, Redl's (1959; Redl and Wineman, 1957) "life space" views the therapeutic space as providing opportunities for transferential reenactment and therapeutic interpretations yielding corrective emotional experiences and identifications. Redl's (1959) concept of "ego lend lease" presages that of Kohut's (1971) tension-regulation function of the selfobject and describes another aspect of the therapeutic space wherein the adolescent borrows tension-regulating functions from the psychosocial environment. These concepts may be extended beyond dyadic interactions to incorporate the dynamics of peer group interactions within the therapeutic space for the adolescent and family (Wineman, 1959).

The physical space itself should be consistent with the aims of the therapeutic space. Generally, characteristics of the physical space should include safety, dimensions and furnishings to accommodate the staff and patients comfortably, opportunities to vary degrees of stimulation, and opportunities for intimate, as well as group, interactions. The therapeutic space can include trips to gymnasiums and community facilities, such as places of natural and artistic beauty, and community and cultural activities. Staff members as well must lend themselves flexibly to function in the therapeutic space and become aware of the theoretical and practical application of these principles.

In Program A, developmental needs are addressed through the use of formal modules. Educationally oriented group therapy modules have been developed in the areas of sex education and sex abuse; alcohol/ substance abuse; and adoptions, divorce, and reconstituted families. These modules were developed to educate adolescents about the major issues and difficulties as well as the normal variations. These educationally oriented groups enable staff and clinicians to assess major areas of developmental deviations because adolescents often spontaneously bring up their major issues during the course of these groups.

In Program A's Sex Education/Sex Abuse Groups, the staff uses such materials as videotapes, films, anatomic diagrams, and brochures to facilitate discussion of sexually transmitted diseases, birth control options, and the use of condoms to provide important information for the purpose of primary prevention. Adolescents are encouraged to reveal personal information and to role play to enable discussions of privacy, body ownership, and intimacy and threats to these in sexual harassment, rape, and date rape. The program requires parental permission for this group. Once parents understand that the group orientation is educational and informational, most do not have a hard time consenting. If an adolescent has been sexually abused, this group may be contraindicated because the patient may be overstimulated. In these cases, a therapist who is very experienced in working with sexually abused children will provide individual or small-group therapy consultations. Therapists aim to facilitate development of cognitive mastery, identity formation, and affective regulation in this important area (Simon, 1986).

In Program A, the second educational group module is the Drug/Alcohol Education Group. This group meets twice monthly to focus on the physical, emotional, and behavioral aspects of substance use and chemical dependency, viewed as diseases. Using educational materials selected from those widely available, the group leader presents facts about the types of alcoholic beverages and street drugs and the natural history of abuse disorders. Primary prevention through strategies for abstinence is emphasized. Role playing of actual situations elicits discussions and provides a lively format. Again, adolescents are given opportunities to write anonymous questions for the discussion in group. This specific attention to prevention of substance abuse disorders offers opportunities for developing mastery and alternative means of tension regulation.

Program A also offers more conventional treatments. The adolescents meet twice daily in group therapy. Developmental needs related to moral development, object relations, identity formation, social interactions, and affect regulation are addressed. Patients spend four hours daily in school, where special education needs are assessed and remediated. Aspects of cognitive development are thereby addressed. Patients are expected to demonstrate increasing success in assuming more initiative and responsibility for their school work as they gradually make the transition back to their regular schools in preparation for discharge. Additionally, enrichment activities such as day trips to museums, shopping malls, and a gymnasium are offered weekly. These experiences offer patients opportunities to integrate and practice behavioral and developmental gains in a variety of normative social contexts.

Program A's attractive, 2000-square-foot physical setting accommodates 12 adolescents and is separate from the inpatient units, with its own entrances. There are private professional and clerical offices, as well as multipurpose, comfortable common areas with adequate storage for classroom, lounging, group and activities therapy, and eating. A full kitchen facility is shared with other programs. Staffing patterns in Program A are conventional with 1.5 full-time equivalent (FTE) teachers, a 0.2 FTE activities therapist, a psychiatric social worker, and a secretary. A teacher with training and certification in working with learning and behaviorally disabled children and adolescents provides leadership and coordination. Staff members interact closely with inpatient staff and meet twice monthly with each patient's attending physician to review care. Individual attention is offered in the school setting and in informal asides with the staff to address individual developmental needs and enable individual patients to utilize the therapeutic space in the service of correcting the developmental trajectory.

Program B resembles Program A in many respects but does not offer formal modules. The areas of sex education/sex abuse, alcohol/substance abuse, adoptions, divorce, and reconstituted families are covered informally as they arise clinically. Group activities are provided daily in three hours of school; 2.5 hours of formal group therapy and meal preparation and eating; and several hours of enrichment and therapeutic activities, which include art therapy, psychodrama, trips to the beach, movies, and museums. Gym and other physical activities promote sensorimotor development. A vocational education module prepares patients with job-seeking and job-retention skills. A high degree of spontaneous individual personal contact takes place between staff and patients that aims at general support, as well as development of psychological mindedness and skills of self-observation.

Program B additionally enlists the adolescent's cooperation in setting personal, academic, and therapeutic goals (individual and familial). A plan to achieve these goals is developed and includes formal measures of behavioral compliance and participation of the patient and family. For example, a goal might be to promote compliance with a medication regimen. The staff and clinicians, as well as patients and families, rate progress and use outcome measures whenever possible. For example, a Beck Depression Inventory (Beck et al., 1961) may be administered several times during the patient's stay. The adolescent and family additionally sign a contract upon admission that itemizes expectations for behaviors necessary for continuation in the program. Program B emphasizes the importance of transition into and out of the program. Since many patients suffer chronic disorders, for example, affective illness, the program supports the development in patients and family members of self-knowledge, insight, and strong treatment alliances with the psychiatrist that would form the basis of long-term compliance.

Program B is located in a general hospital and occupies its own 1000-square-foot space adjacent to the inpatient unit. In addition to a full kitchen, offices, and a small interview room, two pleasant large multipurpose rooms accommodate therapeutic activities and school. Staff includes 1 FTE special education teacher, 0.5 FTE secretary, a psychiatric social worker therapist and director, and a masters-level psychologist therapist. Teachers communicate regularly with the patient's home school and obtain curricular materials that enable the student to continue academic progress. Two devoted mature women, mothers of grown children, volunteer to tutor patients and form supportive relationships with them.

The staff of Program B meets with the child and adolescent psychiatrist medical director several times a week, in addition to at least weekly meetings with each patient's attending physician. Additionally, the medical director performs administrative, program development, and staff support functions on an ongoing basis. Turnover among staff members in this program has been extremely low, with no staff changes over the past six years. This staffing pattern enables a warm and nurturing milieu where there is much opportunity for individual interactions and focus on the developmental needs of patients (Levin et al., 1982).

Treatment of the Family

Because the family is the natural context for the developmental process, it must be a central concern of any therapeutic effort aiming to correct the developmental trajectory of any of its members. A family that functions optimally in the service of development of its members—and all members undergo development along their own trajectories through their own life cycles—is characterized by appropriately evolving role functioning of parents and offsprings. Thus, the family itself undergoes development, and the therapeutic effort must value and respect the family as an entity, itself struggling with its own developmental tasks.

Adolescents with deviant developmental trajectories often come from dysfunctional families. Rigid or chaotic families tend to be isolated within their communities and constricted in the variety of interactions among their members, depriving the adolescent of necessary developmental opportunities. This can result in impoverishment of the adolescent's development of identity within the community, flexible and varied social interactions, and use of leisure time in the service of tension regulation. In addition, parents of adolescents suffering deviant developmental trajectories often feel guilty, defeated, and helpless when their children require professional attention. They may, therefore, resist treatment or fail to support compliance. Empowering parents to restore or newly construct family equilibria, communication, and boundaries is an important goal of any intervention. Therefore, the family must be included in the therapeutic space. The therapeutic space must also provide the family with a temporary holding environment and tension regulation through "ego lend-lease" and opportunities for transferential reenactment, interpretations, and identifications. Although parents often relegate parental functions to professionals, especially initially, when family functioning is severely disrupted, program staff must avoid competition with parents and aim to restore parental responsibilities in order to promote appropriate role functioning and boundaries within the family (Palmer, Harper, and Rivinus, 1983).

Recognizing that the family usually succeeds as the natural context for development, both programs attempt to promote a nurturing therapeutic space and lessen the institutional impersonality described elsewhere (Nakhla, Folkart, and Webster, 1969; Harbin, 1979) by incorporating selected family functions in its procedures. For example, daily meals are served family style with the staff eating with patients and playing parental roles. In one aspect of this rich experience, staff encourages adolescents to bring up at the table a wide range of topics, including important current events and their religious, ethnic, and other cultural values. Developmental tasks thereby routinely practiced include individual identity and community membership, appropriate parent–child roles and responsibilities, coherent peer and sibling relationships, impulse control and age-appropriate communication and behavior, and tension regulation.

The components of the adolescent's daily program are designed to facilitate the reintegration of the adolescent with his or her family, be it traditional, blended, or single parent. In Program A, in order to engage and document full family participation, all family members sign a contract upon admission that specifies in detail the expectations of the program. Parental compliance is tracked and regularly noted in the chart by program staff. The attending psychiatrist is encouraged to use this information in his treatment efforts to assist the family in maintaining compliance. Documenting parental compliance in this manner is well received by staff and psychiatrists because it improves communication and advances the treatment process. Additionally, parents are expected increasingly to take more active roles in setting daily and weekly goals for themselves and their children, gradually taking over from program staff. In this manner, the therapeutic space encourages the development of appropriate family boundaries, roles, and equilibria (Cole and Kelly, 1991).

Program A, unlike Program B, also provides formal modules to promote family functioning appropriate for the adolescent's developmental needs. Because developmental disruptions often arise from the effects of adoption, divorce, and remarriage, adolescents participate in a Family Ties Group or Adoption, Divorce, and Reconstituted Family Issues Group. All patients participate because examination of these and related topics includes understanding of basic issues relevant to all adolescents. Adolescents are assisted in mourning losses; accepting role, boundary, and communication patterns; and developing family identities.

Program A attempts to provide a therapeutic space wherein families can broaden the repertoire of their internal and external experiences. For six hours each Sunday, the Familyfest Group offers the entire family highly experiential naturalistic opportunities to enrich the fabric of its internal life and discover means to interact with the larger community. Arriving at 11 a.m., families of all patients and staff prepare lunch, eat, and clean up together. Assisted by the activities therapist, families then participate in board games, art projects, sports, or musical activities for two hours. These activities increase family cohesion and flexibility, permit the development problem-solving strategies, and allow the discovery of leisure-time interests.

For the next hour, an attempt is made to focus more formally on specific roles and boundaries within the family and address the crisis induced by the adolescent's hospitalization. Parents attend a Parent

Support Group while the adolescent attends a Sibling Group. Goals of the Parent Support Group include empowerment of joint parenting, mutual support between spouses and among couples during the crisis of the adolescent's treatment, and learning parenting strategies. Because they are often effective in offering each other moral support, parents are encouraged to form interfamilial networks that would last beyond discharge. The Sibling Group, meeting simultaneously, also promotes generational cohesion and boundaries. The needs of the well sibling, who often becomes isolated by the patient's illness, are recognized. Once a month the siblings group is co-led by the leader of the Adoption, Divorce, and Reconstituted Family Issues Group.

In preparation for discharge, Program A expects that the adolescent and his family will demonstrate increasing awareness and mastery of specific interactions. These problem areas are identified initially and are progressively clarified during the treatment process jointly by program staff, attending psychiatrist, parents, and the adolescent. For two to three weeks prior to discharge, parents are expected to schedule "working visits" outside of the regular program schedule, when they practice specific newly learned parenting strategies. During such visits, as frequent as four or five times per week and lasting up to an hour, the staff gradually relinquishes responsibility as the parent accepts it. For example, while a staff member may initially actively mediate a conflict between parents and the adolescent around curfew, as discharge approaches, the patient and his parents are expected to utilize the working visit to negotiate this limit successfully themselves and then to describe the process and outcome to the staff member (Javorsky, 1992).

Program B similarly requires family participation and offers the family a therapeutic space that resembles that of Program A in most respects. Program B, however, does not offer formal modules. Problems are identified and goals set with each family upon admission and monitored weekly thereafter, and families are expected to make substantial gains as discharge approaches. Each family is assigned a therapist, psychologist, or social worker who is available for support at any time. Families are also seen as a community in weekly multiple family groups. One evening weekly, all families and staff together prepare and eat a meal. Family topics are discussed spontaneously by adolescents during their daily group therapy. Traditional family therapy, conducted by the therapist, includes siblings and is offered to each family at least once weekly, but a family may be seen several times a week during a crisis. Within this framework, various behavioral techniques may be utilized to assist members in specific problem areas. The staff reviews family matters regularly with the attending psychiatrist. Progress of the family and individual adolescent are monitored and reviewed formally by the staff and medical director and integrated into a developmental context in an ongoing manner.

Conclusions

Both programs exemplify the use of a developmentally sensitive therapeutic space to treat adolescents and their families. Both programs assess and treat psychiatric disorders and address their impact on the developmental process through a spectrum of procedures and activities provided by a multidisciplinary staff. Each program is made up of a coherent set of procedures and clinical activities. Each activity is designed to serve several developmental and clinical needs simultaneously. Program A uses more formal assessment and treatment modules to assure that every patient and family is exposed to relevant developmental opportunities; Program B emphasizes evaluation and response to individual developmental needs, uses formal outcome measures, and relies more heavily on mental health professionals.

Adjustment in adulthood is mediated by the course of the developmental trajectory during adolescence. In both programs, an adolescent whose developmental trajectory has been "pulled" from its optimum course by a biologically, psychologically, or socially based disorder is provided multimodal assessment and treatment. Since disruptions in the developmental process underlie the long-term morbidity of psychiatric disorders, which commonly are chronic, we believe that our developmentally oriented approaches allow both programs to provide ultimately cost-effective interventions by enabling greater compliance, quicker remission, less recidivism, and fewer relapses in the short term, and less lifetime morbidity in the long term (Huestis and Ryland, 1990; Kiser, 1991).

REFERENCES

Beck, A. T., Ward, C. H., Mendelson M., Mock, J. & Erbaugh, J. (1961), An inventory for measuring depression. *Arch. Gen. Psychiat.*, 4:53–63.
Cole, D. E. & Kelly, M. M. (1991), Integrations of cognitive and behavioral treatment of strategies in a group family oriented partial

hospitalization program for adolescents, children and their families. *Internat. J. Partial Hosp.*, 7:119–127.

Freud, A. (1965), *Normality and Pathology in Childhood*. New York: International Universities Press.

Grossman, J. A., Poznanski, E. O. & Banegas, M. E. (1983), Lunch: Time to study family interactions. *J. Psychosoc. Nurs. Ment. Health Serv.*, 21:19–23.

Harbin, H. T. (1979), A family-oriented psychiatric inpatient unit. *Fam. Proc.*, 18:281–291.

Huestis, R. D. & Ryland, C. (1990), Outcome after partial hospitalization of severely disturbed adolescents. *Internat. J. Partial Hosp.*, 6:139–153.

Javorsky, J. (1992), Integration of partial hospitalization and inpatient child/adolescent psychiatry units: "A question of continuity of care." *Internat. J. Partial Hosp.*, 8:65–75.

Kiser, L. J. (1991), Treatment effectiveness research in child and adolescent partial hospitalization. *Psychiat. Hosp.*, 22:51–58.

Kohut, H. (1971), *The Analysis of the Self*. New York: International Universities Press.

Levin, D., Darron, M., Tyano, S. & Wijenbeck, H. (1982), Behavioral and psychodynamic approaches to milieu therapy in an adolescent day hospital. *Internat. J. Partial Hosp.*, 1:341–348.

Nakhla, F., Folkart, L. & Webster, J. (1969), Treatment of families as in-patients. *Fam. Proc.*, 8:79–96.

Palmer, A. J., Harper, G. & Rivinus, T. M. (1983), The "adoption process" in the inpatient treatment of children and adolescents. *J. Amer. Acad. Child Psychiat.*, 22:286–293.

Piaget, J. & Inhelder, B. (1958), *The Growth of Logical Thinking from Childhood to Adolescence*. London: Routledge & Kegan Paul.

Redl, F. (1959), The life space interview: Strategy and techniques of the life space interview. *Amer. J. Orthopsychiat.*, 28:1–18.

_____ & Wineman, D. (1957), *The Aggressive Child*. Glencoe, IL: Free Press.

Schwarz, E. D. & Perry, B. (1994), Posttraumatic stress disorder in children and adolescents. *Psychiat. Clinics N. Amer.*, 17:311–326.

Simon J. D. (1986), Day hospital treatment for borderline adolescents. *Adoles.*, 21:561–572.

Wineman, D. (1959), The life space interview. *Soc. Work*, 4:3–17.

Winnicott, D. W. (1953), Transitional objects and transitional phenomena. *Internat. J. Psycho-Anal.*, 34:89–97.

26 RESIDENTIAL TREATMENT OF SEVERELY DISTURBED CHILDREN

JACQUELYN SEEVAK SANDERS

When I was young, idealistic, and looking for a job, I made inquiry at three of the University of Chicago's centers of precollegiate education. Bruno Bettelheim, at the time a relatively unknown figure, responded for the Orthogenic School, the University's center for the rehabilitation of severely emotionally disturbed children. He suggested that I read his recently published book about the school and its work, *Love Is Not Enough* (Bettelheim, 1950).

This was my introduction to residential treatment. I had known that such children as he described existed, children who had been battered by life either in reality or in their minds. In turn, they battered or withdrew to such a profound degree that they were unable to function successfully in any of the spheres of a child's life—in school, at home, or with friends. But I certainly did not know that a place to help them existed. I was completely entranced by what I read, believing that there could be nothing better than to be one of those people who could help such profoundly miserable children gain the possibility of having fulfilling lives.

Forty years later that belief has not changed, and at my retirement party in 1992 I had the pleasure of experiencing the fulfillment of that early promise of what residential treatment can do: a six-year-old boy who had kicked me in the shins on our first encounter is now a lawyer and came from Colorado to celebrate with me; a teenage girl who had sat immobile in a semicatatonic state when she first came to my office is now a teacher and came from New Mexico for the affair; and a seven-year-old abused boy whose adoptive mother confessed that, despite treatment and years of professional help, she had been terrified and exhausted by him, had just graduated from high school and came from across the street. They and many others on that day gave not statistical but personal testimony of the potential for dramatic efficacy that residential treatment has in changing the course of the lives of children who, by all measure, seem destined for broken lives of misery.

At the time I did not know that this was an innovative form of treatment. I did not know that these children were usually considered to be trash-bucket children that society hid in back closets or dreary institutions; and at the time I did not know that it was considered revolutionary to take the insights of a new psychology and apply them to every detail of ordinary life. I did know that what I read was compelling, both to my intellect and to my emotions; so I applied for the job.

There were, of course, many other things I did not know, my ignorance becoming apparent in varying degrees of alacrity. Most dramatically apparent was how frightening these children were in person. Though it was over 40 years ago, my first impressions of some of the children and my first reactions to them remain vivid. I visited with a group of boys who seemed remarkably well behaved—as long as the experienced counselor was with us. As soon as she left for a few minutes' errand, one youngster jumped from bed to bed brandishing a makeshift sword and expounding on what havoc he was going to wreak upon me. I was immobilized with terror until the counselor returned. I was later to understand that the child's immediate return to tranquility had much to do with her recognition that his outburst was a result of his own great anxiety about being attacked by a stranger, combined with his absolute conviction that she would not permit him to hurt anyone, or anyone to hurt him.

Afterwards, I found my own anxiety in this situation understandable since I did not know that this was a mouse that roared. I was, however, as frightened by a little girl who sat on a swing, endlessly moving back and forth, eyes turned upward, oblivious to all around her, working in her hands a hopelessly tangled ball of strings. I could not account for this terror in myself, for she certainly offered no physical threat to me. Why this ethereal strangeness so frightened me, I did not know.

What I saw that day is not atypical for children's residential treatment facilities—and my reaction that day was not atypical for all who come in contact with our children. It, perhaps, goes a long way toward explaining why these were throw-away children and are in constant risk of again becoming throw-away children. It also goes a long way in explaining the need for very specialized training for those who work with them. These children are difficult to understand and difficult to tolerate. The emotions they arouse in us are difficult to live with. Although it was a great blow to my self-esteem that I had not instantly become one of those people who could help these children, I stayed. And I stayed because it was clear that the ethos of this milieu provided the care and structure that would tame "the wild Indians" and the understanding and respect that makes the bizarre comprehensible. It was also clear that it was possible to learn to contribute to such a milieu.

I also did not know that treatment took such a long time. I and many others, though forewarned by Bettelheim that "love is not enough," could not understand how anyone could fail to respond to our wonderfully good intentions. I believe, however, that once one has had any significant amount of real contact with these children, it becomes more intellectually understandable, even though the constant rebuff we experience from these children never ceases to be a professional and emotional problem. But even impatient youth can realize that, if one does not believe in miracles, to go from hope-less to hope-realized is a long and arduous journey. Further, Bettelheim somehow managed to establish the ethos of looking at these children as a variation on normality, not as an aberration from it; therefore, because they were children they were engaged in the process of growth that is even ordinarily a long and slow process. So I could understand that for these youngsters there could be no "quick cure."

My idealism, however, did not permit me to accept that for some of these children there would never be enough time to grow strong enough to live an ordinary life in society. Even when this painful recognition did eventually come to me, it did not lead me to believe that they were not just as entitled to a growth-inducing environment as were those who would grow strong enough to live in and contribute to society.

It is my task to give you a sense of what such a growth-inducing environment — this thing called residential treatment — is all about. Soon after I entered the field, I found that my lack of familiarity with it stemmed not only from my personal naivete, but also from the fact that it was a very new field. In the first part of the 20th century, there were a fair number of institutions for children, but these were for orphans or for children whose parents could not or would not care for them. There were also reform schools for "bad" boys. The notion of emotional disturbance or mental illness in children was not common — and there certainly was no place to treat those who suffered from it. They had either to be in ill-suited institutions or somehow hidden away. But, with the growing popularity of psychoanalysis, this new understanding began to be applied to children. August Aichhorn (1936) described how a total treatment of young delinquents was effective in their rehabilitation.

The idea of a total environment is at the same time fascinating and frightening. If we stop to consider the influence that the various details of our environment have, we recognize their potency — how difficult it is to listen to even an interesting speaker while sitting on an uncomfortable chair in a hot and noisy room; how hard it is to persist in a task when coworkers are discouraging and constantly critical; how impossible it seems to be optimistic when surrounded by darkness and gloom. It is thus a compelling idea that having total control over the environment of individuals has unparalleled influence on their development. As parents, we, of course, have such control over the environment of our children until we begin to give them over to the care of others and until they begin to have some independence. I think no one would deny the profound influence we have on their shaping. Bettelheim, during his stay in a concentration camp, observed how such influence could totally destroy or restructure the psyches of some people. We who take children into residential treatment have that power and make the commitment to use it wisely and well. There are many institutions of society that have similar, though not as pervasive, power. Unfortunately, those in charge frequently neglect to consider the impact of their practices on the human psyche. We in the United States, for example, are all too familiar with the alienating effect of the huge urban high school on our young people. In the interest of more economically providing education and access to a very broad curriculum to many, large buildings, large staffs, and computer programming are instituted; but personal relatedness in teaching becomes more and more difficult to sustain.

We who are involved in residential treatment — with as much emphasis on the treatment as on the residence — or in therapeutic communities — with as much emphasis on therapeutic as on community — are aware of the power given to us by our ability to control a total environment. Therefore, we pay very close attention to all the details of our environment with a continuous effort to understand the nature of the influence that every detail exerts on the psychic growth of those youngsters in our care. Because that influence is so powerful, we must be very clear about what we wish its nature and effect to be.

I recently attended a meeting of the American Association of Children's Residential Treatment Centers and also visited the Scottish arm of the Charterhouse Group, a British association of therapeutic communities. I find that there are certainly differences among us in regard to the psychological theories behind our methods and differences among us in our methods. There is, however, a very high degree of agreement about what we want to achieve for our residents: self-esteem; mastery of their world and of themselves; the ability to relate well to others; and ethical responsibility to their community. A subgroup of us also believe that we are better able to help our youngsters achieve all of these aims if we can help them master the unconscious effects of the past.

We all believe that the children who come to us, no matter what their psychological diagnoses, familial backgrounds, and academic accomplishments and potential, are uniformly lacking in self-esteem. We all agree that this lack is both effect and cause of their inability to manage in life. How can an environment influence that? The beginning of self-esteem is the esteem of others. The light in its mother's eye is the basis of the infant's self-value. There are many ways that an environment can convey to children that they are valued. The attitudes that I described in my first encounter with residential treatment are significant reflections of esteem. The counselor's viewing the sword-brandishing youngster as protecting himself rather than being bad, even as she curtails his shenanigans, reflected a deep respect; as did the intense after-hours discussions engaged in by the staff about the possible meaning of the tangled strings of the ethereal little girl. These discussions moved her out of the realm of the bizarre and into that of pained but understandable human beings.

The way we choose to house our children reflects what we think of them. Bettelheim (personal communication) said that he had wanted to call his last book about the Orthogenic School "The Secular Cathedral," in reference to the custom in some ancient European cities to have the most beautiful building in the city set aside for the insane. The purpose of doing so was to convey to those who felt least valued that they were indeed highly valued. If the place that is provided for our children is as beautiful as possible, we indeed convey to them the message of our esteem. Further, the message is more strongly conveyed if the building is obviously designed for them, for their use. All of us have had the kind of experience exemplified for me in the glass in our dining room. Contrary to the custom in most children's institutions, we have always used glass rather than plastic for drinks. Quite a few years ago, when we were financially flush, we decided to use more attractive and delicate glassware. To our surprise, the breakage rate seemed to go down rather than up—everyone automatically seemed to use more care. We also changed from metal to glass chandeliers. I was against it, expecting at least occasional downpourings of glass fragments. In 30 years, there has been only one instance of breakage by a child. I am certain that everyone in this field has had similar experiences—that when you give children beautiful things that are clearly for them, they will feel the respect and behave respectably.

There are many ways to convey to our youngsters that we hold them in high esteem: from the personal encounter, as in the way we teach our staff to listen with care and concern, to the institutional ritual, as in the way we celebrate each birthday. Since these youngsters come to us with the deepest conviction, sustained by the reality of their lives' experience, that no one holds them in high esteem, a massive dosage from all areas is required to change that conviction. Residential treatment, like no other form of treatment, has the capability of providing that massive dosage.

The esteem of others is an important beginning, but lasting self-esteem has to come from the individual's own self-evaluation. And this relates to the second achievement we all agree we want for our youngsters: individual mastery. I do not believe it necessary to convince anyone of the importance of the ability to master the challenges of life, both external and internal, in the development of self-esteem. Each of us, I am sure, has had personal experience to support that notion. Some might be surprised, however, at the description of these children as lacking in the feeling of mastery. They often present themselves as "know-it-alls" and seem manipulative and controlling. Even those who suffer from obvious academic failure often present this failure as a deliberate act. And even the misbehavers seem more deliberate in their mischief and chaos than out of control. In fact, they seem to control us. The disruptive youngsters in the classroom get the majority of the teacher's attention if kept in the classroom—and, if kept in the family, demand that the family be organized around them. Suicidal or self-mutilating adolescents invariably seem controlling, keeping those around them in constant anxiety lest something they do or do not do elicit a self-destructive episode.

We are generally of the opinion that for some of these youngsters this kind of acting out is a long and desperate cry for care and understanding. All of us in residential treatment have known a youngster, described as an impossible hellion, who has calmed down almost immediately after being taken in to a warm and nurturing environment that does not impose unrealistic demands. For many others, though, we believe that it is symptomatic of their basically feeling out of control of themselves and their lives and that these actions, which are so controlling of us, are, in fact, the youngsters' desperately frantic efforts to feel some kind of control over their destinies. Often what they present is a challenge that provokes in others a controlling response that only intensifies their need. And what they desperately need is a way to develop inner control and the ability to master their world and, thereby, their fate.

The avenue to that development is first the knowledge that they will not be permitted to exceed certain bounds of destructive behavior. For this they need consistency among adults throughout their lives and the support of a community ethos. Within this context they need the experience of positive mastery. Most youngsters get such experiences in the ordinary tasks of life, presented in the ordinary way. Our youngsters have already encountered failure in these experiences and are afraid to approach them again. We have to use all our resources to help them gain the confidence to try again for such mastery. Some people are afraid that we do not consider academics, for example, important; or they fear that if the "appropriate" grade level is not demanded of a child at the "appropriate time," it will never be mastered.

A very brilliant youngster articulated the fallacy in such anxieties when he explained how he had finally been able to learn to read. Until he was nine years old he had tried unsuccessfully to break the code. Then one year he began to play baseball. He enjoyed it and practiced enough so that on a home visit he was able to play with his brother and demonstrate great improvement. He came back to school and was reading in four months. He explained that when playing baseball he found that "this much" effort (and he held his hands very close together to signify a small amount) led to "this much" results (and he held his hands wide apart to signify a very large amount). And he thought that if it was true in baseball then maybe it would be true in reading, and so he had the courage to try again. The sense of mastery that comes from doing what interests a child is tremendously enabling in the approach to tasks that are not in themselves as attractive.

We also believe that the inner confidence that we aim for is enhanced the more the child can make choices about his or her life. We, therefore, try in every way to give our youngsters the possibility to do so. This, of course, does not mean abdicating adult responsibility. It is as important for the youngsters' confidence that the choices be wise as it is that the choice be his or hers. The youngster who finds repeatedly that his or her choice leads to disaster is not likely to be a confident youngster. This means that the choices that are given must be ones that a youngster has the ability to approach wisely, and it means that we help the child to acquire the necessary wisdom, skill, and information to make a wise choice. This kind of experience is most effective when practiced in every area of life: from choosing the color of one's bedspread, the game one plays, the food one eats, the course one studies, to selecting one's representative on a community council.

We all agree on the importance of developing the ability to relate well to others and a sense of ethical responsibility to their community. One might even call these what is in the United States a current buzzword, "family values." It might seem odd that a primary aim of a kind of treatment that removes children from their families is to foster family values. But, in truth, when we examine how most people define this term, we find that what is really meant are values that enable people to live well in families and in society. Not all families transmit these values, and a family is not the only way of transmitting them. As we help our youngsters develop the ability to relate and to gain a sense of responsibility to their society, we help them to be able gradually to return to their families, if they have any, or to create their own families.

And now I want to talk a bit about that subgroup who believe that we are better able to help our youngsters to achieve all of this if we can help them master the unconscious effects of the past. This does not mean, as caricatured by some, that we insist they lie down and unleash the chaotic forces of their unconscious and relive the bitter memories of the past. Quite the contrary, by our understanding of the nature of those chaotic forces and the bitter memories, we find that we are better able to help our charges harness those forces and lay the memories to rest. To give you at least a sense of the meaning of this, I would like to tell you some stories, stories about three of those youngsters who came back to celebrate with me the memories of a mutually fruitful time — our years in residential treatment at the Orthogenic School. The stories are not their whole stories, nor explications of their whole psyches, just little parts to give a flavor of the whole.

The boy who had kicked me in the shins on our first encounter was referred because his general approach to the world had made him unmanageable. We had some inkling that behind this hostility was a desperate misery, since he had, by the age of six, had to have his stomach pumped three times after swallowing excessive doses of aspirin. He later told us that the reason he had taken the aspirin was that he knew that taking aspirin made him feel better — so taking a lot of aspirin would make him feel a lot better. A youngster who found himself miserable discovered that his efforts to make himself feel better led only to worse consequences. The message that he finally got was that the source of expected comfort turned into the source of destruction. He could not believe it at first, so he continued to try—is it a wonder that he would strike out at a world where that which was supposed to soothe hurt?— and no one protected him from his own disastrous efforts. Most important for this little boy was to be surrounded by an environment that was safe—where he could hurt no one, where nothing would hurt him, and where those he turned to for comfort would not betray him.

We did not impose any demands on him, other than the usual routines of life—getting up with the others in the morning, going to meals on time, going to school, going out to play, and getting ready for bed. There was always a counselor or teacher with him and his group to ease his way in accomplishing these routines. And we saw that, once he could relax and stop fighting the world, he himself found a healthy way to protect himself from its dangers. He learned to read—by asking his counselors to read the words on cereal and other food boxes, and the warning signs in the street. Though not yet receptive to direct instruction from his teacher, he learned by listening to the teacher's instruction to other children in his class. Thus this little boy did not need explicit understanding of the psychological forces working inside him in order to utilize his environment to master them.

The girl who sat in a semicatatonic state in my office at our first encounter was 15 and much more sophisticated. Once she became able to communicate, we found that she herself was driven to understand those psychological forces explicitly. Nonetheless, understanding itself was not enough to enable mastery—the support of a total milieu was required. For example, she was anorexic. After many months of our insisting that she eat, she told us that she deeply believed that her parents did not care about her because they had not noticed many signs of despair that she had exhibited from the time she was very young. Therefore, when her teacher failed even once to notice at the lunch table that she had not eaten as much as we had insisted was necessary for her health, she was sent into a frenzy of despair and ran screaming from the dining room. It was necessary that the staff and she work together; that the staff be always vigilant so that she could gradually come to realize that we really did care about her; and that she come to understand that the lapses in noticing were not lapses in caring, neither for the staff nor necessarily for her parents.

She also needed a way to reintegrate the various parts of her personality that likely had been more intensely torn asunder through a brief experimentation and bad experience in the use of drugs. To do so she was able to make use of our tradition of providing the children with stuffed animals. She gradually gathered for herself a menagerie, naming each for a different quality: "Mr. Bear" was security and protection; "Merlin" was a rabbit of gentleness; a hand-puppet lion called "Bite" represented aggressiveness; a large lion represented the clash of ambivalent feelings; a leopard called "Stink" represented her budding sexual feelings; and a monkey represented integration. Their use, together with the staff's understanding interaction around them, helped her acknowledge, accept, and thus integrate these disparate aspects of herself.

And the seven-year-old abused boy, who had so terrorized his adoptive family, was able to find safe haven, a person with whom to identify, and a way to gain self-esteem in his classroom. This little boy was so unable to acknowledge his attachment openly that he left his parents easily and dry eyed, only to bury his head in his pillow and cry. His mother was convinced that his leaving without looking back meant that he did not care. When he eventually left the Orthogenic School, with cause for hope and pride, he stood before the entire community of the school and wept at the loss of his friends. This boy was unable to approach the pain of his early years. In our experience, it is often of great help to provide experiences that can in a more distant way permit the working through of these trauma. To try to do so more directly can prove unmanageably disruptive to an already fragile psyche. For this young man, a class in animal studies was such an opportunity. He was fascinated by any account of animal babies and the care given them either by their mothers or by humans. This was the kind of early nurturance that he had not had and could not accept in any but distant ways when provided by the staff. Animal study could provide a vicarious satisfaction. The class would often affectionately tease their teacher because of her interest in and love for the barnacle—the strange pest of an animal that clings upside down. No doubt this reflected their response to this symbolic exemplification of her acceptance of strange creatures who make pests of themselves—the most frequent description of our children.

I cannot leave the topic of residential treatment without saying something about the kind of children for whom this treatment is necessary and beneficial. As you, of course, can see from the examples that I have used, the children have a very wide range of diagnoses and behaviors. But not all children with similar diagnoses and similar behaviors require residential treatment. One would like to have a way of determining exactly for whom this treatment should be used and for whom a less all-encompassing form would be more appropriate—since one rightly has to consider the disruption involved in removing a child from his or her place of attachment. In my view, the issue is the fragility of the central core. Unfortunately, this is often very hard to assess—and, unfortunately, children are often tried in various other, less intensive placements before coming into residential treatment. In my experience the best assessment tool is the opinion of those who deal with the youngster on a day-to-day basis in regard to the youngster's ability to manage life and their ability to manage the youngster. Far too often the failure experienced in a variety of inadequate placements intensifies the problems almost beyond repair. There are also a great many youngsters who may not be as fragile as most of those we treat but who have neither a stable family nor a system of services available in their community to provide the support necessary for them to function.

In recent years two groups of children have come more and more into visibility and into our care: these are those who have been severely abused, neglected, or both; and those who suffer from neurological and perceptual disabilities, which frequently are a result of drug or alcohol abuse by the parents. These groups do not change our task, but their particular problems and disabilities make it more complex and more costly, as it becomes essential to have within our facilities more skills and more services.

Much has changed since my first encounter with residential treatment some 40-odd years ago. I am no longer young, not quite as idealistic, and certainly not looking for a job. But, I still believe that there could be little that is more demanding; and less that is more rewarding. Anyone who has ever been immersed in a therapeutic community, even for a very short time, has been deeply moved by the experience. Anyone who has ever had the pleasure of watching a severely disturbed youngster begin to trust, begin to love, begin to grow, has been deeply moved by the experience.

Much has changed in the world, of course, and that means change in attitudes toward residential treatment and change in its sources of funding. Support and understanding of residential treatment from the community around it is necessary both for funding and for the essential connections to accomplish its goal of leading its children back into that community. Unfortunately, residential treatment is not a popular cause. The youngsters that we serve suffer profound pain and often have had great pain, emotional and sometimes physical, inflicted on them. Most often, however, they do not present a sympathetic surface—they cause trouble, look bizarre, and usually are unresponsive to the usual good works and ministrations. It takes not only a good heart, but unusual understanding, to see the profound need and potential for growth beneath the strange and defiant exterior.

In addition there are questions raised about the desirability of residential treatment. There are those who say that many of these children suffer from organic problems that need chemical treatment — as though they, therefore, do not also need to be treated well. Though opinions about the etiology of emotional disturbance range wide, there are no children, whether helped or not by medication, who do not need to be treated sensitively in order to live well. Medication can address the imbalance or the deficit, but it cannot teach the child to master the problems that the deficits have caused.

One also hears about the need for families, as though that were an argument against providing for those youngsters whose families are desperate because they cannot manage or help their children, or for those youngsters who disrupt any family, or for those youngsters who do not have any possibility of a family.

One also hears about "the least restrictive environment" as though having a child in a regular classroom or living situation were a civil rights issue. Is it a child's civil right to be in a place where the majority of children are, or is it a child's civil right to be in a place where he or she can grow to being able to master what the majority of children can master?

And there is the issue of money. One hears that this form of treatment is too costly. One never hears that open-heart surgery is too costly, even though open-heart surgery does not prevent inevitable future costs — a funeral is usually not more costly than the next several years of the patient's life that the open-heart surgery enables. But residential treatment does prevent the inevitable future costs of the next many years of the lives of these children who, without this most intense form of treatment, would become burdens not only to themselves, their families, and friends, but also to society.

Though much has changed, residential treatment continues to be an important component in the array of services available for alleviating human misery and fostering human growth, particularly for those most difficult of youngsters who are continually at risk of again becoming society's throw-away children.

REFERENCES

Aichhorn, A. (1936), *Wayward Youth*. New York: Putnam's Sons.
Bettelheim, B. (1950), *Love Is Not Enough*. New York: Free Press of Glencoe.

THE AUTHORS

GERI ANDERSON is a Research Nurse at in the Anxiety Disorders program at St. Boniface General Hospital, Winnipeg, Manitoba, Can.

IRVING H. BERKOVITZ, M. D. is Clinical Professor in Psychiatry, UCLA School of Medicine.

DAVID J. BERNDT, Ph.D was, at the time of his collaboration with Dr. Feinstein, Senior Clinical Psychologist, Psychosomatic and Psychiatric Institute, Michael Reese Hospital, Chicago, and Research Associate and Assistant Professor, Pritzker School of Medicine, University of Chicago.

ADRIAN D. COPELAND, M. D. is Clinical Professor of Psychiatry, Jefferson Medical College, and Medical Director, St. Gabriels System, Outpatient, Philadelphia, PA. He is a member of the Philadelphia Psychoanalytic Institute.

AARON H. ESMAN, M. D. is Professor of Clinical Psychiatry, Cornell University Medical College, New York City, and is on the faculty of the New York Psychoanalytic Institute.

SHERMAN C. FEINSTEIN, M. D. (Editor Emeritus) is Professor of Clinical Psychiatry, University of Illinois at Chicago; Director of Child and Adolescent Psychiatry, Michael Reese Hospital; and Editor-in-Chief Emeritus, *Adolescent Psychiatry*.

WILLIAM P. FLEISHER, M. D. is Assistant Professor of Psychiatry, University of Manitoba, and Medical Director of the Family Therapy Programme and consultant to the Adolescent Psychological Trauma clinic at the St. Boniface General Hospital, Winnipeg, Canada.

BENJAMIN GARBER, M. D. is Director of the Barr-Harris Center for Study of Separation and Loss; Training and Supervising Analyst, Chicago Institute for Psychoanalysis; and Attending Psychiatrist, Michael Reese Hospital.

BARONESS GHISLAINE D. GODENNE, M. D. is Professor of Psychology, Psychiatry, Pediatrics and Mental Hygiene at Johns Hopkins University and Clinical Professor of Psychiatry at the University of Maryland Medical School.

HARVEY GOLOMBEK, M. D. is Associate Professor, Department of Psychiatry, University of Toronto, and Director of Psychotherapy Training, St. Michael's/The Wellesley Hospitals, Toronto, Canada.

DENNIS C. GRYGOTIS, M. D. is Associate in Psychiatry, Northwestern University Medical School and on the faculty of The Family Institute of Chicago.

KENNETH HOWARD, Ph.D. is Professor of Psychology at Northwestern University.

PHILIP KATZ, M. D. is Professor of Psychiatry, University of Manitoba (Can.), Winnipeg and a past president, American Society for Adolescent Psychiatry.

CLARICE J. KESTENBAUM, M. D. is Clinical Professor and Director of Training, Division of Child and Adolescent Psychiatry, Columbia University College of Physicians and Surgeons, New York City.

MARSHALL S. KORENBLUM, M. D. is Director of the Adolescent Clinical Investigation Unit at the C. M. Hincks Treatment Centre, Toronto, Canada, and Director of Postgraduate Education, Division of Child Psychiatry, and Associate Professor, Department of Psychiatry, University of Toronto.

RICHARD C. MAROHN, M. D. (editor) is Professor of Clinical Psychiatry at Northwestern University Medical School and a member of the faculty, Institute for Psychoanalysis, Chicago.

JAMES F. MASTERSON, M. D. is Director of the Masterson Institute and Adjunct Clinical Professor of Psychiatry, Cornell University Medical College, The New York Hospital.

DEREK MILLER, M. D. is Emeritus Professor of Psychiatry at Northwestern University Medical School and Honorary President of the International Society for Adolescent Psychiatry.

DANIEL OFFER, M. D. is Professor of Psychiatry, Northwestern University Medical School, and past president of the American Society for Adolescent Psychiatry.

LYNN E. PONTON, M. D. is Professor of Psychiatry, Langley Porter Psychiatric Institute, University of California, San Francisco, and a member of the San Francisco Psychoanalytic Institute.

VIVIAN M. RAKOFF, M.B.B.S. is Professor Emeritus, Clarke Institute of Psychiatry, Department of Psychiatry, University of Toronto.

NORMAND ROUX, M. D. is Lecturer in Psychiatry at McGill University and Child Psychiatrist with the Allan Memorial Institute, Montreal, Canada.

JACQUELYN S. SANDERS, PH.D. is Director Emerita, Sonia Shankman Orthogenic School, Senior Lecturer Emerita, Department of Education, and Clinical Associate Professor Emerita, Department of Psychiatry, University of Chicago.

KIMBERLY A. SCHONERT-REICHL, PH.D. is Assistant Professor, Department of Educational Psychology and Special Education, University of British Columbia.

WILLIAM A. SCHONFELD, who died in 1970, was Assistant Clinical Professor of Child Psychiatry at the College of Physicians and Surgeons, Columbia University; a member of the attending staff and Chief of the Adolescent Research Unit of the New York State Psychiatric Institute and Columbia-Presbyterian Hospital; a Past President of the American Society for Adolescent Psychiatry; and recipient of ASAP's first Distinguished Service Award.

411

ALLAN Z. SCHWARTZBERG, M. D. is Clinical Professor of Psychiatry, Georgetown University School of Medicine and Editor-in-Chief, *International Annals of Adolescent Psychiatry.*

EITAN D. SCHWARZ, M. D. is Assistant Professor of Psychiatry and Pediatrics, Northwestern University Medical School, and Head, Divisions of Child and Adolescent Psychiatry, Department of Psychiatry, Evanston (IL) Hospital.

BERTRAM SLAFF, M. D. is Associate Clinical Professor of Psychiatry, Mt. Sinai School of Medicine, The City University of New York, and past president, American Society for Adolescent Psychiatry.

HERMAN D. STAPLES, M. D., who died on October 14, 1994, was a Past President and Convention Manager of the American Society for Adolescent Psychiatry and Clinical Associate Professor of Psychiatry, Hahnemann University in Philadelphia. He also held office in and management positions for the International Society for Adolescent Psychiatry, the Association for Child Psychoanalysis, and the International Association for Child and Adolescent Psychiatry and Allied Professions. Along with his wife, Mary, he was the recipient of ASAP's Distinguished Service Award.

MAX SUGAR, M. D. is Clinical Professor of Psychiatry at Louisiana State University Medical Center and Tulane University Medical Center, and a Past President of the American Society for Adolescent Psychiatry.

PAUL V. TRAD, M. D., who died in the fall of 1994, was Associate Professor of Clinical Psychiatry and Director, Child and Adolescent Outpatient Department, The New York Hospital-Cornell Medical Center. He was also Editor-in-Chief, *The American Journal of Psychotherapy.*

CLAUDE VILLENEUVE, M. D. is Assistant Professor of Psychiatry, McGill University, Montréal, Canada, and Coordinator of Family Therapy Training, Department of Psychiatry, Sainte-Justine Hospital, Université de Montréal.

JULIE WINTER, PH.D. is a Lecturer at Carroll College, Waukesha, WI, and at the University of Wisconsin-Milwaukee.

CONTENTS OF VOLUMES 1-19

417

NAME INDEX

M

MacCorquodale, P., 151, *156*
Mahler, M. S., 16, *21*, 24, *28*, 367, *379*
Malan, D., 302, 305, *306*
Malizio, J., 166, *177*
Malmquist, C. P., 8, 15, 16, *21*
Mandelbaum, A., 367, *379*
Marks, A. M., 166, *177*
Marks, S. R., 120, *123*
Marohn, R. C., 68, *74*
Marriage, K., 182, 183, *201*
Martin, C., 141. 144, 149, *157, 158*
Marton, P., 307, *323*
Masters, W., 141, *158*
Masterson, J. F., 11, 13, 16, *21*, 242, 245,
    249, *251*, 254, 255, *265*, 367, 370, *379*
Mattison, R. E., 361, *363*
Maurer, A., 180, *201*
Mayton, K., 212, *215*
McCann, L., 212, *215*
McCauley, E. A., 184, *202*
McClough, J. F., 272, *282*
McCormack, W. H., 151, *156*
McCormick, D. O., 151, *158*
McDonald, W., 82, *85*
McGee, R., 79, *85*
McGonagle, K., 80, 81, *86*
McKinney, G. E., 369, *379*
McKinney, H., 175, *178*
McKnew, D. H., 7, 11, *20, 21*
McMahon, P., 203, 207, *214*
Mechanic, D., 184, 197, *201*
Meeks, J. E., 297, *298*, 322, *324*, 340,
    341, 373, *379*
Meissner, W., 254, 259, *266*
Meller, I., 175, *178*
Melly, G., 99, *107*
Melon, L., 270, *284*
Mendelson, M., 387, 391, *395*
Mendelson, W., 182, *201*
Menninger, K., 325, *341*
Mesce, D., 143, *158*
Meyer, J., 270, *282*
Michael, S. T., 175, *178*
Miller, D., 242, 243, 244, 247, *251*, 325,
    341
Miller, J., 231, *235*
Miller-Tutzauer, C., 166, *178*
Millsap, P. A., 126, *137*
Minuchin, S., 271, *284*
Mitchell, C. B., 279, *284*

Mitchell, J., 184, *202*
Mitchell, J. E., 259, *266*, 277, 279, *284*
Mitchell, J. R., 175, *177*
Mock, J., 387, 391, *395*
Modolo, M., 100, *107*
Monarca, S., 100, *107*
Money, J., 143, *158*
Monk, M., 182, *201*
Mönks, F., 95, *107*
Moos, R. H., 165, *176*
Morelli, N., 204, *215*
Moretti, M., 182, 183, *201*
Morgan, S. P., 145, *157*
Morris, N. M., 142, 147, 148, *159, 160*
Morrison, I., 186, *201*
Mueller, P., 11, *21*
Muensterberger, W., 96, *107*
Munan, L., 166, 174, *178*
Murphy, D.L., 182, *201*
Murray, D., 100, *107*
Myers, W., 82, *86*

N

Naber, D., 273, *283*
Nadler, A., 165, *176*
Nakhla, F., 392, *396*
Nathan, S., 244, *251*
Nattiv, A., 154, *158*
Neala, M., 81, *85*
Neisser, U., 136, *137*
Nelson, B., 182, 184, *202*
Nelson, C., 80, 81, *86*
Newacheck, P., 81, *86*
Newcomer, S. F., 145, *158*
Newman, P. A., 279, *284*
Nietzsche, F. D., 335, *341*
Nigg, J. T., 126, *137*
Norman, D. K., 277, 279, *283, 284*
Norton, G. R., 208, 214, *215*
Nottelman, E. D., 142, *158*
Noyes, R., 79, *86*
Nurcombe, B., 361, *363*
Nye, F. C., 169, *178*

O

O'Connell, M. O., 145, *158*
Offer, D., 93, *107*, 166, 169, 174, 175,
    177, 307, *324*, 326, *341*, 368, 378, *379*
Offer, J. B., 93, *107*, 174, *177*
Offord, D., 78, 81, *85, 86*

SUBJECT INDEX